Online Marketing Handbook

1998 edition

How to Promote, Advertise, and Sell Your Products and Services on the Internet

Daniel S. Janal

John Wiley & Sons, Inc.
New York • Chichester • Weinheim • Brisbane • Singapore • Toronto

This publication is designed to provide accurate and authoritative information in regard to the subject matter covered. It is sold with the understanding that the publisher is not engaged in rendering legal, accounting, or other professional services. If legal advice or other expert assistance is required, the services of a competent professional person should be sought.

ISBN 0-471-29310-5

Printed in the United States of America.

10 9 8 7 6 5 4 3 2

Dedicated to my mother, Florence Janal.

Table of Contents

Acknowledgments

This book is a collaboration of great minds who consented to share their wisdom and experience. In addition to the people interviewed for the book, I'd like to thank these people who have helped me over the years. We learn from our experiences and chance encounters. Sometimes it amazes me how much we really do learn from each other and how the most trivial of information gained one day can play an important role in our lives years later.

Steve Case and Tanya Mazarowski at America Online. William Giles, Regina Brady, Keith Arnold, Michele Moran, and Kathy Gerber at CompuServe. Carol Wallace at Prodigy. Leslie Laredo, Michael Kolowich, Jennifer Christensen, and David DeJean.

Pam Alexander and Brian Johnson at Alexander Communications. Connie Connors and Lydia Trettis at Connors Communications. Barbara Thomas, Ed Niehaus, Bill Ryan, and Skye Ketonen at Niehaus Ryan. Kim Bayne of wolfe-Bayne Communications. Marty Winston of Winston & Winston. Ron Solberg of PRSIG. Mark Ragan, Bill Sweetland, and Kristin Clifford at Ragan Communications. Shel Holtz of Holtz Communications. Charles Pizzo of PRPR. Craig Jolley of OASIS. Bob Vogel of Consultech. Katharine Paine of Delahaye Group. Susan Morrow of Morrow and Associates, Mark Bruce of GHB, and Bruce Freeman of ProLine.

Greg Jarboe, Charlie Cooper, Ryck Lent, Chris Shipley, Robin Raskin, and Bill Machrone, Lorraine Sileo and Chris Elwell of Simba Information. Jeff Silverstein and Maureen Flemming of Digital Information Group. Kristin Zhivago at Zhivago Marketing Partners. Larry Chase of Chase Online Marketing Strategies. Bob Lash, Wendi Bernstein Lash, Michael Fremont, and Scott Shanks of WebChat Communications. Ameet Zaveri of InfoPlace. Terri Lonier of Portico Press.

George Thibault, Steve Leon, Michael Krieger, Ken Skier, Maurice Hamoy, Brad Peppard, Tom Stitt, Gary Jose, Keith Hendrick, Jim Nichols, Jackie Clark, Eric Robichaud, Lynne Marcus, Mark Bruce, Bruce Freeman, Mark O'Deady, Peggy Watt, Sharyn Fitzpatrick, Pat Meier, Charlie Valeston, Frank Tzeng, Leigh Mariner, Ivan Levison, Larry Parks, Jonathan Parks, Howard Zack, Dave Arganbright, Joe Szczepaniak, Maryanne Piazza, Alan Penchansky, Tim Bajarin, Steve Hersee, Richard Goswick, David Toner, Irv Brechner, Marty Shenman, Jeff Tarter, Jane Farber, Allison Shapiro, Bob Kersey, Colleen Coletta, Jerry Duro, John Cole, Ken Wasch, Dave McClure, Greg Doench, John Kilcullen, Carol Rizzardi, Babbette Griffis, Mary Stanley. Thanks to Joel Strasser and Tom Richmond, who gave me my start in PR.

My mentor, Sandy Hartman. Great friends like Gordy Allen, Wally Bock, and Roberta Morgan.

Friends for life, Steven Kessler, Stuart Gruber, Barry Block, Alan Dauber, Alan Penchansky, and Len Zandrow.

The excellent staff at Van Nostrand Reinhold, especially John Boyd, Angela Burt-Murray, Jacqueline Jeng, and Marianne Russell. Matt Wagner at Waterside Productions.

Special thanks to Susan Tracy. May all your fortune cookies come true.

Preface

ONLINE MARKETING—A STRATEGIC OVERVIEW

"We are betting fortunes on products that haven't been designed and markets that don't exist."

Avram Miller, Intel, quoted in *Forbes*, August 1996

Corporate America is at the crossroads.

Marketing is changing right before our eyes.

The Internet is changing the way business relationships with customers are initiated, consummated, and maintained.

The promise of the Internet is nothing less than a complete rewriting of the marketing rules corporate communications managers have grown up with.

If your company isn't on the Internet it will be left behind. At least that is what is being said by hundreds of newspaper articles.

What is the truth?

"Marketing is marketing because people are people."

Wally Bock, publisher of the *CyberPower Alert*

THE TRUTH ABOUT ONLINE MARKETING

Pick up any newspaper article about the Internet and it will imply that you'll get rich quick. Professional marketers and communicators know that no one gets rich quick either on Main Street or in cyberspace. However, if you have specific goals, adopt a solid plan, measure activities, and modify actions based on results, then you stand a much better chance of reaching your objectives.

The truth is that many companies are making money selling products and services to consumers and businesses on the Internet and via the Internet from their stores on Main Street. They are opening doors to corporate America. Many other companies are saving money by using the Web for prospecting, educating, and closing sales. The only disappointed Web entrepreneurs are those who either think they are going to get rich quick or who don't understand why they are on the Internet anyway and don't have the appropriate corporate support in terms of finance or mindshare. This book will explain how to integrate the Internet and commercial online services into your marketing plan to achieve profits, cost savings, improved productivity, or enhanced levels of customer satisfaction and support.

Why You Need This Book

The *Online Marketing Handbook* is aimed at marketers and communicators who know that their successes are tied to a well-founded, integrated marketing plan that uses as many corporate resources as possible in the most beneficial ways possible for maximum return on investment. Entrepreneurs and small business owners also will benefit from the tactics and insights and strategies presented. This book tries to separate the hype from the reality of marketing on the Internet and online services like America Online, CompuServe, and Prodigy Internet.

By following the guidelines, examples, strategies, and case studies in this book, your company will have a much better chance of maximizing its investment in the Internet.

How to Use This Book

This book is presented in an easy-to-read format. It is a book that marketers can read without having a background in technology.

The book contains six parts covering online marketing strategy, tools, advertising, public relations, selling, and the future. Most chapters feature strategies and tactics for succeeding as an online marketer and include step-by-step instructions on how to carry out each task.

This book is divided into 27 chapters:

- Chapter 1 explains the need for integrating online activities into the overall marketing program. You'll also see how to integrate the Internet into your marketing plan so that it supports all your other marketing efforts.
- Chapter 2 explains how online marketing differs from current marketing and stresses the need to exercise caution and respect the "netiquette" code of conduct.
- Chapter 3 describes how to build an online marketing plan. We'll discuss the benefits of online marketing and how to overcome some of its shortfalls. This chapter can help you make money and help you save money! It describes the factors that should be included in writing an online business plan and offers several examples.
- Chapter 4 explores the issues corporations need to deal with when deciding to go online.
- Chapter 5 gives you a deeper understanding of the Internet and several of the major commercial online services. You'll see the demographics of each service, its major features and benefits, and the sales and marketing opportunities on each.
- Chapter 6 shows you how to conduct marketing online. You'll also learn about online resources to enhance your marketing program.
- Chapter 7 explains how to conduct competitive research step by step.
- Chapter 8 lists online resources for networking with peers and finding solid marketing advice. You'll find out about online news and reference sources and learn how to network with marketers through forums and mailing lists.
- Chapter 9 examines ways to measure the return on your investment in online marketing activities.
- Chapter 10 discusses how advertisers need to think in dealing with an online audience, clarifying how interactive advertising works on the Internet. You'll find out what advertising strategies work and why. You'll learn how to maneuver the corridors of Madison Avenue without getting ripped off.

- Chapter 11 explains the new terms of advertising online, like banner ads, clickthrough, and visits. You'll learn how to buy, sell, and write effective online ads. You'll also discover which measurement techniques are most effective and which ones are outright lies.
- Chapter 12 breaks new ground by showing how advertisers can create online communities of raving fans who bond with the company.
- Chapter 13 provides a framework and tools for creating online publicity.
- Chapter 14 describes how to write and send publicity material.
- Chapter 15 provides you with strategies for building relationships with reporters online.
- Chapter 16 gives you strategies for dealing directly with your communities and the public online, even if reporters throw out your press release.
- Chapter 17 explains how to build relationships with your communities via e-mail and private mailing lists.
- Chapter 18 discusses how to use newsgroups and public mailing lists to create relationships.
- Chapter 19 offers the largest source of proven strategies for publicizing and promoting traffic to your Web site and encouraging repeat visits. Many are low cost or no cost!
- Chapter 20 explores how to use the Internet to solve crises.
- Chapter 21 describes how to use the Internet as a customer support center.
- Chapter 22 shows how to design a Web site to maximize marketing efforts.
- Chapters 23, 24, and 25 explain how to use Web sites to sell consumer and business-to-business products and services online.
- Chapter 26 examines the issues in using the Internet to sell to international markets.
- Chapter 27 looks to the future of online marketing and what to expect as we enter the next phase of the evolution of this dynamic new medium.

This edition of the *Online Marketing Handbook* builds on the groundbreaking work and strategies contained in the first edition but has been revised to include new marketing strategies, tools, and perceptions.

In keeping with the spirit of giving back to the Internet, several chapters have been previewed online and subjected to comments from readers in all types of businesses and industries. While my publisher can't put the entire book online for free (we do have to make money!), I can put my newest thoughts on my home page: www.janal.com. You'll find new strategies, commentaries on newsmakers, and other marketing information that will make your job more productive. Check it out! And feel free to comment on these chapters, or ask new questions. I'll answer them personally and, if you give permission, print the questions and answers on my Web site for all my readers to learn from.

PART 1

Online Marketing Strategy

Adding Online Power to Your Marketing Mix

Market researcher Odyssey's latest study of the home computing market reports household use of online services and the Internet has almost doubled in the last year. Households using online services or the Internet now spend an average of 12.8 hours a week online compared to 6.5 hours a year ago. According to Odyssey's research, 48 percent of U.S. households with computers are now online.

Marketing on the Internet is for real.

The online jury has been sitting on the sidelines for the past three years to judge the pioneers who set up stores, catalogs, and customer service and support centers on the Web. Ladies and gentlemen of the jury, the verdict is in: Companies are benefiting from marketing on the Web.

Companies are making money selling products and services. Companies are saving money by providing sales and marketing materials that cut their costs of getting leads, educating customers, and making sales.

There are success stories among both large and small businesses. There are successes in selling to consumers as well as in the business-to-business marketplace.

While the past three years have been filled with a mixture of hype and promotion, facts, figures, anecdotes, and case studies show that companies of all sizes reaching out to all markets are benefiting from being on the Internet.

Long Island Hot Tubs & Paramount Pools Store's Daniel Harrison says his Web site makes $5,000–$6,000 a week selling supplies for hot tubs via his Web site. His 100 page site offers chemicals, pool covers, pump replacement parts, inflatable dolphins, and other supplies. The address is www.lihot-tubs.com.

American Leasing, www.americanleasing.com, is closing business on its Web site with minimal employee intervention. "We just received the check and contract by Federal Express for a $50,000 notebook computer lease, from an inquiry on our Web site sent to Fisher-Anderson in Iowa, who approved it within two hours after we sent the application, for a major company with a foreign parent corporation. I never spoke to the person who signed the lease. I did this all over the Internet and Federal Express," says Kit Menken, president of American Leasing. "And this wasn't the first time we have gotten business."

Large companies are venturing onto the Web as well. ADP, the $3.5-billion computing company, has leveraged its expertise in electronic commerce applications to create a comprehensive virtual automotive shopping mall with ADP AutoConnect, http://autoconnect.net. With more than 4,000 auto dealers online and more than 800 links to auto manufacturers and other sites, ADP AutoConnect is the largest collection of automotive information on the Internet and a great example of electronic commerce on the Web.

Selling cars via the Internet seems to be a popular choice among America's large companies, such as CUC International, a multibillion-dollar company (AutoVantage, www.netmarket.com). Yet the market seems to be so big that a third company, Auto-by-Tel, www.autobytel.com, also has a large presence on the Internet.

The Internet is changing the way some industries conduct business. A wave of discount brokerage firms set up business on the Internet and forced traditional companies like Charles Schwab & Company and Fidelity Investments to follow suit by offering steeper discounts than those given to their phone customers. A report by a securities industry technology analyst predicts the online stock trading market will account for 60 percent of the total commissions generated by discount brokers and 10 percent of all retail stock brokerage commissions by 2001. Bill Burnham, an analyst with Minneapolis-based Piper Jaffray, estimates those commissions will total $2.2 billion. He expects the online trading market this year will more than double from last to account for 30 percent of discount brokerage trading fees. He says online brokerage E*Trade is rapidly expanding its online presence and that it is now the third largest, with 13 percent of the market. Charles Schwab is first, with 35 percent, and Fidelity Investments is second.

Real estate giant Coldwell Banker estimates 10 percent of the almost 18,000 customer leads developed by its four-month-old Web site have turned into transactions, according to the president of the company, Alex Perriello. At least 90 percent of the company's inventory is available for review on the Web. The site offers customers convenient access to listings and information, he says, which gives customers "the freedom to contact us only when they are ready to see houses after doing some of their research online."

Financial services are booming on the Internet as well. Zacks Investment Research, a well-known investment information company, has added a Web site and delivers three million impressions per month. Clearly, lots of people are on the Internet, despite the naysayers' protestations to the contrary.

Not only are merchants going online to sell products directly to consumers or provide them with the information and motivation to visit retail outlets to purchase products, but they are finding more and more customers are willing to buy directly online.

Companies are finding they can sell more products and sell them more effectively. Wal-mart, www.walmart.com, sells 500,000 products on its Web site but only 80,000 in a retail outlet.

Dell Computers, www.dell.com, says it takes five phone calls to close a traditional sale, but on the Internet, many sales are finished in one sitting.

Insight, www.insight.com, which fills three Federal Express planes with computer products each day from sales via its hard-copy catalog, finds that four percent of its $19 million annual sales come from the Internet.

The top-selling items on the Internet are, according to Forrester Research:

28 percent	computer hardware and software
14 percent	books, magazines, newspapers
9 percent	clothing and personal items
3 percent	entertainment and recreation
2 percent	sports tickets and products
2 percent	financial

Forrester predicts the growth of these items:

	1997	**2000**
Computer products	$ 323*	$ 2,105*
Travel	276	1,579
Entertainment	194	1,250
Apparel	89	322
Gifts/flowers	103	658
Food/drink	78	336

*figures in millions

Entertainment is very a popular item on the Internet. CDnow, www.cdnow.com, which sells music online, reported sales of $2 million in 1995, $6 million in 1996, and $18 million in 1997. Reel, www.reel.com, sold a thousand movies in its first three weeks online.

Dell Computers reports $1 million in Internet sales per day!

Even auction sites generate $500 million in revenue in 1997, according to Jupiter Communications, a research firm, www.jup.com. I say "even" because one would think that these would be the riskiest sites around. After all, you don't know if the buyer will send the money or if the product is in the condition promised. Yet people are willing to take a shot on this buying venture in numbers too large to ignore. Witness First Auction, www.firstauction.com, which has 20,000 members and sold $100,000 in product on its first day and $1 million in its first month. Another auction site, Onsale, www.onsale.com, expects to sell $100 million in 1997 from its 240,000 members!

FreeShop makes available free and trial offers to Web shoppers. If you are wondering if people really are online, just look at Free Shop Online, www.freeshop.com. As of mid-1996, the company had processed two million orders since it went online in 1994. The site has given away 40,000 rolls of film from Seattle FilmWorks and 20,000 trial subscriptions to the *Wall Street Journal*. The company has 130,000 members in its Club FreeShop.

Internet Shopping Network sells more than $1 million in computer products a month and 100,000 people used their credit cards to make purchases, helping to erase merchants' fears that consumers won't use credit cards online for fear of security limitations.

On a wider scope, more and more people are not only using the Internet but are finding that it plays an "indispensable" part of the lives of 20 million people in the United States, according to a 1997 survey conducted by research firm Find/SVP. http://etrg.findsvp.com/internet/findf.html. Some 9.3 million of those surveyed have logged on in the past year but do not consider themselves regular users and nearly half of all users believe the Internet is difficult to use and confusing. On the other hand, half of all regular users and 60 percent of e-mail users go online every day. Online shopping increased from 19 percent in 1985 to 27 percent this year; a third of these shoppers came from ad-clicks. The number of women online has tripled in two years to 9.9 million. Fifty-five million U.S. nonusers plan to go online in the next year. The Internet accounts for 20 percent of total news intake for regular users and use of television, magazine, and radio has drastically decreased for those users.

Furthermore, people seem to be happy with their Internet purchases. Vaidec's 1997 CyberShopper Survey showed that 98 percent of shoppers who purchased something online are satisfied with their purchase. The report conducted for the Internet Chamber of Commerce, based in Denver, showed 52 percent of respondents saying they are online one to two hours a day. They are watching less TV so they can stay online. The average cost of an online shopper's purchase is $142.

Some 51 million U.S. adults are now online compared with 35 million a year ago. Some 17 percent of those are online purchasers, more than three times the level of last year.

For the latest surveys, check out the NUA Internet Survey Web site, www.nua.ie/surveys/, or subscribe to its mailing list by sending e-mail mail to:surveys-request@nua.ie with the word *subscribe* in the body of the message.

Dataquest forecasts 82 million PCs will be Internet-ready by the end of 1997, up 71 percent from 1996. The number will hit 268 million by the year 2001 (a 327 percent increase). See http://dqi2.dataquest.com/info/press/ir-n9744.html.

International Data Corporation says that 50 percent of all U.S. companies have set up Web sites and that companies connected to their customers via the Internet save 50–90 percent in sales, customer support, and distribution.

Internet users are surfing for information and entertainment, for sure, but they are increasingly using the Internet to shop. Forrester Research says consumers spent $530 million in online transactions in 1996 and that total annual consumer sales will reach $7.17 billion by the year 2000. Business-to-business sales was put at $600 million in 1996 and is expected to reach $66.47 billion by 2000. Zona Research predicts sales of goods and services used to build and access the Internet will top $100 billion by the year 2000. See www.zonaresearch.com/newsreleases/II3Report.html.

Yet, these figures might actually be *understated* because no one knows how many people use the Internet to research products they buy in retail outlets.

Consumers around the world are using the Internet for shopping as well. A survey of European Yahoo! users, the Pan-European Audience Survey, shows that 23 percent of users in France, 39 percent of users in Germany, and 38 percent of users in the United Kingdom have made purchases on the Internet in the last six months. The report also disclosed that Yahoo! users in these countries have a higher-than-average income. In the United Kingdom user income was three times the national average (pounds sterling 44,000). In France, user income was 274,000 francs (150,000 francs is the national average) and in Germany it was 96,807 deutschmarks, 36.3 percent higher than the national average. The survey revealed Yahoo! users are keen cyberspace visitors, with 73 percent in the United Kingdom, 71 percent in France, and 70 percent in Germany logging on at least once a day.

More than a few companies in the United States are finding that a significant number of purchasers are from other countries. This makes sense when you consider that American goods, especially books printed in English as well as craft items, might be hard to find in other countries.

Success can be measured in other ways as well. Amazon, a superb online bookstore, has never existed outside the Internet. Within three years of operation the company went public and sold its shares on the NASDAQ stock exchange. Founder Jeff Bezos was worth $324 million on the day the company went public.

Online music retailer CDnow has received $10 million from a private placement managed by investment firm Alex Brown. The retailer's president,

Jason Olim, in a release announcing the infusion, said the money will help fund marketing plans that include becoming "one of the top advertising spenders on the Internet." Alex Brown managing director Thomas Mitchner said CDnow is a business in the right place at the right time. "With local music stores closing and consumers demonstrating more diverse musical tastes, CDnow is experiencing a real convergence of market place trends," he said in a statement.

Start-up capital and a public offering made millionaires of David Filo and Jerry Yang, founders of Yahoo!, the successful Internet search engine and directory. What started as a hobby for two Stanford graduate students during the infancy of the Internet is now a worldwide media venture, with versions available in French, German, and Spanish. Another sign of Yahoo!'s success is its plan to offer its own VISA credit card. VISA holds a 2 percent equity position in Yahoo!

Many large companies are investing in Internet start-ups or are forming marketing alliances. American Express took a minority investment in Info-Beat, a personalized e-mail service providing news, and financial and entertainment information to 1.5 million subscribers. American Express wouldn't provide details but said that it is a "primary" corporate investor, along with the media mogul Tribune Company.

For several years companies have been sitting on the sidelines watching the pioneers to see if they can actually make money. The verdict is in. Companies can profit handsomely by marketing on the Internet.

THE IMPORTANCE OF INTEGRATING THE INTERNET INTO YOUR MARKETING PROGRAM

Is your home page hot?
Is your Web page cool?
Does it really matter?
I am sick and tired of hearing these phrases!
What do they mean? Really?
Cool is a '50s term.
Hot is a '60s term.
Beatniks.
Hippies.

What do they—or their pony-tailed, goateed, tongue-pierced progeny—know about marketing?

These groups are the very antithesis of marketing.

Do you want Maynard G. Krebs and Abbie Hoffman designing your Web site?

Yet their terminology and supposed marketing strategy are taking over the Internet.

How did this happen? How is it possible that dull, boring, geeky technology has suddenly been transformed and reframed like the ugly duckling into a medium that is cool—or hot?

That's a rhetorical question. No answer is needed.

What is needed are data. Hard, cold facts that answer the real question: Does my Web site meet my marketing goals? Does it sell? Does it provide customer support? Does it build and enhance the relationship between customer and company?

These are the questions companies need to ask—and answer.

Case in point: Everyone loves the Ragu site. You can't go to a marketing conference without hearing a speaker extol its virtues. Hundreds of thousands of people have been exposed to this pasta sauce through the Web and at conferences. But no one asks the vital question: Is anyone buying Ragu? Has its sales increased? Has its market share increased? Has even its share of the people on the Internet who buy spaghetti sauce increased? No one has these answers.

While everyone loves cute Momma—including me—why isn't she part of the integrated marketing campaign for Ragu? Why isn't her inviting, motherly face beckoning us from the label of the bottles in the supermarket shelves? Why isn't Ragu taking advantage of its most famous—cool—asset while she is—pardon the expression—hot?

These omissions would not be made by professional marketers.

In the pursuit of knowledge, I sent e-mail to Momma and her minions to find out the answers and told them that I planned to write about the site as well as mention it in my speeches around the United States, Canada, and Mexico.

I promptly received e-mail from Kathy McNally and Momma, who wrote, "We have had many requests on just these same questions. Unfortunately, due to confidentiality, we are unable to answer them."

When I informed them that I intended to write about this, they wrote,

"We are so glad that you liked our Web site. Unfortunately, we cannot respond due to the amount of requests received."

Sounds like a form letter. That's not what I'd expect from a company that prides itself on one-to-one marketing!

When companies plead confidentiality it can mean one of three things:

1. They are making a ton of money and don't want to tip off their competitors.
2. They are losing a ton of money and don't want to scare away their investors.
3. They don't have any way of knowing how they are doing.

I wish Momma the best, even if she won't tell me if her recipe is working.

Putting techies and postmodern hippies in charge of your online marketing program is like putting your architect in charge of designing your house without him bothering to interview you first. He puts in a spiral staircase. Why? Because he has the technology to do so. No matter that you use a wheelchair and prefer a one-story house.

Let's look at the San Diego Zoo and Wild Animal Park, www.sandiego-zoo.org, an organization that understands the value of placing the Web into the integrated marketing program.

The Zoo presents its image through a series of well-crafted pages that include rich, full-color pictures of the inhabitants, easily understandable icons, plenty of useful information, upcoming event schedules, an online guest book, and a custom animal signature prints game.

The site was launched using a live video conference between Joan Embery at the Zoo and Bill Toone at the Wild Animal Park. The conference was attended by students from two San Diego County elementary schools who asked questions about animals. Also participating were several elementary school students who had been using the Web site as a resource for study assignments related to wild animals.

Other companies, like Penguin Books, are integrating their radio advertising on National Public Radio to encourage listeners to visit their Web site.

Car Talk, the popular National Public Radio talk show, extends its information network and product sales by hosting a Web site, www.cartalk.com.

Roche Laboratories uses a print ad in *USA Weekend* magazine to create interest in acne treatments with a startling picture of a boy with a pockmarked face, then leads readers to find out more at its Web site, www.face-facts.com, or to call its toll-free phone number.

Don Johnson promotes himself, the *Nash Bridges* TV show, and an online chat on America Online.

The House of Blues restaurant chain broadcasts its music on the Web under the name LiveConcerts.com with Progressive Networks, developer of RealAudio. This shows how one company is extending its brand identity to a new channel of distribution.

Volkswagen uses the same look and feel of its irreverent images from its print and TV ads on its Web site. The site goes beyond the traditional ads to give users control of site activities, and tries to build community by offering sections of drivers' favorite roads and extreme sports. The site generates e-mail, which staffers respond to within 24 hours.

Disaster can occur when a company doesn't mesh online communication within the company. Apple Computer sent e-mail messages to dealers alerting them to a repair-and-exchange program for a particular computer flaw. However, it failed to tell its telephone support representatives, which led to massive confusion and irritation.

Sadly, while many companies understand their need to have an Internet presence, fewer than 10 percent of Fortune 500 companies realize the importance of integrating their marketing efforts, according to a study by Matrixx Marketing, Inc., of Cincinnati. Some 60 percent of companies surveyed had not yet integrated the Internet into their customer service program. Instead, they think of the Internet only as a sales and marketing vehicle.

Online marketing should support the entire marketing program. Online marketing does not and should not exist in a vacuum because the online component is but one part of the marketing solution—not the only solution. To conduct a successful marketing campaign, online services should be thought of as another distribution channel providing a service to prospects and customers. In that way, the key marketing messages of your company should be seen in the online advertising, publicity, and promotion that your company employs. Companies must use a consistent message, typeface, logo, and other elements of the marketing campaign.

Integrated marketing, a hot buzzword in business schools these days, has three components:

1. **Message consistency:** The consumer finds the same message regardless of the medium used. Colors, logos, and typefaces are

identical so their credibility and connotations create a solid, familiar feeling with customers.

2. **Interactivity:** Consumers conduct a meaningful dialog with the company, obtaining information that answers their questions quickly, accurately, and personally.

3. **Mission marketing:** Everything the company does stems from its definition of what the company is and what its purpose is.

Fortunately, the Internet and commercial online services provide powerful tools for marketers to extend the integrated marketing program to the electronic media.

Question: Can you be hot and cool at the same time?

No, you can only be lukewarm.

As the Internet enters the next phase of its marketing maturity, professional marketers will demand answers on the issues of accountability, return on investment, and message consistency. They will set up reliable tests, surveys, and benchmarks to justify their online existence and to provide the quality of service and information that their customers seek in a Web site.

Won't that be groovy?

Case Study: Microsoft Excel Online Contest

This study shows how publicity, direct mail, advertising, and promotion work together to build relationships with customers and editors in a business environment.

The ten-year anniversary of Microsoft Excel for the Macintosh came on the heels of the Microsoft Windows 95 launch event. In the face of all the Windows 95 hype, Macintosh users and the press were questioning Microsoft's commitment to the Mac platform. The primary objective of the ten-year celebration was for Microsoft to recognize the product innovations and demonstrate the company's loyalty to Mac users. It was important that the campaign be fun, informative, and interactive so that Microsoft could strengthen its rapport with its Mac audience.

Zebra Design decided to turn the celebration into a retro-looking, ten-year class reunion bash that would appeal to the offbeat humor of the Mac audience. Zebra worked with Microsoft and its public relations firm to develop an integrated communications program including a direct mailer to top-tier press, an online contest, advertising in *MacUser* magazine to promote the contest, and a bash at MacWorld '95 with prizes for contest winners.

Only 25 direct mailers were needed to reach the top-tier Mac press. The mailer presented a historic overview of product development milestones for Microsoft Excel for the Mac, blending product information on features and functionality with some wacky stories about the developers.

Zebra Design's online contest was called The Great Microsoft Excel Story Contest. The contest included a call to write a 100-word essay on the coolest application on Microsoft Excel for the Mac and a fun game matching favorite product features with reunion categories. This proved a cost-effective way to involve a large percentage of the Mac audience.

Zebra created an inexpensive business reply card (BRC) to insert next to the Microsoft Excel ad in *MacUser* magazine. The BRC served as another vehicle for promoting the online contest and provided a way for those without Internet access to participate.

The results of the anniversary celebration—as a vehicle for strengthening Microsoft's rapport with Mac users, generating user stories, and increasing awareness for Microsoft Excel applications—exceeded Microsoft's expectations. The Web site had approximately 5,000 hits over a nine-week period. The quantity and quality of contest entries also surpassed Microsoft's expectation. The unique applications provided great fodder for marketing and advertising. The number of entries—approximately 700—was seven times greater than Microsoft's optimistic projections for user participation.

The interest in the online contest brought unexpected media coverage from three large-audience U.S. radio shows (*Online Today,* syndicated nationwide on the WOR radio network; *Business Radio Network,* one of the largest syndicated radio networks; and *On Computers*).

ENTER THE FOURTH WAVE OF INTERNET MARKETING— WHERE'S THE BEEF?

We are entering the fourth phase of Internet marketing. The first phase was characterized by technicians who showed that text and graphics could be distributed over the Internet. The second phase was controlled by technicians who said that commerce could be conducted on the Internet, although they weren't very successful at it. The third phase was dominated by a mix of technicians and marketers posting advertisements and sales literature on the Internet, with mixed results. These marketers replicated the Wild West by charging whatever they thought they could get away with for creating home pages and for selling advertising space. No thought was given to measuring results or targeting audiences. This marketing model made professional marketers cringe.

The fourth phase will be characterized by professional marketers who have taken control of the Internet marketing mandate at their companies and are using the professional marketing techniques of testing and measuring activities to show the highest possible results. This phase will also be the one in which companies integrate the Internet into their marketing plans so that all marketing activities will help each other.

Like a child learning to walk, the first three phases of Internet marketing were full of starts and stops and a lot of falling flat on the face. Companies went online and learned that not all of their marketing efforts paid off. For example, McDonald's placed two files on their forum on America Online in 1984. One video file contained the entire contents of a 30-second TV commercial that had yet to air. The executives felt that the Internet community placed a premium on seeing things before the general public. They thought this idea would be a hit. What they didn't realize was that it would take a consumer 45 minutes to retrieve the commercial—while paying America Online and the phone company for nearly an hour of connect time! This idea proved to be horrible.

You might wonder how the executives kept their jobs after this disaster. The other file they loaded made up for the mistake. This second file was a coloring book that parents could download in about two minutes, which is an acceptable amount of time. Parents could print the coloring book on their printers and give a copy to their children. Look at the genius of this move: McDonald's created a positive relationship between the company and the parent; between the parent and the child; and between the child and the company. The coloring book was a brilliant idea! Only by trying new things will the Internet community learn what works and what doesn't in this brave new online world.

Many companies went onto the Web with visions of dollars floating in their heads. They thought they would become instant millionaires based on the promising demographics of the Internet, which showed the average online consumer to have above-average income and education. What these companies didn't realize is that marketing is as long and hard a process online as it is in the real world.

We are at the point where huge amounts of money are flowing into the Internet. Millions of dollars are being spent on developing and maintaining Web sites, and advertisers are spending millions to promote their wares online. In the first three phases of Internet marketing, companies were so happy to be invited to the party that they didn't realize they were going home by themselves. In this fourth phase, Internet marketing teams will be held accountable for their budgets and for producing demonstrable results.

WHERE IS THE SERIOUS MARKET RESEARCH?

When I teach Internet marketing seminars at company locations and at the University of California at Berkeley, most people are only too happy to learn about the new strategies and marketing trends online. However, there are always two people in the class who ask questions like "Has anyone done a study of A–B splits of home pages?" and "Has anyone shown the effectiveness of promoting a Web page with direct mail advertising?" and "Has anyone tested pricing models on their home page?" In all these cases I say *no*. There is a distinct lack of reliable marketing research to create benchmarks for success on the Internet, rules of thumb for spending plans and returns on investment, and other measurable statistics that marketers can use to justify their online activities compared to other companies or to industry norms.

Even the demographics of the Internet, as reported by reputable companies, show wide divergence in the number of people online and the growth of the online population. In fact, when I wrote the first edition of *Online Marketing Handbook,* every resource I checked, including unbiased journalists, said the Internet had a population of 30 million and was growing like a hockey stick, with one million new users coming aboard every month! At that rate there should be 48 million people online by the time this book hits the stands in January 1998. However, statistics released by several companies in the first quarter of 1996 show about 10 million people online, while another study says 18 million. A professional marketer would immediately question the validity of all these numbers and wonder if anyone really knows the size of the online audience. The answer is: No one knows.

While this may not be good news for marketers writing business plans, I hope it pushes online providers to create definable, measurable, realistic numbers. I hope we see an end to the hype and hysteria that marked the first three phases of Internet marketing. I know this must happen or corporate America will not continue its massive investment in materials and resources to profit on the Internet because the era of the professional Internet marketing manager has arrived.

SUMMARY

The need to integrate online services into the marketing mix is important for companies that need to expand their sales base by building brand identity and awareness of the online world. The online program must tie into the goals of the traditional marketing program, not go off on its own tangent. Building brand identity is important for companies as the race to stake out claims in cyberspace becomes increasingly important because mass market consumers going online will look for familiar names. The online world offers many tools that can build relationships with these consumers, as the rest of this book will show.

New Paradigms of Online Marketing

Imagine you are the marketing manager of a nice-sized business in the early 1950s. One day your college intern rushes into your office and says, "There's a cool new medium through which we can advertise our products. Everyone on campus is talking about it."

"Really? What's it called?"

"Television," he says.

"Television? What's television?"

"It's radio with pictures," he clucks.

If TV were radio with pictures, then we'd see a camera focused on an announcer reading from a script in his hands.

Instead, TV ads today are phenomenal vehicles that use pictures and sounds to create an emotional yearning for products we didn't know we desperately needed. Some ads don't even show pictures of the products and we want them anyway!

There's no way the college student of the 1950s could have foreseen this change.

Now let's fast-forward to the 1990s. You are the marketing manager of a good-sized company and your college intern rushes into your office and says, "Hey, there's a cool new medium we can advertise on. It's called the Internet."

"Internet? What's the Internet?"

"It's like television, with interactivity."

Well, the Internet is no more like TV with interactivity than TV was radio with pictures. As the medium evolves, new ways of using it develop. And it develops in ways we never dreamed of.

This chapter will explore:

- key concepts of Internet marketing and advertising
- how online marketing differs from traditional marketing
- how to be a success online
- netiquette: forbidden marketing activities

KEY CONCEPTS OF INTERNET MARKETING AND ADVERTISING

When I conducted a seminar for Pacific Bell for their small business owners who were new to the Internet, a middle-aged woman asked the first question: "What is the Internet?"

A million ideas flashed through my mind. Do I tell her about the complicated and confusing way in which computers all around the world are linked together to share information so that a consumer in Monterey, California, can read about a concrete company in Monterey, Mexico, and create a business relationship?

Do I tell her about the arcane history of the Internet that includes its beginnings as a communications vehicle to allow the government to send messages in case of a Cold War fallout?

No, I thought quickly. Marketers don't need those technical or historical anecdotes to understand the Internet any more than they need to know the history of the fax machine or how telephones send voices around the world. All they need to know is that *the Internet is the least expensive marketing tool in their arsenal as well as the most cost-effective.* People from around the world can read their message and create a business relationship with them for a fraction of the cost of any other marketing method.

Pure and simple.

Some people are afraid of or uncomfortable with the Internet because they are afraid of high tech or don't think they can understand the jargon. They needn't worry about the intricacies of the technology because that isn't what is relevant to marketing. What is relevant is that the Internet is not just high tech—it is high touch. With the Internet, you can create one-to-one relationships with prospects and build lasting relationships with consumers in a very personal, individualized manner.

"Why is the Internet more effective?" another seminar participant asked.

"You are never going to get more attention from any customer than when they are online. Both their hands are on the keyboard and both their eyes are on the monitor. You are interacting with them. They have preselected you. They want to see you. This is a very intimate selling situation," according to Carol Wallace of Prodigy.

If you are writing a business plan, you might consider using this quote. In the next chapter you will see more than 70 benefits to being online that you also might want to insert into your marketing proposal to convince your bosses or investors that online marketing is the way to go.

Just as it is important to know what the Internet is, it is vitally important to understand what it is not. The Internet is not a get-rich-quick scheme. Success on the Internet requires hard work, attention to detail, and constant promotional activity. Online success is not guaranteed. A study by Network Solutions showed that 30 percent of companies did not renew their domain names in 1996. This can mean that those businesses did not make enough money to justify their investment in cyberspace. Meanwhile, 447,000 businesses were registered on the Internet as of mid-1995, which means there is a lot of competition for attention.

"You have to have a good business plan, be price competitive, and promote yourself," says Marc Fleischmann, president of Internet Distribution Services, Inc., of Palo Alto, California, a marketing design technology company that helps companies market on the Internet (marcf@netcom.com; 415-856-8265). "Companies with bad ideas, poor marketing, or products that didn't work in the real world won't work online either. If it will sell in a mail order catalog, it will work on the Internet."

HOW ONLINE MARKETING DIFFERS FROM TRADITIONAL MARKETING

Yet the Internet is a different marketing medium that requires its own rules and regulations for doing business effectively. Online marketing turns the traditional broadcast methods of advertising on their heads. Instead of sending a message to a targeted audience that acts or dismisses the call to action, online marketing consumers seek out information and advertising. They, not the advertiser, are the initiators of communication.

This means that advertisers need to deliver and create messages in entirely new ways. The key differences are:

- space
- time
- image creation
- communication direction
- interactivity
- call to action

Let's explore these concepts to better understand how to create a message that will appeal to Internet consumers.

Space

Old Advertising—Space is a commodity you buy. It is expensive and finite. No matter how much you buy (even a full-page ad in a newspaper or magazine), you have only begun to tell your story. You are forced to leave out information because of the limitations and constraints and costs of space.

New Advertising—Space is unlimited and cheap. You can post an encyclopedia's worth of information about your company and its products on the Internet for a modest amount of money. Because of this, you can tailor sales messages to different kinds of buyers: information-seeking, money-conscious, value-oriented, and so on. If they are visual, you can post pictures and movies. If they are numbers-oriented, you can post reams of statistics. In fact, consumers can create their own sales scripts as they seek out the information that interests them and avoid information of little interest. Interview your salespeople. They know which techniques work for each kind of buyer who walks into the showroom.

Time

Old Advertising—Time is a commodity you buy on TV and radio. It is expensive and limited. You have a short period of time to convey a message. Advertisers tend to try to create an image of a company or product through visual means because of these limitations.

New Advertising—Time is what consumers spend. It is a valuable commodity to them for two reasons: they are spending hard dollars to be online and they are spending real time away from other business or personal activities that constantly pull at them. In order to attract them to your store, hold them there, keep them coming back, and tell their friends to stop by, you must add value to their experience at your store.

The first step is to have high-quality products and information displayed in an attractive manner. The second step is to add real value to the consumer's experience—and that might have only tangential reference to your product or sales or advertising as we know it today. For example:

- Wells Fargo Bank allows its customers to find their account balances online.
- VISA lets anyone read free information about how to get out of debt.
- Federal Express and UPS let customers find packages for free online.
- Southwest Airlines has free travel information about vacation destinations.

These experiences help create goodwill with consumers by enriching the time they spend online.

Image Creation

Old Advertising—Images are created with static or motion pictures, music, lighting, and action, primarily. Information is secondary. For example:

- A cigarette manufacturer shows a film of a cowboy on a horse lighting up and creates the rugged image of the Marlboro Man.
- A sleek sportscar's door opens, a woman's bare leg emerges, and seductive music plays in the background as the announcer says, "The night belongs to Michelob."
- Teenagers are shown having fun playing volleyball at the beach and drinking Pepsi.

In each of these cases, image is created with words and pictures that trigger emotions. Information is not used at all.

New Advertising—Images are created with information. Because the tools for audio and video on the Internet are still fairly crude, the main way to get information across is through the printed word. The Internet takes full advantage of the printed word! Sales scripts and product information can be written to take advantage of *hypertext,* the feature that allows consumers to go from one piece of information to another at will instead of having to plow through an entire document in a linear format, from top to bottom. Let's say you are selling a product that can be understood on several levels, like food. You could have a picture of a piece of chocolate, a paragraph of copy extolling the virtues of the dark, seductive nature of the candy and its smooth, silky texture. However, a health-conscious person wants to know about the fat and calorie content of the product. You can write that information as well. You can increase sales opportunities by showing gift box options and describing the flavors.

For a more technical product, like phone systems, you could begin by showing the phone and basic information like features, benefits and price. That would probably be enough information for the owner of a small business. However, people buying large phone systems need more detailed information. Will it work with our current system? Will it work with our remote offices? The Internet allows you to create the image needed based on providing as much information as the consumer needs to make a buying decision.

Communication Direction

Old Advertising—TV broadcasts images and messages to couch potatoes who sit by passively and either hear or ignore them. If viewers have questions, answers are not immediately available. For example, if they see the picture of a car and want to know how much it costs, they have to turn off the TV and drive to the dealer. If they see an ad for a bottle of beer and want to know how many calories it contains, they have to turn off the TV and go to the supermarket. Some commercials post a toll-free telephone number to call and begin a relationship in that manner. But that is the exception rather than the rule (except, of course, for infomercials and shopping programs).

New Advertising—Consumers seek out your message. They choose to be at your cyberstore and read the information. Not only that, they expect communication to be interactive. This means consumers can establish a line of communication with the company and find out answers to questions quickly, if not immediately.

Right now, technology allows consumers to find information at your store and send e-mail to your staff. You must respond as fast as possible to build a relationship. The first step is to create an e-mail tool called an *infobot,* which is analogous to a fax-back system. In this case, the person hears or reads about your product, possibly from a print ad, and sends a message to an e-mail address. The infobot immediately sends a prepared note to the consumer that answers most questions they would have. Of course, people always think of a question your staff didn't think of and send another note. At this point, human intervention is required to answer the question. This is good, as the action begins to build a relationship between the company and consumer. From this, good marketers can create a customer for life.

Interactivity

Old Advertising—You are watching TV when you see a commercial for a new car. You like the car and want more information. How much does it cost? How many miles per gallon does it get? Where is the local dealer? The commercial doesn't tell you. There isn't enough space to fit it all in. A toll-free number flashes on the screen. Maybe you'll call. Maybe you'll forget as the next commercial begins.

New Advertising—You see the ad on TV and get really excited by the image. You read the Web address on the TV and sign on to your Internet service to read the home page. You find all the information you need, then switch to a car discussion group and read messages people have posted about that automobile. You post a question of your own and a few minutes later it is answered by a car owner, not a company representative. You get a stream of information on which to base a buying decision.

Call to Action

Old Advertising—Requests are based on appeals to emotions and fears. They're going fast! Last one in stock! This offer expires at the end of the week! Requests also are based on incentives. Buy one, get one free!

New Advertising—Request are based on information. Consumers are looking for answers to specific questions. If you have the right product and describe it correctly, you have a better chance of making the sale than if you appeal to emotion.

The jury is still out on whether traditional off-the-page selling methods work in cyberspace or not. These tools include time-limited offers (product scarcity). No one has conducted a serious study of the extent to which persuasion works on Internet users before they get turned off. Serious marketers will want to test the envelope.

HOW TO BE A SUCCESS ONLINE

"Being the first online will not only establish initiative but will accelerate the learning curve of conducting business online," says Leslie Laredo, an authority on online advertising. "As the old lottery ad stated, 'You've got to be in it to win it.' Participation at almost any level is fast becoming necessary."

Marketers will be most successful when they follow these keys to online marketing success, as defined by Laredo and other experts interviewed for this book:

- Appreciate the new paradigms in online marketing and advertising.
- Mass market is over—customization is in.
- Build relationships one at a time.
- Appreciate the long-term value of the customer.
- Advertising must be interactive.
- Provide reams of information, not persuasion.
- Create interactive dialog.
- Contribute to the community.
- Free products generate interest.
- Adjust to the compression and distortion of time.
- Blend advertising, public relations, promotions, catalogs, and sales.
- Online is a competitive advantage.
- Company size is irrelevant online.

Appreciate the New Paradigms in Marketing and Advertising

Online marketing is a new branch of an old tree—marketing, which can be defined as the process of satisfying human needs and wants with information, services, or products through the exchange of money. To be a successful online marketer, one must know the basics of the marketing process, including needs assessment, market research, product development, pricing, distribution, advertising, public relations, promotions, and sales.

Online marketing has its roots in traditional marketing concepts but branches out in a most important manner—interactivity. Vendors now can deal interactively with consumers in their own homes or office at any hour of the day or night. Conversely, buyers can interact with vendors in a new way. Communication is two-way, not one-way.

However, the most striking contrast between online marketing and other forms is the technology itself. Communicating messages on computers replaces paper with on-screen displays of information, text, art, and sound. Principles of layout, design, typography, and art need to be reconsidered in this context. Also, computers allow communication to become an interactive, two-way process, unlike print and television advertisements, which are one-way processes. Simply uploading ads to online services means your company misses the chance to take advantage of technology and its tools to empower your messages.

Online marketing can take advantage of presenting interactive sale materials that meet the needs of every type of buyer. Instead of creating a message for the lowest common denominator, as does broadcast advertising, for example, online marketers can create interactive brochures that allow consumers to choose the information they want to see when they want to see it. Companies can create individual sales presentations to match the needs of each buyer.

"Cyberads must leverage the online medium by providing more and deeper information, more entertainment value, and faster and more personalized fulfillment than what can be jammed into a 30-second TV commercial or a single page print ad," says Laredo. "What's more, online advertising dictates customized communication, not broad general messages. Target marketing can be exercised in a much finer fashion. Individual message management or one-to-one selling, with ad placement in the context of relevant, sought-after content, is the new rule. Online advertising is more like personal selling than anything else."

Mass Market Is Over—Customization Is In

Online marketing allows companies to target customers in a way that other media cannot.

"For the last thirty years, mass marketing has torn the business away from the customer. We've been advertising mass-produced product to a mass audience. We end up counting the people we reach, not reaching the people who count," says Dan Fine, president of Fine Communications, a database marketing company based in Seattle. "Customers have been bombarded with more advertising messages than they could stand. As a result, they've become increasingly selective as to which messages they give their attention to. We have come to a time when the consumer wants to talk back to the marketing message and a place where individual relationships must be reestablished."

To get an even better perspective of online marketing, perhaps it is best to compare it to mass marketing and direct marketing:

- *Mass marketing* needs a mass market to survive. It reaches consumers through television and magazines. It does best when it sells food, health and beauty aids, beer, and cars.
- *Direct marketing* needs a highly targeted audience. It finds consumers through mailing lists. It is a good vehicle for selling credit cards, travel, software, and catalog goods.
- *Online marketing* targets individuals through online services. It sells travel, stocks, upscale consumer goods, and computer equipment and software.

Think of the Internet as a mass of audiences instead of a mass audience and you will begin to understand online marketing.

Build Relationships One at a Time

Successful online marketers know that businesses are built one customer at a time.

"You must get personally involved in the virtual community. You must invest the time to start relationships," says Carol Wallace, program manager of communications for Prodigy. "Through that process, you will begin to understand how this society operates. Then you will be in a better position to sell to them."

Companies can create warm relationships with prospects by using personalized e-mail, welcome messages on Web pages, and keeping track of their interests, previous orders, and passwords. A flower store can track birthdays, holidays, and anniversaries you celebrate and remind you well in advance so you can order flowers. Stock brokerages can notify you when your stocks hit buy and sell points or when there is news about the companies in your portfolio.

Appreciate the Long-Term Value of the Customer

For marketers, a major change in thinking must occur regarding the value of the customer. For too long companies have regarded consumers as replaceable commodities. Marketers must look to the long-term value of a customer. This concept will be a stretch for many salespeople.

For example, when was the last time you got a call, card, or note from the person who sold you your car? Probably never. Do you have any sense of loyalty to that salesperson or dealership? Probably not. That's too bad for them, because you probably will buy a new car one day and it won't be from them!

What does this cost the company? Let's look at the figures. If you are an average consumer, you'll buy a new car every three to five years. You will be influenced by peers, ads, and other factors. One factor that will not influence you is a sense of loyalty or commitment to a salesperson or dealership. If the average car costs $20,000 in today's dollars and is held for five years, that means the lifetime value of a 30-year-old customer for a car dealership is $160,000, assuming that person buys a new car every five years until he is seventy. You'd think it would be worth $1.50 to send a birthday card or personal note once a year to build a relationship worth that much money. Few car salespeople do this even though they make their living by commission.

For marketers to succeed, they must make additional sales to their installed base of customers. Online communication offers relevant tools. Marketers can create individual sales messages, remember each person's likes and dislikes, his buying patterns, and what kind of persuasion works best for him. Savvy promoters can send targeted communications—newsletters describing new products, sales, and productivity tips—to build relations with customers who approve of that interaction.

Online marketing didn't invent this process—it just made it easier and less costly.

Case Study: Wally Bock

Wally Bock, an author, speaker, and consultant who trains police departments on human relations and procedural issues, uses online services to reach his target audience: police chiefs. He participates in discussions on online bulletin boards and answers questions such as *How do I deal with sexual harassment?* He replies with a message that provides a few examples from his book.

"The last time I did that, I got an individual order from a police chief in Wisconsin. He posted a message praising the book," says Bock. "This led to more orders. An East Coast police chief asked for a review copy and then ordered 50. He promotes his staff every 18 months, so I expect to sell 50 new orders every 18 months. That's the value of long-term customers. Bock also publishes two newsletters for businesses going online, *CyberPower Alert!* and *CyberPower for Business!* (wbock@jcyberpower.com), that place the lifelong value of one of his customers at $500–$5,000.

"That's what the future of this marketing is about," he says. "I am not in the business of one-time sales. That is not smart. If you are a customer of mine, you will be a subscriber for years. You become a prospect for additional businesses and products and consulting. My primary focus is getting quality people who stay a long time. Secondarily, get as many as possible."

For Bock, the key to success is target marketing. "We tailor what we have to specific people," he says of the forums and newsgroups and mailing lists that have tightly defined readers. "What I can do on the Internet I can't do with paper mailing lists. There is no other technology that lets me do this as well."

Advertising Must Be Interactive

Customers of online systems have a style all their own. They are not typical consumers. According to demographic information supplied by commercial services, the average online consumer is better educated and has more disposable income than the average American. They also have little tolerance for in-your-face advertising, ads that suddenly appear on their computer screens, and ads that masquerade as messages.

Because the online consumer is not average and because the technology of online systems offers different message formulation possibilities, the entire advertising/marketing focus must undertake a major paradigm shift from traditional methods.

In traditional advertising, the purpose is to disseminate the message to as many people as possible for the lowest possible cost. Generally speaking, the advertiser buys space in a medium that claims to reach the desired demographic audience—for instance, placing an ad in a skiing magazine to sell ski equipment or airing a commercial on a children's cartoon show to sell a doll. The communication is one-way: The advertiser presents information and persuasion to convince the consumer to purchase the product. Appeals to logic and emotion are made. If the ad is successful, the consumer buys the product. If the consumer has a question she can ask the company for more information, receive it in two weeks, and make a decision.

The online medium uses a different strategy. Consumers request information from companies, which respond quickly. Consumers search for more data, pictures, testimonials, and the like, which the company has carefully placed in accessible places online. A company representative might even interact personally through private e-mail to answer questions. When the consumer has finished her research, she has built a relationship with the company that propels her to want to buy, and she places the order.

This strategy works because the request for information was created by the consumer, not the advertiser. The two keys to remember are that information is at a premium and that it must be requested.

"Interactive advertising would best be defined as a sort of digital infomercial if you will," says Jonathan Pajion, executive vice president of marketing for 2-Lane Media of Los Angeles, which won wide acclaim for its *Forrest Gump* advertisement. "A typical digital ad, if done properly, will convey much more information than an ad in any other medium and do it in a much more friendly manner. An interactive ad will allow the consumer to pick and choose what information he/she wants to view and the order in which it is viewed. Additionally, if properly executed, the ad won't really seem that much like an ad that the typical consumer is used to."

2-Lane Media has created promotions for films including *Undercover Blues, Fatal Instinct, Addams Family Values, Naked Gun 33 1/3, NBC Spring/Summer Preview, City Slickers II, Angels in the Outfield,* and *The Mask.*

"With Gump and the other Hollywood Online kits, you don't really feel like you're viewing a blatant ad for the film, though you are. Instead, you feel like you're exploring and finding out exciting preview and insider information about the film and the stars and crew. Under the guise of obtaining information and perhaps playing a game, the consumer is also repeatedly given the sales message in some form or another. Any of these kits we've done for Hollywood Online fit the above description very well," Pajion says. "As other examples, there are interactive kiosks that promote certain sales messages and other online and floppy-based kits for music and ads on the new generation of digital magazines."

Provide Reams of Information, Not Persuasion

The stereotype of the overbearing salesperson is the antimodel for online marketing. Online consumers are information seekers and are persuaded by facts and logic. The medium itself is mostly text-based, which attracts an educated audience used to making decisions based on reading reports. Users go online to find information from company databases and peer discussion groups. These are not people who are persuaded by the classic techniques of image advertising, which is based on irrational and emotional messages such as appeals to ego and sex. Online consumers are turned off by hype and oversell. The successful online marketer has a better chance to succeed if she offers information and rich content instead of self-serving materials.

This is good news for online marketers because space on the Internet and forums on commercial online services are inexpensive or free. Companies that were forced to condense their messages to fit printed advertisements on half a newspaper page will enjoy the freedom of virtually unlimited space online to post file after file of product information, complete with text, picture, and sound.

"You are not constrained by pages like print magazines. Advertising becomes more interactive and creative," says Marcos Sanchez, a marketing consultant. "With magazines, you had to match your message to a limited space. On the Net, you can use an inverted pyramid. Start with overview and then go very broad or deep. The ad becomes an amorphous space."

Another advantage is that you can find out what people are really interested in. Let's say you are selling cars and have information stored on separate pages listing options such as air bags, stereos, J.D. Power ratings, safety tests, and colors. By counting the number of times a page is read, you can see that more people are interested in air bags than, say, colors. These data can be used to fine-tune advertising messages online and in other media.

"This changes the model of how we look at advertising," Sanchez says. "It is no longer a 3-by-5-inch ad that goes out to 20,000 people. It is unlimited space going out to the world, limited only by the capacity of your server."

Companies can also use information to build relationships with existing customers. For example, NBC and ABC both have forums on America Online (keywords *nbc, abc*) in which readers can find out which guests will be on *Good Morning, America,* download pictures of their favorite actors, and find out how to get tickets to the taping of the *Seinfeld* show. The CBS forum on Prodigy allows viewers to read about David Letterman. All these services build interactive relationships with viewers by allowing them to send e-mail to the companies.

Another example of information content is GE Plastics, www.ge.com, which placed more than 1,500 pages of information on its site on the Internet's World Wide Web. Customers can find information and answers to their questions 24 hours a day from any spot in the world.

Remember, hard sells don't work.

Create Interactive Dialogue

After the prospect has read your online information, you must create a way for him to continue developing a relationship with the company. E-mail provides a great way to create a new dialogue. Customers should be encouraged to send questions to the company—and the company should be equipped to send a prompt reply.

Technology allows several reply methods. A customer support representative can respond to e-mail as soon as a message is received in the company mailbox. Automated mail responders on the Internet (called *mailbots* or *infobots*) act like fax-back systems, sending the desired information immediately to the requester at any time of the day or night.

Companies can also create relationships by having representatives scan online forums for conversations concerning their company, products, or product area. When they find these messages they quickly provide information, answer questions, and dispel rumors with the goal of finding new prospects and building loyalty to the company and brand.

Contribute to the Community

Online marketing is a two-way, interactive process. You are asking for the consumer's time and money. In return, you must offer valuable information *free,* releasing surveys, reports, and impartial information packets that contribute to the greater good of the online community. For example, an insurance agency could post files about saving money on insurance, a real estate agency could explain how to choose a house, and a swimming pool installer might post an article about how to select a pool manufacturer.

Companies can also offer free samples of their products, such as online newsletters and reports and demo versions of software. In addition to being useful to the consumer, these products cost nothing to deliver via e-mail and file transfers.

Free Products Generate Interest

If *location, location,* and *location* are the three magic words of real estate, then *free, free,* and *free* are the three magic words of the Internet. If you give people something for free, they will come visit your site, participate in a survey, or try your product. Marketers should think of giving away free information, free software, or free samples, depending on their business. For example, the Windmere Real Estate company in Seattle builds credibility by giving away free articles on such topics as how to improve a home's curbside appeal. Prospects can then select homes based on price, location, and amenities. The interaction starts with a freebie and could end up as a sale.

The Seattle FilmWorks company at one time gave away two free rolls of film. To get the film, people had tell the company where to send it. Violà! The company got the name and address of a prospect for its database.

The Bob Dole for President home page offered free wallpaper and screen savers to the candidate's followers, showing that you don't have to be a computer company to give away free software, which is something that everyone on the Internet appreciates because everyone has a computer!

Adjust to the Compression and Distortion of Time

Remember the first time you searched your computerized address book for the name of a colleague? You were so amazed that the computer could sort through so many names so quickly. The same act would have taken much longer if you had done it by hand. Then you got used to the speed of the computer and would complain if the operation took longer than two seconds. This example shows how people's perceptions of time have changed, thanks to the computer.

Fast is a relative term. In the world of online marketing, fast can be measured in seconds. People get impatient when their questions aren't answered by support staff in minutes. These same people might once have been happy with a 24-hour call-return policy. Companies that conduct business online must deliver information quickly because the customer demands it and because the technology can make it possible. For example, automated mail systems can send information-packed files to customers who request specific information. This is the norm, not the exception.

Blend Advertising, Public Relations, Promotions, Catalogs, and Sales

While researching this book, I was constantly asking questions that turned into conundrums. Is a home page an advertisement or a catalog? Is posting a message on a forum public relations or a promotion? Is information an advertisement? The answers are that the distinctions between these forms of marketing blur in online environments. Online marketers must get used to new definitions and new uses for trusted strategic marketing elements. Time will shake out these strategies and determine what works and what does not. Undoubtedly, new communication forms that we can't even comprehend today will be created and seem obvious in 18 months. Online marketers must keep their minds open. Probably the best strategy is to see what other companies are doing online and adapt the most reasonable tactics to your own use.

Online Is a Competitive Advantage

Having a commercial presence online presents a competitive advantage to companies. It provides them with an alternative and an additional distribution channel for its products and services. For computer and software companies, not having an online forum to offer customer support can be seen as a distinct disadvantage. If a prospect wants to buy a modem or flowers or coffee and searches through Yahoo! and finds 50 companies but yours isn't listed, you can't possibly make the sale. If you *are* one of the 50, you might please a new customer if your marketing materials and prices fit their needs.

Company Size Is Irrelevant Online

When you drive past a shopping center, you can tell the big players from the start-ups; online, you can't. In many ways, online services are the great levelers of companies. At this stage in online marketing, small companies can compete effectively with large companies. This will change as more large companies come onto the Web and bring the power of their famous brand names. There is a short window of opportunity for new or small companies to establish a brand identity on the Web.

"Small companies with a well-designed home page can look every bit as professional and credible as a large, multinational company. Small companies can build instant credibility with a Web home page," says Wendie Bernstein Lash, president of WebChat Broadcasting Network, a large chat system on the Internet. "People can't tell if you do business from a 90-story office building or a two-room rented suite. Web home pages level the playing field for small companies."

Although online marketing is still in its infancy, quite a few small companies have become big companies by using online marketing to sell flowers, T-shirts, novelties, and computer software. In some cases, online marketing was their only sales method and distribution channel.

In this stage of the Internet's development, people are willing to give business to companies they have never heard of. People buy wine at Virtual Vineyards and books from Amazon Books. What will happen when large companies and well-known catalogs go on the Internet? Will people be loyal to the brand names or try new cybercompanies? Time will tell.

If you follow these steps, you will enhance your chances for success. However, read the next section to make sure you don't mess it all up by violating a cardinal rule of marketing online.

NETIQUETTE: FORBIDDEN MARKETING ACTIVITIES

You are attending a cocktail party. You want to relax and have some fun, or meet some future business contacts. From across the room, you see an attractive stranger who smiles at you and gives you good eye contact. You move closer together. You say "Hi." The stranger says, "Want to buy some life insurance?"

You find out that everyone there is selling life insurance! Sure, there is no law prohibiting them from selling life insurance, but you didn't attend the cocktail party to buy life insurance. If you had known that you would be pitched, you would not have attended the party!

The same is true with online services. People don't go online to receive broadcast advertising. If they want to find commercial information, that's fine. But they don't want to find their e-mailboxes filled with get-rich-quick schemes or ads for products they don't care about. The same is true with the electronic bulletin boards called forums, newsgroups, mailing lists, and clubs. People go to those areas to exchange relevant information, not to find unwanted commercial notices.

Effective marketers observe the unwritten rules of *netiquette,* the etiquette of the cyberworld, which says that unsolicited material is unappreciated.

Companies that violate this simple policy risk being flamed—that is, bombarded with hate mail filled with four-letter words or threats.

Idiotic marketers say they have thick skin and don't care about offending tens of thousands of people as long as they get a buying response rate that justifies their efforts. This group is despised.

If your company is planning a marketing campaign that violates netiquette, you might find yourself trying to stamp out a crisis of global proportions. If your outside marketing company suggests renting a list of e-mail names, fire the company before the online world throws flames at you!

SUMMARY

Being an online marketer requires you to take a fresh look at the Internet and treat it as a new medium with different benefits and limitations. In some ways, marketing on the Internet is like marketing at the mom-and-pop grocery store, with an emphasis on customer service, interactivity, and an appreciation of each customer's long-term value. At the same time, online tools make marketing more efficient and easier.

CHAPTER THREE

Constructing the Online Marketing Business Plan

Sad to say, many companies that have home pages on the World Wide Web don't have a clue as to why they are online or a reasonable set of goals to judge whether or not the site is effective. That's because serious marketers were not involved in the planning and implementation of this generation of home pages. To put your company ahead of the pack, you need to create a solid business basis for your online marketing plan.

In this chapter you will learn:

- 10 essential steps toward creating an online marketing plan
- 100 reasons to go online to promote marketing goals
- 5 business models for online companies

ONLINE MARKETING PLAN—OVERVIEW

Definition: Online marketing is a system for selling products and services to target audiences who use the Internet and commercial online services by employing online tools and services in a strategic manner consistent with the company's overall marketing program.

Every company that intends to go on the Internet needs to have a marketing plan so it can be assured of outlining common goals and objectives that meet the company's needs. Too many companies (even Fortune 500 companies) have ventured onto the Internet without a clear goal and wondered why their efforts were not effective. Here are the ten essential steps to creating an online marketing plan:

1. Define the marketing mission by setting reasonable goals and objectives.
2. Get the buy-in from various departments.
3. Determine budgets.
4. Assign areas of responsibilities.
5. Create the marketing materials that support the mission. (See Chapter 2, New Paradigms of Online Marketing; Chapter 11, Understanding Interactive Advertising; Chapter 23, Strategic and Operational Issues for Online Selling; Chapter 24, Selling Consumer Products and Services Online; Chapter 25, Business-to-Business Selling Online.)
6. Create the Web site to present the marketing materials in a friendly and efficient manner. (See Chapter 22, Designing Your Web Site To Increase Sales.)
7. Connect to the Internet. (This topic is beyond the scope of this book.)
8. Promote the Web site. (See Chapter 20, Promoting Your Web Site.)
9. Test and revise the effectiveness of the home page. (See Chapter 10, Measuring Results from Online Marketing.)
10. Meld the Web site into the corporate structure. (See Chapter 4, Corporate Policies for Web Site Content.)

DEFINE YOUR MARKETING MISSION—YOUR SUCCESS BLUEPRINT

The first step of going online is to decide what you want to accomplish. From that decision you can plan your budget and personnel assignments. Here are 100 reasons to go online and benefit from a marketing perspective.

100 Reasons to Be Online

The Internet is the world's least expensive and most efficient marketing tool and helps companies of all sizes from all parts of the world disseminate sales and marketing messages, create one-to-one relationships, educate prospects, and support existing customers on a worldwide scale.

General Benefits

1. Deal with an audience that wants to hear your message. Unlike a TV commercial that blasts a message to a large general audience, the Web site attracts a specific prospect who is clearly interested in your company. He chose to view your site, unlike the passivity of TV.

2. Reach a worldwide audience. People everywhere can read the information on your site and decide to start a business relationship with you.

3. Be completely accessible. Your site never closes. People can read it 24 hours a day, seven days a week.

4. Deal with an affluent market. All reports show that the first wave of Internet citizens make more money and have completed higher education levels than the average American.

5. Deal with a market that has sought you out to compare products. Unlike television, the Internet is customer driven. Prospects read your materials because they need to find out about your product. Other media can't pinpoint their messages and audiences.

6. Deal with customers when they are ready to buy. Customers come to your site when they begin the buying process. Either they are comparing your product to competitors' or they have the desire to buy directly from you.

7. Create specialized sales scripts appealing to each type of consumer, using their unique buying buzzwords. With the advantages of hyperlinking information, pictures, sound, and video, merchants can create customized sales presentations affecting several senses and appeals to logic and benefits. Consumers can pick the sales presentation and information they want.

8. Appeal to customers who hate pushy salespeople and manipulative sales pitches. Consumers can use the Internet to find the products they need and to place orders without fear of manipulation by aggressive sales personnel.

9. Enjoy low cost of entry. The World Wide Web is the least expensive printing press ever invented. Merchants have an unlimited amount of space to describe and demonstrate their entire range of products. Companies can spend as little as $100 for a software program to create their site.

10. Enjoy low rent, especially compared to storefront. Internet service providers charge $30 a month to host your site, and consumers

can read it any time of day from anywhere on the planet. Opening a store in the real world requires thousands of dollars to fix, paint, carpet, and outfit the property, as well as to obtain insurance. These limitations don't exist on the Internet.

Competitive Advantage

11. Doing business online costs less. As it costs so little to go online compared to opening a store on Main Street, merchants can pass the savings along to consumers.
12. Lack of salespeople online means lower overhead costs for merchants. Automation features like autoresponders, e-mail, and Frequently Asked Question (FAQ) files can reduce the need for salespeople to answer redundant questions, thus enabling them to be more efficient with their time.
13. Without the need to warehouse products, inventory and warehousing costs as well as shipping costs decline. Companies can order products from suppliers when they receive customer's payments. Emusic, www.emusic.com, offers CDs for about $3 less than retail outlets. Trucost, www.trucost.com, offers computer hardware and software products at dealer cost.
14. Enjoy access to a large inventory of product. As online merchants don't have to have products on hand, they can offer a wider range of products to the public. Online bookseller Amazon, www.amazon. com, claims to offer the largest number of titles in the world.
15. Cut out distributors. Companies that sell direct make more money because they don't pay middlemen.
16. Beat competitors who aren't online. Thanksgiving Coffee, www.thanksgiving.com, was online 20 months before Starbucks, www.starbucks.com. Guess who made the sale.
17. Engage customers' senses (and business) by using audio, video, and multimedia to create relationships.
18. Compete on an equal footing against larger companies. Online, no one knows how big a company you have or how long it has been in business. Consumers only care that you have the product they are looking for at an attractive price.

Competitive Research

19. Find out what is going on with competitors. You can visit their Web sites and find out what new products they are offering. By

reading messages in specialized newsgroups and mailing lists, you can find out what people think about your competitors' products as well as your own.

20. Find out what is going on in your industry. By using online news services and specialized newsgroups and mailing lists, you can read about breaking news and discern trends.

21. Form alliances with companies. Dealers, vendors, and distributors who read your material might want to represent your company in new channels around the nation and the world. Your research might turn up companies that you could be a supplier to or engage in other relationships.

Customer Research

22. Conduct consumer surveys. With feedback forms, consumers can tell companies what they like and don't like.

23. Conduct market research. Companies can determine customers' preferences for new products and services.

24. Determine which products are most popular. Merchants can look over consumers shoulders and see which products are most frequently considered and purchased.

25. Find out which features and benefits are requested most.

26. Find out how long it takes to convert a prospect. By capturing keystrokes and counting time spent online learning about and purchasing a product, companies can understand the buying process more accurately.

Prospecting

27. Generate inquiries. People who read the information on your home page can let you know if they are interested in learning more.

28. Qualify prospects. Your Web site can ask questions of prospects to find out their buying power, interests, and needs.

29. Create lists of qualified prospects. Prospects who visit your home page or request information via e-mail can be added to your e-mail lists and databases.

30. Follow up on leads from ads in other media. Prospects who see your Web address or e-mail address in advertisements in print and television ads can read more on your home page or ask for a call.

31. Make appointments via e-mail or phone.

32. Answer questions via e-mail or phone.
33. Fulfill literature requests. Literature can be sent via e-mail or the customer can be directed to the Web site for more information.
34. Invite prospects to seminars and product demonstrations.

Sales

35. Sell new products to new markets.
36. Sell old products to new markets. Ketchum Kitchen, www.recipes.com, targets younger adults, especially men, not being targeted through other media.
37. Sell old products to new international markets.
38. Sell products that have a hard time moving through the distribution channel.
39. Sell products in your catalog with more description than available in print. Online catalogs have an unlimited amount of space to create sales messages that answer virtually every question posed by prospects.
40. Sell products that wouldn't normally fit in your catalog. Companies with large product lines might not be able to describe all products in a printed catalog because of the price of printing and mailing. These costs are minimal online so companies can display and describe their entire product line.
41. Quickly and easily distribute time-sensitive information about price changes, sales, and new products. E-mail is virtually free, so communication with prospects and customers is easy.
42. Test sales prices and products. Information on a site can be updated quickly and inexpensively so companies can test every variable imaginable.
43. Rotate featured items. Companies can test the product selection and change the display for any kind of audience. For example, a clothier can show one page for teenage girls and others for their mothers, brothers, and fathers. Companies that sell internationally can offer products depending on the seasons.
44. Distribute product information (news, software, reports, financial information) electronically. This is much less expensive than traditional printing and mailing.
45. Make sales directly on the Internet or through your inbound sales department. You have the option of taking orders in the manner that best meets your needs and those of your customers.

46. Lead people into stores locally. Kodak doesn't sell products from its site but rather leads prospects to local dealers.

47. Amass and distribute inbound leads for telemarketers and outbound sales professionals. People who respond to your ads via e-mail leave their e-mail address when they correspond with you.

48. Further the sales process by providing more content and demonstrations. The Internet offers companies the opportunity to present an unlimited amount of information to close the sale.

49. Make sales directly over the Internet, or by phone, mail, or fax.

50. Drive sales by offering coupons that can be redeemed at the store. Sites can include coupons for prospects to print and redeem.

51. Sell to targeted audiences with special interests (i.e., fishing, gardening, vacationing).

52. Sell to targeted audiences with lifestyle interests (i.e., children, education, parents).

53. Increase business-to-business sales. Many businesses use the Internet to find products and suppliers.

54. Educate customers. Use your site or e-mail to provide prospects with background information that helps make the sale.

55. Show products in action with video and sound. Prospects can learn more about a product by seeing it in action.

56. Supply maps and directions to your stores or offices.

57. Handle catalog sales more efficiently. Attitudes, www.attitudes .com, shut down its 250,000-copy print catalog and eliminated 12 employees because its Web site was so efficient.

Publicity

58. Build rapport with reporters by responding to their online queries, send information quickly via e-mail, and tailor messages to each reporter's needs.

59. Build relationships with your stakeholders (employees, stockholders, local residents, etc.) by sending them press material, financial statements, and demonstration products.

60. Notify reporters and customers of new policies. E-mail is a quick and efficient method of distributing information.

61. Distribute press materials inexpensively to reporters, employees, stockholders, and vendors. Xerox saves more than $100,000 a year with Internet and fax delivery of annual reports.

62. Warehouse press material for retrieval by reporters and various publics.
63. Spur word-of-mouth campaigns to sell products or create buzz about a company.
64. Manage crises. Communications professionals can manage reports sent to the press and stakeholders with information presented on the site, sent via e-mail, and stored in data libraries.
65. Debunk misinformation. By monitoring and participating in news-groups and mailing lists, company representatives can set the record straight if people write inaccurate information.
66. Hold press conferences and annual meetings online for reporters or stakeholders. People who cannot travel to attend a meeting can view the proceedings online. If the proceedings are recorded, people can listen at their convenience.

Collateral

67. Distribute materials inexpensively. Sun Microsystems says it saves more than $1,000,000 a year by referring people to its home page instead of sending out literature. Tandem Computers says it saves the same amount of money and reaches five times as many people as before.
68. Create targeted materials. Pages can be created on the fly so consumers interested in certain products can get clearly targeted information.
69. Create targeted materials more economically. Online brochures are much less expensive to produce than print versions, so companies can create pages clearly labeled for targeted audiences.

Customer Relations

70. Establish one-to-one relationships with customers and prospects using e-mail.
71. Send targeted messages and advertisements to customers who request them.
72. Build long-term relationships by responding to customers' initial requests and then sending newsletters and notes about new products, upgrades, and sales.
73. Answer frequently asked questions in a cost-effective manner. As most questions are asked by large numbers of people, standard answers can be sent via e-mail for a cost-effective response system.

74. Find disgruntled customers and deal with their concerns. By monitoring newsgroups, you can identify customers who are bad-mouthing the company and deal with the situation.
75. Build a base of evangelists. Customers who love your product can be recruited to solve peoples' problems online, answer technical questions, and alert the company to loud-mouthed troublemakers.

Advertising

76. Test ads. Because of the low cost of updating information, companies can test their advertisements and all factors involved in the sales process.
77. Test prices.
78. Test headlines.
79. Test offers.
80. Measure response. Every action on the Internet can be tracked, so companies can review each consumers' decision process.
81. Test to determine why prospects didn't purchase.
82. Integrate ad sales with other media (i.e., direct mail, postcard, TV, and print ads). Many companies print their Internet and e-mail addresses on ads in other media. Sporting goods cataloger REI received as many requests for catalogs through an online promotion with *Outside* magazine on ESPN's SportsZone site as it ever had through traditional media.
83. Deliver more information online to prospects who were initially attracted by ads in other media. Once prospects are attracted to a site, companies can present more information than could ever fit into a print ad or run on television.
84. Generate income from selling advertising on your Web site.
85. Build mailing lists of purchasers and build long-term relationships with them.

Cut Product Support Costs

86. Cut costs of support. Online support techniques can answer most routine questions without human intervention. Netscape, www.home.netscape.com, saves more than $10 each time a person uses the online support system instead of talking to a human being.

87. Reduce human cost. As consumers become accustomed to using online support, companies might be able to reduce support staffs or train their human staff to deal with higher-level problems.

88. Savvy customers want to use online support centers. Macromedia, www.macromedia.com, reports that 80 percent of its customers phoned the customer support center in 1995 but only 20 percent did so in 1996, preferring the Web site instead. Hewlett-Packard, www.hewlett-packard.com, gets one million customer questions on the Web per month compared to 600,000 on the phone.

89. Provide 24-hour support. Online service centers are open around the clock, unlike many in the real world. This increases customer satisfaction as questions are resolved at the customer's convenience.

90. Educate customers after they've found their answers. By receiving additional information about a product, customers become more knowledgeable and can solve future problems.

91. Lead people to purchase upgrades and new products. Once consumers resolve their problems, they are interested in learning more about your product line.

92. Let customers find solutions to problems without high-priced staffers. Federal Express and UPS let customers trace their own product shipments. Wells Fargo lets customers find their account balances. Many mortgage companies offer online mortgage calculators.

Brand Building

93. Extend brand image through a new medium. Customers who are loyal to companies and products with trusted brand images will follow them online.

94. Preempt position from virtual competitors. A first wave of online entrepreneurs is selling wine and books, and holding online auctions. Companies that sell these products in the real world will need to go online to recapture lost sales. Customers of these new companies will need to be targeted to buy from established companies with deep brand recognition.

International Sales

95. Sell products to an international audience.
96. Build and extend brand identity.

General Business

97. Post job notices online. Companies that have done this report they find better-qualified applicants than they do from advertisements in newspapers.
98. Distribute reports to employees quickly, even if they operate in satellite offices.
99. Revise price lists quickly via e-mail or updates to home pages.
100. Test products. Customers can download new versions of software tools or first drafts of information-based products like books, newsletters, and reports. They can give the company their opinions via forms sent by e-mail.

GET THE BUY-IN FROM VARIOUS DEPARTMENTS

It is essential for everyone in the company to have a say in the online marketing program. This is a fundamental business step. It is not important that everyone agrees on the final results, but it *is* important that everyone connected with the project feel that his comments were at the very least listened to. From a management perspective, it is important to listen to as many ideas as possible because good ideas can come from any source. If you follow this step, you might avoid ruffling feathers and even sabotage.

DETERMINE BUDGETS

Deciding which departments will pay for the online marketing plan is a tricky issue whose outcome will vary from company to company. While it seems that everyone wants to take responsibility for the project as it is new, exciting, and cool, no one wants to have the money come from his department's budget.

While it is possible to construct a basic Web site for $100, there are additional manpower costs for designing and maintaining it. Forrester Research reports these figures as average costs for going online based on interviews with 50 consumer-oriented Web sites:

Type of site	Costs	Time to launch (months)
Promotional	$304,000	2
Content	$1,312,000	6
Transactional	$3,368,000	4

NOTES:

A *promotional site* promotes a company's product or service.

A *content site* publishes constantly updated news, weather, or entertainment information.

A *transactional site* lets viewers shop, bank, or get customer service.

Source: Forrester Research, Inc.

It should be noted that many companies run their sites for a fraction of these figures.

OTHER QUESTIONS TO CONSIDER

The marketing staff and Internet team need to consider these questions when creating their online blueprint:

- *Do your online marketing materials carry the same image, message, and tone of your other marketing materials?* Do they add multimedia, virtual reality, and other forms of interactivity that enhance the shopping experience? The online message should be consistent with the rest of the marketing program.
- *What materials are needed to support the message?* Sales sheets, customer testimonials, reports from testing labs, awards, and the like can help build credibility.
- *How can these materials be interactive?* By using hypertext, e-mail, contests, surveys, and free products, you can create an interactive dialog with customers.
- *Why would customers buy online instead of through another channel?* You need to create a reason-to-buy-online statement, considering first if you want them to buy online or to go to the store.

Will you damage channel relationships if you sell direct? Should online marketing be a stimulus to generate in-store traffic?

- *Who will create the campaign, including message, art, and technology?* Does your in-house staff have the expertise to plan a campaign or should they manage an outside agency that understands the nooks and crannies of online marketing? Should part be conducted in-house and part farmed out?

- *Will the materials be updated? How often? By whom?* Updating a print catalog can be expensive, with production and mailing costs. However, online catalogs can be made current with new prices and products very quickly and usually at a lower cost. Sites should have new information added on a regular basis to attract customers and encourage repeat visits.

- *How does the message reinforce the company's mission?* Is the message consistent with the company's goals? Does the online marketing campaign tie in with the entire marketing program?

- *How do you respond to questions?* With a short message or a multi-page information kit? "The more you tell, the more you sell" is the operative phrase online.

- *Which delivery medium do you use to respond?* E-mail or snail mail? People buy when they are motivated. With online services, companies can close the sale while the customer is still hot. If they send information packets by mail or overnight courier, the customer's thirst for the product might be quenched.

- *What do your materials look like?* Do they take advantage of interactive tools and multimedia? Are they static text documents reprinted for mass consumption? Truly innovative companies that understand the medium will use it to its potential.

- *How do you ask for the order?* What persuasion techniques can be applied without going over the top? Remember that hard sells don't work online.

- *Do you use special promotions, discounts, refunds, and upselling techniques?* Online consumers like free samples of products.

BUSINESS MODELS

There are many ways to make money on the Web. Operating a mall, renting space on your server, and providing consulting services to companies entering the market have been explored. Here are additional business models to consider:

- *Business Model: Sell Promotional Space on an Information Product*
  Best for: Information Providers

  A popular Internet business model is creating frequently updated product information, sending it free to subscribers, and charging sponsors a fee for a special listing. For example, a mailing list on a given topic can be sent to 30,000 people and contain a sponsor's message at the top of the document. One could charge $20–40 per thousand readers.

- *Business Model: Create and Distribute a Sample Product; Charge for the Full Version*
  Best for: Software Publishers

  Software publishers can create their own Web sites to offer free downloads of new software programs. These files can contain complete software programs, shareware versions of full programs, or demo programs. To make money, the publisher attaches an unlocking code to the file. This code allows the consumer to try the product for a period of time and then locks the program so it cannot be reused. If the consumer wants to use the product again, he has to call the publisher, pay for the product, and receive the keys to the lock.

  Using the Internet and commercial online services has been a boon for many publishers of software distributed as shareware. Examples of products that began as shareware and have become retail products selling hundreds of thousands of copies include Procomm, Virus Scan, Doom, PC Write, and AutoMenu. Now it seems like every piece of software intended for Internet use is released online for a trial period.

- *Business Model: Create Editorial Content; Sell Advertising Space and Subscriptions*
  Best for: Information Publishers

  Publishers of books, magazines, 'zines, newsletters, and reports can make money on the Internet by creating Web sites where readers can read current and historical issues. While some publications offer only a few key articles, others print the entire issue online. This strategy introduces new readers to the publications. The publishers hope to make money either by selling subscriptions to the print edition or by selling online advertising in the form of cyberads or paid sponsorships.

The Knight-Ridder Science Base, a collection of thousands of articles and abstracts from scientific publications, charges a monthly subscription fee of $50 and an access charge to search the database. However, if you want to read an article, you must pay an additional fee ranging from 10 cents to 5 dollars, with the former being the norm. The fee is split between Knight-Ridder and the publisher of the original work. Subscribers give their credit card or billing information to Knight-Ridder in advance, so there is no problem collecting money.

Many information providers are having a difficult time selling subscriptions. *USA Today* and the *New York Times* dropped their plans to charge for subscribers, perhaps because so much news and information is already on the Internet and people felt there was no reason to pay a premium for those articles. As the Knight-Ridder Science Base shows, if you plan to charge for access, you must have information that is highly valued and difficult to obtain otherwise.

- *Business Model: Create Information Products*
  Best for: Consultants, Speakers, Trainers

  By writing informative articles and reports, consultants, speakers, and trainers can build credibility and gain exposure that can lead to revenue from selling their services. Such articles can be posted to mailing lists, newsgroups, and Web sites—the author's and others'—to create links between complementary sites.

- *Business Model: Sell Products Online*
  Best for: Companies that sell products either in the real world or only online

  Estimates of sales of goods and services ordered online by the year 2000 range from $7 billion, according to Forrester Research, to $189 billion, according to International Data Corp., 1996. Companies are selling lots of products today.

"Internet users planned the following online purchases, according to O'Reilly and Associates, Sebastopol, California.":

57 percent music

57 percent application software

38 percent computer peripherals

35 percent modems

20 percent travel services

14 percent financial products/services

12 percent automobiles

SAMPLE BUSINESS PLAN

EVEREST ADVERTISING
Internet Business Plan
By Supriya Padmanabhan
goopumsy@aol.com

Overview

This document describes the potential of Everest Advertising using the Internet as an advertising medium for itself. The questions of why and how are explored in the following pages to help us reach the decision: Should Everest Advertising develop a presence on the World Wide Web?

Who Are We?

Everest Advertising is a publicly owned multinational advertising agency. The company develops and implements marketing and advertising strategies for large and small corporations worldwide. The company has been doing this successfully for the last 20 years in North America, 15 years in Europe, and has extended its offices to Asia and Australia during the last 10 years.

What Do We Do?

- development of marketing and advertising strategies
- creation of ad works in all media: print, TV, radio, point of purchase (POP), Internet

- media planning and buying services
- promotional activity: direct mail, trade shows, event sponsorships, etc.
- publicity services: press releases
- corporate services: logos, annual reports, etc.

Our Marketing Mission

We provide marketing opportunities and solutions that take our clients to the peaks of success. Using innovative and creative strategic planning we successfully bring our clients and their customers together.

Corporate Advertising to Date

Prospecting by Everest Advertising in the form of advertising as been done using the following media:

- print advertisements when entering a new market
- direct mail to marketing teams of prospective clients
- word of mouth
- participation in advertising pitches on invitation from clients

The new option is going online.

- What does going online mean?
- Why should we go online?
- How do we go online?

What Does Going Online Mean?

For Everest Advertising, this means developing a presence on the World Wide Web in the form of a Web site—a three-dimensional representation of the company.

- It would serve as a forum through which clients looking for an advertising agency could learn about us and see what we are all about and what we have to offer.
- It would serve as a forum for advertising professionals to meet and interact.

- It would serve to develop a marketing community that sees Everest Advertising as a prime example, and the host, of success in the advertising arena.
- It would serve as a tool for the company to stand behind its marketing mission.

Today the Internet boasts over 35 million users with a million new users signing on every month. Never before has a medium offered so much interactivity between the customer and the provider. By going online Everest Advertising would become an easily accessible agency; prospective clients would be introduced to the gamut of services and the quality it provides.

This is a medium that is here to stay and is beginning to be an integral part of large service industries. The pushy salesperson attitude has never been an option for company promotions, nor has the 30-second world of TV advertising been for us, and we certainly have not been able to use POP to attract potential customers. However, a presence on the World Wide Web would attract people who are looking for us and want to find out more about us. We will be helping them make an intelligent buying decision.

Why Should We Go Online?

1. To increase our client base.

- By developing a Web site that is captivating, creative, informative, and intelligent we can attract clients looking for the same approach to their advertising.
- People browse the Web looking for information. Anyone looking for information or help on advertising, marketing, etc., would be able to visit our Web site if we register with the correct search engines or advertise appropriately.

2. It is a medium that will work for us, not against us.

- We have used that approach with our clients—very successfully. Why not practice what we preach?

3. To showcase our portfolio.

- By showing our portfolio to prospective clients visiting our site we will be able to guide them through our successes, offering proof of our high caliber. This gives us a chance to introduce Everest Advertising to people who come asking for the information, people at whom we do not have to thrust information.

4. Investor information can be offered online (e.g., annual reports, stock and shares data, annual meetings, etc.)

5. For our own public relations.
- We can use this as a forum for our own press releases, award announcements, new clients, etc.

6. To keep a lookout for new talent.

We can also create a community around the company and its clients through chat rooms, information on the making of ads, announcing release dates of campaigns, contests, etc.

Today, companies of all shapes and sizes are using the Internet as a starting board. On the Internet the actual size of a company is not noticeable. What does come through, however, is the quality of the company and the services it provides. There are several case studies of home-based outfits that have grown beyond expectation and all these are our potential customers. We have to keep in mind that there likely will come a time when the Internet will develop its own set of advertising rules and regulations like every other medium.

This is a medium that is accessible in every corner of the globe. As Everest Advertising is a global company, it makes sense to be a part of this global community.

Finally, the firsthand knowledge of the day-to-day schematics involved in successfully establishing and operating a Web site is invaluable.

How Do We Go Online?

On the following pages are detailed the list of services and sites we need to provide on our Web site. However, to ensure the success of the site it must be publicized and promoted by:

- Including the Internet address on all company literature (e.g., mailers, business cards, annual reports).
- Registering the Web site with at least two search engines: Yahoo! and Infoseek.
- Registering with keywords that are related to our work in any form (e.g., *advertising, marketing, success, innovation, creativity, promotions, TV, radio, press*).
- Issuing press releases in all relevant countries/geographical locations.

The Cost

The cost of maintaining a Web site using direct connection rates, not including standard installation charges, would be as follows:

Level of Service	Monthly Charge	Installation	Reconfiguration
64kbps	$1,000	$300	$300
128kbps	$1,500	$300	$300
256kbps	$1,700	$300	$300
384kbps	$1,800	$300	$300
512kbps	$2,000	$300	$300

The Competition

Several of our competitors are online with successful Web sites. The assumption that these sites are successful is based on the following:

- Over 100 advertising agencies are listed on Yahoo! and Infoseek each.
- The competition has several intelligent and creative Web sites that can only be helping provide a positive image to the company.
- Most chat rooms are filled to capacity during lecture sessions and preannounced guest speaker visits.

Competitive sites to visit:

- www.cks.com
- www.glness.com

These are examples of intelligent, creative, and informative sites.

Blueprint for the Everest Advertising Web Site

The blueprint for the Web site highlights aspects of the site that should be included. This is to be used as a guideline in the development of the Web site—no creative or storyboard planning.

Welcome Page:

- The Company
- Services and Clients
- Company Highlights
- Talk to Us
- The Funnies
- Investor Information
- Job Opportunities
- Site Map

This page should have on it the company logo, the marketing mission, and a creative theme to be carried through the entire site.

The Company:

- Who We Are
  - Welcome Letter
  - History of Company
  - Key Personnel (list personal achievements)
- What We Do
  - List Services (link to services and clients)
  - List Departments
- Where We Are
  - List Sites (link to sites)
  - Maps and Addresses

Services and Clients:

- List of Services
  - Examples of Work
  - Contact Persons for Each Service (provide e-mail links)
- List of Clients

- Portfolio of Work
  - By Country
  - By Language

Company Highlights:

- Press Releases
- Achievements
  - Awards
  - Expansions
- New Clients

Talk to Us:

- Suggestions (what people would like to see)
- Comments (remarks on ads)
- Chat Rooms
  - For Creative Ad Enthusiasts
  - For Marketing and Advertising Strategists
  - For Advertising Aspirants and the Pros
  - International Sections (Europe, Asia, Australia)
  - For Ad Watchers/Viewers

The Funnies:

- Bloopers while Shooting Ads
- Funny Ad Stories/Jokes
- Jingles to Download
- Favorite Ads to Download
- Ads We Like that the Competition Made
- Your Favorite Ads
- Ad Quizzes and Contests

Investor Information:

- Annual Reports
- Wall Street News

Job Opportunities:

- Now Hiring (permanent, temporary, freelance)
- Internship Programs

SUMMARY

The first step in going online is to create a master plan that sets realistic, definable goals. There are many reasons to go online to fulfill a variety of marketing goals. It is essential that the organization get the buy-in from as many constituents as possible for the Web site to be a success.

CHAPTER FOUR

Corporate Policies for Web Site Content

The Internet is the hot new prize in corporate America. It seems as if everyone in the company wants to control this new status symbol. Yet the issues for effective use of a Web site go well beyond turf battles. Serious decisions need to be made to avoid having the Internet turn into a hot potato.

This chapter discusses policies for decision-makers and suggests guidelines for a successful Internet master plan.

MANAGEMENT ISSUES TO CONSIDER BEFORE YOU EVEN GET ONLINE

Who Owns the Web Site?

Marketing wants it and so does the information technology group. My vote is for marketing. Why? Because marketing knows the overall picture of the company, its products, and its mission. Marketing knows where the company is headed. Technology understands the tools to make the Internet operate; marketing knows how to make it sing. Technology departments that have put up Web sites in the first phases of marketing have shown they don't understand how to write marketing copy that sizzles without being offensive, don't understand the fine points of tracking return on investment, and have a propensity to add time-consuming toys to the site even at the risk of burning relationships with prospects who have shown that they don't want to waste time watching pictures slowly unfold on their screens. However, marketing must work with technology to understand the new technological tools and toys, their strengths and limitations. The technology staff should be involved in planning meetings to keep the marketing staff up to date on developments, but marketing must call the shots.

What Are Your Goals?

Too many companies go on the Web without a set of goals. This is a recipe for disaster not only for the company but for the marketing manager responsible. Without a clear purpose in mind, you can be assured that when management looks at the results in three or six months, they will be disappointed because they have no numbers to which to compare activity. You might be thrilled that 100 people placed orders, or 1,000 people visited the site to build brand awareness in your niche market, but if management wonders why there weren't 1,000 sales and 10,000 visitors, then your job is history. It is essential that marketers responsible for the Web site create clear, achievable goals early in the process and revise them as events warrant.

There's More to Marketing than Sales

If you attend any conference on Internet marketing, the first question you are likely to hear is *Is anyone making any money?*

This is usually met with a mix of laughter, sneers, and blank looks. People joke that no one is selling on the Internet. That's not true. Many companies are. Some will even tell you. Others keep their mouths shut so their competitors won't find out. When 800-Flowers announced it was selling millions of dollars of flowers via online services after starting out as a two-person flower store, hundreds of two-person flower stores suddenly opened shop on the Internet! Others might not have answered the question because they are not online yet.

For the large majority, the purpose for going online is not to sell products but to improve marketing activities by gathering prospects and converting them to customers via online and offline activities, building brand awareness, providing customer retention techniques, or by a host of other marketing activities designed to save time and money.

Who Signs Off on Web Site Issues?

Each bit of information on the Web site is an official piece of business correspondence and should be treated as an important part of the company's history. If a site is sloppy, filled with typos, or contains outdated price information, the company's image will suffer both in public perception and even in a court of law. It is essential that companies create a policy on who has access to updating information on the Internet and who has sign-off authority. Policies will vary based on a number of factors such as company size, status of the marketing department, or charisma of the founder. It isn't necessary to debate the merits of each factor here, as long as a clear line of decision-making can be used to approve and post pages. Having such a policy in place ensures that disgruntled employees can't malign the company on its Web site and that people who don't have the latest marketing information cannot post inappropriate, inaccurate, or misleading information.

How Are Incoming Messages Handled?

The interactive nature of the Internet demands that each site have an e-mail address so customers can talk to the company. The question is, *who handles those messages?* The answer depends on what kind of company you run and what the mission of the site is. For some companies, the answer is a product manager; for others, a customer support representative; for larger companies, the answer might be both. In fact, there might be a need for a mailroom supervisor to sort the mail to each department. A simpler approach would be to have separate e-mail addresses for each major department, such as media relations, product information, product support, and investor information.

How Long Should It Take to Answer E-mail Questions?

Autoresponders can send preprinted information within seconds of receipt of the inquiry, so people are beginning to expect this kind of service, which works well for requests for product literature. However, as it is impossible to provide answers to individual questions in seconds, companies can build brownie points by sending a message that acknowledges receipt of the initial inquiry and a promise to respond within a certain time frame—usually 24 hours.

How Do Employees Refer to Themselves Online?

Employees have lives; they participate in online activities like submitting questions and answers to newsgroups and mailing lists. If they identify themselves as working for your company either in their messages or in their signature files, then their views will reflect upon the company, to whom this can present a dangerous situation. For instance, do you want the world to know that an employee is a member of a list your company finds in questionable taste, or represents a controversial political point of view?

Another serious issue is employees' participation in newsgroups when the discussion turns to competitors. Do they present the company point of view or do they report on the discussion to product managers or executives? How do they introduce themselves to the discussion? Let's assume that your product manager for the seat belt division enters a discussion about a car manufacturer's performance and offers his views about the safety of the car. Should he identify himself by company and title, as his opinions could be biased? Or is he a private citizen entering the discussion because he is a car nut? These issues need to be addressed by companies before damage is done.

Whose Budget Is It?

Who pays for the Web site? Marketing? Customer support? Public relations? Advertising? A combination of all? The answer will vary based on the company and the size and marketing mission of its Web site. While it is beyond the scope of this book to suggest a hard and fast rule, companies certainly should decide who will pay for the site.

Franchise Relations with Franchisees

For franchise companies, officers must decide if local franchisees can have their own Web site and what statements they can make. The design, look, and feel of the local site must reflect positively on the corporate image.

If the franchise decides to offers a host service to local franchisees, it must declare these issues, as well as decide how much space to devote to each business.

The method of handling inquiries and referring leads must also be determined.

What Is the Job Description of the Web Master?

Businesses must write a job description for the Web master. Here is the view of Brian Flanagan, supervisor of Internet projects for Molson, the leading Canadian brewery.

> My job description is similar in scope to that of a magazine editor and more. Depending on what you are trying to accomplish and the scope of your site, the responsibilities of your Web master will vary substantially. The following qualities are what I would look for:
>
> - Ability to handle multiple tasks/brands/initiatives simultaneously.
>
> - Ability to manage an existing budget and plan one for the future.
>
> - Being well versed in HTML and understanding technology well enough to work with system administrators, etc.
>
> - Design sense. This will vary with the amount of HTML you do in-house.
>
> - Strong communication skills. Report writing is vital to informing the unwired masses!
>
> - Good interpersonal skills, public speaking (if required for presentations), etc.
>
> - Some media background is helpful if you plan to advertise unconventional media.
>
> All in all, a generalist is what you really need. The more experience that the candidate has, the better. I suspect that a production assistant from the film world would have many of these qualities.

What Role Does the Web Master Play?

While Web master is the coolest title on anyone's business card these days, no one can agree on the role or responsibilities of such a person. At some companies, Web master is synonymous with king. At others, masters are propeller heads who tinker with hardware and software either to the relief or consternation of the marketing department.

The role of the Web master will change radically in the short term, the power shifting from the technician to the thinker. While HTML programming skills and knowledge of network servers seemed like a task for rocket scientists a few months ago, new software is making these tasks less daunting, even transparent, to many Web masters.

The situation compares to when I was a news editor for the Gannett Westchester Rockland Newspapers, which were the first in the country to have full-page composition systems on their computers (this was years before PageMaker brought the same results to desktop computers). I was among the first 12 editors in the country to use this system. In the beginning we were high-level editors and treated with great respect for our mastery of layout chores that formerly took minutes to accomplish. However, as the technology spread and more editors learned to use the systems, the tasks became routine. In less than a year, a new job category was created for "paginators" who worked under news editors and merely followed orders to lay out the papers. They had almost no discretion on placing articles or writing headlines. The same will happen to Web masters.

Here's the view of Joel Maloff, president of The Maloff Company, a strategic marketing consultancy to top-tier corporations. Maloff has viewed the growth of the computer industry and the Internet for more than 20 years, much of that working for telephone companies. (See www .maloff.com.)

Enterprisewide Coordination: The Case for a Web/Internet Resource Executive (WIRE)

The case for establishing an individual or possibly a group of individuals as electronic commerce (EC) coordinators across the enterprise can be made via the following points:

- Having multiple electronic commerce plans and programs is likely to be redundant, whereas community efforts may be able to benefit from economies of scale.
- It is unlikely that there are qualified enterprise personnel with excess time waiting to be assigned to these tasks within their own business units. Engaging in these tasks will be a full-time responsibility for some of the assigned personnel. Part-time efforts will be less than successful. New hires are likely to be needed by each group that engages in electronic commerce efforts.
- Institutional memory can be very valuable in assisting the efforts of less experienced groups and to help avoid common mistakes.
- In the absence of a clear enterprisewide electronic commerce philosophy, administered in a consistent fashion, each unit will evolve along its own path. Having a single, credible voice represent the views of the enterprise will stimulate creative approaches based upon the successes of others—both internal to the enterprise as well as external.

The arguments against a central EC authority are equally clear:

- It creates another layer of management.
- The more successful business units will be watched by their enterprise colleagues and learn from their efforts. Having a central management structure is more than enough—WIRE may not be required.
- Having a centralized Internet coordinator may slow down the process and remove authority from the lines of business.
- The existing lines of business are too disparate and there is unlikely sufficient synergy or overlap to require a common WIRE.
- Finding the right person(s) to staff this function will take too much time—we need to move ahead NOW.

The arguments both for and against the creation of a common Internet coordination role are compelling. The benefits of such a role are not without their costs. The fastest business units will find themselves somewhat impeded by the coordination process. The less adept units may be intimidated and taken aback by the forcefulness of their more advanced brethren.

The concept of a central, enterprisewide coordinator is a good one, but it can only succeed if a very clear delineation of purpose, role, and authority is provided at the start.

The WIRE should work closely with existing top-level management, and it must be clearly understood that the WIRE does not have the authority to approve or disapprove any programs. Rather, she is in a position to offer assistance, institutional memory across the entire enterprise, and to provide assurance to top management that good business practices are in place.

At a minimum, the person(s) acting as WIRE for the enterprise should have the following attributes:

- excellent interpersonal skills, including written and oral communications
- substantial knowledge of the Internet and electronic commerce concepts
- considerable business knowledge
- proven project management and coordination skills
- ability to effectively work with senior management
- ability to act as both a leader and a facilitator
- excellent listening and information assimilation skills

Given the ability of the enterprise to implement the role of WIRE, the company will likely be much more able to respond to environmental change, organize efforts internally, and maximize the productivity of its electronic commerce initiatives. The alternative is a lightly coordinated and distributed set of efforts throughout the enterprise. If it is possible to implement effectively, a well-coordinated approach seems to be preferable.

SUMMARY

To avoid problems, corporations must set policies regarding mission, content, and public persona before going online.

CHAPTER FIVE

Marketing Opportunities on the Internet and Commercial Online Services

How many small businesses are using the Internet and how are they using it? Well, according to a report from FindSVP, http://entry .findsvp.com, small business employees now account for more than 40 percent of work-related Internet users in the United States—not including home business operators. By comparison, midsized businesses account for about one quarter and large businesses account for nearly one-third of all work-related Internet users. Delve into these and other small business Internet statistics, courtesy of FindSVP.

Every online system has its own personality, rules of procedure, and advertising policies. It is important that marketers know the demographics of each system so that they can find which one(s) attract their target audiences. This chapter presents an overview of each major system, including its demographics, where available, its ability to provide marketing opportunities, its technical prowess, and the attitudes of its subscribers toward advertisers. At the end of this chapter you will have a better understanding of which online services can meet your marketing objectives.

In this chapter, you will learn:

- what an online service is
- about targeting your audience
- interesting statistics
- the truth about online demographics
- about marketing opportunities on the Internet and major online services

- reasons to use a commercial online service
- about negotiating the deal to go online with a commercial online service

WHAT IS AN ONLINE SERVICE?

An online service is a computer network composed of information libraries, shopping and commercial services, and e-mail that can be used by consumers who have personal computers, modems, and software. America Online, CompuServe, Prodigy, and Microsoft Network are examples of commercial online services that are owned by companies. The Internet is a network of networks that is not owned by anyone.

Online marketers can use several vehicles to reach consumers. We'll go into each topic in greater detail later in the book. Here is an executive overview:

- **Forums** are company-sponsored areas that allow the company to interact with its customers and prospects. Forums can include message areas, libraries, conference centers, and online stores. They may be private or public. Private forums, like the Toyota forum on Prodigy, can be used only by current customers. Public forums, like *Time* magazine on America Online, can be accessed by any online subscriber. Both types of forums can be profit centers for information providers, who take a percentage of the connect time (the amount of time each consumer stays on that forum) and a bounty for each new customer it lures to the online system. Companies can also sell products on some forums. The Internet's USENET newsgroups are discussion boards covering more than 18,000 topics. These groups cannot be used for blatant commercial activities. However, company officials can find targeted groups of consumers interested in certain products and join in the discussion by providing information, not salesmanship.
- **Message areas** enable consumers to talk with one another or with company officials to create relationships. Online services call them by different names: CompuServe features forums, America Online calls them forums and clubs, Prodigy names them bulletin boards (BBSs), and the Internet has newsgroups and mailing lists. Message areas are powerful communications tools that online marketers can

use to cultivate goodwill, dispel rumors, and build brand awareness. Although advertising is prohibited, there are several subtle ways to create the kinds of dialogs that are permitted. For small businesses and consultants, these informal chats can lead to long-term clients.

- **Libraries** are repositories of files that contain materials the company wants its customers and prospects to read, such as press releases, data sheets, and advertisements. Libraries can also be used by software companies to house software programs, demos, updates, and fixes that consumers can retrieve.
- **E-mail** is the primary communications vehicle between consumers and companies. Online services offer a tremendous amount of flexibility for online marketers, who can automatically respond to customers' e-mail information requests and product orders 24 hours a day. You won't lose sales because your e-mail operator is always on duty.
- **Automated e-mail**, also called **infobots** or **mailbots** (think robots) are like automated fax systems that send prewritten messages describing your product or service in response to consumers' e-mail requests. You can have any number of mailbots.
- **Electronic malls** are places where marketers can sell products. They can be part of a commercial online service or part of the Internet's World Wide Web. Merchants can also lease space from a new breed of electronic landlords who package offerings from companies. Electronic malls give consumers the opportunity to read about products and see pictures or hear descriptions before placing orders. Consumers can also send e-mail for more information—and receive it almost instantly, thanks to automated mail systems.
- **Conferences** enable marketers to build relationships with consumers by providing information, speakers, or access to famous personalities (such as Mick Jagger and William Shatner). Companies can also feature their CEOs or product managers in order to build relationships with employees, consumers, dealers, and investors.
- **News and financial services** provide consumers with information from wire services and more than 1,000 newspapers worldwide.
- **Reference databases** include government sources and hundreds of colleges and universities.
- **Internet telephony and video conferencing** enable marketers to create a relationship with a customer, provide support, and distribute sales information at the customer's convenience for the cost of a local phone call to the Internet service provider (ISP).

On the Internet, these terms are synonymous: *home page, Web page,* and *Web site*. No one can agree on the capitalization or spacing of *Web page* or *Web site*. The terms *World Wide Web* and *the Web* are synonymous. In this book I define the terms as follows: *home page* is the very first page of the Web site only, the front door; *Web site* is the whole site; and *Web page* is any page of the site that is not the home page. The terms *Internet* and *World Wide Web* are used in place of each other frequently, but this is not technically correct. The Web is a subset of the Internet, as are such tools as newsgroups and mailing lists. However, consumers seem to treat the terms *Internet* and *Web* the same.

These tools help online marketers create an informative, entertaining, and interactive experience for consumers.

TARGETING YOUR AUDIENCE

Marketing has been described as the process of making selling easy. This is especially true of online marketing. Convincing consumers to buy can be easy if you know which service they use and which messages will influence them. You will fail if you don't understand how the services differ and how they attract different audiences, or if you present a message that is inappropriate for that community.

This is especially relevant in the evolving field of online marketing. One of the great benefits of online marketing is the ability to target an audience. Each commercial online service has demographics on its average user so that you can see the differences between the services. Also, thanks to forums, bulletin boards, newsgroups, and mailing lists that cover every imaginable interest, online services attract people with varied tastes. Your job is to find your audience so you can convince them to spend time at your Web site.

INTERESTING STATISTICS

Here are statistics that will help you make your case for going online to your superiors or investors.

Source: Jupiter Communications, 1996

- The number of U.S. households online by the year 2000 will reach 35 million or 34 percent.
- At the end of 1995, the number of online households stood at 9.6 million and will reach 13.2 million at the end of 1996, a rise of 37.5 percent.
- Advertising revenue totaled $54.7 million in 1995 and could hit $5 billion by 2000.

Source: NetSmart of New York City, June 1996

This survey of 500 adults who use the Internet and online services for more than one hour per week, not including time spent reading e-mail, yielded the following statistics:

- 97 percent of people on the Web said becoming an educated consumer is a primary goal.
- 81 percent use the Internet to research products and services, with 46 percent buying the goods at retail and 46 percent buying online.

Source: Georgia Institute of Technology's Fifth World Wide Web User Survey, 1997

(www.cc.gatech.edu/gvu/user_surveys/)

- 60 percent of respondents use the Internet from their home.
- 31 percent are women.
- 45 percent are married.
- Average household income is $59,140.
- 40 percent shop online.
- 70 percent gather information for product purchases made offline.

Source: Hambrecht and Quist

	2000
E-mail accounts	300 million
Web users	200 million

Source: Decision Analyst, Arlington, Texas

More than 12 percent of the 98 million U.S. households subscribe to online services:

- West—15.2 percent
- Northeast—14.2 percent
- South—12.5 percent
- Midwest—9.5 percent

THE TRUTH ABOUT ONLINE DEMOGRAPHICS

The problem with demographics as a whole is that no one identifies himself as a white male between the ages of 30 and 45 who earns between $50,000 and $75,000 a year.

Think about how you identify yourself. You might be a father of two who coaches soccer on Sunday, gardens on Saturday, and takes a two-week backpacking vacation in the Rockies every year.

People don't put themselves in neat little boxes. Demographers do. Neat little boxes don't come to your Web site. People do.

The question is not who is online. The question is how to build a Web site that attracts your key targets by offering them so much value to enhance their personal or professional lives that they beg you for an account to get online!

This is not a farfetched idea. It is actually the business plan that helped America Online (AOL) grow from 500,000 members to 10,000,000 members in less than four years. AOL created relationships with publishers of magazines ranging from *Business Week* to *Popular Science* to *Better Homes and Gardens,* then offered free trial subscriptions to the magazines' readers. Each magazine created compelling areas online and attracted members by telling them they could read more articles online than fit in the printed publication, read the articles before the printed edition was available, send e-mail to reporters, participate in conferences with newsmakers, and network with other readers. Given those benefits, millions of people signed up for accounts! That should be your mission as well.

The beauty of the Internet is that audiences identify themselves.

THE INTERNET

Executive Summary

The Internet has the potential to expose your company and products to a vast worldwide audience. Even the commercial online services are hooking into the Internet, offering a rich new source of possible buyers. The Internet offers the best multimedia tools for presenting information through the World Wide Web, a multimedia environment (a place where marketers can present their information with photographs, animation, sound, and text). Because of the simple tools needed to create a Web site, or virtual storefront, any business can, for a modest investment, create an online presence, showcase its products, and take orders. As with other systems, advertising is prohibited in USENET newsgroups and mailing lists; however, many newsgroups have been overrun with spam and there is serious concern as to whether newsgroups will continue to be effective forums as members abandon the groups for fear of wasting time reading spams.

The Internet is slow to use. Because of this, marketers might want to restrict their use of pictures, multimedia, audio, and video.

The Internet's culture must be respected. The feeling among users is that the system is a big democracy in which governing principles come from the grass roots, not from a central authority. Information and software are exchanged freely. Old-timers resent companies that abuse system resources by spamming the network (placing the same message in many different newsgroups) or by placing ads in improper locations. Companies that give resources back to Internauts are welcomed. Therefore, marketing must be conducted in a new, noninvasive, nonthreatening style that is full of information: two-way interactive dialog. Users' feelings about spamming—the junk mail of the Internet—is reaching a fever pitch of hate. Marketers who think about using spam in their efforts are advised to rethink their marketing plan.

Overview

Founded in 1968 as a Defense Department project to develop a worldwide communications system, ARPANET (the Internet's original name) connected computers located in seven universities. Today more than two million host machines link more than 25 million people in 154 countries. The Internet is expanding rapidly, with some growth estimates reaching one million new users a month, although this is difficult to prove. Further, the commercial online systems CompuServe, America Online, and Prodigy are creating accessways for their members to use the Internet.

The Internet is a network of networks. It has no central authority, no governing body, and no official policies on anything. It is as free-form as an amoeba. Customers can create anything they want, such as a virtual store on the World Wide Web or a private mailing list—provided they have the technical ability.

Since late 1994, commercial interest from business consumers has grown considerably. As more businesses go online, the composition of the Internet community will change dramatically. The most important note is that commercial activities will be welcomed, not dreaded, by those new members who are attracted to the Internet because of commercial opportunities.

Demographics

When I wrote the first edition of the *Online Marketing Handbook,* every expert, journalist, and survey said there were 30 million people online and that one million more were joining every month to create a hockey-stick chart showing the explosive growth of the medium. Based on those projections, you would think that more than 50 million people would be online today.

However, the latest surveys show just the opposite! One survey says there are 13 million people on the Web, another ten million, and a third six million! How can so many smart people come up with such radically different numbers?

First, you must look at what is being measured. Is it the population of the Internet, the World Wide Web, e-mail accounts, or subscribers to commercial online services like America Online? Some news reports mingle and mangle the figures so they make no sense whatsoever.

Second, you must look at the source of the company issuing the study, especially if that source is a Web site interested in your advertising dollars. Ask yourself: What are they selling? Would that motive influence the report? Most of these surveys are used to convince companies that the Internet is a rapidly growing audience of highly educated and highly affluent consumers who want to shop online. That might very well be true, but how do they prove it? After all, there isn't any independent, third-party source to confirm these studies. Shady operators are free to claim any figures or demographics without fear of reprisal.

A great deal of Web demographics is inaccurate. Here's why:

- **People lie or don't remember.**
  People don't answer surveys correctly. Why? Any number of reasons. Some people give inaccurate information because they don't want the surveyor to know how much or how little money they make. They might be motivated by the need for privacy, or they might want to confound the surveyor's figures.

  They might want the surveyor to think they are smarter or more interested in loftier areas of the Web than they really are. When I was in journalism school, our professor told us that a survey showed that people said they read the front page, editorial page, and business pages of the newspaper, in that order. However, when the surveyor went to the subway to see what people really read, the results differed radically. People read the sports pages, horoscopes, comics, and front page. They didn't read the editorials or business sections. They just wanted to give the impression they were smart.

  People might honestly not remember the answers to such questions as "How much time do you spend online?" After all, do you keep a watch on your bedstand to let you know how much time you spend watching television? How would you keep accurate track of your online time (without referring to a meter set by the ISP or online service)?

- **Many survey participants are self-selected.**
  Some surveys phone a random sampling of the population at large, some a random sampling of people on the Internet. However, some studies that are widely quoted, like the Georgia Institute of Technology World Wide Web User Survey, are self-directed. Most of the demographics issued by individual Web sites are self-directed as well. This means that the people who filled out the surveys actively decided to go the survey site and answer the lengthy questionnaires. Such surveys can be misleading because they attract a specific slice of the audience that doesn't have anything better to do than fill out lengthy forms. It is no wonder that very busy people don't fill them out.

- **People have multiple accounts.**
  People have multiple accounts and are counted several times. For example, I have accounts with CompuServe, America Online, Prodigy, and my local Internet service provider. I am counted as four accounts even though I am one person. Should these organizations look at my zip code and make interpretations about my income or lifestyle, they would be multiplying the answers by four. I am not alone here. Other people might have an account issued to them by their company and a personal account that they pay for. How many times are we counted? Too many.

- **Surveys might not count kids and spouses.**
  When you sign up for an account, the order taker doesn't ask if you have a spouse or kids. They count you as one person. But your spouse and kids may sign on and buy everything from lingerie to college preparation programs to rap music CDs. How do those sales purchase patterns jive with the buying habits of a 40-year-old male subscriber? An astute demographer would realize that something is wrong, that an unknown number of persons aren't being counted, but would not know how many.

- **Information is outdated when it is published.**
  Because of the lag time in collecting, analyzing, and publishing data reports, they may very well be outdated when you read them. Check the online versions for updated information.

- **Women aren't counted.**
  This leads to the most damning statistical fallacy of all—that two-thirds of the people on the Internet are male. This makes absolutely no sense at all when you consider that:

  - Women have been using computers for many years in corporate America.
  - Women in college have free access to the Internet and use it.
  - Women are represented in equal numbers on many newsgroups and mailing lists, as judged by the number of messages posted.
  - Women comprise at least 50 percent of the people in my marketing seminars.

Certainly many of these observations are qualitative rather than quantitative, but qualitative information is no less important than numerical.

Women aren't counted for a variety of reasons:

- They don't have time to participate in self-selected surveys.
- The Internet account they use might be listed in the name of their spouse.
- Some women hide behind initials ("E.G. Smith") or use masculine names to avoid unwanted sexual attention or harassment.

- Even the companies that conduct surveys don't believe each other's numbers.

  In the high-stakes, high-rewards game of selling surveys, companies are doing their best to discredit each other's reports. No sooner does a survey come out than a competitor rips apart the methodology or interpretation of the figures. University of Vanderbilt business professor Donna Hoffman shook the survey industry on its head by disclosing faulty survey procedures used by a company that was getting the lion's share of the headlines.

DEMOGRAPHIC FINDINGS AND RESOURCES

Having totally debunked and denuded the demographics of the Internet, I hope to have created a healthy skepticism in your mind so that you have a realistic picture of who is online. However, I also realize that the truth frequently lies in the middle, just as where there is smoke, there is fire.

Perhaps the most reliable figures to date have come from highly credible organizations, Louis Harris and Associates and Baruch College of the City University of New York, printed in the May 5, 1997, issue of *Business Week*. This study shows that Web users are wealthy, educated, and white. The survey claims there are 40 million Internet users in the United States and that 42 percent have household incomes greater than $55,000 compared to 33 percent of the overall population. Seventy-three percent attended college compared to 46 percent of the overall population. Their figures show 59 percent of users are male and 85 percent are white. More importantly, 10 million people have bought something online. That's 25 percent!

Other sites that compile surveys and statistics about the Internet include:

www.cyberatlas.com
www1.mids.org/ids2/.index.html
www.cc.gatech.edu/gvu/user_surveys/
future.sri.com/
www-personal.umich.edu/~sgupta/hermes/
www2000.ogsm.vanderbilt.edu/site.statistics.cgi

Demographics of Commercial Online Services

Unlike the Internet, which has no central repository of information on its users, the commercial online services keep user demographic data. Because each person signs up for an account directly with these providers, they are able to maintain accurate account records and demographics based on internal surveys or studies of members' zip codes. These figures might suffer from the same problems as Internet studies in terms of how many people are online and who is actually using the account (did the mother buy an account so her teenage son can do homework online?).

MARKETING OPPORTUNITIES ON THE INTERNET AND MAJOR ONLINE SERVICES

The Internet offers many tools for marketing. The World Wide Web offers companies a way to put their entire inventory online to a worldwide audience, 24 hours a day. Web sites can be multimedia and interactive. Just what the futurist ordered! In this system, the business structures and posts its files as hypertext links that allow customers to browse and search for information to their heart's content. Consumers can click on a main subject area, such as toasters, and see pictures of every toaster in stock, followed by short descriptions. If they want more information, they can click on the term and find more detail. Whatever the business puts online, the customer can read. Marketers can add pictures, text, and sound to their Web sites. It is way cool. For marketers, the Web has become the place to post brochures, press releases, data sheets, and information about their businesses—as well as to take orders.

E-mail and mailbots can also help marketers create relationships and get the word out.

USENET newsgroups and mailing lists can be used by marketers to find out what people are talking about on more than 20,000 topics. Company officials can use these message areas to answer consumers' questions but may not advertise or promote their products or companies.

WHY USE A COMMERCIAL ONLINE SERVICE?

With all the talk about the Internet in the news media and around water coolers, you might wonder why anyone is even looking at commercial online services to transact business in an online world.

Here are a few compelling reasons to use the online services instead of the Internet, or in addition to the Internet:

- Reach more people. By using more services, you will reach more people. *Consumer Reports* uses several online services and the Internet. *Reader's Digest* uses AOL and the Internet.
- Reach a clearly defined market with proven demographics. The commercial online services do a much better job of identifying their subscribers than the Internet can.
- Gain revenue from connect time. Subscription services on the Internet have not worked. Online services, however, are subscription-based, so forum operators generate revenue each time someone browses. The money is split between the online service and the forum operator on a case-by-case basis. *George,* John F. Kennedy Jr.'s political magazine, and Century 21 chose AOL instead of the Internet as revenue is generated for the publisher every time someone visits the site. Some companies have used AOL as a launching pad to use before going on the Internet. Motley Fool began as a service on AOL, then added a Web site. Hoover's business guides are available on AOL and the Internet. On the Internet, revenue is not realized until someone buys something. Viewing is free.

NEGOTIATING THE DEAL TO GO ONLINE WITH A COMMERCIAL ONLINE SERVICE

When you consider all the benefits that accrue to an information provider, you might be surprised to learn that online services pay information providers to be online! You might think that companies would pay the commercial online services for the expertise and computer space to serve their customers. As a matter of fact, on the Internet you have to pay an Internet presence provider a fee to create and maintain the forum as well as pay for the storage space your forum's data occupies on a computer server. However, because the commercial online services make money from information providers' customers, your company can operate a forum and make a profit.

The commercial online services were hesitant to reveal financial terms for this book. Each deal is different, they say. Analysts believe the average split on royalties is 80–20 in favor of the commercial online service.

However, the commercial online services are eager to sign new information providers to attract new customers and to give them a competitive advantage over the rival services, so you might have considerable leverage in negotiating.

If you decide to create a forum online, here are the steps to take and the factors to consider:

Step 1: Decide Which Online Service to Use

The most important factor in deciding which online service should house your forum is determining which service currently has members who match your target market. For example, CompuServe has a large business market; Prodigy has a large home, children, and women's market; and AOL seems to appeal to people at the cutting edge of technology, literature, and the arts. Before signing on with an online system, find out much more about the demographics of their subscribers.

Step 2: Negotiate the Best Deal

There are two revenue streams to discuss. Online systems make money when members sign on to the system. The longer they are online, the more money the system makes. Your company could get a slice of both those pies—new member enrollment and online time. How much money you receive is determined by many factors. Every deal, representatives say, is different. Here are some factors that affect the terms of an agreement with an online service:

- **Can your forum recruit new members to the online service?**
  If it can, the service will pay a bounty for each new member.

Bounties can vary from a few cents to several dollars. Newer services are more likely to make sweetheart deals than older, established online services.

- **Can your business help promote the online service by bartering services?** For instance, a radio station, television station, newspaper, or magazine can offer to trade advertising space for additional financial consideration. A large association could send notices to members or place an ad in its newsletter or magazine.

- **Is the information provider exclusive to one service?** If so, the commercial online service will offer more favorable terms. Some companies would rather extend their reach. For example, *Consumer Reports* is on CompuServe, Prodigy, and America Online.

- **Does the forum provide information that can't be obtained from competitors?** If so, you have an enviable bargaining position.

- **Does the forum attract highly desirable consumers (high-income) or hard-to-attract consumers (women)?** Women have been slow to sign on to online commercial services and are poorly represented. If your forum can draw women, you have an impressive bargaining chip.

- **Does your forum appeal to a large number of members?** Operating the tiddlywinks forum might not give you as much bargaining force as having information that many people want, like baseball statistics for a fantasy league.

- **Does your forum have a high degree of name and brand awareness?** If consumers know your company instantly, you bring credibility to the online service. Members have a preconceived notion of the quality of products your company makes and could spend time in your forum.

- **How stable is your company and its commitment to online services?** Has your company been around for a while, or is it a relatively new start-up? The longer your company has been in business, the better. Start-ups have a much more difficult time bargaining with the commercial online services.

- **What will happen if the hourly rate charged to consumers falls?** Online services once charged like a taxi—the longer the time online, the more money you paid. Forum operators stood to make a lot of money in this plan. Now the commercial online services charge users a flat rate regardless of how much time they spend online. This will cut into the profits of the online publishers who depended on time as a revenue source. The average flat rate pricing plan is $19.95 per month, but that could fall as competition heats up.

Step 3: Maintain the Forum

Maintaining the system involves issues of technology, user interface, personnel, and content.

Technology involves creating the look and feel of the forum, connecting information to the server, and other nerdy issues. Unlike on the Web, these factors are out of your control. The online service creates the software, interface, and other tools and training needed to operate the forum. It also maintains billing records.

You need to consider what the user interface looks like. Will you have any say in the way it looks or will it look the same as every other forum? Using an online service's software is a double-edged sword. It is a blessing because these services know what works and what doesn't, so you get the benefit of their knowledge and experience. You also don't have to create tools from the ground up or spend massive amounts of time learning to program new software. Your readers, familiar with other forums on that service, will easily be able to use your forum's tools, which are identical to every other forum's way of doing things.

On the other hand, your forum will look pretty much like everyone else's forum—a distinct disadvantage to companies and publishers that have their own corporate look and feel. For that very reason, the *San Jose Mercury News* created an Internet World Wide Web site in addition to its forum on America Online. The company wanted to create a unique look and feel. The technical and artistic tools on the Web allow the publisher to reach its goal.

Online systems probably will adapt to a hybrid forum that allows information providers leeway in designing their forums. For example, America Online permits Hollywood Online to maintain a unique interface designed to take advantage of its multimedia offerings.

Human factors also must be considered. If your company hires a system manager to create content and organize the forum's messages, libraries, and conferences as well as to check files for viruses, answer readers' questions, and perform other housekeeping tasks, the employee is your responsibility; a salary must be paid and the work schedule defined. Nuts-and-bolts issues about manpower must be discussed. How many people will be needed to maintain the forum? Who will they be? Is this a primary or secondary part of their job? How much time should be devoted to this forum each day? What happens when your system manager goes on vacation? How will employees be trained?

Finally—and most important—content must continually be created. People will not go to a forum where nothing is going on. You must do interesting things that draw people to the forum. For example, CompuServe featured a press conference with Vice President Al Gore. Forums on America Online have hosted Jay Leno and Jerry Seinfeld.

The creative issues include: What content will be provided? What will the names of the sections on the message board and library be? What information can be installed by the first day of operation? What information can be added and when? Will special events, like conferences, be held?

Step 4: Keep Members Coming Back

The more times people return to your Web site, the more money you will make. This model works if you are selling advertisements because the more people read the ads, the more income will be generated. If you are building brand or selling product, the more exposures are made to your audience, the greater the chance that results you seek will be generated.

Here are several ways:

- **Be interesting**. If you have new information, lively discussions, contests, and promotions, people will come around regularly.
- **Promote discussion**. People like to chat online. They like to interact with people from around the world who are interested in the same topics they are. To increase the chat function, the moderators should ask questions of readers. Even when he answers a reader's question, the final line should invite a response, such as "What do you think of this?" or "What else have you tried?" or "Let me know if you need additional information." These types of messages can generate more conversation and more entry points for other readers to join the conversation while the meter runs.
- **Promote controversy**. People love to talk and debate online with other members. To stimulate conversations, you should create controversial messages that people can respond to. Typically the

moderator raises a question about an arguable issue from the day's news that would be of interest to the forum members. For instance, a health forum could ask people what they think about some feature of the managed care issue. A forum for business professionals could ask people what they think about the effects of the economy on their business. People also like to discuss current trends in their industry, such as new technology and salaries, as well as personalities.

- **Create interesting files**. Libraries are collections of files of documents, sounds, and photographs. These files can be retrieved by members at their discretion. The more interesting files you have, the more retrievals you will inspire.
- **Offer free samples**. Software is a great giveaway online for obvious reasons—everyone has a computer! Borland introduced its Sidekick for Windows personal information manager program by offering 5,000 free downloads of the entire working edition. By the end of the first day, that number had been reached and the company extended the promotion to 10,000 downloads! Borland won on at least three counts:

  1. It built a large installed base of users who will pay to upgrade to new versions in the future.
  2. These people will tell their friends and company peers, who will buy the software.
  3. The promotion created a large number of articles in daily newspapers, trade publications, and online discussion forums.

- **Conduct conferences with famous people**. Each online service regularly schedules online conferences with sport starts, actors, writers, and celebrities.
- **Host conferences and educational seminars with leaders in your industry or with people who can provide value to your members**. The Public Relations and Marketing Forum, CompuServe: Go PRSIG, has online seminars. Recent topics covered were "How to Write a Press Release in the Electronic Age," and "Crisis Communications."
- **Build interest in a forum with contests**. America Online hosts a stock market contest in which subscribers are given $10,000 in play money and told to build an ideal portfolio. To play, they must sign on and check prices regularly. They probably also chat with other

members and leave messages. They can also invite other friends to play, thus increasing traffic even more.

- **Build online time with surveys**. Prodigy conducts surveys on current event topics, such as "Is IQ related to race?" Survey respondents can spend even more time online to view the results, which are contained on several computer screen pages, by age, race, gender, and educational level. Prodigy uses this tactic frequently on topics ranging from politics to sports. Not only does it build time as readers respond to the questions, but also additional time clicks on the meter as people view the results of previous polls.

America Online

America Online
8619 Westwood Center Drive
Vienna, Virginia 22182–2285
703-448-8700
800-827-6364

Executive Summary

The corporate mission of America Online, which was founded in 1985, is to create electronic communities. When the service was launched, it called its customers *members* when other services referred to their patrons as *users*. AOL has experienced rapid growth since 1994, growing from 500,000 members to more than 10 million in 1997. Despite the growing pains that have been chronicled on the front pages of newspapers everywhere, AOL is clearly the number-one player in this marketplace. Its subscription base is growing rapidly, while CompuServe has stalled and Prodigy Internet has nose-dived. As this book is going to press, AOL announced its purchase of CompuServe.

America Online focuses on interactive communities and provides a wide variety of features including e-mail, newspapers and magazines, weather, sports, stock quotes, software files, computing support online classes, and forums to discuss lifestyles and sports.

Demographics

- Primary members are 69 percent male and 39 percent female, in contrast to the U.S. population, which is 48 percent male and 52 percent female.

- Over half of primary members (56 percent) report that someone else in their household uses America Online, an increase over the 49 percent other household users reported in a survey done in November 1995.
- America Online's 6,000,000 member households equate to over 11,000,000 users.
- Women and girls make up 41 percent of all household users.
- In households with children, 54 percent (ages 6-17) use the service; boys are slightly more likely than girls to be users, 57 percent to 51 percent.
- 68 percent are married, compared to 61 percent in the U.S. population.
- Almost half of AOL households have children—46 percent versus 34 percent of the U.S. population.

Age

Age	AOL Primary User	U.S. Census
18–24	8%	12%
25–34	20%	20%
35–44	30%	21%
45–54	25%	15%
55+	13%	32%

The median age for a primary member is 42.

Education

- 37 percent are college graduates versus 15 percent of the U.S. population overall.
- 26 percent have attended or completed graduate school.
- Another 22 percent have "some college."
- 13 percent of AOL members indicate high school degree or less, compared with 54 percent of the U.S. population.

Employment

- 75 percent of primary members are employed full time versus 67 percent national average.

- 65 percent of spouses are employed full time and 10 percent part time.
- 19 percent report they are self-employed, compared with a U.S. figure of 9 percent.
- 39 percent are in the executive/manager or professional categories.
- 11 percent are employed in a technical category, 6 percent in sales.

Income

- 4 percent of AOL households are in the under-$25K category versus 40 percent of the U.S. population.
- 41 percent report household income of $50–$100K versus 23 percent of the U.S. population.
- 16 percent report over $110K versus 6 percent of the U.S. population.
- 46 percent of AOL households are married/dual income; 24 percent single/no children.
- 18 percent are married/single income, and 8 percent single parents.

General

- 79 percent report having a personal computer with CD-ROM.
- 41 percent of primary members use AOL for both personal and business.
- 56 percent use AOL for personal interests only.
- 14 percent of households use modems 9600 baud or less, down from 25 percent last survey; 51 percent use 14.4 or 19.2, compared to 56 percent six months ago.
- 27 percent of households are using a 28.8 modem, up from 11 percent six months ago.
- 31 percent use AOL e-mail for business communications.
- 29 percent of AOL households have installed an additional phone line for their modem.

Opportunities for Marketers

America Online began offering shopping services in late 1994 with 2Market, a company that provides interactive shopping services for CD-ROM and online. Some 25 companies offer products online, including Lands' End, 800-Flowers, Crutchfield, Hammacher Schlemmer, the Metropolitan Museum of

Art, the Museum of Modern Art, Sony Music, Windham Hill Records, Sharper Image, and Spiegel.

Classified advertising is available in a company-sponsored area, as well as with several online newspapers, including the *Chicago Tribune* and the *San Jose Mercury News*.

America Online forums and clubs do not permit advertising.

Companies can create their own forums that can include advertising, information, customer support, and other materials to build relationships with customers.

America Online does not discuss growth figures, revenues, dollars spent, and so forth, a company spokesman says, nor does it speculate on the future of this market, the costs of operating an online store, or shopper demographics (the last because of privacy concerns).

CompuServe Information Services

CompuServe Information Services
5000 Arlington Centre Boulevard
Columbus, Ohio 43220
614-457-8600
800-848-8199

Executive Summary

Founded in 1969 as a computer time-sharing service, CompuServe is a leading global provider of computer-based information and communications services to businesses and personal computer owners. Its goal is to develop problem-solving computer services that provide companies and individuals with reliable, cost-effective access to host server and data communications services.

The oldest commercial online service, with more than 3.3 million subscribers, CompuServe (CIS) pioneered virtual retailing with the Electronic Mall, which features catalogs and ordering from more than 100 companies, including J.C. Penney and Lands' End. CompuServe introduced a CD-ROM add-on that helps merchants present multimedia catalogs to potential customers. CompuServe offers forums as profit centers for information providers like CNN and *U.S. News & World Report*. Support forums are featured from nearly every major, and many small, computer hardware manufacturers and software publishers. CompuServe also maintains a classified advertisement section.

At press time, AOL announced it has purchased CompuServe, but plans for integrating the services were not yet known. For this reason, the most recent CompuServe statistics, demographics, and marketing opportunities for marketers are presented here. Be sure to check for the latest updates with AOL as you pursue marketing opportunities.

Demographics

CompuServe has more than 3.3 million members in the United States and 5.1 million worldwide as of the second quarter of 1996. An independent survey of its users conducted in January 1996 by Matrixx Marketing, Inc., shows members tend to be well-educated professionals with a relatively high household income. Other interesting results:

- 84 percent are male.
- Median age is 39 years.
- 75 percent have completed at least a four-year college degree program.
- Nearly 75 percent are married.
- Average household income is $84,500.
- 80 percent are employed full-time, while over 50 percent of spouses are employed full time; 33 percent hold the position of executive or officer; 20 percent are in professional or technical positions.
- 35 percent have a home-based business.

CompuServe provides a worldwide market, including 500,000 subscribers in Japan and 140,000 in Europe; it has subscribers in more than 140 countries.

SUMMARY

The Internet and commercial online services offer tremendous benefits for consumers in terms of shopping convenience. Consumers have responded by purchasing an estimated $50 million in products. The Internet and commercial online services can offer a rich supply of tools to reach and influence targeted demographic groups. Each service has its strengths, weaknesses, and audiences. By understanding these differences, online marketers can find the right markets for their products. In some respects the online services function as gateways to the Internet itself. In the case of America Online, its original content offers a strong editorial base to keep readers inside the service instead of going to the Internet, but the handwriting is on the wall. The Internet is the king of online commerce and all small businesses should be headed in the direction of the Internet.

PART 2

Online Marketing Tools

CHAPTER SIX

Market Research Online

The interactive nature of the Internet and e-mail gives marketers an economical and easy way to gather information from prospects and customers. The Internet can be a terrific tool for conducting focus groups. In this chapter, you will learn:

- *how to find out who your visitors are*
- *how to conduct market research on your Web site via e-mail and traditional media with feedback loops through e-mail*
- *other methods of conducting focus group research*

FINDING OUT WHO IS AT YOUR WEB SITE

One of the most perplexing problems of the Internet is that you don't ever really know who is visiting your site. When someone enters your cyberstore, you have no initial way of knowing if the person is young or old, male or female, rich or poor. A store manager at the mall can see the people who enter her shop, but online merchants don't have a clue. They must use clever tactics to identify these visitors. As Internet culture is clearly opposed to manipulation and guards the privacy of individuals, simply asking visitors to tell something about themselves is not an easy task—especially when you consider they are paying money to be online and spending time away from other enjoyable or productive pursuits. They might not be in the best frame of mind to fill out a 20-page questionnaire about their likes and dislikes. This reaction is no different than a typical consumer response to a registration card that accompanies consumer electronics products like toasters and vacuum cleaners. Most people don't fill out the card, which asks dozens of questions about their income and buying patterns.

Here are several strategies for gathering user name and demographic information from customers and prospects via the Internet:

Ask Readers for Feedback

Discussion: A prime benefit of the Internet is that it provides an interactive way to create relationships with prospects and customers. By asking for feedback, the beginnings of a relationship can be formed. The tools to make this happen are e-mail and guest books. E-mail can be set up on a Web site with the HTML command *mailto:*, which allows the customer to click on the text and fill out a preaddressed e-mail message to the company. A guest book is a form that customers fill out and send to the company. Comments can be read by all customers, if the company wishes. By using these tools marketers can gain valuable anecdotal insight into the minds of respondents. If a statistically significant number of people respond, then other assumptions can be made. **Action:** Add *mailto:* forms, text input boxes, and guest books to your pages and encourage people to interact with the company. You should always acknowledge the interaction so people feel they are being heard. An autoresponder can be set up to acknowledge receipt of the letter with a simple thank-you. If the letter warrants a follow-up, then e-mail can be used.

Ask for a Zip Code

Discussion: As people will reach a burnout factor and not want to answer too many questions (no one knows how many is too many), try to compress knowledge. For example, if you know a person's zip code, you also know the city and state they live in, and can make a good guess at their income. To find that information the hard way, you would have to ask three questions instead of one.

Offer a Contest or Free Product

Discussion: For people to receive a prize or free product they must tell you where to deliver the goodies! You will then know their name, street address, e-mail address, and that they are prospects for your product. This strategy also reduces the amount of inaccurate information posted by people afraid of having their privacy invaded and works well at consumer, service, and professional sites. For example, Cliff's Notes, the publisher of literary study guides, offers high school and college students a free "Hot Tips" study disk and a list of all titles and prices.

Require Registration to Access Deeper Levels of the Site Page

Discussion: If you entice people with greater information and access to software, they may be more willing to tell you about themselves. Industry.Net, www.industry.net, which publishes industry-specific trade publications, offers a smash of free, useful information to establish credibility and then asks prospects who want to search the site and download software to identify themselves by name, title, company, industry group, and buying authority. This strategy could work well for other business-to-business sites.

Try Bribery

Discussion: Several sites that offer money or discounts to people to read ads require the consumers to fill out more than seven screens of information about their hobbies, interests, vacations, and sports and business interests. Because they dangle an enticing carrot (money), thousands of people have completed the forms. Goldmail, www.goldmail.com, and Cybergold, www.cybergold.com, are two such sites.

Check Submissions for Completeness with a Software Check

Discussion: People might leave information out either by accident or on purpose. A quick check by a software program will ascertain whether or not they have filled out the form correctly. If they have not, the form will return with a prompt for the missing information. If they have, they will get a confirmation notice on the screen, perhaps by e-mail, and then gain access to the site. Be aware, however, that complete forms are not necessarily accurate. Marketers face the same problem in other venues, such as telephone interviews and prospect forms at trade shows.

Don't Ask Questions that Will Irritate Prospects

Discussion: While respondents might not mind filling out basic mailing label information, they very well may balk at such personal information as net worth, salary, or—my all-time horror—mother's maiden name. While the first two could be merely offputting, the latter is *never* needed by a marketer. This sensitive information could be extremely hazardous if it fell into the wrong hands, as bank accounts and credit cards can be accessed with this password! *Hot Wired* asked for this information and then rescinded. However, the *Wall Street Journal* requires a mother's maiden name to register for their site. This kind of invasion of privacy in a medium not known for security is equal to waving a red flag in the face of a prospect.

Conduct a Survey

Discussion: People like to take part in surveys and opinion polls, especially if the questions are short. A clever (sneaky) tactic is to create a form with two buttons (Yes/No) that respondents click on to show their feelings. The buttons are really *mailto:* commands that send the respondent's e-mail address to your mailbox. You still won't know who john@mycompany.com is, but you *will* know that he prefers chocolate to vanilla ice cream.

Test the Number of Questions People Will Answer before Giving Up

Discussion: Be aware that people didn't come online at great expense to serve as guinea pigs. The more questions you ask, the less likely they will want to participate unless you offer a really great reward. No one has done research to find out what the magic number is and whether or not it is swayed by the weight of the offer involved. The findings might vary from industry to industry. To find out what works on your site, test various options and numbers.

Fill the Form with Required and Optional Information

Discussion: As responses will fall off based on the number of questions asked, you need to limit the number. However, you might be able to get the information you want without turning people off if you make certain information required and other information optional. For example, you might require name and e-mail address so you can correspond via e-mail but make the mailing address optional.

Require All Information

Discussion: If you are in a business-to-business company, then you might not mind risking a drop-off by requiring additional information, based on the theory that if visitors can't qualify themselves properly, then you don't want to waste your resources dealing with them.

CONDUCTING MARKET RESEARCH ON YOUR WEB SITE

You can find out a great deal about your customers by using your Web site. Here are several nonintrusive techniques:

Monitor Online Visits

Discussion: Software programs can track online usage by your visitors and customers. You'll see which products they select to review, which they buy, and how much time they spend looking at each page. By studying these data you can identify those products that are capturing attention and how they sell by time of day and region of the country. You will also find where your visitors reside by region of the United States, as well as in all countries on the globe. Based on this information you might decide to ramp up production of surprising models that are selling beyond expectations. If you can track demographics, you might find that one color appeals to a certain group while another appeals to a second group. Your advertising department might alter the color of the products in their print campaigns targeted for separate groups.

Test Prices, Headlines, and Advertising Copy

Discussion: Because revisions are so inexpensive on the Internet compared to print or broadcast media, you can test your message, prices, headlines, and other factors to see which elements are most effective.

Ask For Feedback

Discussion: Customers know what features they want in a new product and where your product falls short. They will be glad to tell you— if you ask them. Give them a chance to voice their opinions by filling out a survey or sending you e-mail. You might encourage them by selecting winners and posting their entries.

Send Appropriate Messages to Targeted Audiences

Discussion: If you find out where people last visited before coming to your site, you can send them pages specially geared for their needs. For example, if they came from a competitor's site, you could quickly point out the advantages your product or service offers. If they came from an advertisement in a magazine, you could send them a different set of pages than that given to a person who entered via your direct mail campaign. In this manner you can tell parents that your car has the latest safety features for children while you tell college students that it goes from 0 to 60 faster than any other car.

Send E-mail Request Forms to Targeted Audiences

Discussion: Send your prospects and customers an e-mail notice asking them if they are interested in receiving your new products. They could select different price ranges, colors, patterns, and the like. By studying the resulting information you would be able to see patterns and trends. You also will have succeeded in having the readers define their interests to you. Based on this information you would know that a certain person, for instance, would pay between $25 and $50 for a shirt. They would get your material for the midline catalog instead of the high-end catalog. Information-based companies can also use this method to test prices and to create an ordering mechanism.

Use E-mail Surveys

Discussion: If you have developed an e-mail list of customers and prospects in your target market, consider querying them to find out what they like or dislike about your product, what products or services they would like to see, and other market research information. Lilly Walters, coauthor of *Speak and Grow Rich* and a principal in the Walters International Speakers Bureau, sends her readers, professional speakers, and meeting planners a brief survey to find out about new trends in the marketplace. She reports a whopping 40 percent response rate. "We get a very high response rate if we keep the questions *very* simple and only ask one or two questions."

Here is a sample questionnaire:

Walters International Speaker's Bureau

We are taking this very quick survey from a list of 1,500 professional speakers, seminar leaders, and speakers bureaus (if that's not you, please disregard this).

The results of this survey are published in the second edition of *Speak and Grow Rich* by Lilly and Dottie Walters (Prentice Hall) and in our magazine *Sharing Ideas for Professional Speakers*.

Question: Are you a speaker or a speaker's bureau?

Question: Which publication do you make time to read?

Question: Membership in which association has proved the most beneficial for education and information for you as a professional speaker?

Question: Membership in which association has proved the most beneficial as a source of bookings for your speaking?

Question: Which book has been the most helpful to you as a professional speaker?

Question: If you could ask 1,500 professional speakers a question, what would you ask?

Thank you!

Lilly Walters,

e-mail: LillyW@Walters-Intl.com

Author:

Speak and Grow Rich (Prentice-Hall, 1996 and 1988)

What to Say When You're Dying on the Platform! (McGraw-Hill, 1995)

Secrets of Successful Speakers (McGraw-Hill, 1993).

Pose Questions or Present Surveys in Newspaper Ads or on TV and Ask for Response via E-mail

Discussion: *The San Francisco Chronicle's* Business Section asked readers to vote on how stock information should be displayed (decimals or fractions) and respond via e-mail, fax, or phone. Other businesses can ask questions in any medium and direct respondents to answer via e-mail or to go to the company site and receive a gift or free information reports for responding to the survey.

Host a Chat Session on Your Web Site

Discussion: Many company Web sites now feature software that allows people to chat. You could invite customers or employees to such a session and conduct a focus group online.

OTHER METHODS OF CONDUCTING FOCUS GROUP RESEARCH

Use Newsgroups to Find Out What People Are Saying about Your Products

Discussion: People use newsgroups to find recommendations about buying products. It is not unusual to find novice classical music fans asking for suggestions on which albums to buy to create a collection or car owners posting messages to find out which tires they should buy; computer users are always asking for tips. People also post their grievances online. By typing the name of your company or product on a search service like Deja News, www.dejanews.com, you will find out what people are saying about your company. In one seminar I conducted, a woman from a well-known sneaker company found to her horror that customers were complaining that her company's products were falling apart! Another possible strategy is to post questions in appropriate newsgroups. However, this should only be done after making sure the group allows this kind of questioning. If you post questions without first ascertaining the permissibility of this venture, or not, you might run the risk of alienating a large audience.

Hire a Company to Monitor Newsgroup Activity

Discussion: Monitoring newsgroups and making sense of the discussion can take time that you don't have. If that's the case, consider hiring a company that specializes in monitoring and evaluating these discussions. Two such groups are eWatch, www.ewatch.com, and The Delahaye Group, www.delahaye.com.

Focus Group Tools

One of the best ways to conduct focus groups online is with a new tool called PlaceWare Auditorium, which is produced by PlaceWare, Inc., www.placeware.com, a spin-off of the highly regarded Xerox Palo Alto Research Center (PARC). The product is a highly interactive Java-based multimedia Web auditorium that lets organizations conduct seminars, present sales and training materials online to a live audience, and gather customer feedback in real time.

PlaceWare Auditorium provides companies several tools to monitor feedback. For example, a marketing manager could present the company's new product line to an audience of salespeople. After showing slides and presenting the spoken part of the presentation via the Web, he could then ask the salespeople to vote on which products they thought would be most widely accepted by the customers. Audience members can vote on any number of issues in real time, so the company can see the results immediately. Similar applications could be conducted with employees, consumers, dealers, and other members of target audiences. In addition, participants can give spontaneous feedback, and a presenter can gauge audience response on the fly.

Intel Corporation created the MediaDome to present compelling content and multimedia events. The company integrated PlaceWare technology as a component of the MediaDome site and uses it for live interaction and large-scale events.

PBS Learning Adventures raves about the potential applications of PlaceWare technology. "The education and training implications of the PlaceWare Auditorium are enormous for PBS ONLINE," says John Hollar, executive vice president. "With PlaceWare's capabilities, we see a world of opportunity to strengthen our mission to educate and entertain the millions of parents, students, teachers, and adult learners who use PBS ONLINE every year."

The United States Golf Association (USGA) hosted discussions and special events in the PlaceWare Auditorium during the recent U.S. Open golf tournament. "Events in the PlaceWare Auditorium added a new dimension to the Web for golf fans," says Corey Shelton, USGA manager of Internet service. "Not only could the fans review information on our site, but they were also able to interact with U.S. Open golfers, ask them questions, and get live feedback."

The Hewlett-Packard (HP) Desktop Classroom is a fully integrated and interactive Intranet-based application for training HP customer service professionals in a live, global community setting. Using the PlaceWare platform as the underlying technology, a group of HP software engineers has developed a dynamic virtual desktop classroom for training thousands of frontline support engineers. HP finds that PlaceWare integrates into one package all the functionality necessary to run the Desktop Classroom. Says engineer and scientist Gary Orsilini, "With PlaceWare, we've found something that is as easy as picking up the phone. And its robust set of features makes it incredibly more powerful than any other combination of software solutions we have experienced."

A support organization can use the PlaceWare Auditorium to provide just-in-time training at the support engineer's desktop. In the Auditorium, experts can display slides to communicate complex material, annotating slides to focus the audience's attention. By using polling slides, experts can test user understanding and identify potential problem areas.

The PlaceWare Auditorium also provides spontaneous response facilities that let the expert receive constant feedback and that allow the audience to directly question the expert at any time about any subject.

Customer Seminars Marketing professionals work hard to attract and qualify potential customers. The product seminar is a valuable tool in this process, but it is expensive and often requires that customers travel to the seminar.

With the PlaceWare Auditorium, marketing professionals can bring product presentations directly to the customer's desktop, without leaving their own offices. Customers don't need to wait for the next scheduled trade show or make arrangements to attend a special hotel seminar.

Marketing Focus Groups Getting quantified customer feedback on product features can be time-consuming and expensive. Often it is difficult to get the right customers to spend time evaluating a product.

With the PlaceWare Auditorium, customers can easily and conveniently review and evaluate product features, and marketing professionals can efficiently collect customer comments. Marketers can use a multimedia presentation to promote key features and emphasize customer benefits. And by using polling slides, marketers receive quantified voting information about an audience's preferences. Audience questions help a marketer design collateral and future products.

Improve and Simplify Sales Seminars—The PlaceWare Auditorium is seamlessly integrated with the Web, so it's easy and convenient for customers to attend a product demonstration. And because the PlaceWare Auditorium has no physical boundaries, events can serve audiences ranging in number from tens to thousands.

Get Fast Customer Feedback with Online Focus Groups

Online focus groups conducted through the PlaceWare Auditorium can provide an extensive sampling of customer response. The Auditorium is a valuable marketing tool for directly contacting the customer with little expense and effort.

SURVEYS AND E-MAIL

E-Mail Survey: Testarossa Vineyards

Hello Testarossa E-mail Members,

We are contemplating adding the ability for our mailing list members to order wine and pay for it using a VISA or Mastercard. The cost is not insignificant so we want to get your feedback before we sign up for this service.

Would you, as a consumer, like the option to pay with a credit card?

Would there be circumstances where you might purchase wine with a credit card from one of our mailings where you might not send a check?

Say you were to purchase wine from one of our mailings. Please rank in order of most likely (1) to least likely (4) the way you would prefer to pay:

___ A. Fax in order form with credit card number.
___ B. E-mail order with credit card number.
___ C. Send U.S. mail order form with credit card.
___ D. Send U.S. mail order form with check.

___ E. E-mail/fax/U.S. mail order form and be invoiced (this option would only be valid on second and subsequent orders).

Thank you very much for your responses and past support.

Our 1995 wines are now in the marketplace at several top restaurants and wine shops including:

- San Francisco:
  - Rubicon
  - Boulevard

- San Mateo
  - 231 Ellsworth

- Palo Alto
  - STARS (soon to be Spago)

- San Jose
  - Paolo's

- Los Gatos
  - Cafe Marcella

- New York City
  - Windows on the World at the top of the World Trade Center
  - Le Bernardin—New York's longest-running four-star restaurant
  - Montrachet—one of the top seven restaurants in New York (Wine Spectator)
  - Jean Georges in the Trump International

- Boston
  - L'Espalier
  - Ambrosia
  - Biba
  - Grill 23

- Santa Barbara
  - The Wine Cask—Wine Spectator's Grand Award Winner

For a complete list check out our Web site at www.testarossa.com and click on "Where can I find Testarossa Wines?"

We will have a Spring Winery letter coming out soon and sincerely appreciate your feedback.

Cheers,

Rob & Diana Jensen
Testarossa Vineyards
wine@testarossa.com
www.testarossa.com
408-739-5033

SUMMARY

Your Web site can yield a tremendous amount of terrific information about your customers and prospects.

SUMMARY

CHAPTER SEVEN

Customer Service and Support Online

"Answering support questions on the forum is far easier, quicker, and less expensive than answering letters or phone calls," says Eric Robichaud, president of Rhode Island Soft Systems, a software publisher of screen savers, fonts, and games. "You can support customers when it is convenient for you instead of having to drop everything when they call."

In this chapter you will learn:

- the benefits of online customer support systems
- how to create an online support center
- strategies for creating a successful support center

BENEFITS OF ONLINE CUSTOMER SUPPORT

The Internet and commercial online services can help your business build relationships with customers by creating online support centers to answer people's questions. Companies that respond to customer's queries quickly can build loyalty that lasts a lifetime. Also, happy customers tell potential customers—so do unhappy customers!

By creating a customer support center online, your company can benefit from:

- **Increased loyalty from customers:** Consumers who get technical support quickly will remain happy and might see no reason to switch products.
- **Reduced returns from customers who experience problems:** Consumers who can't get support quickly can become frustrated with your product and return it for a refund.

- **Reduced bad word of mouth:** Studies have shown that happy customers tell three friends while unhappy customers tell eleven! One way to reduce bad word of mouth is to have good customer support that helps dissatisfied customers before they unleash a torrent of ill will.
- **Faster response to customer questions:** Some companies with small support staffs are overburdened and can't respond to customers' questions in a timely manner. By using online support centers, they can answer people's questions faster. With the use of libraries of stored text files and software patches, consumers might be able to find what they need without speaking to a support rep.
- **Lower support costs:** Customers can find information that addresses frequently asked questions. Service reps won't have to return expensive phone calls. Toll-free phone numbers won't be used as much. Questions can be answered in batches, thus making more efficient use of service reps. Questions can be delegated to people who have the right degree of skill to answer.
- **Customers helping answer other customers' questions:** This will lighten your staff's workload and build camaraderie among consumers.
- **Market research:** Customer complaints about certain features might lead to development of new products or features, thus aiding research and development. Dan Bricklin, who invented the first computer spreadsheet, VisiCalc, handled customer support calls and learned of customers' needs, which led to significant new features in other products.
- **Profit center:** If your support center generates a significant amount of traffic, your company might actually make money from the arrangement contracted with the commercial online service. Smaller companies probably won't make any money, but larger ones can do well.

"There is some residual payback, although it is not major. Maybe a couple hundred bucks a month," says Craig Settles, senior strategist at Successful Marketing Strategists, of Berkeley, California. "However, there is no cash outlay for returning phone calls."

Another way to turn the support center into a profit center is to train the service reps to sell additional products to customers. For example, people might call about a product that has been replaced by a new model. The rep can sell the new model. Reps can also sell service contracts, additional copies of the product for friends or colleagues, other items from the product line, and complementary products from other companies.

The computer industry has embraced this concept, as most major hardware manufacturers and software publishers have forums. In fact, several companies, including Microsoft, Lotus, Borland, Symantec, Compaq, Hewlett-Packard, IBM, and Apple, offer support forums on multiple services to ensure that they make their support centers available to as many of their customers as possible. Many smaller companies also offer support centers online.

Case Study: Computer Chronicles

Computer Chronicles is a television show that discusses numerous computer products each week to a national audience. The company operates a forum, CompuServe: Go Chronicles, as a service to its viewers, not to make money. The forum provides information about the show, its editorial calendar, topics covered, and a bulletin board.

"The primary purpose is to provide an avenue of support for our customers and an outlet for them to get the products they want in a cost-effective manner for them and for us," says Stuart Cheifet, executive producer of *Computer Chronicles*. "They see lots of neat toys and ask, 'How can we get that? What does it do? How much does it cost?' If they miss information on the show, they can find it on the forum."

Viewers called the program before the forum came online. The company devoted a full-time employee to answer questions. The forum receives about a hundred calls a week that are answered at the convenience of a staffer.

"We can answer questions in one sitting instead of having a person be on call all day to answer," Cheifet says. "It saves us one full-time person and a lot of telephone costs. It is a real solution to a problem."

Because online members are a friendly lot, they frequently answer each other's questions, thus saving the staff even more time.

Case Study: Road Scholar Software, Inc.

Road Scholar Software, Inc., of Houston, is a leading publisher of digital maps. With a large customer base, the company found its two-person support staff overwhelmed with support calls for its product, City Streets for Windows.

"The problem was the constraints of telephone and fax. Technical support is labor-intensive and expensive," says Jim Nichols, product manager. This led to issues with consumer satisfaction. "The average support call might run 25–30 minutes, and response time can suffer when calls stack up. At peak periods, sometimes 80 customers were awaiting callbacks. It could take several days to help customers.

"Furthermore, support is expensive because nearly all the support calls are callbacks, which the company must pay for."

Road Scholar prides itself on maintaining close contacts with its consumers, and so the delays were unacceptable to the company as well as irritating to users.

The company first set up a fax response system. It created 45 topics for all its products that consumers could select from a menu. Topics ranged from installation to screen displays. They were written in a friendly, readable format with such titles as "My screen is distorted. What should I do?" Answers ranged in length from half a page to three pages. The material featured troubleshooting tips and step-by-step instructions—the same material that support personnel were giving people on the phone. Instead, customers could get the answers without waiting for a human to call them, and the company could save manpower as well. And they could get the information well after business hours. "This echoes what we tell them on telephone tech support," says Nichols.

Based on this success, the company decided to expand its customer support to its customers who are CompuServe members to complement its support center.

"The idea was to get on CompuServe's PC Vendor Forum to improve support and increase accessibility on the part of users to enable them to get answers quicker to their questions," Nichols says. "The goal with the online services was to take that fax response system and put it out there online to make it more effective. CompuServe members can read the questions and answers online or download the files and read them offline via CompuServe: Go RoadScholar. They can get help without talking to a person."

Dealing with the online services was painless.

"It was easy. They have people who handle the vendor forums. They are very accessible and responsible. The process itself is straightforward," says Nichols. "There is a little bit of paperwork, but not much. We had to write a company overview and some explanatory material for the online version, but the help sheets remained the same."

CompuServe also wants its vendors to publicize the forum by listing information in manuals and by providing brochures or postcards in the product packages. With CompuServe providing templates for the material, all Road Scholar needs to do is fill in the blanks. "It is the logical thing to do," says Nichols. "Having a forum and promoting it enhances the value of your product."

Getting online—from initial inquiries with CompuServe to writing the material to posting it online and going live—took less than one month. Road Scholar is not paying for the service, although all contract terms vary from company to company.

The project has been a success.

"This has helped our staff by allowing them to handle the exceptional calls that aren't covered by the printed topics. It helps customers get support in the middle of the night without waiting for a support technician. It is more cost-effective for us as it frees up manpower who can concentrate on new problems and difficult situations."

Road Scholar saves money by not having to return support phone calls. "It dramatically reduces telephone bills," says Nichols.

The company plans to expand the services offered in its support forum to include posting bug fixes that consumers can download. Road Scholar also will post demonstration versions of new products that can be downloaded. An ordering mechanism will be included so that people can buy products.

"We've been able to reduce our support costs while improving customer service," says Nichols. "What could be better than that?"

PRACTICAL CONSIDERATIONS FOR CREATING AN ONLINE SUPPORT CENTER

While many aspects of establishing a customer support center are outside the realm of this book, online marketers should address several questions in planning one:

- **Online services:** Which online service should be used? Many hardware and software companies have customer support centers on each major online service because their customers use only one service. Plan to do the same. This might add to your costs but will guarantee a wider area of coverage for your customers and create more opportunities for positive interactions between the consumer and the company. Associations and companies that are not in the computer business might limit their online participation to one major system. This choice can be based on which online service offers them the best terms or which service is currently used by most of its members.

- **Manpower:** The support center must be staffed by competent professionals who not only know the ins and outs of the product but can build rapport with people online. This is important, as people who call support centers are frequently angry and frustrated because they cannot get the product to work properly. Consequently, their messages might be caustic. Support staffers must be able to deal with the situation by diffusing the anger, solving the problem, and building bridges to positive communications with the consumer. The company cannot afford to have one angry customer tell his experiences to thousands of people online!

- **Content:** Online libraries can store a great deal of technical information. Having consumers find this information by themselves can help the company save a great deal of time and expense. This can be accomplished by carefully organizing the information by the appropriate classifications. For example, a software company can have these file folders: product, installation, usage, printing, upgrade, common errors, error codes explained, how do I accomplish task *x*?, and many others. Material can be cross-referenced and hyperlinked so that consumers can jump from one area to another with ease.

- **Cost:** The budget for an online support center will vary by company. While planning the budget, don't think of it as a drain on expenses. Instead, think of it as a way to save money by unburdening other forms of support—telephone, mail, and fax. Also, think of the benefit in positive customer relations. Finally, create ways to turn the support center into a profit center by encouraging messages that create sales opportunities for new product versions, complementary products, and long-term support and training contracts for large companies.

Case Study: IntelliSystems Knowledgebase Provides Customer Support Over the Internet

Companies that need to provide customer support via the Internet, phones, and fax can use the IntelliSystems proprietary system created by IntelliSystems of Reno, Nevada, www.intellisystems.com. This knowledge-based system is used by such industry leaders as Netscape Communications, help.netscape.com, developer of the world's most used browser, and SunSoft, a leading software publisher, access1.sun.com/gateway/knowledgeview/mfirstpg.htm.

Customers with questions can get instant worldwide access to product support information. The IntelliSystems knowledgebase contains the answers to most of the questions most frequently asked by customers. Its format was designed for distribution to end users. The information is complete and is fully tested and reviewed before it is made available to customers.

The cost of handling a customer online is a fraction of the cost of live support. More than 3,700 people visited Netscape's help center in its first day of operation and accessed more than 100,000 pages of information, making it the most visited area of the Netscape Support Page, company officials said. As the industry average cost for a call handled by a customer support technician is $10, Netscape saved nearly $40,000 in the first day of operation.

"The World Wide Web has emerged as a new and viable option for providing support to customers of high-technology companies. The same knowledgebase that offloads calls by phone and fax can now be leveraged further to answer the questions of customers electronically," says Michael Beare of Intellisystems. "Customers now have access to online support without taking up support reps' time by sending e-mail back and forth. By adding the IntelliSystems knowledgebase to the options offered from a Web page, support calls and questions can be offloaded before they reach the support department. This increases customer support availability and reduces costs."

To make the knowledgebase easily accessible via the Internet, IntelliSystems developed a conversion process that takes the content of the knowledgebase files and turns them into hundreds of "intelligently" (and automatically) linked HTML files. These files can then be simply loaded on an existing Web server and a start-up link provided from the index Web page. Access to existing support information can be provided immediately with minimal involvement of support staff resources. The IntelliSystems knowledgebase conversion process can usually be completed in a few days.

"IntelliSystems' Smart Site is easy to set up and to maintain," says Beare. Although the expert system contains answers to thousands of questions, Netscape was able to create it in a matter of days because the company had been using the same expert database on its IntelliSystems phone system.

Netscape is able to resolve more than 10 percent of its support calls using the IntelliSystems telephone phone system, according to Bob Beaulieu, director of tech support for Netscape.

"This system takes customer support to the next higher level," Beare says. "Not only does it leverage their investment in the phone help system, but it provides the fastest possible help for their customers."

Previously, customers who needed customer support had to search through FAQ (Frequently Asked Questions) files, use search engines, or send e-mail to the company. All these solutions had problems. FAQs can be difficult to search. Search engines found many possible answers, but the customer had to dig through a maze of possibilities to find the correct information. E-mail questions might go unanswered for a day or two (or longer).

"By our interactive system, with our Q and A format, we drive you to your answers quickly, unlike a database search engine, which gives you 100 possible answers. This is a very effective way of doing support," Beare says. "We wanted to make it easy for the user and make it the least frustrating experience possible."

"IntelliSystems is the nationwide leader in providing automated customer support systems. As such, we have acquired pertinent experience in the development and implementation of this technology in support environments across several industries," says Beare. "During the consulting process, this experience is applied to create the first knowledgebase for the system. The first step is to look at the current caller requirements from an information standpoint: 'What do our callers need to know?' This is done by a close look at current operations including call logs, call-tracking reports, fax documents, and any established Q and A databases, and through close cooperation with support department personnel. The process is a team effort requiring complete and honest cooperation in identifying and determining what information to place in the knowledgebase. A series of problem identification forms is filled out in the process. The next step involves the organization of the problem identification forms into a structure suitable for voice-system delivery. This provides the format of the initial menu structure presented to callers.

"Intellisystems worked very closely over the past several years with some of the nation's largest call processing centers to establish guidelines to make this a very quick and efficient process. A meeting with the knowledgebase engineer is held to discuss the emerging knowledgebase structure and design. No two knowledgebases are alike; each is heavily customized to the client's specific requirements.

The third step is for the IntelliSystems' knowledge engineer to perform the original coding of the knowledgebase. This lays the foundation for future growth and establishes the first conventions for the knowledgebase. The structure is prepared for customer review several times during the process and full explanations of the work done are given. The actual information is then added into the knowledgebase framework. The completed knowledgebase is finally delivered and explained to those responsible for its ongoing maintenance. The end product is a refined and complete knowledgebase covering some predefined knowledge domain that customers must have access to as soon as possible. A typical first knowledgebase contains from 200 to 300 troubleshooting rules, although this number may vary.

"Although the initial knowledgebase can be created without help from IntelliSystems, the process is shortened and improved greatly by bringing to bear our accumulated experience. We strongly recommend that customers utilize our knowledgebase consulting services to ensure a quick and efficient installation and to guarantee that IntelliSystems will become an integral part of their support environment as soon as possible."

The IntelliSystem has a number of options that allow further leveraging of the information contained in the product knowledgebase and provide logical extensions of the phone interaction:

- The IntelliSystem Phone Server multilanguage module is designed to provide service to customers in several languages from one single knowledgebase. The knowledgebase is developed and maintained in one language and then translated into other languages.

- IntelliFax adds an intelligent fax retrieval capability to the system. Making use of the inference capability of the expert system, the IntelliSystem determines the exact fax document that a customer needs to resolve a difficulty, requests the fax number to which the document should be sent, and delivers it within a few minutes. Support representatives can also initiate fax delivery requests from their own PCs by simply entering the document number and the customer's fax number in a software utility provided with IntelliFax.

- Although the IntelliSystem has excellent problem-solving capabilities, not all callers will find a solution in the knowledgebase. For these callers, the IntelliSystem escalates the call to a live support representative. SessionView allows the information that the IntelliSystem gathered during an interactive session with a caller to be transferred to a live representative. The representative then picks up troubleshooting where the IntelliSystem left off. This benefits the caller because he or she does not have to restate the problem, and benefits the support organization because of the productivity gains associated with reduced talk time for support representatives.

STRATEGIES TO PROVIDE CUSTOMER SUPPORT

Many tools exist to help online marketers support their customers. This section discusses popular strategies.

Use E-mail and E-mailboxes to Help Customers

Benefit: Provide fast response to customers at a low cost to the company.

Discussion: Most people on online systems have access to e-mail and use it. Unlike other tools, like file downloads, there is virtually no barrier to learning to use e-mail, nor is there any hesitation in using it. Because many companies require e-mail usage, this tool is nearly universally used by online consumers.

To help support customers, companies should promote the use of e-mail as the preferred way of communicating with the company. In this model, the customer sends a note to the support department, where the support representative fields the query promptly and courteously. The company benefits from decreased support costs and the customer benefits by fast response time. E-mail addresses can be listed in manuals, fliers, and advertisements, or can be spoken aloud on the telephone messaging device.

To use online services to their potential, consider this scenario. Create multiple e-mailboxes that deal with separate products (e.g., printers@mycompany.com). Consumers send e-mail to the mailbox of their choice, where the right expert can field the question. This removes a step in the sorting process. If every e-mail note went to support@yourcompany.com, a secretary would have to read each message and send it to the proper technician.

Create Mailbots to Respond to Common Questions

Benefit: Reduce or eliminate personnel costs in handling certain inquiries; customers receive answers faster.

Discussion: Many consumer questions are identical. Support personnel spend a great deal of time repeating the same information. By creating e-mail files of these questions and hooking them to a mailbot, companies can help people find and receive information faster.

For example, if a company publicized a list of topics, consumers could send e-mail to printers@mycompany.com and receive data almost immediately.

Although the Internet can provide mailbot service, the commercial online services do not. However, operators can manually send e-mail files to consumers.

Create FAQs

Benefit: Reduce or eliminate personnel costs in handling certain inquiries; customers receive answers faster.

Discussion: The problem and benefits are similar those in the preceding discussion. Posting FAQs—files containing frequently asked questions and their answers—to your company's forum, Web site, or other archiving service enables consumers to find the information they need without drawing on your company's personnel resources.

Action: Interview support personnel for information. Write the FAQ.

Keep Track of New Questions

Benefit: Creates new material for FAQs; alerts company to new problems.

Discussion: Questions that aren't answered in the files can be handled individually. The files can then be updated with new information. This makes good use of the support representative's time. Also, by learning of new problems, companies can uncover bugs in the product, flaws in the instructions, or the need for new features and products to make the existing merchandise more useful.

Use File Libraries and Archives for Software Downloads

Benefit: Solve customers' problems without incurring expensive production and shipping charges.

Discussion: Product upgrades, software patches, and bug fixes can be stored in file libraries and consumers can download them at their convenience. As the company is not manufacturing the new version on a disk and mailing it to hundreds of thousands of customers, this move can save a considerable amount of money.

Create Training Tapes

Benefit: Consumers become better educated about your company's products without burdening staffers.

Discussion: Companies can create self-running computer programs that teach people how to use their products more effectively. As they become more conversant with the program, customers will depend less on calling for technical support, thus saving money for your company.

Create a Mailing List of Customers

Benefit: Quick distribution of important announcements.

Discussion: Mailing lists can be created to send notices to registered users about program updates and bug fixes as well as special notices about sales and upcoming products. For netiquette, ask people if they want to be on the list.

SUMMARY

Making the sale is the beginning, not the end, of a relationship with a long-term customer. To keep customers happy, every effort should be made to ensure that questions are answered quickly and courteously. An upset customer can tell an online audience of thousands about his misfortune faster than you can ever hope to repair the damage. By following the strategies in this chapter, you can help build bridges to your customers that can last forever.

CHAPTER EIGHT

Competitive Research Online

A well-orchestrated marketing program begins with solid research. The very foundation of a business plan or marketing plan is accurate, up-to-date information about the consumer, competitors, and the market-place. Good market research enables the company to create effective product and company positioning, marketing messages, and pricing strategies. Depth of information will guide the marketer in brainstorming and creating effective advertisements, publicity, and promotions. In fact, if marketing research is conducted properly, selling becomes almost superfluous because the company has created a product the market needs and wants. The Internet and commercial online services provide powerful tools to let you research competitors.

In this chapter, you will learn:

- how to conduct competitive research online
- what information is available online and where to find it

COMPETITIVE RESEARCH

ResearchMag, www.researchmag.com, is an excellent starting point for corporate research, as the site houses in-depth information on more than 10,000 companies and industries. Visitors can browse through investment research data, take advantage of portfolio tracking services, and dabble with lots of other extras designed to keep tabs on competitors and investments.

18-STEP ACTION PLAN FOR CONDUCTING COMPETITIVE MARKET RESEARCH ONLINE

You can find out a great deal about your competitors and your industry by using the Internet and online services. Here is an approach to finding information in your niche:

Step 1: Use Search Engines to Begin Your Quest

Search engines are electronic indexes that can instantly find references to your competitors and your industry. These devices read, analyze, and store information contained on millions of individual Web pages. Information is indexed on a series of keywords and other parameters, like beginning and end dates. In this manner you can search for all information about a competitor that has been printed since last year or since your last visit. Information can be stored on your hard disk, inserted into reports, and printed for use (copyright restrictions apply).

There are hundreds of search engines on the Internet covering general topics, including Yahoo!, Lycos, and Alta Vista, and specialized search engines that provide abstracts of information pertaining to vertical market industries, like biotech and astronomy. A list of hundreds of search engines can be found at www.mmgco.com. A collection of the major search engines can be found at www.search.com.

While it is beyond the scope of this book to talk about the relative merits of each search engine, all the major engines can find company and industry information by keywords typed by users.

Let's look at how several of the most popular engines can help you find the goods on your competitors in a matter of minutes.

The most famous search engine is called Yahoo! (as in "Yahoo! I found it!"), which can be reached by using your browser to type www.yahoo.com.

You can search for information in several ways:

- You can type the name of your competitor's company and have Yahoo! search all the pages of the World Wide Web. The service will show you pages on which the search term is printed. The material will be displayed as a hyperlink, or shortcut, that allows you to see the information in full simply by clicking on the text, which appears as highlighted or underlined text, depending on your computer system.

- You can drill down through the menu structure to find out about companies or products that you didn't even know existed. For instance, you could go to the business section and drill down to products, then to software, then to psychologists to find software of interest to that audience.

TIP: *Use software tools to reduce redundant information.*

As every search engine uses a different technique for finding and displaying information, it stands to reason that each engine will have information that the others do not—as well as a lot of the same information. While it is to your benefit to search several engines to find the widest possible sources of information, you will also waste a lot of time dealing with duplicate listings.

Software products like Web Compass from Quarterdeck and Web Seeker from Forefront Group search several engines and report the findings to you as one report, eliminating the duplicates. Programs of this type will save you time and money.

Step 2: Search Your Competitor's Web Site

You can go to your competitor's Web site and read all the information made available to the public, such as annual reports, quarterly statements, biographies of executives, product information, press releases, and job openings. By analyzing this information, you might be able to see strengths, weaknesses, and areas for your company to exploit.

Just in case you are wondering—yes, your competitors will look at your Web site as well. The rule of thumb for deciding what information to print is: Print only information you are comfortable with. This is the same rule you would use at a trade show at which your competitors can—and do—hear your presentations, read your literature, and talk to your salespeople and engineers.

Step 3: Use an Automated Software Program to Notify You of Changes to the Site

Once you've found the sites you want to monitor, consider using a software program that downloads updated pages (including text and images) to your hard disk according to a schedule that you create. Products that do this task include:

- WebWhacker, www.ffg.com
- First Mate, www.documagix.com

Step 4: Hunt for Trade Associations

Trade associations could post a treasure chest of unbiased information and statistics that may give you an advantage over competitors. Use the search engines to look for addresses of trade associations and nonprofit groups in your industry.

Step 5: Search for Personal Pages

Personal pages are Web sites created by individuals who want to connect with the world. These people create pages that include information about their special interests. You might be pleasantly surprised to find that a personal page contains information and links about your subject. You might be enthralled that this individual actually commands the respect and attention of a large audience that matches your interests as well. You should search for personal Web sites of people in your target group to find news, gossip and other interesting information. You'll find personal home pages by using the search engines. While conducting research for a psychologist and author of books on eating disorders who wanted to post a new site on that topic, I found several sites operated by ordinary people and other psychologists. These sites contained a great deal of useful information for my client.

Step 6: Ask Your Target Market

Send queries to online VIPs at Web sites, personal pages, newsgroups, and mailing lists. In the previous example, the people who put up personal sites on eating disorders even answered questions we asked via e-mail.

Step 7: Search Newsgroups and Post Queries

Newsgroups are online bulletin boards for people interested in specific topics such as baseball, computer programming, and parenting. More than 20,000 newsgroups operate via the Internet. These groups very well could discuss your industry, company, or competitors.

If you want to find out what people are saying on the Internet's USENET newsgroups about your company and its products, or about your competitors, you should use DejaNews, www.dejanews.com. This free service will scour each newsgroup for the terms you specify. For example, you can ask it to look for references to Ford, Chrysler, General Motors, Toyota, Honda, and the car industry to find out what is going on. This tool is invaluable for finding and tracing rumors and trends.

The search report displays the e-mail address of the person who wrote the message, the name of the newsgroup in which the message was posted, and the headline of the message. You can search on each of those factors to read the exact message and all responses, other messages in the newsgroup, and all the articles the person has written. As you can imagine, this is a powerful tool for marketers, not only for competitive intelligence but also for public relations and crisis communications.

By reading the articles, you will find out what is hot in the industry. You can also post questions yourself. If the message is not commercial, a great many people might join the discussion and provide you with invaluable information.

"Simply reading newsgroups and forums can be the most effective market research around. Monitor the comments of your target market to learn what features matter and what causes folks to love or hate a product," says Christina O'Connell, an online marketing consultant.

Step 8: Read Mailing Lists and Post Queries

Mailing lists are like newsgroups in that they are a community of people who send messages to the group on issues germane to their interests. Unlike newsgroups, each day's messages are sent to your mailbox and cannot be searched by DejaNews.

You can find a list of mailing lists at www.neosoft.com/internet /paml.com. You might find some while scouring Web sites or search engines.

Just as with newsgroups, you can post queries for information, as long as those messages don't violate the netiquette of the list.

Step 9: Read Online Financial Information

If you are researching a public company, you'll find lots of financial information online. Here are resources on the Internet:

- Daily Stocks, www.dailystocks.com, should be your starting point for all information about publicly trade companies. It contains links to dozens of Web sites that contain almost everything you would want to find out about a company. Such sites included:

  - Zacks Investment Research, which shows how many analysts are recommending stocks and whether that number is increasing or decreasing.
  - Thomson Tipsheet, which notes if company officials are selling or buying the company stock.
  - Securities and Exchange Commission filings and reports.
  - Discussion groups from Silicon Investor Forum and Motley Fool Message Board.
  - News from CNN, Reuters, Dow Jones, *Fortune, Forbes,* the *Los Angeles Times,* the *Washington Post,* and the *New York Times.*
  - Public Register's Annual Report Service, which has 3,000 annual reports available online for free (see www.prars.com).

- Silicon Investor, www.techstocks.com, contains stock charts and chats for technology issues. Check the messages for comments about your company.
- StockSmart, www.stocksmart.com, lets you compare stocks in the same industries so you can see trends.
- Investors Edge, www.irnet.com, offers business news and corporate profiles with historical data on companies.
- Competitive Intelligence Guide, www.fuld.com, is Fuld and Company's area that offers analytical tools and links to other intelligence sites.

Step 10: Read Online Competitive Information

Hoover's Online, www.hoovers.com; AOL: Keyword: Hoover, profiles more than 1,100 of the largest, most influential, and fastest-growing public and private companies in the United States and the world. Directory listings are searchable by company name, industry, location, and sales figures.

Step 11: Study Demographic Reports

Demographics can tell you where your customers live and which markets are emerging.

Internet

- The U.S. Census Bureau, www.census.gov, lets you find information using maps or zip codes. You can find how many people in a geographic area earn a certain income or belong to a specific race. This information can help you pinpoint your marketing efforts. Information can be printed as a Web page or an ASCII file for a spreadsheet.
- Easy Analytic Software, Inc., www.easidemographics.com, creates fast demographic reports that include household income, race, and age.

CompuServe

- Business Demographics Reports, go busdem, are designed to help businesses analyze their markets. The reports are based on information from the U.S. Census Bureau. Two types of reports are available:

The Business to Business Report includes information on all broad Standard Industrial Classification (SIC) categories. Each report provides the total number of employees in each category for a designated geographical area.

The Advertisers' Service Report includes data on businesses that constitute the SICs for retail trade. Each report breaks down the total number of businesses for each specified geographical unit in relation to company size. Reports of either type can be requested by zip code, county, state, metropolitan area, ADI (Arbitron TV market), DMA (Nielsen TV market), or the entire United States. Sample reports are available online.

- SUPERSITE, go supersite, enables you to produce a variety of demographic and sales potential reports for the entire United States, any state, county, zip code, SMSA (metropolitan area), ADI, DMA, or aggregation.
- ACORN Target Marketing, go supersite, provides information on these industries: apparel, appliances, automotive, baby products, beverages, cameras, credit cards, electronics, furniture and furnishings, garden and lawn, grocery, home improvement, insurance, investments, leisure activities, mail order, media, restaurant, shoes and footwear, sports, tools, toys, and travel.

Step 12: Scour These Useful Resources

Here are listings of other useful information sources for marketers:

To contact just about anyone on the Internet or on the phone, use Who Where, www.whowhere.com, or Four11, www.four11.com. You can even find physical addresses.

If you'd like to see where a company is located, use Mapquest, www.mapquest.com, to view and print a map.

THOMAS, www.thomas.loc.gov, offers the most current source for full text of Congressional bills.

Step 13: Set Up a Personalized Daily News Service

One of the key advantages of online services is their ability to find news articles and deliver them to your e-mailbox or pager on a minute-by-minute basis so you find out about new developments quickly and can make informed decisions.

Your first step is to identify the companies and topics you want to find and then specify the publications or newswires you want to search. For example, you might want to search for stories about the oil and petroleum industries and Exxon in the Associated Press, Reuters, and PR Newswire. All stories containing those words from those news sources would be delivered in your private e-mailbox. In the future, these services will be able to beep your pager or print the stories on your fax machine.

Here is a summary of some of the more powerful or popular tools that can help provide you with a daily source of targeted, up-to-date information for decision-making:

- Lexis-Nexis InfoTailor Service, www.lexis-nexis.com, is a personalized daily briefing service that gathers information from more than 7,100 sources of news and business information, including the *New York Times,* the *Washington Post, Fortune,* and *Business Week.* More than 100,000 new articles are added each day from worldwide newspapers, magazines, newswires, and trade journals.

- Point Cast, www.pointcast.com, provides a customized news retrieval service that gathers information from the Associated Press, Reuters, *Money* magazine, and CNN. It displays news about companies and industries on demand, or as a screen saver, so information displays on your screen whenever the machine is idle. It also offers stock quotes and charts.

- Nearly every major search engine offers a free daily news service. To create your personal newspaper, simply go to the search engine, find the link to the free service, register, and select the keywords and topics you want. Each day you can return to the site, type in your password, and read your customized newspaper. Also consider using Crayon, www.crayon.com, which searches hundreds of newspapers and magazines for free.

Thousands of news databases are available for the online marketer. Virtually every magazine, newspaper, government publication, and census abstract is online. Intrepid researchers can find data from the historical archives of the *New York Times* to tiny trade journals, from unpublished college Ph.D. dissertations to citations from the Library of Congress. Another advantage of online research is that you can save the information to your computer, insert it in reports, and print it. You save the time of taking notes and typing them into the computer. Of course, copyright laws require you to note sources and comply with regulations.

Investigators have access to companies' press releases—original source material in the form that the company wished to present. You can read quotes, figures, and background material that the paper either omitted, reworded, or, perhaps, garbled. These press releases are invaluable sources of original business information. Because newspapers don't have the space to print each press release, information from even large, publicly traded companies is never seen by the general public. However, the online researcher can find this information and make more informed decisions because of it.

Two companies, Business Wire, www.businesswire.com, and PR Newswire, www.prnewswire.com, print such press releases online for a fee. These sites can be accessed by the general public or marketers for free.

Marketers should ask these questions when evaluating news services:

- Where does the service get its news from?
- Are those sources providing information that meets my needs?
- How often is the news updated? Once a day or several times an hour?
- How much does the service cost per user?
- How is the news delivered? Is it available on a platform that my company uses (e.g., Lotus Notes, cc:Mail, e-mail)?
- What are the royalties, if any, for distribution over a network, or for reprints?

Step 14: Monitor Special Interest Publications and Other Media

Although the personalized news services are great tools for online researchers, they are only a beginning. That's because numerous newspapers, TV and radio stations, and trade publications are not part of the databases of these monitoring services. You need to determine which publications you need to monitor and set up a bookmark service or visit every day.

The Internet has more than 1,000 daily newspapers available including the *New York Times,* the *Wall Street Journal,* and *USA Today.* For listings, go to:

- Webovision, www.Webovision
- Crayon, www.crayon.com

Many news and business magazines for consumers and trade are now online. Not only do they offer the full text of the print edition but frequently include original content that didn't fit in the hard copy. Electronic editions might also contain links to related stories, charts, and historical information. Further, some online editions add a bulletin board where readers can post questions for reporters and engage in discussions with other readers. Some offer online conferences with editors and newsmakers; viewers can ask questions as well. Several are printed online before the print edition hits the newsstands; others are updated daily online but only once a week at the newsstand, so online readers get more information delivered faster!

Step 15: Conduct Historical Research

News of the recent past and the past few years can help marketers get a perspective on events and discover the history of their competitors as well as see how the field has advanced. Here are four great databases on CompuServe:

- **Computer Database Plus**, go compdb, lets you retrieve computer-related articles from more than 230 magazines, newspapers, and journals. You'll find news, reviews, and product introductions in areas such as hardware, software, electronics, engineering, communications, and the application of technology. Comprehensive coverage includes popular, trade, and professional titles. Full-text publications include *PC Week, PC Magazine, Macweek, InfoWorld,* and the *Newsbytes* news service.
- **Business Database Plus**, go busdb, lets you retrieve full-text articles from more than 1,000 business magazines, trade journals, newsletters, and regional business newspapers.
- **Magazine Database Plus**, go magdb, lets you retrieve full-text articles from more than 140 general-interest magazines, journals, and reports. The database contains a wealth of diverse publications from *Time* to *Atlantic Monthly, Forbes* to *Kiplinger's Personal Finance,* the *New Republic* to *National Review, Good Housekeeping* to *Cosmopolitan.*
- **Health Database Plus**, go hbd, lets you retrieve articles from consumer and professional publications on health care, disease prevention and treatment, fitness and nutrition, children and the elderly, substance abuse and smoking, and just about any health-related topic. The core of Health Database Plus is a collection of publications with coverage oriented to nonprofessional readers. Core publications range from newsstand titles such as *Men's Health, Parents* magazine, *Prevention,* and *Runner's World* to more specialized reports and journals such as the *AIDS Weekly* from the Centers for Disease Control, *Morbidity and Mortality Weekly Report, Patient Care,* and *RN.* The collection also includes pamphlets issued by organizations such as the American Lung Association. Augmenting

this coverage is a collection of technical and professional journals such as the *Journal of the American Medical Association, Lancet,* and the *New England Journal of Medicine.*

Step 16: Research the Encyclopedias

The granddaddy of all encyclopedias, the *Encyclopedia Britannica,* is available at www.eb.com.

Grolier's Academic American Encyclopedia (AAE), CompuServe: go aae; Prodigy: jump encyclopedia, contains the full text of the print classic, including over ten million words in over 33,000 articles. It is updated quarterly, making it the most current encyclopedia available. A general-interest, short-entry encyclopedia, the *AAE* is an indispensable source of information for marketers.

America Online members can use *Compton's Encyclopedia,* keyword: encyclopedia, which consists of more than nine million words, 5,274 long articles, and 29,322 concise articles.

Step 17: Hire a Professional Researcher

A professional online researcher might be able to find information faster and more economically than you or your staff can. For referrals and references, contact Mary Ellen Bates, past president of the Association of Independent Information Professionals, mbates@access.digex.net. Professional researchers also have experience with private databases, which are difficult to use and expensive.

These sites either offer links to competitive intelligence or provide such services:

- Babson College Library, www.babson.edu/~navigator.
- Montague Institute, www.montague.com.
- Society of Competitive Intelligence Professionals, www.scip.org.

Step 18: Learn More about Conducting Online Research

These books can help online researchers craft fast, efficient searches on the Internet, commercial online services, and private databases:

- *The Online Deskbook,* by Mary Ellen Bates, ISBN: 0 9010965 19 6, Pemberton Press, 1996.
- *Secrets of the Super Net Searchers,* by Reva Basch, ISBN: 0-910965-22-6, Pemberton Press, 1996.
- *The Internet Searcher's Handbook: Locating Information, People and Software,* by Peter Morville, ISBN: 0-55570-236-8, Neal Schuman Publishers, Inc., 1996.

SUMMARY

Great marketing starts with great research. Online services provide up-to-date virtual online libraries you can find information quickly about your industry, competitors, and trends. In many ways, online research is better than printed materials because the information is revised more often, is distributed faster, and is easy to integrate into reports. If you conduct online research, your marketing plan will be much more solid.

CHAPTER NINE

Online Resources that Make You a More Effective Marketer

If you think you know it all, think again. There are ideas, visions, and dreams you have yet to experience—especially in the rapidly changing Internet. Fortunately for you, your online peers are ready, willing, and able to serve as mentors, advisors, colleagues, and reality testers.

In this chapter, you will learn:

- how you can learn from the online community
- about online professional forums
- about online professional resources

LEARNING FROM THE ONLINE COMMUNITY

The playing field in online marketing changes dramatically from one day to the next. Yesterday's truths might not apply to today's problems. New players enter the game and new technologies take hold to change life as you know it. You need to keep up with the changes and to learn from others' successes and failures or you will waste a great deal of time and money.

The best places to keep in touch with changes in marketing strategies are online marketing forums, bulletin boards, newsgroups, and mailing lists. The Internet and commercial online services have forums devoted to helping marketing professionals working at large companies, associations, and local businesses, as well as work-at-home professionals and service providers. These areas are great places to learn about the new dimensions of online marketing by posting questions to noncompetitive and helpful peers. After all, who can teach you about the online community and its mores better than the people who actually use the systems?

These repositories also hold vast libraries of reference material that can teach you just about everything from how to fund your company to how to prepare a disaster plan for crises resulting from product tampering. Most files are preceded by dialog boxes that describe the material in the file (see Figure 9-1). By viewing dialog boxes, you can see if the material in the file is really what you want to read before investing the time to download or view the entire file.

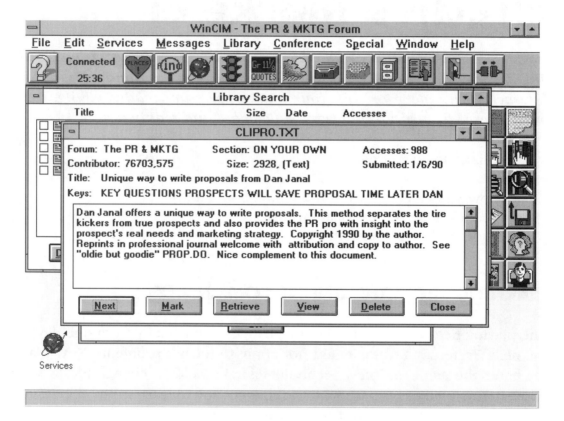

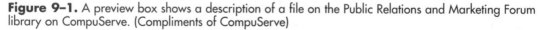

Figure 9–1. A preview box shows a description of a file on the Public Relations and Marketing Forum library on CompuServe. (Compliments of CompuServe)

Bulletin boards are staffed by helpful system administrators, whose titles are different on each system. Internet's USENET newsgroups are staffed by moderators, mailing lists are run by owners, and Web sites are run by Web masters. CompuServe's forums are headed by forum administrators and sysops (system operators). America Online has hosts. Prodigy features board leaders. Some forums are hosted by one person, others by a dozen. Each person lends his or her expertise and time to help newcomers. The commercial online services tend to be friendlier to newcomers and to dispense advice about how to use the tools effectively. The Internet's USENET newsgroups and mailing lists tend to be a bit grumpier in welcoming newcomers, who are expected to lurk or read messages for a few days or weeks to get the flow of the conversations, and also to read FAQs (files containing Frequently Asked Questions) to learn their culture.

Forum operators hope that participants not only ask questions but also contribute their knowledge to others who raise questions.

Information is unbiased and free of commercial advocacy. In fact, strict warnings are posted that prohibit advertising and self-promotion (except to say what kind of work you do, so the host can make points relevant to your industry).

As a result of these online networking sessions, strong personal friendships can form between people who have never met face to face. One group, the Public Relations Special Interest Group, meets once a year at the annual meeting of the Public Relations Society of America and has planned dinners and special outings.

The areas also let you learn from your customers and prospects. "You can learn from the online community," says Christina O'Connell, coco@ pcnet.com, president of O'Connell and Associates, an online public relations consultant.

Finally, by participating in conversations with opinion leaders, industry sages, and VIPs who frequent these areas, you can develop lasting relationships with them.

Netiquette

The rules of netiquette apply to these forums. That means no advertising or solicitation of members. There are slight variations on the rules for self-promotion in that people can describe what they do as a means of introducing themselves to the community.

NETWORKING ONLINE WITH HELPFUL PEERS

Need to network? Here are forums, descriptions, and access codes for bulletin boards for marketers who can answer your marketing questions—if you promise to help the next person who comes along.

- The Public Relations and Marketing Forum, CompuServe: go prsig, which has more than 45,000 members, provides a message board and libraries of files on the following topics: PR online, speechwriting, technologies, online seminars, advertising and marketing, the International Association of Business Communicators (IABC), employee communications, hyperspace, jobs, direct marketing, research, crisis communications, video and multimedia, international public relations, selling, and Web wizardry.
- The Working from Home Forum, CompuServe: go work, provides information for people who run small businesses from their homes—or want to. Moderated by Paul and Sarah Edwards, who have written several best-selling books about working at home, the forum offers messages and files on more than 20 topics. The Working from Home Forum contains the following reference libraries: running a business, information professionals, getting business, health specialties, accounting and tax, jobs/telecommuting, legal matters, word processing and desktop publishing, home office hardware and software, management consulting, auditing businesses and import/export, training and human resources, and home office organization.
- Cybermarketers from any industry or profession can find camaraderie and information in these self-explanatory forums filled with messages and library files on CompuServe:
  - Internet Commerce Forum, go inetcommerce
  - Internet Publishing Forum, go inetpub
  - Internet Resources Forum, go inetresource

- The Small Business Center, AOL: keyword small business, contains information for small business owners (or people considering starting a small business). You can also get personalized help for your small business from the Service Corps of Retired Executives (SCORE). Finally, you can post messages to the Small Business Center message boards to see what other small business owners are talking about or to raise your own issues for discussion. A critique of advertising sites on the Web is featured at www.theeditors.com /adsite.htm.

- The Internet hosts several mailing lists devoted to marketing and advertising. New ones are being added all the time, so be on the lookout for references to other mailing lists. To get the most current list, visit www.wolfBayne.com. The list is maintained by Kim Bayne, president of wolfBayne Communications, a public relations and marketing consultancy. Here are two good mailing lists for marketers:

  - HTMARCOM discusses high-tech marketing issues. To subscribe, send the message *subscribe htmarcom your name* to the e-mail address majordomo@listserv.rmi.net.
  - Internet-Sales is a good newsletter in which to find out about new technologies and strategies used by marketers. You can post questions, state your observations, and join a lively community of online practitioners trying to figure out how to sell products more effectively on the Internet. You can find a FAQ file, information, and archives at www.mmgco.com/isales.html. To subscribe, send any message or no message via e-mail to i-sales@gs2.revnet .com.

Tips on Joining Mailing Lists

To join a mailing list, you must send an e-mail note to the list operator with the message *subscribe listname your name*. That's it. Don't type anything else, like "Please add me to this list. I hear it is great!!!" This note will confuse the software and result in your receiving an error message instead of a subscription. When your subscription has been accepted, you will receive a confirming note and information about the list, which includes instructions for unsubscribing. Save this in case you decide to cancel.

Members of commercial online services can join mailing lists as well. These instructions should work. However, as software is always being refined, please read the instructions on each system to make sure.

You might also find newsgroups that talk about your concerns. You can hunt for these groups by going to Deja News, www.dejanews.com, and using its search tools to find groups listed by interests.

Your peers might also create their own private mailing lists. For example, Speakernet is a weekly publication sent by e-mail to professional speakers. Recipients submit news postings that are edited by two volunteers who also mail the publication. Ask your peers if a newsletter for your industry exists. If not, consider starting one yourself. For more information on this process, read Chapter 18.

MARKETING RESOURCES

You can find a lot of free marketing information on the Web sites of consultants, electronic editions of print publications, and newsletters sent via e-mail. Here are starting points:

Web Sites

- *Dan Janal's Online Marketing Magazine,* www.janal.com, lists new articles from the author of *Online Marketing Handbook.* You can find out the latest trends and read new articles specifically targeted for online marketers at this site. It also contains updates to *Online Marketing Handbook.*
- *Guerrilla Marketing Online,* www.gmarketing.com, offers articles about online marketing from the authors of the popular Guerrilla marketing books.
- *Inc. Magazine,* www.inc.com, includes useful articles and neat tools like interactive spreadsheets.
- *Larry Chase's Web Digest for Marketers,* www.wdfm.com/index .html, provides marketers with a brief but insightful critique of new marketing sites. Not only is this weekly update must reading, it is fun reading.
- The Small Business Administration, sbaonline.sba.gov/, has useful information.
- *The Smart Business Supersite,* www.smartbiz.com, is one of the largest how-to business resources on the Internet, with more than 60 categories of free information on such topics as advertising, raising money, and managing human resources. It also provides useful articles, checklists, reports, and worksheets geared for business executives, managers, and employees.

- *Who's Marketing Online,* www.wmo.com, has many thought-provoking articles about marketing and Web site creation.
- *Working Solo,* www.workingsolo.com, is an online searchable database of more than 1,200 valuable business listings based on the popular *Working Solo* and *Working Solo Sourcebook.*

Electronic Editions of Print Publications

Print publications that cover the online world publish online editions to keep you up to date with new marketing trends and other online intelligence. Bookmark these sites:

- *Ad Age,* www.adage.com/imm
- *Ad Week,* www.adweek.com
- *DM News,* www.dmnews.com/web_marketing.html
- *Interactive Age,* techweb.cmp.com/ia/current/
- *SIMBA/Cowles Communications,* www.mediacentral.com/
- *WebWeek,* www.webweek.com

Newsletters Sent via E-mail

Several e-mail newsletters keep you up to date on the Internet and marketing strategies:

- *A Clue to Online Marketing,* published by veteran journalist Dana Blankenhorn, is a weekly newsletter that highlights companies that are doing well on the Internet and those that are not doing so well. To request a free copy, write to dana.blankenhorn@worldnet.att.net. Back issues are located at www.tbass.com/clue and www.ppn.org /clue.
- *Newslinx* is a daily news service that provides headlines of dozens of Web-related articles and links to the full text. There's always a good article about online marketing and advertising as well as fascinating trends of online use, such as online addiction and the latest on the spam wars. Subscribe at www.newslinx.com.
- *EduPage* is a thrice-weekly summary of news items on information technology published by Educom, a Washington, DC–based consortium of leading colleges and universities seeking to transform education through the use of information technology. To subscribe,

send mail to listproc@educom.unc.edu with the message *subscribe edupage your name.*

- Netsurfer Digest is a weekly newsletter offering Internet news and marketing information. To subscribe, send e-mail to nsdigest-request@netsurf.com. Include one of the following commands in the body of the message:

  - HTML format version (subscribe nsdigest-html)
  - ASCII version (subscribe nsdigest-text)
  - You can also read the report at the Web, www.netsurf.com/nsd/index.html.

PR/RESOURCES

- The Web site prindustry.miningco.com features a weekly public relations column and a resource list with more than 150 links.
- The National PR Network has compiled a listing of 2,500 Web sites covering public relations, marketing communications and advertising companies on the Internet, www.usprnet.com. To join the National PR Network free put *subscribe* in the body of an e-mail to: mailto:Webmaster@usprnet.com.

SUMMARY

By joining professional groups on the Internet and commercial online services, online marketers can hone their skills and learn new strategies. To get the most out of these forums, you have to do more than just join—you must participate. You can exchange war stories, stay abreast of new trends, test ideas, get advice, and impart wisdom. Chances are, the more you contribute, the more benefit you will receive.

CHAPTER TEN

Measuring Results from Online Marketing

Every action on the Internet can be counted, tracked, and traced. No other medium allows for such precise measurement of the effectiveness of every piece of text or image. Unfortunately, most companies online have not implemented these tools nor instituted measurement and tracking systems to test the effectiveness of their marketing campaigns. The online industry needs to establish standards of measurement, performance, and metrics as well as create an unbiased, objective source to verify Web site demographics and statistics.

This chapter will explore:

- why companies need to track their messages across all communications platforms
- the problem with hits and log files
- the next generation of Web site measurement
- benchmarking the Web
- the birth of the direct-response Web site
- expanding on the direct-response model
- accountability and metrics for online communications

WHY COMPANIES NEED TO TRACK THEIR MESSAGES ACROSS ALL COMMUNICATIONS PLATFORMS

During a seminar I conducted in Des Moines, a delegate asked if anyone had ever bought anything over the Internet. In the crowd of 70 people, about 15 raised their hands.

I asked one person what he bought. It was a Kodak digital camera. I asked him to describe the steps he took in buying this expensive piece of equipment.

He said he read about it in a magazine.

I asked if he was reading an advertisement or an article. He said he didn't remember. (Marketers, note that people do not always remember how they heard about your product.)

However, he saw the address for Kodak's Web site and went online. He read about the family of products and decided which one to buy. Kodak has a policy of not selling products directly to consumers. Instead, it supports its dealer network with ads, both in print and online. He found the toll-free phone number of the nearest dealer, who was in Chicago. He called the number and placed the order.

Notice how many different media he used: magazine, Internet, and telephone. Internet marketing was but one piece of the marketing puzzle.

Now let's go back to the actual transaction. When the dealer picked up the phone, were his first words "How did you hear about us?" or "What's your credit card number?" You bet it was the latter! He didn't know or care how he got the order, as long as he got the order.

Let's go to the next scene. It is the next day at Kodak headquarters. The director of marketing calls the person charged with Internet marketing and asks, "How is our Web site doing? Is it making any sales? Is it paying for itself?"

The Internet manager has no idea that they just sold a thousand-dollar piece of equipment via the Internet because no one asked either the buyer or the dealer!

Therein lies the fatal flaw of most online marketing activities today. No one is tracking sales, let alone tracking brand awareness or image or goodwill. These Web sites might be doing marvelous jobs in reaching those goals, but no one will know if they aren't counting—and counting over all media platforms!

THE PROBLEM WITH HITS AND LOG FILES

The first measurement technique you've probably heard of in relation to the Internet is *hits*. Your friends probably asked you how many hits your page gets, or you might have seen a Web page display an odometer that displays how many hits the page has received since a certain date.

These measurement techniques are dead wrong.

Hit is a very misleading term. A normal person would assume a hit refers to a person visiting a Web site. In reality, it means each time a *file* on a Web page has been accessed. So, if your front page has one text file and four picture files, that adds five hits to your counter. If the visitor goes to read your press releases on a new page and returns to the front page, five more hits are added to the counter. What happens if he leaves the page after the third file loads? Are we at 15 hits or 13 hits? And what difference does it make anyway? Hits don't buy things; people do. If you look at your hit counter, you'd think 15 people visited the site and only one person bought anything. That's not a very good percentage. But, in reality, only one person visited your site and he bought something. That's a pretty good percentage. Unfortunately, you'd never know it by looking at hit counters.

Another problem with Web measurement is the dependence on log files. Log files are records of visits that are kept by your Internet service provider (ISP), or by a software program, dedicated to that service, that sits on your Web server. These log files record such facts as the number of visitors, their IP (Internet Protocol) number, their domain extension (i.e., .com, .edu, .gov), the geographic location of their ISP, and the time of day they entered your site. This log file might contain useful information, but chances are you won't learn a thing about your users or if your site is accomplishing its goals.

That's because the information is basically irrelevant. You really don't learn much more about the person or the quality of her visit to your site from it. Only in rare cases will you benefit by knowing that your site is most heavily visited at 1 P.M. Wednesday (as one stock brokerage company discovered), or that people with the .edu extension are immediately shown information for college students, as a financial aid company does. You might even find out that a good number of visitors are from Japan, so you could decide to translate your Web site to Japanese. However, for most Web site operators, these statistics are meaningless at best and misleading at worst. Consider that a viewer spends three minutes on a certain page. You are delighted that he spent so much time there. What you don't realize is that the page took 2:45 to load and the reader actually saw the page for 15 seconds before leaving!

Another problem with log files are that prospects are anonymous throughout the entire visit. Log files can't tell you the name of the visitor, let alone where she came from or her demographics. Because log files are compiled, not individualized, you can't tell the paths every person took on your site. So you can't see which pages worked and which pages didn't. You can't tell if the users are reading your message or taking action based on it. Furthermore, log file reports are tedious affairs that require a lot of manpower to understand. If you have mirror sites (several servers house your content across the country or the world), each log file for each site is separate, so you have to merge the information. As you can guess, this is not an easy process, and even under the best of circumstances it yields information of marginal value.

Log files were an inevitable and necessary first step in measuring activity on web sites. However, their usefulness has been surpassed by next-generation tools that track the total user experience so marketers can gain accurate information about the user transaction.

State-of-the-art Web measurement tools provide network-level analyses that account for content and delivery information. Accrue Insight, www .accrue.com, measures server activity and response time so you can see how much time a consumer spends reading the page and whether or not your server is acting efficiently. The program provides live, real-time reporting, so equipment errors can be spotted and remedied quickly and content like prices and calls to action can be measured and corrected. It also can compile reports from mirror sites so the Web master gets one report, not dozens. Yet, each visit can be analyzed to the point of seeing where users came from (an ad, a search engine, a competitor's site) and which pages they viewed at your site, in what order, and for how long. Armed with this information, a marketer can benchmark specific messages. If the messages aren't delivering the right amount of leads or sales, the marketer can change messages and compare the results. On a broader scale, marketers can use this information to justify their entire Web marketing activity, as they will be able to see where their sales are coming from.

The next section shows how the user's experience can be measured. Also, be sure to read Chapter 6 to learn techniques for encouraging visitors to identify themselves to you so you can begin one-to-one marketing tactics.

THE NEXT GENERATION OF WEB SITE MEASUREMENT: BEYOND LOG FILES

White Paper Presented by Accrue Software

Accrue Software, Inc., provides online user response analysis software to improve the effectiveness of high-end Web sites. Developed in answer to the demands of sophisticated clients, Accrue's patent-pending, on-the-wire technology gives organizations comprehensive understanding of user behavior. Located in Sunnyvale, California, Accrue Software can be reached at 408-542-8900, www.accrue.com, or info@accrue.com.

Web sites are increasingly mission critical for businesses and organizations using the World Wide Web as a strategic marketing and distribution channel. Web site managers need tools not only to assess performance but also to enhance the effectiveness of their sites. In order to do this, they need to have information about user behavior at the site, where user behavior can be affected by both the site content and the content delivery issues. User behavior as related to site content can be observed by watching the paths taken by visitors, the pages viewed, the links followed, and the time required for downloads. Content delivery factors that affect online user behavior include server and network performance. This type of information is necessary for improving Web site performance. Understanding online user behavior and what affects (drives) user actions at a site is the key to improving user response to the site.

Currently available tools attempt to analyze Web site traffic by looking at server log files. This provides some information about how much of the content is being requested and how often, but no information about delivery factors that may have affected the user's experience. Log file data are neither comprehensive nor accurate enough to provide a clear and useful picture of a site's true effectiveness. For example, a log file may indicate that a Web server sent a page when in fact the user may have canceled the request during the download process and never received it. The log files would still indicate that the page had been viewed.

Before accurate deductions can be made about a site's efficiency or the quality of the users' responses at the site, more complete and accurate data must be collected. Furthermore, to understand the implications of the information collected and actually use it to enhance a site and improve online user response requires an understanding of what factors influence a user's behavior. Why do users respond to content and make the navigation choices they do? More importantly, why do they take those actions at a specific site, on a specific page? Until now there has been no technology capable of collecting the data required to learn about user behavior, or to use that knowledge to improve user response to the site.

Online user behavior is the sum of choices made and actions taken by a user at a Web site. These include actions such as viewing a page, downloading information, following a link, and even making a purchase. User behavior at any site is influenced by a combination of site content and delivery of that content. Content can be controlled by site administrators. The site content is what the user sees while navigating through pages and links, the content of downloaded material, and the actual route chosen. Content delivery involves server and network performance, including speed, quality, and reliability. Together, content and delivery influence what the user chooses to view, how long he views it, how he navigates through the site, and whether or not he will return to the site.

If accurate and comprehensive data are collected and useful relationships between user action and site content or delivery factors are analyzed, user behavior trends or patterns can be discovered. For example, user data may show that users will wait only an average of 15 seconds for an image to download before hitting the cancel button. This can be further examined to show that people with certain psychographic, demographic, or technographic attributes (for example, children or those using slower modems) may not wait as long.

For example, performing user response analysis at a site may reveal that users are not waiting for, and therefore not viewing, certain pages. More data might suggest that the problem is server speed, and either the server should be upgraded or the problem diagnosed and fixed. However, the data might suggest that the server is fine but that the page contains too much data and graphics should be simplified. Once this problem is identified and its cause pinpointed, changes can be implemented.

Organizations that have come to rely heavily on their Web sites and site-related business need powerful tools that can handle high traffic volumes and help site managers improve user responses.

Corporate Marketing Web Sites: Corporate online marketers at sites such as Levi or Federal Express need to continually improve their sites' effectiveness and user response in order to continue to grow and compete.

Advertisers and corporate marketers traditionally work with large quantities of data and information when field testing ideas and developing marketing programs and strategy. Until now no tool has been capable of processing the Web site user data necessary for making effective online marketing decisions and obtaining feedback on the effectiveness of changes.

Internet Service Providers: In the competitive ISP market, the ability to provide functionality that can help customers improve their sites is a value-added differentiator.

Web-based Businesses: These businesses were founded on the Web and conduct their business primarily online. For them, understanding user response to their sites is nothing less than imperative—it is the core of their business!

Advertising-supported Sites: Web navigation services and content providers such as Yahoo! and HotWired are supported largely by advertising money. Convincing advertisers to continue sponsoring them requires that they can prove a return on the advertiser's investment. This involves providing statistics about which mechanism (navigation tool or site) brings users to specific ads and which ad brings users to the advertisers' site. Additionally, they must constantly enhance their own service and functionality.

Most current Web site analysis tools are Web server statistical analysis packages, installed in the application space of the host server, that analyze data deposited in the Web server log file. Several problems and limitations are inherent in this approach. Being located in the application space means they can collect and analyze only the data that reach the HTTP daemon. Much of the data useful in understanding and analyzing user behavior either stops at the IP (Internet Protocol) layer or loses accuracy on the way up to the application layer. Because of this, Web site log file analyzers are not able to detect:

- client-initiated disconnects (for example, users hitting the stop button in mid-download)
- busy signals—requests ignored by the server due to overload
- network problems—server retransmissions due to overloaded networks the time the server took to respond to each request

Another shortcoming of solutions that rely solely on server-based log file data is that the measurements are only accurate to the level of one second. Much finer time accuracy is needed to perform many useful calculations, such as determining the precise point at which users tend to cancel a request. In a system potentially capable of executing a hundred million instructions per second, the mandatory one-second time resolution imposed by the application layer will prevent accurate measures of system performance.

Another limitation of existing tools is their inability to factor in additional information such as demographic data, as discussed above.

DoubleClick Tracks In-Depth Online User Response

DoubleClick, www.doubleclick.net, in response to increasing industry demand for accurate site trafficking data, created a product called Spotlight that fills the gap between who's visiting a site and at what points users take specific action within that site. Spotlight tracks the number of pages clicked through by individual users and at exactly what point in their click-through they either requested additional information or made a direct online purchase.

This represents a significant marketing tool for gauging and maximizing user impact, documenting which pages motivate action and which do not. DoubleClick's Spotlight delivers on the promise of true interactive marketing by helping advertisers accurately pinpoint effective advertising, according to company literature.

Prior to the creation of Spotlight, the most extensive site activity that advertisers could track was the number of users visiting the site over a specific period of time. With Spotlight, advertisers can access the profile of users who purchase a product online or generate a lead, delivering a closed-loop marketing feature for sales and accountability. Users are identified not by name but by a set of user profile characteristics. Advertisers can access Spotlight data on a daily basis through DoubleClick's advanced online reporting system.

Spotlight data also helps advertisers determine which Web sites delivered the most user activity overall and can be matched against specific advertiser needs. For example, DoubleClick's Spotlight can determine what percentage of Canadian users asked for more information on a particular product and what percentage of .edu users actually made purchases.

BENCHMARKING THE WEB

By Katharine D. Paine, CEO and Founder

The Delahaye Group, Inc., www.delahaye.com, 603-431-0111
© The Delahaye Group, Inc., 1996
Reprinted with permission.

No matter what your business, chances are there is money to be made or saved in a Web site.

First of all, you must remember that the Web is one of the few communications tools that the customer *and* prospects pay to use. So think of it this way—if 10,000 people spent an average of six minutes each on your site last month accessing the product help section, that's 60,000 minutes that your customer service folks didn't have to spend on the telephone or $xxx dollars you didn't have to spend on a toll-free number. How much it will do for you depends entirely on what objectives you have for it.

It's all a moving target. Anything that pertains to the Internet and communications today is a moving target. For example, one ongoing debate I've had recently asks what model we should use when we talk about the Internet—is it more like a trade show, a magazine, or a mall? The truth is, the Internet differs from any other medium. Its use has grown faster than that of any other new technology in history—that includes the telephone, television, and the car. The Internet has already spawned hundreds of new businesses. It promises to do for the high-tech economy what Lotus 1-2-3 did in the early 1980s—gave people a reason to buy a PC, thus spurring the growth of thousands of peripheral businesses.

The Basics of Measurement

Yes, Virginia, there is a way to measure it.

The simple answer is that you measure your Internet activity the same way you measure any other communications activity—you get everyone to agree on objectives, you establish specific criteria, you measure those criteria, you look at the results, you take action, then you measure again.

And really, it's just as simple as it sounds.

Before we get into the specifics of measuring online marketing, let's review the basics of measurement. Those of you who have heard me speak

before know this old litany, but it still applies. No matter what you benchmark, your success depends on following six basic rules:

1. **Establish objectives**. Reach an agreement between all the parties
   involved about what you are trying to achieve.
2. **Determine criteria**. Define success specifically—number of hits,
   percentage of people more likely to purchase, rave reviews in
   Interactive Age. At the end of the day, what will convince you and
   your superiors that your Web site is a success? Decide on a benchmark. Benchmarking above all is a comparative process. If you tell
   me that 1,000 people a day are hitting your site, you haven't told
   me anything of value. I have no way to know whether 1,000 is a
   good number or a bad number until I know how many hits you
   received last month or last year and unless I know how many hits
   the competition gets. And how do those numbers compare to the
   number of people reading your ads?
3. **Select a benchmark**. There is no shortage of criteria against
   which you can benchmark your progress. The key to valuable
   benchmarking is your choice of the right criteria. Are you going
   to compare your progress to yourself over time, compare yourself
   to the competition, or compare the Web to other forms of communications? Select the right measurement tool! Only after you've
   identified your objectives, criteria, and type of benchmark can you
   really decide what technique you should use to benchmark your
   program.
4. **Compare your results to objectives**. Once you've conducted
   your benchmark, don't get carried away by numbers. Instead,
   examine them in relation to your original objectives to decide if
   your online marketing has succeeded.
5. **Draw actionable conclusions**. You've received one million hits a
   day, but what do you do with that information? No one in business
   today needs more numbers. People need interpretation of numbers to know what actions will help them become better, more
   efficient, or more cost-effective.
6. **Deliver on time**. Work backward from planning sessions, strategy
   meetings, or quarterly review meetings. Don't just pick an arbi-
   trary time period to measure. Pick one that will give you critical
   information for your upcoming meetings.

Now, with those rules in mind, let's get into the specifics of Internet benchmarking.

Definitions of Success

To know if your Web site works, you have to know its specific purpose. Otherwise, you can't define what marks its success. Why is your company bothering to put up a Web site? What do you want to accomplish? In the past few months I've been boggled by how many different things companies try to do with their Web sites. Here are a few examples:

- **The "Hello, I'm Here" Site**. Some companies believe that it's better to have something out there than nothing at all. Frankly, I can't argue with that logic. It's what I call your basic place holder—something out there so that someone can call up widget.com and find you. This type of online presence typically includes basic company background information, a list of products, maybe a newsletter and a feedback form. Success in this case is measured by evidence that no one is flaming you and you're not on anyone's worst-of-the-Web list.
- **The customer service substitute**. Most fully operating sites probably originated from customer service departments to answer customers' questions online and therefore ease the workload of customer service phone banks. Success for these is measured by the reduction of wait time on phone lines and increased number of people contacting you for very efficient help.
- **The "Hello, I'm Cool" Site**. Some companies (or technowizards within companies) decide that the Web is the coolest thing around and they're going to join cool by putting something on it. Whether such a site is consistent with anything else in the company's communications program is irrelevant. Success for such an objective is measured by whether the site tops the best-of-the-Net list in *Wired* magazine.
- **The image-enhancing site**. Image builders also appear in Web sites. These companies see their presence on the Internet as part of their larger image. They use their sites to enhance other communications strategies. Success for them is measured by consistency of messages across various media, from publicity to newsgroups to advertising. Ultimate success is measured by users' awareness of the

company's key messages and preference for the company's products.

- **The international marketing site**. Actually, this Web site goal is redundant because by its very nature the Web is the most international of communications media. Companies that don't bear this in mind can get into major trouble. Witness the small instrument company that, after putting up a Web site, was instantly flooded with international orders years before it planned international distribution. But if your primary purpose for a site is to target international customers, your site design and definition of success will be quite different.

- **The revenue-producing site**. Some companies see the Web as a new advertising medium. While sites make information available to a phenomenally large population, the Web needs a lot more time to develop and a lot more T-1 lines (designated Internet connections) before it can substitute for Murphy Brown. But never underestimate the power of Coke's and Ford's marketing departments. For these folks, success is measured by the Web equivalent of gross rating points and/or audited circulation figures. Trouble is, we haven't quite figured out what the equivalent is yet.

The Mechanics of It All

But how do you measure anything in this great chaotic environment? The same way you measure any other type of communications. You have to look at communications from two angles:

1. **Output measurement**. Lurk and learn. This is equivalent to monitoring your press coverage. It means thinking like members of your target audience and getting online to surf the Internet, newsgroups, etc. Once you're there, you need to scan the postings to determine message, tone, content, and type. Then, to make sense of it all, you need to put it in a file and begin to compare to results from other media and to the competition.

2. **Counting hits**. A lot has been said about defining hits these days. Doing so really is a lot like defining circulation figures. Before two large, well-known providers of circulation figures ABC (Audit-Bureau of Circulations) and BPA, International, stepped in, no standard definition of circulation figures existed. That's essentially where the Web is today. One hit really is just one user's access to

one of your files; one person listing your site may generate a dozen or more hits by accessing different files. So your first 5,000 hits may be nothing more than a few of your employees checking things out.

Those hits are like the numbers for pass-along readership that some magazines and newspapers want you to include.

Software is available that gives very specific information about what your specific hits entail, where they go on your site, and how long they stay there.

Ultimately, you must know how effectively your online marketing moves people to prefer or purchase your products, just as you need to know how effectively your trade show, publicity program, or advertising campaigns do this. Today's big debate is whether you find out by online surveys or by more traditional phone surveys.

The advantage of the Web's interactivity is that to some extent it's like direct mail. If you have the right kind of product, you can solicit sales and/or leads right there on your site. That's a great measure of impact. But what if you're not marketing a product that lends itself to that type of catalog sale? You still need to know what image the site leaves with your target audience or the impression it makes on them. One way to find out is with online questionnaires. But these sometimes meet with resistance on the grounds of intrusiveness and violation of privacy. The jury is still out about the accuracy of online questionnaires. We're sticking with the tried-and-true methodology of gathering your site visitors' phone numbers to call them later and ask.

The So What Department

There's no shortage of ways to collect data, nor is there any shortage of data to collect.

The real shortage occurs in analysis of what all that data means. To determine what it really does mean, you have to return to your original objectives. What do you do if you're getting 100,000 visitors a week, your server is overloaded, and you need a $100,000 investment to upgrade? First, you have to look at who those 100,000 people are, what percentage are in your target audience, what percentage are asking for more information, and what percentage are ready to buy.

Maybe your results are right on the edge. You're getting good but not great response. The numbers are good, but you're trying to decide whether or not to put other types of information on the site. Now you need to look at your competition, what else is available to your target audience, and what revenue potential exists for those additional products or services. You also need to assess the quality of other ways you reach your target audiences, and at what cost. Then you can determine cost per contact so that you can compare the effectiveness of your online marketing to other forms of marketing.

The point to remember is the specific value of benchmarking: Whether you benchmark online or with more traditional forms of marketing, the process enables you to use the data you collect to improve all segments of your communications program. If your data doesn't do that, you're collecting the wrong data.

Thank you very much. I'll see you in cyberspace.

BIRTH OF THE DIRECT RESPONSE WEB SITE

By Bob Vogel, ICI/SoftMail Direct, 120 Defreest Drive, Troy, NY 12180, 518-283-8444

softmail@icisolutions.com
© Bob Vogel
Reprinted with permission.

The World Wide Web is the fastest-growing segment of the Internet, with nearly 1,000 businesses posting new Web sites every week.

That's the statistic that tells us the commercial world is rushing to stake out its claim in this yet unknown frontier, even though the latest estimates suggest that fewer than 10 percent of households in the United States have Internet-enabled PCs (and the vast majority of those are using the Internet exclusively for e-mail).

How far the Internet has come in so short a time is staggering. It's not unusual these days to see URLs (Universal Resource Locators—Internet jargon for electronic addresses) mentioned in print and electronic advertising for everything from automobiles to vodka. Even television shows—soaps, cartoons, and prime-time dramas—have millisecond invitations to visit their Web sites. You'll also find Internet addresses posted on highway billboards, inside paper catalogs, even in some direct mail pieces.

The Web site is fast becoming an additional selection in the call-to-action response vehicles, right there by the phone, mail, and fax options. Unfortunately, in the rush to construct these Web sites—usually in some vain attempt to beat the competition and claim First in Cyberspace—most companies do not carefully think through exactly how best to integrate the Internet into their overall sales and marketing programs.

Now this is not surprising when you look at who within most companies is given the responsibility to create the site. Most often, it is one of three types:

1. Technical consultants, who provide advice on Web site content based on what the Internet culture was, not what it is or can be.
2. Graphic designers and advertising types whose focus is generally sizzle rather than content, and generating hits rather than generating results.
3. Computer programmers who have no clue about marketing communications, or marketing people who have no clue about Web site programming and flow chart diagrams.

It's not surprising that only a handful of islands in the ocean of Web sites have any true economic value to their owners.

From where I sit, as a direct marketer of 15 years serving technology clients, the paradigm for creating a successful, meaningful, and profitable Web site is crystal clear: the Direct Response Web Site.

If you haven't heard the term before, don't feel like you missed something. I just invented it. The operative word here is *response*, and the underlying key is to design and structure the site as a response vehicle to all other forms of outreach, including advertising, PR, mail, telemarketing, even the Internet itself.

While I may have invented the term Direct Response Web Site, I did not invent the time-proven direct marketing techniques behind the concept, namely:

- Carefully target your market.
- Create a compelling offer to get people to respond.
- Use graphics and copy to direct the flow of the message.
- Build fail-safe mechanisms for measuring response.
- Test. Test. Test.

Carefully Target Your Market

As I'm a direct marketer, I'm not so much concerned with the number of hits at my site as I am in accomplishing a clearly defined sales objectives, whether that is closing a sale or creating a qualified lead, or something in between.

With direct mail and telemarketing, this starts with selecting the best lists that match the profile of your target market. For direct response TV, radio, and print ads, it means matching the demographics of the program, time slot, or circulation to your target market. For the Internet, it means linking your site only to those places where your target markets might be poking around.

There is no magic to this. In fact, if you are doing your job right with your conventional direct response tools—advertising, direct mail, telemarketing, trade shows, PR, and the like—adding a conspicuous URL for your Web site is probably all you need to do to get started.

Create a Compelling Offer to Get People to Respond

If you have done your targeting job correctly, you'll want to capture the name and at least contact information of every person who visits your site.

Unfortunately, the way the Internet is structured, most people can visit your site pretty much anonymously. You can tell what server they came in from but not necessarily the identity of the individual.

Most companies have a so-called guest book as a standard feature, where people can voluntarily put themselves on a mailing list (or opt in, as they say in the mailing list world). But there is usually no compelling reason for them to do so, especially if the promise is a vague indication of keeping them informed of new developments.

Again, there's nothing magic or new about how to accomplish this: The very same tricks of the trade we've always used in conventional forms of direct marketing work on the Internet too. Try contests, premiums, sweepstakes, promotions, special prices, and the like. Just be sure to structure your offer in such a way as to generate a qualified prospect—not every Jane and Joe in the world who happens to be wired.

Remember, as the Internet is so open, the URL you carefully targeted to a limited audience could quickly get passed on through e-mail and newsgroups to an enormous number of people in no time. And if you're giving away free T-shirts, for example, you'll probably end up giving away the one off your back before you are through.

Here's a good example of how to keep control: To promote a new service being offered by SoftMail Direct, we might take out an ad in a trade publication offering a free Web site critique—a $1,000 value. We would offer it to 100 people selected at random from all people who visit our Web site between December 15 and December 31 and register at the special URL mentioned in the ad. Qualified prospects would jump at this opportunity, as they would otherwise have to pay $1,000 for our critique. Anyone who doesn't have a Web site for us to critique, or sees no value in having the site critiqued, is not a prospect.

Use Graphics and Copy to Direct the Flow of the Message

Unlike any other response vehicle—like phone, fax, or mail—there is no practical limit to the amount of information you can provide your prospects and customers once they hit your Direct Response Web Site.

Think how much more effective your sales communications would be if you could afford to send the answer to every possible question about your product or service that the prospect might have. Wouldn't it be great if you could afford to send a one-inch-thick color brochure, or a three-inch-thick color catalog, or a five-inch-thick technical manual, to every single qualified prospect?

Thanks to hypertext and the low cost of electronic storage media, the amount of information you can post is limitless. But this is both a blessing and a curse. If you put the wrong kind of information up on your site, or if it's not perfectly segmented and linked, you will quickly overwhelm (or underwhelm!) your prospects, and they'll jump off your site with the click of a mouse button.

When building (or revising) your Web site, take a look at every single page as a stand-alone entity. Ask yourself how this page is furthering your marketing objective. Then, carefully inspect each link on each page. Every single link should move the prospect one step closer to your objective, be it capturing a name, closing a sale, further qualifying the prospect, or expanding awareness of your product, company, or brand.

Also, contrary to conventional wisdom, it is a big mistake to make it easy for people to leave your site by embedding links in your Web pages to other sites. Many people put links to other sites as a hook or feature to attract people to their sites. That's the worst kind of incentive you can provide. They should come for your content, or they're probably not worth knowing.

Build Fail-Safe Mechanisms for Measuring Response

Even if you do a great job of targeting your outbound activities, you will find dramatically different costs and response rates associated with each. As with any form of direct marketing, you want to be able to measure response by source of the inquiry or sale.

Most people designing Web sites today create a single home page address that they use in all marketing and communications activities. That's like using the same source code for all mailing lists, direct response ads, PR hits, and so on. Direct Response Web Sites have many home pages, all identical in every way (or maybe not) except for their URL.

The best way to track response by source is to create a separate URL or home page for each place you advertise your Web site, including the Internet itself. This is incredibly simple. All you have to do is make a copy of your current home page and save it as a new filename in the same directory as the original.

For example, the standard URL for SoftMail Direct is www.softmail.com /index.html. However, in the example above with my special offer for a free Web site critique, I could have a duplicate home page at www.softmail.com /NewPubAd.html. That way, when I get my hit report, I know exactly how many people came to my Web site as a result of my ad in *DM News*. If I send out a direct mail piece with the same offer, I'll create another home page (for example, www.softmail.com/NewMail.html), giving me a clean way to measure cost versus response for each outreach vehicle.

And, if I'm really smart, I won't send my carefully targeted and segmented prospects to my home page at all. Other things go on there that could distract them from taking the action that drove them there in the first place. Instead, I'll send them to a special page relating to my offer, then give them the option to jump to the home page after taking the desired action (say, completing a form).

Creating unique URLs for each offer may sound cumbersome. But the data is critical, and it's a lot easier, less expensive, and much more accurate than creating unique telephone extensions for phone orders or separate P.O. boxes for mail responses.

Test. Test. Test.

The amount and level of data you can obtain about what people do when they get to your Direct Response Web Site is unprecedented in the world of direct marketing. Imagine sending out a direct mail piece and being able to find out exactly how many people actually opened the envelope, how many read the letter (and which pages they read), how many read the brochure, which pictures they looked at, and how many people looked at the order form—all, even if they never responded to your piece. Wow!

With these finely calibrated measurement tools at your disposal, you have a unique opportunity to test product positioning, offers, and creative—in real time!

In addition to setting up separate URLs for separate sources, you can set up separate URLs for different offers, creatives, and product positions—just about anything. And, if you already have a lot of traffic at your site coming in to a single URL, you can turn it into a Direct Response Web Site by measuring the hits for the current offer, creative, or product position and then making a change to one of the variables and measuring what happens.

Again, using my example of our free Web site critique service, I might create a new ad with a more generalized promotion like, "Visit our Web site and qualify for a super deal on our new Web Site Critique service." (I have set up a special URL for this test—www.softmail.com/Weboffer).

For the first week of response, I use my control offer of a free Web site critique. Then, after one week of response, I might change the offer to 50 percent off a Web site critique—just $500. The next week I might offer the Web site critique at the standard price, with a $1000 rebate off our regular fees if we are subsequently retained to redesign the Web site.

Depending on your normal Web site activity, you might be able to change promotions daily (or even several times a day). The important thing is that, whether you are talking to consumers, a technical audience, or business to business, you keep testing different parts of your site, removing parts that are not working hard for you and retaining and enhancing those sections that are.

EXPANDING ON THE DIRECT RESPONSE MODEL

As good as the direct response model is as offered by Bob Vogel, it only gets better. Once you have people coming to your direct response sites, you know how many people are coming from each ad. Now you have the starting point for creating relationships with each customer and for measuring the effectiveness of each magazine's readers. For example, let's say you have placed ads in *Fortune, BusinessWeek,* and the *Wall Street Journal*. Readers are from the same demographic profile, so you have one ad message copied to three distinct URLS: www.mycompany.com/F1, www.mycompany.com /BW1, and www.mycompany.com/WSJ1. You place counters on each page, so you know how many people are coming in from each magazine ad. You finally have a tool that measures cost per lead.

On one level you now know how effectively each ad pulls. If 10,000 came from *Fortune,* 1,000 from *BusinessWeek,* and 100 from the *Wall Street Journal,* you'd have a good idea that *Fortune* is the magazine for you to continue advertising in!

However, that might not be the case. Let's take the next step in creating a relationship. You ask each reader to take action: Ask for a sample or download software, read more about the product, have a salesperson call, or buy the product. Now let's look at those figures. How many readers from each magazine took which course of action? You might find that the *Wall Street Journal* readers, who were fewer in number, actually bought more product than the *Forbes* readers! You can now track the cost per sale for each magazine.

Let's take this a step further. If you are in charge of public relations at your company, you can tag each press release with a distinct URL so that one newspaper tells its readers that more information can be found at www.mycompany.com/pr001, while a second paper can send its readers to www.mycompany.com/pr002. Now you can track leads and sales by publication. Finally, public relations can show its impact to the bottom line!

METRICS

You can employ several formulas and tactics to measure the effectiveness of your online marketing campaign.

WebConnect suggests that its clients spread their advertising dollars over several Web sites, tracking the click rates for each Web site where an ad is placed. Within a month the client can see which sites are most effective for its particular purpose and concentrate its money for greater effectiveness.

The banner ad itself needs to be tested, as a slight variation might double the click rate. Some Web media brokers allow clients to test various banners for a somewhat higher fee.

Here is a set of measurement metrics developed by the Delahaye Group:

- If your objective is *targeted exposure,* count the:
  percentage of visitors from the targeted audience
  percentage more inclined to purchase
  cost per minute spent with prospect
  cost per qualified lead
  cost savings for literature and mailing
- If your objective is to *strengthen customer relations,* count the:
  cost savings of literature, support, and printing
  percentage of positive and negative postings
  percentage of visitors in target audience
  percentage of positive versus negative feedback
- If your objective is to *improve internal communications,* measure the:
  cost savings of literature, support, and printing
  percentage of personnel accessing the site
  impact on productivity, loyalty, and turnover

Objective	Criterion	Tool
Reach new markets.	Percentage of visitors in target audience.	Track visitors' demographics.
Sell ad space.	Influence of page on purchasing habits.	Track visitors' habits.
Create affinity between brand and event.	Visitor opinion of brand.	Survey visitors.
Sell product.	Dollar volume of Web page sales.	Isolate and track Web page sales.
Be cool.	Yahoo! and HotWired put it into their "what's hot" list.	Track number of mentions in hot lists.
Convey information.	Amount of literature sent.	Isolate and track Web page sales.

Source: The Delahaye Group

RETURN ON INVESTMENT

Customer Support

Measure the costs of a support call in the real world. Compute the cost of creating and maintaining a online support center. Divide the cost of the system by the calls handled to determine the cost of service on the Web. Compare that figure to the office costs.

Netscape pays $10 per call to a service company to handle telephone customer support calls. If customers use the Web instead, there is no human cost. If the Web site gets 3,000 hits a day, that's $30,000 not spent in support costs. That figure goes a long way toward paying for the Web site.

Saving Customers' Time

One of the hidden benefits of the Internet is the time companies save for their customers. Instead of hanging in voice mail jail on the phone, customers can find the answers they need by themselves on your Web site. This could also translate into improved customer satisfaction and increased brand loyalty.

Measure Customer Satisfaction

Each piece of e-mail to FedEx is coded. Complaints, compliments, and the like are all assigned codes. The Web master can quickly tell the voice of the consumer by counting the numbers in each coded category. The responses are then matched against similar codes of telephone surveys to check for trends and discrepancies.

Customer Education

Companies can save a great deal of money by providing educational material such as brochures, white papers, and press releases online. If the price of printing and mailing collateral is $10 per prospect and the price of creating online versions is $1,000 per page, the payback comes after only 100 visits.

Lead Generation via Advertising

Advertising provides several ways to measure effectiveness: The cost-per-lead model takes the number of dollars spent on advertising and divides it by the number of leads. For example, you pay $3,000 for an ad and get 3,000 leads. The price per lead is $1.

Another measure is the sales per lead. To find this number, take the amount spent on advertising and divide it by the number of orders. For example, you pay $3,000 for an ad and receive 300 orders. The cost for each order is $10.

A third tool is the profit per sale. This might be the most important figure, as profit is what you are really seeking. To find this number, take the amount of money spent on the ad and divide it by the profit per order. For example, you spend $3,000 for the ad and make $21,000 profit. You have a 7-to-1 return on your investment. In other words, for every dollar you spent, you received $7 in return.

Online Sales

This figure is easily computed by measuring the number of sales or the profit for all sales. Divide that figure by the cost of your Web site and to see if the site is profitable. For example, you've sold $1 million of products with a 50 percent margin, so you've netted $500,000. If your site cost $250,000 to build and maintain, you've made $2 for every dollar invested.

Public Relations

You can measure the effect of public relations on the company by creating a chart showing the number of visits per day and overlaying bullet points representing the announcement of news such as product introductions, earnings reports, and management changes. You will probably produce a chart that shows spikes at those events. If that's the case, you can show your management that public relations is having an effect on the interest in the company.

Another way to use the Web for public image management is to review comments made on newsgroup postings. Do the recurring themes contrast with the company's key messages? What percentage of the postings is positive, negative, neutral? What issues are on the top of users' minds? Are these issues long term or do they appear only once or twice? "By analyzing comments made in chat rooms and newsgroups, you might identify issues that need to be addressed, such as customer support. After making changes to that area, you can then go back to the users and see how and if they are commenting on that topic," says The Delahaye Group's Katharine Paine.

SUMMARY

An effective online marketing program is one that can be measured, tested, and improved based on specific number targets and realistic objectives. The testing field today is in its infancy, though new tools are being developed to accurately record consumer response. This chapter presented several realistic techniques, including benchmarking and the Direct Response Web Page, to give marketers useful tools by which to determine the effectiveness of their online marketing programs. It also explored metrics for determining success.

After it is all said and done, remember this quote from Larry Chase of Chase Online Marketing Strategies: "It is not about numbers. It is about conversions."

PART 3

Online Advertising

CHAPTER ELEVEN

Understanding Interactive Advertising

Interactive advertising is as different from traditional advertising as TV commercials are different from radio commercials. This chapter explores how the new online medium adds interactive features to the marketing mix and how marketers can best take advantage of these new paradigms.

This chapter will help you understand:

- integrating online advertising into the marketing program
- what "interactive" advertising really means
- tips and techniques for writing effective Web sites

INTEGRATING ONLINE ADVERTISING INTO THE MARKETING PROGRAM

Integrating traditional and online advertising is a new phenomenon that will change over time. In the past few years, the two media existed separately. As companies became more conscious of the Internet, they began to see the possibilities for synergy.

At its very best, a 30-second commercial on TV or radio can only begin to tell a company's story. The Internet serves as an integrated tool to help tell the rest of the story. More and more ads on TV and radio and in newspapers and magazines print the Web addresses of the advertisers so prospects can find as much information as they need to make intelligent buying decisions. Remember, these people buy on intelligence, not on fear or emotion.

Savvy companies realize that many people who don't have Internet access do have e-mail accounts, so they get their messages across by printing e-mail addresses on their ads so viewers can write for more information.

By sending e-mail to an infobot or autoresponder, viewers will receive text files that answer most, if not all, of their questions. The infobot is an automated process and does not require human intervention beyond the time to initially write the answer file and load it onto the computer. Meanwhile, viewers can receive these messages whenever they are exposed to offline ads. Not only does this procedure cut costs of printing and distributing information via the mail but it also puts answers into viewers' mailboxes seconds after the request is received. In other words, viewers get answers to their questions when they are most interested in your product. Unlike under traditional advertising conditions, consumers won't have time to cool off or to forget about your product if you tie online advertising to your integrated marketing program.

Many companies are tying traditional advertising to Web sites and e-mail accounts. Every Hollywood movie has a Web site address posted to the ad. That Web site usually has an online press kit with information about the movie and the stars as well as an online game based on the movie, which kids can play free, and a store where viewers can buy branded merchandise. Car companies print their Web addresses in magazine ads, as do real estate and financial institutions.

Companies also place ads in special Web advertising sections in print publications like *USA Today, Wall Street Journal,* and *BusinessWeek.* These directories print display and line ads pointing readers to Web sites. Most ads just list company names, although some small display ads try to lure people to the site by pitching free samples, information, or contests.

Clearly, the trend is to use traditional advertising to create traffic on the Web site, where consumers learn more about the company and its product or service, and make a buying decision.

WHAT "INTERACTIVE" ADVERTISING REALLY MEANS

When one thinks of interactive advertising, the first agency that comes to many minds is CKS Interactive in Cupertino, California, which virtually created the term. To give you the best view of interactive advertising, I interviewed Pete Snell, general manager of CKS Interactive, which has conducted advertising campaigns for Apple Computer, Ziff-Davis, and many others.

Janal: What is interactive advertising?

Snell: There are so many definitions. I would use this one: *Interactive advertising is the ability to interact with the source of the message you are receiving to either stop the playing of the message, to divert it to another area within the message for additional information, or to have the source of the message respond to your desires.*

For example, let's take an interactive advertisement aimed at direct response. The prospect looks at it and says, "I've seen enough. I want to buy." She can get information on where to purchase the product. The delivery of the message must be able to react to the message recipient's desires.

We much prefer interactive information delivery. Our belief is that whether we are using online or interactive television, the emphasis must be on information delivery and not on classical persuasion. The term *advertising* has come to mean things that people see on TV: a commodity product that delivers little information but attempts through images and persuasion techniques to get people to buy the product. For example, beer ads feature bikini-clad women playing volleyball on the beach. Infiniti ads don't even show the car; they create a *feeling* about the car.

That is inappropriate for online services and interactive TV.

Marketers who want to get a message across should not think absolute persuasion but rather serving the online service's customer through the efficient and intuitive delivery of information about the product.

The first things a marketer must understand are the expectation and mindset of the users of this communications medium. The Internet is the classic example at the farthest end of the spectrum. It has grown due to the sharing of information. The people who use it are engineers, scientists, UNIX programmers, the university community—and now business-oriented professionals are coming online. The Internet is a fantastic place for people who want information. They see strings of messages on a BBS, engage in a chat, or download files. They go to the Internet to get unbiased information—pure, honest information on a product, hobby, or lifestyle. What facilitates that is that people can hide behind a screen and not reveal their true identities. These people are information seekers and absolutely will not tolerate the Internet as a delivery mechanism for commercialism.

Janal: What guidelines should marketers use to create effective messages that avoid crass commercialism?

Snell: The marketer needs to blend his objectives and messages to meet the users' needs. For example, an engineer needs information on chips to design a board. Rather than rely on the manufacturer's printed information, he can download detailed information, including a technical manual, schematics, and performance models. By putting current technical literature and product information online, the chip company does a service to the customer.

Janal: Does this model work for the commercial online services as well?

Snell: The commercial online services are more family oriented. Something happens in the minds of users when they move away from the TV to the computer. They are in control and don't want to be interrupted by commercials. A fast way to create ill will is to interrupt their work with a commercial. People don't want more intrusions. In their minds, the computer is one of the last areas where they are in control and can make decisions about what they want to see. On the other hand, online services can create sales, but not in the way that TV has done. Marketers must think about how to interact very, very differently.

Janal: How?

Snell:

1. *Throw away the commercialism.* The marketer must think about how he can deliver information in a reactive, not proactive, mode. Establish a forum or area where people can go, using ads to attract people to the forum, where you can create one-to-one or one-to-many dialogs.

2. *Exploit the power of word of mouth.* This is the best way to sell a product. Online services give marketers that ability. The recommendation of satisfied users is essential. Amplify that a thousandfold to a millionfold. Unbiased, unsolicited people going on a forum and saying, "I love this thing and love the customer service and if you have this problem, I'd recommend this product." You have 5,000 people on a forum who'll see that message! What an incredibly powerful way to sell a product! It gets back to the idea of serving the customer—an idea that has been lost in this country.

3. *Serve—don't manipulate—the consumer.* Be accessible.

4. *Create a forum for people who have a passion* (for such topics *as Melrose Place, The Simpsons, and Seinfeld*). Enthusiasm is infectious. If you are a facilitator who creates excitement, people will want to check out your forum. Manufacturers can create an environment where happy customers can tell everyone else about their great transaction with the company.

Janal: Is this really advertising?

Snell: It is not advertising at all. It is the delivery of information and customer service. It is a spin-off of event marketing—creating a forum for excitement.

Janal: What concerns should marketers have over the design and interface?

Snell: First, no shovelware. Don't take the stuff you've done in print and put it up on the Internet without any thought to the medium and how people will access the information. A print brochure has a layout that shows what information you want to deliver to the customer. The same questions must be asked when you place electronic information—for example, product information, a message from the president on the vision of the company, investor relations information, press releases, FAQs from customers, seminar schedules, training schedules, and customer testimonials.

In regard to interfaces, there are no manuals for your forum. Consumers can't read how to use it. So it must have these elements:

1. It must be intuitive.
2. It must look good.
3. Icons must do the communicating.
4. It must integrate into the rest of the marketing pieces, which must all have the same messages.

TIPS AND TECHNIQUES FOR WRITING EFFECTIVE WEB SITES

With all the new technology tools and toys available to jazz up a Web site, you'd think that successful marketers would be blinking, wallpapering, and shockwaving their way to success. However, one of the software industry's leading direct mail copywriters, Ivan Levison, has a different point of view for making direct sales on the Web.

Levison, ivan@levison.com, is one of Silicon Valley's hottest marketers, having written successful pieces for Adobe, Advanced Micro Devices, Apple Computer, Hewlett-Packard, and Intel. So he knows how to sell in a crowded, competitive environment.

Janal: What new paradigms do you see developing for direct marketers on the Web?

Levison: The World Wide Web inverts the way communications really take place. I am a writer of direct mail. I knock on people's doors. I push my way in (with logic, benefits, facts, and emotions) and make them a terrific offer, and I'm in the house.

The Web changes this.

The inversion is that I am sitting in my house (my Web site). I am the salesman and I am waiting for people to knock down my door. Rather than an aggressive push into their houses, they have to come to me. It is an interaction process instead of an intrusion process. What flows from this is that you really have to attract. From this you need the creativity to get them to come.

For example, MicroProse software promotes its Across the Rhine game with a trivia game with prizes. The answers can be found in the manual. They have turned the game experience into another Internet game experience.

Because we have to attract, we have to be creative.

Janal: Does this mean a back-to-the-basics approach?

Levison: You will be more effective if you use proven direct response techniques. That means getting people to order now or get more information now. The idea is that immediate action is called for to break through the inertia. You have to force people to act.

Janal: What is the single most important point to bear in mind for making sales on the Web?

Levison: For all the talk of the graphics and so forth, the World Wide Web really is a text-based medium. A very important statistic is that 40 percent of Internet surfers disable their browsers so they never even see graphics because they do not want to wait. They are voting for text, and we have to acknowledge that this is a text-based medium.

Right now, you better write well, or the back button is always lurking and you are one click away from oblivion.

Janal: Should marketers be concerned about the multimedia, audio, and video capabilities of the Internet?

Levison: Yes, in the future, when we have giant bandwidth; then they can have full-motion video and audio. But right now most people are using 14.4 modems and they are sitting around knitting while they wait for graphics files to download.

Janal: What skills should marketers have?

Levison: Marketers must be good writers. Spunky writing. Writing with personality. Writing with humanity is what you need. Retreads of your brochures and press releases ain't gonna make it.

For example, write, "Check out my terrific clients." Don't write, "See my clients."

Ivan Levison's Tips on Writing for the Web

- When possible, give your readers choices. Let them feel in control. Interactivity (giveaways, incentives, and questionnaires) makes them feel comfortable on your site.
- Include your contact information at the bottom of every page so people can write, fax, phone, or e-mail you. If people print out only a selected page or two, they will see the contact information.
- Use a strong call to action (e.g., "Act Now"), just like in direct response.
- One of the most popular features is links to other sites. Create reciprocal links to their sites. Some marketers might be afraid of losing customers. However, to not have links presents a feeling of being locked in. If you have good information, people will be back.
- Make sure the important information is at the top of the page. Don't bury it. If they choose not to scroll, they will still get the most important message.

The Need for Call-to-Action Statements

Most Web sites fail because they don't have a strong call to action. There is simply no incentive to move people from being curious to being committed.

Advertising in print publications works in part because they use off-the-page selling techniques like coupons, fill-in forms, and once-in-a-lifetime offers. Web marketers can learn a lot from this example.

On the Web, most sites ask for the order by weak calls to action such as order and select. These words don't cut it. "Order" is as weak a sales tool as a retail clerk asking "May I help you?" Sounds good in theory. Doesn't work in practice. "Select" also sounds good in theory, but what does it really mean? Select the product and buy it? Select this icon to read more information? It is confusing.

Marketers must offer incentives to get people to order. Consider these calls to action:

- Order today and get a free dingbat!
- Order today and get two for the price of one!
- Order today and get a second for a penny!
- Order today and we'll pay the shipping and handling!
- Limited time only!
- Supplies limited!
- Exclusive offer for Internet customers only!

Starfish Software, www.starfish.com, has some of the best copywriting on Web sites. Consider this example: "A power-packed collected of over 25 essential utilities. Your choice: CD or download for only $29.95."

Try to find a word that doesn't belong in that sentence or doesn't help the sales process. Notice that every price is preceded by the word "only." It makes the price sound reasonable. This technique can make almost any price sound reasonable.

Make sure that you write enticing copy. How many products have you seen that have skimpy or neutral copy writing? An example would be "20-ounce jar of tomato sauce." That doesn't sound appealing in any manner. You might be saying, "But it *is* a 20-ounce jar of tomato sauce." Yes, but there's no life in that kind of writing. Think back to a time when you were in a restaurant and read the menu. French fries weren't written as French fries, but as "crispy, golden-brown French fries made from fresh Idaho potatoes." See the difference? Your mouth waters at the second description.

Try to get the consumer interested in the product by personalizing the copy. Show the benefits of the product, not just the features. Show how each feature will benefit the consumer.

Tell a story about the product. Paint a picture of how the consumer will benefit from using the product. Place yourself in the shoes of the consumer. Imagine what he would want to use your product for and what fears he has about ordering the product. Now you're in a better position to sell.

Next, you must build trust for your product and company. If you work for a company with a positive brand image, that should be easy. But for many of you who don't represent well-known companies, you must convey in your message a sense of trust. This can be accomplished by reducing the risks of buying. Offer consumers a money-back guarantee, no questions asked. That message can reduce their fears of buying from a company they had not heard of until a few minutes ago.

Consumers will wonder why they should buy from you instead of a competitor. You must point out the benefits of doing business with your company. You might point out that you've been in business for a long time, that the product has won more awards than competitors' have, or that the product has certain key features and benefits that other products lack.

Finally, you must clearly explain the steps the consumer needs to take to buy your product. This step is especially important on the Web site, where consumers can get lost or distracted all too easily. Also, because many people still are uncomfortable ordering via the Internet, you need to spell out how they can order by phone or mail. Wal-Mart even displays TTY information for people who are hearing impaired. Talk about attention to customer's needs!

If you follow these steps, you should improve your sales efforts substantially.

WRITING EFFECTIVE ONLINE ADS

Because of the interactive nature of the online services and people's intolerance of intrusive advertising and their decreasing patience, writing ads for online advertising requires a new set of skills.

"The nature of the medium begs for interactivity," says Larry Chase, president of Chase, Online Marketing Strategies, an online advertising consultant and publisher of "Larry Chase's Web Digest For Marketers," www.wdfm.com. "To not do that is like putting radio commercials over TV. You could do it, but it would look stupid because you are not using the visual aspect of the medium."

Advertising online is a series of actionable requests seeking closure. Closure means different things to different companies. For companies selling products, like flowers or books, closure is the sale. More complex items, like insurance and high-ticket items, end in a request for a salesperson to call the viewer or to put the viewer on a mailing list. Other companies want to create repeat visits so they can sell the impressions to advertisers.

Chase criticizes most Web sites because they don't go for closure of any kind. This might be a throwback to the fear of the hard sell, but professional marketers agree that the tools of traditional marketing must be employed on the Web site to get action.

Without a call to action, it's no wonder owners complain their sites are not effective.

Case Study: Sample E-mail Copy

This is an actual e-mail message I received. The names of the product and company have been erased. It is a good, but not great, example of e-mail advertising copy.

Hi, I thought this might interest you.

ABXD Company specializes in Gourmet Gift Baskets and Corporate Gift Programs. We would like to help you build your business.

Our Gourmet Gift Baskets can be customized with your promotional products and they come gift-wrapped and shipped with your own message.

Gift Baskets are great for building and promoting your business, thanking customers, appreciating employees, or just showing someone you care.

E-mail your snail mail address or call 1-800-555-1212 to receive our FREE "Making Memories" catalog of Gourmet Gift Baskets.

Visit our Web site at www.mycompany.com/html/corporate_gifts.html to view our complete line of products.

Mention this e-mail and receive 10% OFF your first order !!

Thank you.
Best Regards,
Jon

Case Study: If You Want to Write A Killer Web Site, Don't Whisper

by Ivan Levison

A lot of Internet gurus are giving out lousy advice about writing Web sites. They say you should keep the tone of your Web copy flat, sober, and subdued. Forget about writing with personality, they say. Keep your copy bone dry and you can't go wrong.

Believe me, if you're selling software on the Internet, the last thing you want to do is sound like your software is the new cure for insomnia.

O.K. I agree that you shouldn't sound like you're selling Ginsu knives, but let's get real! The Web today is a text-based medium and you've got to quickly capture the reader's interest and attention.

In other words, as always, you have to establish a relationship with the reader and therefore write with energy, enthusiasm, and personality. If you don't, you may wind up sounding like this flatter-than-a-pancake Web copy that introduces the reader to Lotus Notes:

Notes Product Information

Lotus Notes has defined a new breed of software called groupware that enables an organization to realize the full potential of its networks and its people. Now teams can work together in smarter, faster, more productive ways, and get more done with fewer resources.

What a yawn-inducing waste of time. This isn't soft sell—It's no sell!

For an example of Web copy that's alive and kicking, check out the lead to Abacus Concepts' page on StatView V4.5:

A statistics package that's easy to use? You've heard this before ... only to realize there's a five-volume library to read before you can get any work done. Not so with StatView. While other packages make lofty claims about ease of use, StatView really delivers.

Since 1985, StatView has been the leading statistics package on the Macintosh. And from the very beginning, StatView's goal has been to provide researchers with a software tool that makes statistical analysis a seamless and sensible process. One that works the way you do.

Nice and smooth. The writer at Abacus knows what she is doing.

The bottom line? If you're taking text from your brochures and press releases and using it as filler for your Web site, you're going about things all wrong. Visitors to your site are looking for an involving, entertaining experience, and if your writing is dead, they'll hit the back button fast!

If you agree that your Web site can stand a little improvement, here's a one-two punch that will knock some life into your cybercopy:

1. *Improve your headlines.* You'd never, ever write an ad or a direct mail piece that had a lousy headline or no headline at all, yet you see terrible headlines littering cyberspace everywhere.

    Don't settle for blah, vanilla headers. Give them a little snap and don't be afraid to have some fun. Here are some examples:

A while ago, Netscape came to me with a very special assignment. They asked me to create a series of high-impact success stories for their Web site that would explain how leading businesses and institutions put Netscape products to work.

(When your Web site gets over 80,000,000 hits a day, you want to make sure it's well written!)

One of the stories I wrote focused on the College Board. Instead of just throwing away the headline with the boring two words "College Board" I wrote a spunky little headline and subheadline:

The road to a college diploma starts on the Internet. The College Board puts valuable educational resources online.

For the Chicago Board of Trade story I kicked things off with:

Good news for bulls and bears. The Chicago Board of Trade helps information seekers cash in.

And for the story on the *New York Times*:

Hot off the press and onto the Internet.

Now the *New York Times* delivers your morning newspaper (and more) online.

Isn't it possible you could put a little more energy into your cyberspace copywriting?

2.   *Humanize the body copy.* Writing on the Web doesn't have to be uptight, so don't let your cybercopywriter get overly formal. (Hey, it's still O.K. to sound like your company is staffed by human beings, even if they are selling bits and bytes!)

Listen to how relaxed my body copy sounds leading in from the College Board headline quoted above:

These days, high school seniors aren't just hanging out at the local mall. You'll find growing numbers of college-bound youngsters, their parents, guidance counselors, educators, and other professionals logging on to College Board Online. It's the exciting new Web site created by the College Board in partnership with the Educational Testing Service....

Or how about the lead-in from the Chicago Board of Trade story:

At the Chicago Board of Trade (CBOT), information is the most important commodity. Fortunes can be made or lost depending on what you know, when you know it, and how you limit risk. No wonder tens of thousands of people from more than 50 countries visit the CBOT's innovative Web site every day, with more logging on all the time....

(If you want to check out these and other Web site stories I've written for Netscape, you can get to them directly via www.levison.com/pg12.html.

One last thought. Remember, lots of people are out there telling you to stay cool and distant when you're writing your Web site. I say, hold your ears and don't listen to them. Spirit, energy, personality, warmth, friendliness, and honesty have always worked in print and they will continue to work in cyberspace!

OTHER TIPS TO INCREASE SALES

People shop on price, so offer them the best price on the Internet! Even though it costs less money to make a sale on the Internet, you'd be surprised how many companies don't pass along the savings. A recent survey of software programs showed that some publishers actually charged more for sales on the Internet than in retail outlets, where their product was considered a loss leader to get people into the store! Successful companies will be the ones that pass along the savings to the customers.

The shopping experience must be pleasant for the online consumer. The fastest way to upset customers is to make navigation difficult. Carefully consider how the consumer will navigate the site. Successful product companies use analogies. For instance, the catalog companies use the analogy of a supermarket by having people select "aisles" that contain specific merchandise. Smart companies also use search engines so consumers can find products by simply typing the product name.

To increase sales, smart companies suggest add-on purchases. When consumers search for the albums of a particular recording artist, CDnow, www.cdnow.com, which sells CDs online, presents the names of other artists who might appeal to the buyer. In this way, the buyer can consider the other artists' works and decide whether or not to buy the CDs. In the case of CDnow, buyers can even hear sound clips from many albums. At some bookstores, buyers can read sample chapters from books. Both these examples illustrate how easy it is to make add-on sales.

In retail outlets, the box is the silent salesman. Many stores don't have enough salespeople, or knowledgeable salespeople, who can answer questions, so manufacturers print lots of descriptive information on the box for consumers to learn about the product's features and benefits. On the Internet, there is no box, so manufacturers need to print long, detailed descriptions and offer pictures for consumers to view. Don't force the consumer to guess what the product will do. They will get it wrong every time!

SUMMARY

Interactivity is the key difference that separates online advertising models from traditional models. As tools for the online world evolve, this difference will become more evident, and interactivity forms will grow beyond anything we can think of today.

CHAPTER TWELVE

Buying, Selling, and Creating Online Ads

In this chapter you will learn about:

- objectives of online advertising
- advantages of online advertising
- integrating online advertising with your traditional media
- key terms
- creative models
- banner ads
- pricing models for banner ads
- advertising rates and resources
- negotiating strategies for getting better ad rates
- new adventures in advertising
- increasing income by selling ads on your Web site
- challenges to online advertising
- future trends in online advertising

OBJECTIVES OF ONLINE ADVERTISING

Online advertising can be used to achieve four basic objectives:

1. **Build brand**. Many Fortune 500 companies, from Kodak to IBM, use the Internet to tell the world about their products, support their deal channels, and educate the public about their companies or products.
2. **Drive traffic to the Web site**. Online advertisements offer a proven way to steer interested buyers to your Web site, where you can tell them more about your products and services.

3. **Develop qualified leads**. While at the Web site, your best copywriting and photographs can convince prospects they should do business with you. Your questions can determine how best to follow up with each qualified prospect.

4. **Conduct sales**. As the prospects become warm, you can close sales either online or direct the buyers to your dealer channel, if that is your sales strategy.

As you can see, online advertising can be used to help your company make money.

ADVANTAGES OF ONLINE ADVERTISING

The benefits of online advertising have been discussed at length in this book, especially in Chapter 2. In summary, online advertising offers advantages over other media in that:

- It is interactive. Consumers can pick and choose the information, sales message, and buying modes that fit their individual needs.
- It offers the best of push and pull advertising in that merchants can pull consumers in based on their advertising and push material out to them once they have created a relationship.
- Because users select the sites they visit, advertisers are almost guaranteed highly qualified prospects.

Once the prospect identifies himself to the merchant, they can engage in a one-to-one relationship that can last a lifetime.

INTEGRATING ONLINE ADVERTISING WITH YOUR TRADITIONAL MEDIA

Major corporations as well as small businesses and home offices should consider using the Internet as part of their integrated marketing program. Because paid advertisements on TV and radio and in the newspaper can tell only so much about the product (or rather, so little), the best they can hope is create interest. Traditionally, that interest is intended stimulate a consumer to call the company or visit a store to find out more about the product and buy it. Online marketers know that they can save time and money by using their traditional ads to steer traffic to their Web sites, where consumers can read and hear about the products when it is convenient for them. If the Web site is designed and written properly, it can do an admirable job of playing the role of salesperson. When the consumer is ready to buy, he can order in the manner he is most comfortable with—online, by phone, or by visiting the merchant's store.

Examples of this tight integration can be seen daily on TV and radio and in newspaper display and classified ads by nearly every type of company. Hollywood movie studios run ads on TV and always include the Web address for that movie. Business-to-business companies place the Web address and e-mail address in print ads in trade publications. Consumer companies do the same with their newspaper advertising. Even smaller consultants, tax preparers, and home-based businesses use their classified ads to draw people to their Web sites.

KEY TERMS

Before entering a general discussion about the opportunities and risks of banner advertising, let's look at key terms you need to understand.

Hits

The first wave of Web entrepreneurs pointed with pride at the number of hits their site collected. You could see these people at trade shows telling potential customers that their site had 10,000 hits this day, or week, or month.

The trouble is that the term *hit* is very misleading. You would think that 10,000 people had visited his site. In fact, the number is far smaller. A hit refers to the number of times each file on a page has been accessed by a consumer. For example, if your home page has a text file and three picture files, it has four files. If a consumer visits the page, the number of hits counted is four. If he goes subpage and then returns to the home page, the counter is increased by another four.

As you have probably surmised, hits are not a good measurement of activity or popularity of a site.

When sites try to sell you advertising and tell you they have a gazillion hits, ask them how they define the term.

Page Impressions, Page Views, and Visits

A much better statistic is page impressions, page views, or visits, which all refer to one person visiting one page or many pages during one session.

If the visitor goes from the home page to another page, each page is recorded as one visit. When she goes back to the home page, that counter is not increased.

If the visitor comes back the next day, the counters will increase, unless you have a program that identifies her as an individual. If she comes back a second day to look for more information, the computer will realize she has been there before and count her as a repeat visitor.

Visits are a much more reliable measure of activity than hits.

CPM

CPM stands for cost per thousand impressions. This is a standard advertising term used in the real world. Advertising is bought and sold based on the CPM. For example, if an advertising site on the Web charged 2 cents per viewer or $20 CPM and claimed 100,000 readers, the cost to advertise would be $2,000.

Cookies

Cookies are electronic identifiers that enable Web servers to record and track user activity on a site. For example, if I visit an online bookstore and go to the John Grisham section and the online marketing section, the cookie records this on a file on my computer's hard disk. An integrated marketing site would then realize that I am interested in these topics and show me information and ads about these topics when I return to the Web site. The benefit is that the targeted information is conveyed by the marketer to the consumer. In other words, I read ads about products I am interested in, and I don't receive ads about things I am not interested in, like quiltmaking and fishing. We both benefit by using targeted information and advertising.

However, some consumers have misunderstood the role of cookies and consider cookies an invasion of privacy.

Term	Definition
Ad clicks	number of times users click on an ad
Ad click rate	also called *click-through,* percentage of ad views that resulted in users clicking on a banner
CPTM	cost per targeted thousand impressions
Gross exposures	number of times an ad was seen
Impressions	the number of times a reader sees the sponsor's banner image
Inventory	the total amount of impressions that an individual page generates

Source: DoubleClick, Worldata.

CREATIVE MODELS

There are many creative expressions of advertising on the Internet. The Web site is the single most effective advertising tool online. In fact, when the World Wide Web first was seen as a marketing tool, the Web site was considered your ad, brochure, catalog, store, and media center. Web sites offer a great deal of information, including corporate data, brand promotion, customer service, lead generation, and sales.

When we talk about online advertising, people now generally think of banner ads instead of the Web site. In reality, the banner ad is simply a vehicle to draw people to the Web site itself. We will look at Web sites as advertisements and sales tools in Part 5. This chapter focuses on what is considered advertising in today's terminology.

Banner Ads

Banner ads are advertisements that companies buy and place on other companies' advertising vehicles, such as search engines, chat rooms, online magazines, and Web sites. For the sake of simplicity, we will call the companies that sell advertising space "publishers" and the companies that buy the ads "advertisers."

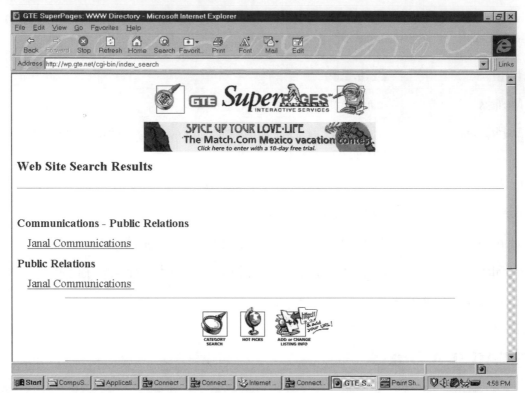

Figure 12-1 A banner ad for a travel destination is featured on the GTE SuperPages Web site. (Copyright 1996, GTE Directories Corp.)

Because of their rectangular shape, these ads are called *banners*. Banner ads range in height from one inch to the entire computer screen (or page) and are five or six inches wide. Banners can contain several colors or even a picture. They can be placed at the top or bottom of the screen. Some ads are smaller and placed along the sides of pages as well.

Although there is no standard size, which is a considerable problem for both advertiser and publisher, a banner ad is measured in pixels and is generally 400–468 wide by 60–65 high. The file size is about 7–12K. Any size could conceivably be offered or purchased. Some sites impose dimension standards so ads fit into their makeup. They also may restrict file size so that the page doesn't take a long time to display on the screen.

Banners can be static or interactive. Static banner ads present their message in the brief space allotted. As space on the banner is limited, the message must be written so that each word counts. This can be useful in presenting a simple message or for branding purposes—for example, "Think Company X. Think Safety."

To get around the limitation of space, interactive banners are hyperlinked to the advertiser's home page or to another page containing additional information and an offer. For example, if you bought an ad on an e-'zine targeting a youthful market, you could link the ad to a follow-up page using words, images, and psychology that appeal to that audience. In this manner, you can create targeted messages for different demographic groups attracted to your product. When an ad is displayed, it is called an *impression*. When a consumer wants to learn more about the ad's message, he clicks on it to see the Web site. That is called a *click-through*.

Because some publishers don't want the consumer to actually leave their Web site (after all, it cost so much to get them there in the first place!), they sell additional space to advertisers. When the consumer clicks on the ad in an e-'zine, he sees the follow-up page, but it exists on the magazine's computer, not the advertiser's. When the consumer finishes reading the ad, he is at exactly the same spot as when he clicked on it in the first place. Another tactic used to retain readers is to let them click through to your advertisement on your home page, but when they press the back button they are transported back to the magazine's home page. Other variations exist as well.

While banner ads offer the benefit of attracting customers to your Web site, naturally there are costs as well. There are so many banner ads that people filter them out mentally. They almost don't see the ads, much like passing a billboard on the highway. They also might use filtering software that hides the ad from view. Or they might turn off the picture-loading feature on their browser so the ad doesn't even display on their screen! There is a problem with ad measurement as well, because the commercial online services cache, or store, the most active Web sites on their computers. When the page is displayed, neither the advertiser nor the publisher has a record of this activity, so the advertiser gets a free ad and the publisher is deprived of income. Also, if the advertiser changes the ad, the commercial online service might not be showing the current page with the current ad.

Not only are there no size standards for banner ads, there is also disagreement on the definition of certain key advertising terms, like *page views* and *impressions*.

Increasing the Effectiveness of Banner Ads

While the typical click-through rate for banner ads is between 1 and 4 percent, which mirrors direct mail response, advertisers always want to do whatever they can to improve the response to their ads. This section presents various studies that have shown how to do just that.

The University of Michigan claims that moving the banner from the top of the page to the lower right (near the right scroll bar) increases response 228 percent, according to legendary researcher Sunil Gupta and his graduate students. Moving the banner from the top to a third of the way down the page increased response 77 percent

I/PRO and Doubleclick, www.doubleclick.net, 212-271-2542, the largest ad banner network, conducted an exhaustive study of the effectiveness of banner advertisements. Here are the highlights from this 1996 study—Doubleclick's ten lessons for increasing effectiveness:

Lesson 1: Target, Target, Target

In traditional advertising, you want your message to be seen by your target audience. You try to select the medium that attracts the audience most similar to the one you are trying to reach. But you don't know for sure exactly who is viewing your ad.

The Web, however, offers the ultimate in accountability. By utilizing the Web's ability to target, you can recognize and reach your target audience to the exclusion of others. You can deliver your message to specific industries, include or exclude specific geographic regions or cities, target by user interest, and even control frequency. This eliminates waste and makes your campaign more effective.

Taking advantage of the Web's ability to deliver highly targeted audiences creates the one-to-one relationships that extend and build your brand.

Lesson 2: Pose Questions

Don't just make statements or show pretty pictures. Use questions ("Looking for free software?" "Have you seen?"). They initiate an interaction with the banner by acting as a teaser. They entice people to click through. More importantly, they can raise the click-through rate by 16 percent over average.

Lesson 3: Use Bright Colors

Colors affect the eye differently. Using bright colors can help attract a user's eye, contributing to higher response rates. Research has shown that blue, green, and yellow work best, while white, red, and black are less effective.

Lesson 4: Home Is Not Always Sweet

All Web pages are not created equal when it comes to eliciting consumer responsiveness. While the home page often performs very well, a site may have other pages that outperform it. This can vary by advertiser. Certain pages can deliver a more targeted audience than others. By carefully analyzing individual pages, you can increase your response by placing your banner on a page that better attracts your target audience.

Lesson 5: Location, Location, Location

According to research, banners that appear when a page first loads are more likely to be clicked on. Negotiate ad placement at the top of page when buying space. The best possible scenario is having banners placed both at the top and at the bottom of a page.

Lesson 6: Use Animation

Animation can help you catch a user's eye. Strategic use of movement grabs attention more effectively than static banners. Using simple Java or .gif animation can increase response rates by 25 percent.

Lesson 7: Use Cryptic Messages

What did that ad say? What did that mean? Cryptic ad banners can help involve a user in the message. Because the sponsor of the message is not revealed, cryptic messages can be very intriguing. But there is a downside: Branding is forfeited on the ad. This may not be an issue if branding is not your main objective. Cryptic messages typically increase click-through by 18 percent.

Lesson 8: Call to Action

As in traditional direct response, telling consumers what to do helps raise response rates. Simple phrases such as "Click Here," "Visit Now," and "Enter

Here" tend to improve response rates by 15 percent. These phrases should be strategically placed in the ad, preferably on the right side. This is where the eye will be drawn.

Lesson 9: Avoid Banner Burnout

After what number of targeted impressions does click-through rate significantly drop off? After how many impressions do people start ignoring your banner? Doubleclicks' study concluded that there indeed is a sweet spot for user response. After the fourth impression, average response rates dropped to under 1 percent is called *banner burnout,* the point at which a banner stops delivering a good return on investment. These findings are incredibly significant. Controlling your frequency extends your reach and maximizes your ad dollar.

Lesson 10: Measure Beyond the Click

Click-through is not always the best measurement of campaign effectiveness. It depends on your objectives.

If you are simply trying to drive traffic, the click-through is great. If you are trying to gather leads, the best measurement is the number of people who clicked through and filled out a lead form. Three percent click-through and 80 percent lead fulfillment is better than 10 percent click-through and 20 percent fulfillment.

LinkExchange

LinkExchange, www.linkexchange.com, is a service that allows people to place banner advertisements for their Web sites for free if they agree to place advertisements of other members on their sites in turn. The number of advertisements you receive is directly proportional to how many times you advertise other members. The busier your site, the more free advertising you receive.

When the service first began, ads were not targeted—that is, your ad could appear on any site that might or might not reach your target market. Everyone knew the service was working to overcome this limitation and provide targeted marketing. In late 1997 it began offering targeted ads across a network of 100,000 Web sites. Advertisers can choose markets in 1,600 categories. For example, a sporting goods manufacturer can place ads on 4,000 sports-related sites, on 417 Web sites about outdoors sports, and even on 43 Web sites specifically about climbing and hiking, the company said.

The new targeting engine is fully automated and equipped with a self-service interface, according to the company. Network members can participate in LinkExchange's free cooperative advertising service by exchanging ad space on their own sites in return for targeted advertising across the rest of the network. Advertising can also be purchased from LinkExchange. This option works well for companies that don't want advertising to appear on their pages or don't generate enough traffic to support their advertising program, or for companies that have large budgets.

Sound Advice

People can zap your ad in a heartbeat. "This sends a very clear message to marketers," says Larry Chase, president of Chase Online Marketing Strategies, larry@chaseonline.com; www.chaseonline.com. "Your commercial message has to be as compelling at the content it sponsors, or people will fast forward past you."

"Your banner is the outer envelope. It has the offer. Does it say 'Zima' or does it say 'free six-pack,' or 'for lovers of hops?'"

One of Chase's clients, Hotel Discounts, www.hoteldiscounts, runs a banner ad offering discounts on airlines. "Consumers aren't going to want to miss that link," Chase says.

He recommends that the banner ad have a strong offer that encourages readers to take action. As the banner is quite small, you don't have a lot of room to work with, so every word and picture must count. Ads that say "Visit Our Site" or "See What Is New" won't attract action. No one drives to see a billboard on the highway, and no one goes on the Internet to read billboard ads. Banner Ads must be compelling. To get action, you must offer readers something that benefits them.

"The commercial messages will have to be in the best interest of the reader," says Chase. "This is no place for weak-kneed slogans like those printed on highway billboards or newspapers. They won't go for it online. What they need are affinity-type offers." For example, offer coupons, a chance to win a sweepstakes, a month's subscription for free.

Chase placed a banner ad for his publication on InfoSeek, a search engine, that read "Free Early Bird Edition of Web Digest for Marketers Available." His subscription rate increased to 2,000 from 250 in a few weeks.

To create a good banner, make a strong call to action and include an offer that addresses the self-interest of the consumer.

PRICING MODELS FOR BANNER ADS

The pricing system for online advertising is still in transition, but three models are gaining favor: CPM, flat fee, and click-through.

CPM—The cost per thousand model (CPM) used in traditional advertising seems to be taking hold. In this model, advertisers pay a set price for every 1,000 times the ad is shown. Each time the ad is shown is called an impression or a page view.

Flat fee—Advertisers pay a set fee for a set time period, regardless of how many people see the ads. Advertisers can buy days, weeks, or months of time.

Click-through—Advertisers pay only for each time the consumer *clicks* on the ad, not when he *sees* the ad. This model assures advertisers they are reaching more highly qualified prospects. Procter and Gamble (P&G), the largest consumer advertiser in the United States, forced this model on publishers, who reluctantly agreed. As the limits of banner advertising are being reached, more publishers are offering the click-through pricing model to assure advertisers they can deliver the right audience.

P&G's move also meant that online advertising outlets were put on notice to qualify their audience, produce reliable demographics, and justify the media purchase. They had been getting a free ride until this point. Now they must be accountable—just as their counterparts in traditional media are. What a concept! Online advertising outlets are quick to say that they don't want to be penalized for a bad ad that doesn't attract click-throughs. They do have a remedy: not to take the advertiser's money if they think the ad won't work. This is called consultative consulting. If the client is going to do something stupid, tell him before he wastes their money. That's good business and results in a win-win situation. If your advertising outlet doesn't care about your success, then you might want to look elsewhere for a partner.

Other advertising venues are following suit. PointCast created PointCast Direct, which follows a pay-per-click advertising model. This service guarantees click-throughs for its advertisers. Internet advertising network DoubleClick has 300 companies eager to test a pay-per-action pricing scheme that gives Web sites a commission if they refer someone who buys a product.

Other Pricing Models

"Cyberadvertising introduces a new set of paradigms to advertising. It is different in every way from print and broadcast advertising—creatively, functionally, and economically," says Leslie Laredo, www.laredogroup.com, a noted online advertising authority. "The interactive capabilities of cyberads offer key advantages for vendors to establish and maintain dialogues with customers."

The traditional method of buying advertising on the cost per thousand readers, CPM, does not apply to cyberspace, she contends. "There is no easy answer," Laredo says. The price of an ad changes based on each medium's main attribute. For example, computer ads are more valuable in a computer section, where they are more likely to be read by interested buyers.

That's why you might pay a higher price to reach targeted buyers.

Questions linger as to how to charge for ads. Is it by the time consumers spend on the system? Number of screens? Number of times a person accesses the information? What about offline usage, in which customers copy and send information ads to colleagues?

Another problem arises from the commercial online services' ability to store or cache pages of popular sites. These pages and the ads are displayed on the consumer's computer from the American Online computer or the CompuServe computer. The advertiser or the Web site publisher has no idea how many times pages are displayed in this way. The advertiser does not pay for these additional page views but derives additional benefits. The Web site publisher does not receive income for these page views, and thus loses money.

Many areas still need to be addressed in this rapidly changing environment.

Effectiveness Formula

Is your ad purchase effective? Here is one yardstick to measure the response: Take the cost of the ad and divide it by the number of clicks to get the cost per lead. If your ad cost $5,000 and you received 1,000 visitors, the cost per lead is $5. How does that compare with your other marketing costs for lead generation? If the figure is favorable, you've got a winner; if not, then you need to evaluate your ad and its message and whether or not you are advertising on the right site. Mark Kvamme, chairman and CEO of CKS Group, says, "Ultimately, the measure of all Web advertising will be cost per lead."

ADVERTISING RATES AND RESOURCES

The price for banners varies all over the board. I'd like to say that advertising rates are based on sound demographic research, but they're not; they are so random that they are more likely based on how much money the Web master has outstanding on his college loans or her house payments!

Most sites that accept advertising charge from 2 to 5 cents per banner view or $20 to $50 per thousand viewers. For example:

- **Geocities**, www.geocities.com, which builds and operates themed virtual communities on the Web, charges $30 CPM.
- **Happy Puppy**, www.happypuppy.com, a game site, charges $30 per month.
- **Lycos**, www.lycos.com, a search engine, charges $20–$30 CPM.
- **Nando Times**, www.4nando.net, a newspaper, charges $27–$34 CPM for sports, $34–$42 CPM for entertainment, $36–$45 CPM for travel, and $34–$42 CPM for business.
- **Netscape**, www.netscape.com the publisher of the popular Web browser that is the starting page for many users, charges $17–$25 CPM.
- **The Dilbert Zone**, www.unitedmedia.com/comics/dilbert, a popular cartoon, charges $70 CPM on average, but charges $15,500 per week for an ad on the masthead, $6,000 per week for the archive, and $1,750 per week for the Sunday strip.
- **Yahoo!**, www.yahoo.com, a search engine, charges $20 CPM, but $30 CPM for a fixed category, $60 CPM for the top hundred keywords, and $1,000 per week for a Web launch special promotion.

However, premiums of all amounts are charged for placement and position, keyword, targeting, duration, and number of impressions. Further, ad rates can be discounted off rate cards, although no sales rep will ever admit to this in public. There are no set rules and everyone seems to be charging whatever they think they can charge.

Media buyers want to compare sites and advertising opportunities. Given the large and growing nature of the Web, that research could take a great deal of time. However, these two sources should provide accurate information quickly:

For trends in the Web advertising industry, go to *WebTrack* at www.Webtrack.com. The site provides both free information and advertisements to its reports. You can freely browse the Advertiser Index, which lists major advertisers on the Web (over five hundred hyperlinked sites and rising) and the AdSpace Locator, which lists over eight hundred sites that accept sponsorship.

MarketMatch, www.marketmatch.com, categorizes content and lists rates for five hundred Web sites that accept advertising. A free demo shows how you can save time and plan more precisely for buying ad space on the Internet. With MarketMatch, you design and control site searches that best define your target audience and yield the most accurate, cost-effective results possible.

Checklist for Buying Advertising

Here are questions you should ask to evaluate advertising opportunities:

- What is the rate?
- Is the rate negotiable?
- How does this rate compare to other sites that reach the same market?
- What are the demographics of the site?
- What auditing procedure is involved?
- How will the publisher report activity?
- Is the contract cancelable if the performance doesn't match the promise?
- Can the publisher create the ad?
- What are the printing dimensions of the ad?
- What are the deadlines for art copy?
- Can the art copy be replaced in mid-run to test different messages or prices?
- Will additional charges be incurred for switching ads?
- What are the start and end dates?

- Are special orders included in the contract?
- What is the payment schedule?

NEGOTIATING STRATEGIES FOR GETTING BETTER AD RATES

Because the quality of Web demographics is questionable, the quantity of targeted consumers in many fields is low, and because publishers are dying to make money—any money—media buyers have a considerable amount of negotiating power when buying advertising space. The wise communication manager strikes a firm negotiating stance with Web publishers. Chances are the publisher will blink first. Of all the publishers vying for Web advertising dollars, only a handful have any experience in the field. The traditional publishing companies (*USA Today, Wall Street Journal,* Hearst, Time-Warner, etc.) know how to price properly and stick to their guns at the bargaining table. However, as any 16-year old who knows HTML can open an e-'zine, you can negotiate quite favorably because the e-'zine has a different economy of scale—to make a profit or simply keep the doors open or buy a new modem. This can be a boon to a company because the 16-year-old might publish an e-'zine that reaches your audience more effectively than the large publishing companies! For example, if you sell boogie boards, there might be a vigorous e-'zine that reaches that small but essential marketplace, a marketplace that large publishers won't touch because the numbers aren't large enough to be massively profitable.

The commercial online services also leave room for negotiating, but they are in a much stronger position because they know their audience and are more sophisticated marketers. As the major services are all more than 10 years old, they have a wealth of statistics, case studies, and proven track records for companies in certain industries.

NEW ADVENTURES IN WEB ADVERTISING—BEYOND WEB SITES AND BANNERS

Of course, there is a world of advertising possibilities beyond banners. As good as they are, other methods can be used and are being used. As the Web evolves, other advertising formats are being used as well. Time will tell which method will win, or which method is best for your type of business. We'll look at these new forms of online advertising: keywords, interstitials or intermercials, push technologies or Web casting, coupons, mailing lists, and sound.

Buying Keywords on Search Engines

Advertisers can buy keywords on search engines to increase their exposure. When a consumer types in a keyword, like computers, airplanes, or hotels, he sees a banner ad paid for by an company that sells computers, airplanes, or hotels. This is a great concept because users are identifying themselves as being in the market for those products at that time. This is one of the great advantages of advertising on the Internet. Yahoo! charges $1,000 per month to buy a word on their search engine and guarantees 10,000 impressions (a CPM of $100, or 10 cents per impression). Lycos charges $500 minimum per month per keyword, at 5 cents per impression over 10,000 impressions for a CPM of $50.

There are two parts to this advertising strategy. The first part is that the consumer sees the banner advertisement. The second part occurs when the consumer clicks on the banner. They are connected to your site, but where in your site? That's the central question. For a long time, advertisers led consumers directly to their home page. However, this is not necessarily the right place for them to be. If you have a good many products, they will have to wade through the clutter to find the material that related to the ad. It is like going to a hotel to attend a seminar. You arrive at the hotel lobby, search for the roster of the day's events, find the room where the seminar is located, search for the elevator, get off at the right floor (making a wrong turn), and eventually find your way to the room. The same scenario applies to the Internet. If someone comes to your front page, they might not make it to the advertising page because of all the confusion.

The answer is to link the banner to a specific page on your site. That way, when the consumer clicks on the ad, she will see a message created just for her: "Hello traveller, need a place to stay?" an ad for a hotel might read. That is so much better than "Welcome to Our Hotel Home Page. Click on any of these icons to read about us, our mission statement, a message from our chairman, letters from our guests, press releases, and a list of our properties." Whenever you have an ad linking to a site, it should link to a specific page.

If you are really clever, you will create different pages for each ad so you can track the effectiveness of each one in the sales process. After all, if everyone sees the same ad, you won't know if readers from ad 1 are more likely to buy than readers of ad 2. Of course the ad can be the same; only the URL needs to be different. This concept is discussed in detail in Chapter 10.

Infoseek, a search engine, claims it is getting up to 9 percent click-through rates on banner ads by combining keyword screens with its new Ultramatch technology. Ultramatch observes what sites an individual consumer visits and records the information on a cookie stored on the consumer's hard disk. From the sites visited, Ultramatch builds an individual's profile. Behaviors are categorized into twenty-two broad segments, such as health and entertainment, and further refined into 300 micro-interests, such as soap operas and lacrosse. This information is used to target banner ads. Privacy is protected in that advertisers don't know consumers' names or e-mail addresses. Compared to standard banner ads, Ultramatch can lift response by 25 percent. When combined with keyword screens, some Ultramatch ads get up to 9 percent response.

Interstitials or Intermercials

An intersitial ad is one that pops up when the user loads a new page. In other words, when the user hits a button to link to a new page, the interstitial is displayed. It disappears and the new page is loaded. This type of ad begins to follow the format used in television advertising in that you see content that you want to see and then they throw in an ad before letting you see more of what you want to see.

Interstitials began showing their ugly heads in early 1997 and are not widely used—yet. I believe the public will see these ads as annoying and will leave sites that have them. People hate the slowness of the Internet now (that's why they call it the World Wide Wait) and will think that the interstitial ad is slowing things down even more. But that's just my thought.

One big interstitial advertiser thinks the ads work fine. Berkeley Systems runs interstitials for its "You Don't Know Jack" trivia game. The software publisher claims these types of ads "generate higher brand recall than online banners" and "are more effective than traditional media such as television and print." This might be because the site is run like a game show and people are comfortable with the idea of taking commercial breaks. I don't know if people will adopt this same benign attitude when they are viewing an auto dealer's site.

A study conducted by MBInteractive shows that consumers exposed to a single interstitial were 64 percent more likely to recall seeing advertising for a specific brand compared to an average 30 percent increase seen in traditional banner advertising, Berkeley Systems said. Interstitials are twice as effective as traditional online banners and three times as effective as television, according to the study.

This approach is being embraced by Internet chat network Talk City, www.talkcity.com, which uses what it calls Chat Intermercials in an attempt to give advertisers greater ability to tell a story and create relationships with customers through one-, two-, and four-minute advertisements.

Because Talk City consumers use the service for an average of 30 minutes—five times the time spent on typical content-based Web sites—Chat Intermercials give advertisers the time and space to engage their customers, the company said.

As an example, the Toshiba Chat Intermercial educates users about the benefits of the company's Infinia line of computers by enabling the user to interact with the computer's features over the course of two minutes. The Sears Intermercial extends the "Many Sides of Sears" television advertising campaign. Diamond Multimedia's ad explains in detail the technical advantages of its 56K modems.

Talk City claims more than one million hours of chatting a month (equivalent to over 250 million Web impressions), over two million chatters to date, and more than ten thousand active chat rooms each week.

Push Technologies or Webcasting

The biggest headlines these days seems to be reserved for push technologies or Webcasting. This model basically tries to mimic television in that consumers subscribe to "channels" published by advertisers, who send information and ads to the consumer on a schedule determined by the consumer. In other words, I can subscribe to a news channel and read business news updates every half hour or 15 minutes. Along with the news comes ads. That's where the publisher makes money. If the publisher asks me to identify my interests, I can receive targeted ads. In other words, I will read ads for skiing and gardening instead of ads for cooking and sailboating. Promoters of this format think merchants will create their own channels and that interested consumers will subscribe. Only time will tell if this idea takes root.

Netscape says it has signed publishers of more than 700 channels of news and information for home and business users. It further says its software will allow almost any Web site to become a "channel" that delivers information to the desktop. Web users will be able to subscribe to any site and specify when they would like information sent over the Web. Among new business channels being developed are those from CNNfn, Gartner Group, Federal Express, News Corp., ABC News, and IndustryWeek. Targeted at home users will be new channels from Disney, Excite Personal, and TV Guide Entertainment Network. In addition, many large corporate customers are taking advantage of Netcaster internally to create Webtops for their corporate intranets and channels to push key business information to their employees. With the Netcaster Channel Wizard, a feature of Netcaster, enterprise customers and Web content providers alike can transform Web sites into Netcaster channels.

CASE STUDY: PointCast

One of the first publishers to pioneer the concept of push technologies is PointCast, a free editorial product containing ads that appear as screen savers. Each screen view contains news, a stock ticker on the bottom, and an unobtrusive ad. Consumers can select the news categories, companies, and industries they want to monitor. They can even select their favorite sports teams, daily horoscopes, and state lotteries. The articles and information can pop up at a predefined time, like a screen saver, or on command from the user. With these attractive, interactive features, PointCast has created an entity that consumers welcome.

PointCast makes money by selling advertisements that appear alongside the editorial copy. The company bets that consumers will not find the ads intrusive but rather the price of getting their news for free, much like television or radio (magazine and newspaper viewers must pay for their periodicals but don't object to advertisements appearing next to articles).

PointCast also hopes that consumers not only see the ads but act on them. The ads are hyperlinked to the advertisers' sites so viewers can click on an ad and find more information. In this way the ads surpass their static, one-way cousins in the analog world. They accomplish the goal of creating awareness for a company or product for viewers who don't click and provide targeted information for those who do click.

The ads are displayed in these formats:

- Moving ads, which appear as one square divided into four boxes. A message draws and displays in each box, one after the other.

- Animated ads, which feature moving icons or words.

While these formats won't rival TV ads, they are a step up from the static banner ad because more information can be displayed to build brand identity and product awareness that could lead people to click on the ad and visit the Web site.

- **Rewards:** PointCast could be a cost-effective way to reach your audience. If PointCast can allow viewers to select their news and categories, they might be able to provide the beginnings of a targeted audience that would delight advertisers.

- **Risks:** Until the ads are targeted, advertising messages could be wasted on glazed-over eyes.

- **Analysis:** The PointCast system has tremendous opportunities for advertisers who create their own content. Imagine using this kind of program to deliver news and advertisements to your targeted markets, investors, employees, prospects, and current consumers. This business model could be a great way to build communities and maintain relationships.

For computer and software advertisers, PointCast offers a ready marketplace because the one demographic we can all agree on is that everyone on the Internet has a computer and wants software. It is no surprise that early advertisers included hardware manufacturers and software publishers.

Until we see hard numbers on leads generated and sales closed, we'll have to wait to see if this is the most effective use of the new medium or just an interesting transition point along the way.

E-coupons

Distributing coupons can be a valuable method of:

- attracting customers to your site
- attracting customers to your store in the real world
- building a database of prospects
- getting people to sample your product
- building product awareness
- tracking leads

Most online consumers want coupons, whereas most offline consumers don't, according to a survey by Market Facts of Arlington Heights, Illinois.

You can create coupons at your Web site that people can print and redeem at your physical store.

Third-party companies also offer coupon distribution services. These companies attract consumers, find out their interests, and offer them coupons or free offers accordingly. For example, e-coupons, www.ecoupons .com, asks visitors which business magazine they would like to see on a free trial offer— *BusinessWeek* or *Forbes*. E-coupons forwards names and addresses to magazines' circulation departments for fulfillment—and follows up to make sales.

Similarly, the service could e-mail coupons for kitty litter to consumers who have cats. In both cases, companies get prospects' names and addresses for their database.

Coupon.Net, www.coupon.com, distributes coupons in a target geographic area or by brand. Consumers can search for coupons by product type, brand, and manufacturer. With dedicated state and regional directors, travelers can access coupons for, and information about, products, restaurants, hotels, and entertainment. The company also has a similar service for rebates. Consumers can download and print forms and send them to a redemption center with the appropriate attachments. Internet-illiterate companies can put a coupon online without even having a Web site.

These strategies ensure that only customers who want your coupon will receive it. This is a great way to implement one-to-one marketing.

Sponsored Mailing Lists

Mailing lists offer advertisers highly targeted audiences that gather to discuss specific interests. Rates tend to be very low, less than 10 cents per reader. A carefully targeted ad can produce results. A travel sponsor to the Internet Sales mailing list received close to 3,000 additional hits, over 250 e-mails, and $34,000 in sales. A source of mailing lists that accept advertising is compiled by copywriter Al Bredenberg and can be found at www.copywriter.com.

INCREASING INCOME BY SELLING ADS ON YOUR WEB SITE

An interesting thing happened when a friend of mine published a small magazine on artificial intelligence. He covered his costs with his 5,000 subscribers. But he found he could make a small fortune selling the list of names to companies that wanted to reach those subscribers.

One of your goals could be to make money by selling advertising on your site to other companies. The two key ways to do this are to sell banner ads to other companies and to sell links from your site to other companies' sites.

Let's say your Web site attracts 50,000 viewers a month. If you were to sell those eyeballs to advertisers at the conservative rate of 10 cents a view, you would receive $5,000 for each ad you sold. Several publishers rotate ads among six or more advertisers each month. If you were to sell each of your six spaces for $5,000, you would generate $30,000 a month, or $360,000 a year.

(Of course, some companies wouldn't want to sell advertising on their site because it might send the wrong message to its community or dilute the focus of the site.)

To sell space, you have to convince ad space buyers that you have a market that meets their demographic objectives. To do this, you must keep a log of users and capture their demographic information. You must be able to prove to potential advertisers that your audience is composed of likely consumers of their product.

The best way to find out who is on your site is to entice them to tell you. Merely asking them will not draw a response, as people have better things to do than fill out survey forms on every Web site they visit. Imagine going into the mall in your home town and having a teenager with a clipboard standing by the entry to the shoe store who won't let you in until you tell her your age, income, travel plans, and family size. You wouldn't go inside that store! Same on the Web. However, you will get answers to a short questionnaire if you offer people something of value, like a free sample of your product, information, or entertainment. Consumer sites as well as business-to-business sites can put free information on the doorstep but only allow access to the meaty files after the viewers identify themselves. This method is effective.

Charging for your ad space or links should be done based on the CPM model, as most advertising buyers are familiar with it and can compare it to other advertising choices. The rate will depend on how targeted your audience is and how hard it is to reach.

The process of selling the ads can be done in two ways:

1. You can hire a staff to call on customers, create an advertising sales kit, and the like. The advantage is that you will keep more of the money and have a tighter control over the process. The disadvantage is that you have to hire, train, and create sales tools from scratch.

2. You can hire a rep firm to sell ads. The advantage is they have a staff in place, are familiar with the Internet and its advertising norms and practices, and might even have contacts at advertising agencies or potential advertisers. The disadvantage is that you have less control over the sale and take a smaller share of the income than if you had an in-house staff.

Hiring and Managing an Ad Rep Firm

Media buying agencies, or rep firms, sell ad space on company Web sites. This is a service to companies that want to generate revenue from their site without investing in the manpower to conduct the operation. Good agencies bring expertise and contacts to the table. Some advertisers prefer working with agencies because they can make their entire media selections by dealing with just one or two firms instead of dozens of people at individual Web site companies.

Agencies charge anywhere from 30 to 50 percent commission on each ad they sell. Some firms also charge expenses for office charges, travel, and entertainment, which can be considerable. Make sure you are aware of all possible expenses before signing a contract.

Companies that offer this service include:

- **Burst Media**, www.nerdworld.com/burst, 800-876-4352
- **DoubleClick**, www.doubleclick.net, 415-919-0500
- **Softbank Interactive Media Sales**, www.simWeb.com
- **WebConnect**, www.worlddata.com, 407-393-8200

Here are several issues to consider when retaining an ad rep firm:

- Can the firm run the entire operation from start to finish?
- Can the firm create a department that your company can phase in after learning the ropes?
- Can the task of selling ads be done more efficiently or cost-effectively in-house?
- Will the firm recommend prices for ads and discount schedules?
- How much latitude does the firm have to negotiate a deal?
- Are the printed ad prices fixed or negotiable?
- After ads are established, can they be managed in-house for a lower fee?

- How long has the firm been in business?
- What accounts does it handle?
- Are those accounts complementary or competitive to your business?
- Will other accounts handled make your site look good or bad?
- Should the firm also maintain traffic and auditing reports?
- How long is the service contract in force?
- Are commissions paid after a contract ends?

Ad Networks

Ad networks are cooperatives of sites that have an inventory of advertising banners to sell. Like a farm cooperative, they can leverage their merchandise and marketing efforts and reduce duplication and costs. Advertisers benefit as well because they can buy ads on many sites that reach their target markets with just one phone call.

Ad Auctions

Companies that have excess advertising inventory auction off their wares. Adbot, Inc., www.adbot.com, provides an Internet advertising network in which all media transactions occur by means of an organized, impartially mediated auction market. "Our mission is to provide the industry's most efficient way to buy and sell ad space on Internet-based publications. We are committed to assisting Internet content providers in maximizing the potential revenues of their publications while making it possible for advertisers to reach their target audiences with effective and affordable media placements," according to company literature.

Companies can target their advertising on four content networks: music, movies, personals, and news, at prices ranging from 60 cents to $3 CPM.

Traffic Measurement and Analysis

Leading companies in this field include:

- **Accipiter**, www.accipiter.com
- **Accrue Software**, www.accrue.com
- **Bellcore**, www.bellcore.com
- **Broadvision**, www.broadvision.com

- **Firefly Network**, www.firefly.com
- **Focalink Communications**, www.focalink.com
- **I/PRO**, www.ipro.com
- **Interse**, www.interse.com
- **NetCount**, www.netcount.com
- **Net.Genesis**, www.netgen.com
- **NetGravity**, www.netgravity.com

CHALLENGES TO ONLINE ADVERTISING

Of course, online advertising faces barriers and challenges. Chief among them are:

- **Personal filters**. People might not want to see ads, or act on them. Just as in other media, only a small percentage of people will ever buy your product. That's okay. The key is to target your message so that people who are interested in your product will buy it.
- **Technology filters**. Software programs like Internet Fast Forward, www.privnet.com, are being created to filter out advertisements such as banner ads. Your ad might never reach its target.
- **Lack of good writing and marketing techniques**. Many Web sites don't use the tried-and-true methods of selling off the page. Merely presenting features and benefits is not enough to sell in the online world. You must make a compelling offer that is irresistible to your prospects.
- **Holding the Internet to a higher standard than other advertising**. What is your response rate for cold calls? For direct mail? For advertising? For walk-in traffic? Use those yardsticks as measurements for online advertising. To expect the Internet to be the all-in-one answer is foolhardy.

FUTURE TRENDS

Dynamic Page Creation

A key advantage of online advertising is the ability to create one-to-one relationships with customers. One way of doing this will be through the process of dynamic pages—that is, Web pages created for each individual user based on that user's preferences. No longer will one static page be served for each customer. Instead, when a person signs in to a site, the database will be contacted and gather information and ads that are relevant to that user. So if a person is interested in golfing and tennis, he will see ads for those products instead of ads for gardening and cooking.

CONCLUSION

Many new advertising opportunities are on the World Wide Web. Because online advertising is so new, prices and paradigms have yet to evolve fully. There is much debate over the effectiveness of banner ads and how they should be measured and paid for. Meanwhile, new advertising models are percolating. Time will tell which formats prove most effective.

CHAPTER THIRTEEN

Using Online Advertising to Build a Community

While some companies do well with only an e-mail presence or a simple Web site, the companies that want to break away from the pack create content and communities to win raving fans for life. The Internet offers new interactive tools for advertisers to build one-to-one relationships with consumers for the purpose of creating lifetime customers. If you can create a community that feels enhanced by being at your site, you will be able to attract the consumers who can make your business grow. This chapter shows how companies are doing that.

WHAT IS A COMMUNITY?

At this point it is important to define community. Let's use this definition: A community is a group of:

- like-minded people who band together
- for frequent interaction
- because it is mutually beneficial
- and provides a sense of safety
- and a sense of identity.

Online Chatting Fosters Communities

The Internet, commercial online services, and BBSes (private bulletin boards) have the ability to attract people interested in meeting and chatting with others who have the same interests and, hence, create a sense of community. Chatting is the number-one reason given by online denizens for subscribing to America Online. That message is borne out by the amount of connect time devoted to community-building areas such as chats, e-mail, and places where people can exchange information and opinions. These interactions can be done in real time, where members type messages to one another and get responses as soon as the recipient has time to think and type. Meetings can be done in store-and-forward mode, in which one person leaves a message for another person who might not be online at that moment. The message is stored on the computer system and forwarded to the recipient, who reads and responds when he uses the online service. If messages are posted to the entire list, then anyone can read and respond to the discussion.

Users Create Their Own Communities

People have banded together to create communities since the beginning of the online revolution. From the earliest days, online denizens have used their own initiative to create communities of like-minded people to discuss topics of mutual concern. Groups range from computer programmers to devotees of *Beverly Hills 90210* to parents of children with dyslexia to people with eating disorders to lawyers, public relations professionals, and other professionals, to people who identify themselves by hobbies such as gardening, cooking, flying model airplanes, and photography. The Internet has more than 18,000 such communities in the form of USENET newsgroups as well as countless mailing lists; the commercial online services have another 2,000 or so communities grouped in forums, clubs, and special interest groups. No matter what the name, the purpose is the same: to provide a sense of community for members.

It is important to note that people create the community on the Internet—the Internet did not create the community. The Internet merely contains the tools that allow these communities to form. Without advertising or publicity these groups coalesce; members tell their friends and colleagues, who in turn decide to join. On the commercial online services, information providers create the communities, which are held together by paid staffers, volunteers, and the more vocal members of the community who lead discussions, arrange for articles to be contributed to their libraries, and prevent merchants from posting intrusive advertising.

Community members participate as often as they want. On some forums, people come once to search for files or ask questions and are never seen again. On other forums, people come, ask questions, answer others, and do so several times a day or a week. People contribute at the level they decided is best for them. Even today, some newsgroups have only a few vocal members who post articles, but those articles are read by 30,000 lurkers who read and never comment.

Community Members Benefit from Participation

Community members give freely of their time and expertise because they feel the interaction is mutually beneficial. If they answer a question for a stranger today, then someone will answer a question of theirs tomorrow. For some members, the mere thought of helping people is reward in itself. Others know that if they answer a question, people will see them as experts and might hire them. CompuServe's professional forums are rife with anecdotes of consultants who have gained clients or sold products in this manner—all done with the intent of helping people, never with the blatant sales pitch that violates the netiquette of the online world.

People ask personal questions or list the problems of their companies in a public forum because the sense of community gives them feelings of safety. On the Internet and commercial online services, it is easy to hide behind a mask so that no one knows your name or where you live or work. This sense of anonymity also contributes to the feeling of community. Online, no one knows if you are old or young, able or disabled, white or black. They know you only by the content of your character as expressed online. In this manner, people become fast friends, or feel they know one another, or are able to open up to each other. The online world has hundreds of stories of people who met and fell in love online, as documented in many newspapers across the country.

It should be noted that community membership is not necessarily based on geography, like communities in the real world. People who are interested in gardening can be from all over the world, be of any age, sex, or race, and get along marvelously. These communities are based on interest, not merely on geography or demographics. People who are interested in fishing can talk with one another, even though they might not look at one another in the real world. Communities based on geography can exist as well, as people in one town go online and discover each other, just as in the real world. However, an advantage of online communities is the ability to meet people who you might not normally run across in your geographic community.

From this mutual caring and concern arises a feeling of identity. People who contribute a great deal become well known. These online VIPs are courted by advertisers who seek their opinions, their feedback on new products, and their endorsements. They become opinion leaders in their niche market. Other members of the community come to trust their opinions and seek their advice. IBM noticed a number of computer consultants giving free advice to people in their forum. The company decided to support these people by giving them advance information on products and provided them with advanced training not normally available to the general public. These VIPs, in turn, were able to offer high levels of support to the online community. Why did these consultants offer their time for free? That's a question for sociologists exploring this brave new online world.

Advertising and Online Communities

These communities have evolved without the help of advertisers. In fact, advertising has long been abhorred online in the private messaging areas. The early dwellers on the Internet felt that intrusive advertising and the hard sell are repulsive.

Now, as more consumers and businesses go online, the dread of advertisers is subsiding to a mere tolerance. People have long been conditioned to accept advertising in limited doses in return for getting free or subsidized content (look at newspapers, magazines, television, and radio, for example).

Advertising is effective in the online world only when it adopts the principles of the soft sell, where advertising is based on information instead of emotion and where messages have an attitude or personality that makes the company and its mission come alive.

The Deliberate Development of Communities

Smart advertisers are taking this common bond of community and making it their own. While the first wave of online members created its own community and content, the new breed of advertiser is deliberately creating community and content in an attempt to establish relationships with people and make them customers for life.

Examples of communities sponsored by companies or associations include Toyota, the Arthritis Foundation, and WRAL-TV in Raleigh, North Carolina. Other communities are being created by companies, professional organizations, or by the people and professionals themselves who are interested in such topics as sports, politics, religion, parenting, health, and sexuality.

Let's look at a few examples of companies that have created online communities:

- **Absolut Vodka**, which is known for its inventive ads showing its bottle in various designs, uses its Web page to show artists creating the ads. People can see the artists at work (using video clips) and ask them questions. In this way people who come from a variety of backgrounds and interests can interact with one another based on their common interest in art, creative design, and advertising.
- **WRAL-TV** in Raleigh, North Carolina, prints a village square image in cartoon strokes on its home page. People in that geographic community can find the local news, sports, and weather, talk with each other in chat sessions, and buy things in local stores.
- **Molson's beer** has created a pub atmosphere to attract a community of twentysomethings who have a need to meet others and chat about music and sports.

In each of these examples the advertiser presents content that draws people together to discuss issues of common concern. The advertiser is not blatantly selling a product, as on television. Instead, the advertiser seeks to create an environment or an experience for the target audience. These examples show that advertisers can create a sense of community without violating the Internet's ban on intrusive advertising.

Case Study: Reebok

Reebok's online mission is to create a community of people united in their common interest in sports fitness. To create the site, Reebok had to first identify its community and marketing mission. "Preparation is the link between fitness and sports, and every athlete is driven by his own personal motivation as he prepares to compete at his personal best," says Dave Ropes, senior vice president of integrated marketing for Reebok. "The message Reebok is delivering is that everyone who participates in sports or fitness can attain a feeling of confidence, of being in control through the proper preparation."

Reebok's Web master, Marvin Chow, is a 23-year-old wunderkind of the online world who is able to create a feeling of community at the Reebok Web site, www.planetreebok.com. In setting up the site, Chow studied the attitudes and perceptions of his target audience and found they had a great many things in common.

"The generation growing up today is accustomed to heavy advertising and sponsorships. All athletes are owned by companies. They are walking billboards." He decided to take that feeling of manipulation by the athletes and large companies and turn it to Reebok's advantage. "You have to take that connection and utilize it. We bring athletes to them in a live chat. We've sponsored chats with Emmett Smith and Frank Thomas." He notes, "We will target people with similar interests, feed them information, and give them a way to discuss data."

This creation of content fits in well with the Internet's philosophy of providing free information. "You have to give them something back, such as information or physical stuff. They say 'What are we getting out of it?' Information is the answer," Chow says.

Reebok is among the first advertisers to create an online community and content. "Because kids are bombarded by ads, the Web site has to create an entire content area. For Reebok, that area is sports fitness. We are doing more than sponsoring it. We are creating the content. We have turned from a sponsor into a content creator. We can offer them so much more," Chow says. "In every other medium we are a sponsor. On the Internet, we are a content provider. We can't show our expertise on TV. We can show it on the Net."

Reebok has been most successful in appealing to women. The Web site has a wealth of information on the growing field of versatraining, a combination of aerobics, gymnastics, step master, tai chi, and other forms of exercise that women participate in several times a week at their local fitness centers. Such women search for information about their sport of choice. As their daily newspapers cover only professional sports, these women have no other source of information. Reebok has wisely chosen to fill this void. The Web site contains articles about versatraining, interviews with leading coaches and trainers, and schedules of upcoming events and meets—information newspapers do not provide, thus giving greater value to the information.

The company also wisely chose women as one of their key audiences. As women control 80 percent of the consumer dollar in the United States, advertisers who want to be successful must create content and community that appeal to women's interests. For many companies, thoughts about women's interests seem to be limited to cooking and recipes. Reebok shows that they can appeal to more diverse pursuits.

By adopting the "Planet Reebok" theme on its Web site and its television advertising, Reebok makes use of the Web as a worldwide medium. It offers chats with soccer and track stars in countries where they are heroes.

Chow says the Web site is a success. "We get tons of comments. It is truly the best grassroots communication there is. We have gotten tremendously good feedback from this." Companies should also note that not all the comments are positive. In Reebok's case, viewers have debated the company's morals and actions.

This points out a situation that marketers who venture onto the Internet must deal with, whether they host a community or not: They no longer control the message in this two-way medium; consumers can create messages as well. Marketers must learn to recognize and deal with this new reality of the online world.

Case Study: Parent Soup

Parent Soup, www.parentsoup.com, is one of the finest examples of creating an online community. The site is devoted to the needs of parents—no matter how you define a parent. A parent can be a 14-year-old high school student or a 70-year-old grandparent who is raising children, and everyone in between. The site makes money by selling advertising space to companies that are trying to reach an audience of parents.

Members contribute most of the site's editorial matter. Parents write reviews of movies and products for kids. Would you rather read a movie review for *Alladin* by Siskel and Ebert, two old men, or the mother of two preteens? Now you understand why people read the comments of their peers.

The site offers dozens of chats for parents on such topics as breastfeeding, picking a day care center, and how to be a better single parent. These chats are offered virtually every hour of the day to attract the right audience at their convenience. As noted before, the chats are designed to appeal to every possible type of parent, from teenager to senior, from traditional families to blended families and everything in between.

Another way to get people to come back is by offering a poll, which Parent Soup conducts every day on such topics as getting along with your in-laws" and what the appropriate discipline should be in various situations. The results are announced as soon as each new person votes. About 1,000 people vote each day.

The site does a wonderful job of creating a warm, inviting community, as witnessed by their members' willingness to post pictures of their kids and families online. Considering the paranoia many people have about invasions of privacy, this is truly remarkable.

As a result of this intense community building, Parent Soup has attracted advertising from such companies as Pampers and Ford, the latter for its Windstar van, aimed at families.

Case Study: Storksite.com

Launched in April 1996, Stork Site is the premier pregnancy, fertility, and infant parenting community Web site. Stork Site was started by Victoria "Tori" Kropp, a registered nurse and pregnancy expert, as a way of providing emotional support and a wealth of pregnancy-related resources for expectant parents. The site was designed and is maintained by Lot 11 Studios, Web Community Architects, located in Hermosa Beach, California.

Many of Stork Site's state-of-the-art capabilities are proprietary creations of Lot 11's Nucleo technology and are found exclusively at www.storksite.com. Stork Site derives its revenue from third-party advertising and plans to merchandise Stork Site–branded baby products. Here is the story:

Storkies. Sound like bird-shaped snacks? Actually, Storkies are very human and very real...all 26,000 of them (up from 8,000 in March 1997). They are the self-named life force behind Stork Site, www.storksite.com, and fiercely loyal to this place they call Home Sweet Cyberhome. Why? Because Stork Site is the cutting-edge example of a complete virtual community—the best place on the Web to talk and learn about infants, pregnancy, and infertility. And it's free.

When you visit Stork Site you meet Storkies from all over the world—from as far away as Singapore and as close by as your next-door neighbor. These women and their partners roost at Stork Site more than once a week for an average of 40 minutes (the industry average is only 10 minutes). They come for the features and information; they stay for the community. And Stork Site is thriving—as Storkies are always in touch, they rack up 3.2 million page impressions per month.

Visiting Stork Site is unique because it is not a solitary experience. Unlike most other Internet communities, on Stork Site members can actually see who is on site with them. Storkies are even alerted when their friends arrive. Members don't just visit Stork Site, they actively participate—over 80 percent return to the site once a week and some have even chatted from the delivery room. They share the adventures, joys, and challenges of pregnancy and parenthood in today's world. They support each other through the rough times—infertility, miscarriages, and postpartum depression. Just like in a face-to-face community, Storkies come through for each other no matter what.

For example, Sonya, a long-time Storkie, has her own story: "Stork Site was a real lifesaver. Eight weeks into my pregnancy, my doctor put me on total bed rest. For two months I was barely even allowed out of bed.... I would have gone crazy without Stork Site's monthly bulletin boards! I had no family around to keep me company, so it was especially fantastic to see other women going through the same stages of pregnancy as I was. This was my first baby, and my daughter Sarah was born two weeks late, so you can bet I was on Stork Site all the time!"

There are hundreds of stories just like this. Vicki Smitz of Wasco, Illinois, a Storkie since the start of her pregnancy in October 1996, lives in a small town outside of Chicago with her husband Dennis and their five-week-old son, Joseph. She says: "I think Stork Site is great. I even recommended it to my Lamaze instructor! It is so helpful to see so many other women who have had the same concerns and feelings that I have had. My husband is wonderful, but he couldn't relate to me like the women I've met on the site. Everyone's really nice on Stork Site and people make a genuine effort to be supportive and kind to one another."

Storkies are so involved in Stork Site, they have reached out offline to meet other Storkies in their neighborhoods and hometowns. They call each other and meet for coffee. They have even built their own Storkie Web sites. Texas Storkies at www.startext .net/homes/bailey1/texstork.htm, is one such site. Here Storkies post family information, arrange real-time festivities such as picnics and barbecues, and make plans to hook up when they travel. This summer, Storkie gatherings are in the works in Texas, Indiana,

Florida, and Ohio. As Ellen, an Australian Storkie, puts it: "Stork Site has been the greatest resource for knowledge and friendship a person could have during a time of uncertainty....Not only am I less afraid, but I made a friend in my own home town who I never would have met—and a whole bunch of other friends who live all around the world."

The Technology: Stork Site requires no downloads or plug ins and is multiplatformed and accessible through all popular Web browsers. Any first-time Internet surfer can easily connect. Users enjoy sitewide and private chat rooms, free e-mail accounts, and real-time messages.

The Face Behind Stork Site: Tori Kropp, RN, an obstetric nurse for over 13 years, is the publisher and founder of Stork Site. It's Tori's personality and presence that have helped create this safe and intimate community. All members have access to Tori via e-mail, scheduled chat sessions, and her weekly "Ask Tori, RN" column.

The Content: Storkies can read daily and weekly articles on health, pregnancy, and parenting in *Storkzine,* Stork Site's online magazine. Members receive daily newsletters full of personalized information based on the stage of their pregnancy or their newborn's development.

The members themselves create, foster, and invest in this community, both on and off line. Stork Site's dynamic content is what brings people in; it's the other Storkies that bring them back.

ACTION PLAN FOR CREATING AN ONLINE COMMUNITY

Benefit: You will create customers for life and be known as the key authority on your subject on the Internet.

Action: The first step is to decide what your company really does and who you want to appeal to. For example, it would have been too easy (and ineffective) for Reebok to say it was in the business of making and selling sneakers and to post a site that told about the history and manufacture of sneakers. As ludicrous as this sounds, many companies on the Web use exactly those tools—as if anyone really cares about the arcane history of a humdrum, everyday product. Instead, Reebok focused on the benefits of its product and the common interests of people who buy it. It thought of its market as people who use sneakers for participating in weight control, sports, fitness, and fun; then it created content for these areas, writing objective articles, creating interviews between members and famous athletes, and sponsoring chats among the community.

Action Steps:

1. Decide what business you are really in and how that translates to an online community.
2. Brainstorm on the kinds of content (articles, information, graphics) that will entice people to your Web site and enhance their personal or professional lives.
3. Add interactive elements, like chats and conferences, that will make people feel a part of the community.
4. Consider other activities outside of the Web site that will add value to people's lives, like an e-mail newsletter, discounts and coupons on your products, usergroup meetings in person, and the like.

Note: The answers could be different for each company and still be effective.

ISSUES FOR MOLDERS OF ONLINE COMMUNITIES

The challenge for marketers is that they need to think outside the box to create an online community, a new venture for many of them. Also, they will be forced to create content, which will expand their current duties. Some companies will be able to use the same materials they produce in paper format (like newsletters, magazines, and case studies) and retrofit them for the Web or e-mail. Companies must begin to budget the personnel, time, and materials for this marketing task.

As more companies realize that the Internet is about content and community, there will be more competition to create Web sites that realize these goals. Your company might be able to stake out the pioneer's position as the first on the Web in its area, but competitors will be on your heels. Just as Molson set up its Web site—the ultimate metaphor for a community where everybody knows your name—other breweries opened their virtual bars as well. Marketers must be on the prowl for competitors.

Keeping the site fresh is another key concern. If your mission is to maintain long-term relationships with customers, you must add new articles and activities. However, no one knows how often this update must be done. Should it be once a day, like a newspaper; once a week like a news magazine or trade publication, or once a month like a magazine? Some argue that the site must be updated every minute or hour, like news radio or TV news. Others wonder if consumers are getting too much information and are drowning in frequent updates. As the Internet evolves, the right time for each industry will become apparent.

"As with any product and service, Web sites will do well if the focus starts and remains with the market. Constant market research (no matter how qualitative) and visitor interaction is the only route to continuous improvements on the Internet," says Marcia Olmstead, director of internal development and communications for Southam New Media.

"Keep your users coming back. Always offer the user something new—you must find a way to constantly update your site without straying from your master plan, or changing the site so much that the user becomes frustrated and never returns," says Kim Silk-Copeland, communications resource coordinator for the Discovery Channel. "Original content, prizes, free downloads, and updated services are a few great ways to attract attention. Always leave them wanting more—always keep them thinking they might miss out on an opportunity if they don't return often."

Marketers also will be placed in the unfamiliar position of managing opinion. What will happen if community members violate netiquette? How will the content provider deal with errant community members without alienating them from the fold? Companies need to establish policies on acceptable online behavior as well as stake out the action steps for dealing with violators.

CONCLUSION

The most powerful paradigm shift in online advertising is that the advertiser is adopting the role of the magazine publisher and becoming responsible for creating content. Because the hard sell and overt advertising tend to put off an audience burned out from commercials, advertisers can gain influence by creating a sense of community for their target audiences.

PART 4

Online
Public
Relations

CHAPTER FOURTEEN

Interactive Media Relations

Online communications give public relations professionals and corporate communicators new tools for building relationships with reporters and communities in a timely and cost-effective manner.

This chapter helps you build relationships with reporters by providing you with information on:

- what public relations can do for you
- advantages of online PR versus traditional PR
- how the media use the Internet
- how to meld online media communications with integrated marketing
- how to build a world-class site for media use
- measuring the effectiveness of publicity efforts
- new publicity opportunities online

WHAT PUBLIC RELATIONS CAN DO FOR YOU

The most cost-efficient weapon in the marketer's arsenal is public relations (also called publicity and PR). For a fraction of the cost of advertising, public relations can help accomplish the following objectives:

- Build a more favorable image for the company or product.
- Expose the company or product to new audiences.
- Reinforce images and messages within an audience to create demand for products.
- Build relationships with new customers.
- Cement relationships with old customers.

You achieve these goals by implementing a public relations campaign—a targeted marketing tool—that begins with writing down your goals and ends with reporters writing articles about your company or product.

Public relations can build credibility for products and services in a way that advertising cannot. When reporters write favorable articles, they implicitly or explicitly endorse your product, company, or cause. Advertising doesn't carry that same weighty endorsement.

Public relations can't make up for a bad product. It has been said that publicity for a bad product will just let the world know that much faster to avoid that product.

ADVANTAGES OF ONLINE PR VERSUS TRADITIONAL PR

Online publicity offers distinct advantages over traditional public relations (conducted in newspapers and magazines and on television and radio). With online services, corporate communicators can take PR into their own hands and influence their public directly as well as build relationships with reporters. Online publicity puts the public back in public relations.

In the traditional media, there is a gatekeeper—an editor, reporter, producer, or host—who decides whether or not your message will see the light of day and in what context the message will be viewed. The gatekeeper can kill the story because she doesn't think the message would interest her readers, because there isn't enough room in the day's program even though readers would be interested, or she's just having a bad day and wants to take it out on a PR person (stranger things have been known to happen).

Online systems offer tremendous opportunities for companies to boost image and sales through publicity. The online world lets you broadcast your message directly to the audience without the intervention of the media. This is an important distinction. Companies can accomplish this by disseminating their messages through forums, bulletin boards, newsgroups, e-mail, and other methods discussed in this chapter. Public relations, used correctly and in full compliance with netiquette, can be an asset to you and your customers.

In summary, with online public relations you have tools to influence reporters and your publics. You have the best of both worlds!

The New Deadline

One of the most profound changes the Internet is having on the news media is that traditional daily or weekly deadlines are dissolving. The media can disseminate news around the clock on their Web sites. Instead of once-a-day newspaper printing deadlines, online newspapers have deadlines akin to those of news radio: Publish it when the news is fresh.

This move has great benefits for PR people. The new publishing cycle means reporters need more news, so more opportunities for placing stories crop up.

However, PR people need to be aware that this opportunity poses a challenge as well. They used to plan press tours so that stories would break at the same time. For example, if you visited a reporter of a weekly publication on a Tuesday, you knew he couldn't print the story until the following Monday. Now you can be assured that the story can be printed on the Web site before you arrive at your next appointment.

This move has dramatic implications for communications professionals because they no longer control the timing of the story. They must also be more sensitive to releasing information to all reporters at the same time or the reporters at the tail end of the tour will feel slighted at being given yesterday's news.

Credibility

"Credibility in cyberspace will be hard to establish. It will also be easy to lose. Remember, it will be easier for reporters and editors to check the validity of material online. As a result, they may even penalize companies for accurate but incomplete data," say Steven Ross and Don Middleberg, who conducted a definitive study of the online activities of journalists.

Public Relations versus Advertising

Public relations beats advertising hands down in forums because advertising is prohibited in forums on commercial services. Messages can be killed by system administrators so that your intended readers never see slick ads. On the Internet, there are no specific rules against advertising but there is a strong cultural bias against blatant advertising. If you posted an advertisement on an Internet USENET newsgroup, recipients would see the message and probably send flames—vicious hate mail—to you. Public relations works online in a way that advertising cannot.

Online publicity also has the advantage of creating a one-to-one relationship between the company and the customer or prospect. Thanks to e-mail, results can be nearly instantaneous. E-mail is a phenomenal tool for developing targeted marketing campaigns.

As with traditional publicity, companies must continue to follow up with prospects to make the sale. However, the next step for the online marketer might involve a combination of cyberspace and traditional methods. For example, you might receive a request for more information. You can follow up either by sending e-mail alone or by sending e-mail along with printed materials via the post office or overnight courier.

HOW THE MEDIA USE THE INTERNET

The Internet is changing the way reporters gather and disseminate news.

In a seminal study of reporters, Steven Ross and Don Middleberg interviewed 6,000 writers, editors, and investigative reporters at daily and weekly newspapers and business magazines. Their findings and conclusions are must reading for professional communicators.

The survey showed that journalists used online services at these rates:

- 16 percent daily
- 33 percent weekly
- 50 percent monthly

"What we are eyewitnesses to is nothing less than the birth of a new way to communicate. The study highlights that the impact on journalists is real, growing, and must be understood by all of us interested in being communicators," they wrote in August 1994. The study has been updated every six months and rings even more true as time passes.

The Internet allows people to get raw data from companies and governments. The journalist's role will always be to filter the news and put it in perspective. However, the Internet is giving rise to a new breed of reporter who writes with an attitude but backs it up with facts. This differs from print reporters, who strive for objectivity or at least to present both sides of a debate. TV reporters like to tell stories with a beginning, middle, and end that show two sides clashing.

How do they use online services?

Editors can search the online world for news, controversy, consumer comments, and research.

The media can find the latest press releases printed on company Web sites. While many companies have a press center feature on their sites, companies can post breaking news on their home page as well. For example, when IBM completed the purchase of Lotus on a Sunday, the story was plastered on the home page hours before the daily newspapers could print the story in their Monday editions. Reporters who went to the site found information and quotes from officials at both companies.

Editors can read original source press releases in online versions of PR Newswire, Business Wire, and Canadian Corporate NewsNet, services that are paid by companies to distribute material to reporters. With the advent of the online medium, consumers and business people can also read these press releases on the Internet and commercial online services.

Reporters for trade publications search online forums and newsgroups for controversy or consumer complaints about companies or new products. If people find problems with new computer hardware or software products, they are sure to post notices in company forums on CompuServe, which has more than 800 company-sponsored help forums. It is not unusual for a company that says their new product is perfect to find a story on the front page of InfoWorld quoting customers who point out bugs.

Monitor Discussion Areas for Comments about Your Company

Benefit: Build relationships, quell rumors, correct facts.

Discussion: It is important for PR professionals to monitor newsgroups and forums for negative comments so they can provide answers and solutions quickly. Not only will this dispel negative news, it will build customer loyalty and reflect positively on the company.

It would be impossible for any PR staff to read every message in every newsgroup to search for customers with complaints. Fortunately, there is a tool called DejaNews, www.dejanews.com, that searches every newsgroup to find articles that mention keywords you choose. In just a few minutes you can locate every mention of your company posted in any given time frame. Reporters use this tool as well to find examples of controversy.

Action: Assign this task. Create keywords to use for the search. Respond to comments. Not all the news is bad. Reporters also look in discussion areas to find unbiased sources to comment on companies and products. They frequently post notices in newsgroups and forums asking for people who have experience or knowledge in certain areas.

Ask Usergroup Members and Loyal Customers to Be Active on Message Areas

Benefit: Reporters could use them as sources.

Discussion: This is not a violation of netiquette so long as the users are not compensated by the company.

Action: Identify loyal, articulate customers. Ask them to help you.

Other Ways Reporters Use the Internet

Reporters use the online services to network with other journalists. The Jforum for journalists on CompuServe has more than 35,000 members who talk about current issues and finding jobs. Private mailing lists on the Internet for reporters also provide a way for reporters to talk privately about issues of concern. Pitching reporters in these areas is a violation of netiquette.

Smart reporters use the Internet to create relationships with public relations officials and other sources. They might print their editorial calendars on their own sites, so PR people can contact them with relevant information. Others post their articles online so PR people can understand what they write about. It is a way of saying "Here's what I'm interested in. If you can help me, get in touch."

Several reporters print their own newsletters online, including Gina Smith of *Good Morning America,* Yael Li-Ron of the Contra Costa (CA) *Times,* and Dave Duberman of the *Daily Spectrum*. The contents include what articles they are working on, industry gossip, and editorial calendars.

In summary, the media use the Internet and online services to gather news and publish it. They enjoy greater control over the flow of information and the ability to find additional sources from online libraries, competitors, and consumers. Communications professionals must learn to be a resource to these reporters.

HOW TO MELD ONLINE MEDIA COMMUNICATIONS WITH INTEGRATED MARKETING

When I gave my first talk on publicity on the Web, a person in the audience asked an incredible question: "How much longer after I send out a press release should I post it online?"

The answer, of course, is that the press release should be posted on your Web site at the same time as it is made available to every medium. Today, very few people would think of asking such a question.

Online press campaigns should be part of the general strategy for every product launch or other newsworthy story because reporters and your targeted audiences will expect to find information on your Web site. All press releases should be placed in the press room area of your site. In addition, the release can be sent via e-mail to customers, employees, shareholders, and the like who have told you in advance they want to be notified of all announcements.

It is important to target the online media and online press release distribution networks because people will increasingly get their news from the Internet, according to Intel Corp. People born after 1971 believe they will get news from Internet (59 percent), radio and TV (31 percent), and print media (10 percent).

Yet, the Internet is, for now, just one part of the PR program.

"You can use the Net to manage public relations, but as a medium it is still far too immature to rely upon as your sole vehicle," says Chip Hall, vice president of marketing for Release Software Corp., chip@releasesoft.com, 415-833-0200, who conducted public relations campaigns for Yahoo!.

"People like John Verity at *BusinessWeek,* Peter Lewis at the *New York Times,* Ellis Booker at *Web Week,* and Mitch Wagner at *Computerworld* will continue to help drive significant traffic if you can convince them yours is a story of importance," he says. "I can honestly say your best return will still come from the physical—not cyberspace. Example: A Peter Lewis column is worth about 100,000 visitors to your site."

"That said, you should still continue to use the Net for things like e-mail and newsgroup postings, and you should research who to contact at online information areas like c|net, Web Review, Daily Spectrum (David Duberman), Interactive AgeDigital (Gary Brickman), WEBster, Netsurfer Digest, and Nando Times," he adds. "The PR landscape is slowly changing and you should keep up with it. But do not quickly disregard the power that remains with the traditional media. I would say that the best PR campaigns still have 85 percent of efforts being directed at traditional media and 15 percent to the online world of new media influencers."

Case Study: Intellisystems

Intellisystems, a leading manufacturer of customer support systems via telephone and Internet, wanted to announce that Netscape decided to use their system to provide Internet customer support. Here is a review of its media program, which encompassed traditional and online public relations. This format could serve as a checklist for your public relations campaign.

1. Write press release.

    - Research via the Internet.
    - Copy/paste key documents into draft of press release.
    - Interview key speakers via telephone.
    - Write press release.
    - E-mail press release to key speakers for comments and approvals.

2. Send out press release.

    - Send to regular mailing list via U.S. mail, fax, and e-mail.
    - Send to PR Newswire via fax; then distribute via e-mail and online databases.
    - Send to appropriate newsgroups and mailing lists.

3. Post press release on company site.

    - Add links to client sites.

4. Call "A-List" reporters by phone.

5. Respond to other reporters who read the release and contact you.

Notice that this strategy used the following media: online, print, mail, fax, and phone!

Case Study: Blanc & Otis

Blanc & Otis, one of the largest public relations firms in the San Francisco Bay area, conducted a media campaign for a client's product launch. Due to scheduling conflicts, all of the scheduled in-person meetings for the press/analyst tour had to be done via teleconference. Among other problems, the phone meetings would not allow for the kind of relationship-building that face-to-face meetings offer. Furthermore, the product could not be demonstrated over the phone. The latter issue seemed an especially high hurdle, as none of the press had ever seen the client's type of product and questioned its ability.

To get over this hurdle, Blanc & Otis provided the press with the address of the client's Web site, which contained screen shots; these were discussed during the phone interview. As a result, the demos were conducted during the phone tour with 11 analysts and 8 editors.

The launch was a huge success, as the client was able to speak with more industry influencers than it had on any previous tour and received articles in such publications as *BusinessWeek, Web Week,* and *Interactive Week.*

HOW TO BUILD A WORLD-CLASS SITE FOR MEDIA USE

Thanks to the interactive nature of the Internet, communications professionals find themselves in a new role: They are content creators. In effect, they are now publishers of news and information for reporters—their *stakeholders,* a term communicators use to describe all key audiences, such as investors, employees, dealers, distributors, vendors, and the community at large.

The key tool communicators have is the Web site. Reporters are coming to realize that companies will have the latest updates and background information and pictures on their Web sites—even as the story breaks.

Reporters come to rely on these tools as a way to get information quickly and accurately. Several reporters have told me they wished that all company press releases were in a searchable database online. When they get an assignment to cover a product or company they are not familiar with, they are able to get a quick read from the company's perspective. They don't want to rely on other reporters' articles! Even reporters realize that errors and bias could enter stories printed in the trade magazines and daily newspapers. Yes, hard as it is to believe, some reporters actually value press releases!

The task here is to create a world-class Web site that helps reporters and stakeholders tell the company's story. Be sure to add navigational links to each page so reporters can find information easily.

The site should have a link to the *press center,* which can be called media center, press room, press release, or the like. The first press page should contain an overview of the material that can be found and links to press releases, case studies, etc. The first page of each of those categories should contain the headlines, date of publication, and any other relevant comments. Icons indicating new material can be added as well. Each headline should be linked to the story. The story itself ought not be merely a reprinting of the paper press release but an interactive version.

An online media center should contain the following eight elements:

1. Contacts
   - Names, titles, and areas of specialty of each contact person, along with desk phone number and e-mail address.
   - Bios of contacts so reporters can understand the person's background and develop rapport. (Yes, it is important for reporters to know if the contact person has a degree in engineering, for example, so they can better trust the information. You also might find that a relationship can be built if the reporter has something in common with the media contact.)
     "This enhances the relationship building. Bios are personal. I have what influenced me growing up. They can get a sense of who I am as a person and it breaks the ice," says Skye Ketonen of the PR firm of Niehaus Ryan Group in South San Francisco.

2. Press releases
   - Title page, including headlines sorted by date and/or topic and links to full text.

3. News
4. Product information
   - New products
   - Updates
   - Recalls
   - Case histories
   - Testimonials
   - Reviews
   - Competitive analysis
   - White papers
   - Charts and graphs
   - Audio and video clips (variety of formats)
   - Pictures (variety of formats for IBM and Macintosh computers)

5. Company news
   - Hiring
   - Promotions
   - Layoffs
   - Financial news
   - Annual reports
   - Quarterly financial statements
   - Forecasts and updates
   - Case histories

6. Company background
   - Message from the chairman (Some reporters have labeled this tactic as corny, but these messages can begin to show a company's personality.)
   - Executive bios and contact information
   - Photos

7. Stock price (updated every 15 minutes)
8. Offer to join a private mailing list. This list can be used to identify your stakeholders and send them update notices of news releases and newsletters.

EXAMPLE

CHAT ANNOUNCEMENTS
http://www.iagency.com
INTERACTIVE AGENCY
FROM THE INTERACTIVE AGENCY NEWSWIRE, LOS ANGELES

FOR IMMEDIATE RELEASE

Dear Daniel Janal:

As always, thank you for your support as we continue to pave new ground in the online marketing industry. As we grow and improve upon the integrated marketing services offered by iagency, we plan to host more client promotions at www.iagency.com and online events in our virtual offices, palace://palace.iagency.com.

The first of these events will happen TODAY AT 2 P.M. PST, when we feature WORLD WIDE WORD MegaZine Publisher Donald Rose for a dialog about online journalism in the press room of the iagency Palace.

This WEDNESDAY, AUGUST 27, at 4 P.M. PST, Symantec's VIRUS MASTER Alex Haddox will kick off a series of online chat events in the new "Symantec Lounge" we've added to the iagency Palace. The event is first of several VIRUS MASTER online conferences that will be held in our Palace and other online forums to educate users about the threat of viruses.

LOGGING ON IS EASY!

If you're not already using The Palace, take a few minutes to download it at www.thepalace.com. Download all of the iagency Palace artwork from the CHAT section of our Web site and you're set! In the coming weeks we'll be hosting a panel about online advertising and the first of many online networking events for the Los Angeles area interactive entertainment community.

Any questions? Don't hesitate to give us a call at 310-664-6710 or mailto:palace-help@iagency.com. SEE YOU ONLINE!

The iagency Team

MONDAY, AUGUST 25, AT 2 P.M. PST

Editor-in-Chief/Writer/Host DONALD ROSE
WORLD WIDE WORD MegaZine

Every week or two the MegaZine is delivered to your e-mailbox. Issues feature articles on entertainment and technology, with a mix of humor and commentary. Several hundred folks, from the creative forces at *Star Trek* and *Good Morning America* to the head of Microsoft, get the 'zine each week!!

About DONALD ROSE, Ph.D., computer science. Expert in artificial intelligence and Internet technologies. Computer consultant and film/TV/interactive scriptwriter.

Books authored: *Minding Your Cybermanners on the Internet and Internet Chat Quick Tour;* co-author, *CyberLife!* and *Internet Roadside Attractions.* In 1996: Head writer and segment producer on *CyberLife,* a daily Discovery Channel TV show on technology.

WEDNESDAY, AUGUST 27, AT 4 P.M. PDT

Meet Symantec's Virus Master ALEX HADDOX at the GRAND OPENING of the Symantec Lounge !!!!!

Alex Haddox is the Product Manager for the Symantec AntiVirus Research Center (SARC), one of the industry's premier antivirus laboratories, as featured in *Fortune* magazine. He is a leading member of the global team deciding the future for Symantec's AntiVirus products and team. Mr. Haddox oversees the direction of the Center and is responsible for the monthly Norton AntiVirus updates in which new virus definitions are added to the Norton AntiVirus and Symantec AntiVirus for Macintosh databases of known viruses. His team researches new virus technology worldwide with SARC satellite offices in Tokyo, Sydney, and Leiden, The Netherlands.

Mr. Haddox is a world-recognized computer virus expert (the Virus Master), has spoken internationally on virus topics, and has appeared on hundreds of national television and radio segments including interviews on *Good Morning America,* CNBC, the Discovery Channel, and ABC and CBS radio. He has been interviewed by numerous national magazines and newspapers.

Mr. Haddox is a member of the Advisory Board for Virus Bulletin, one of the industry's leading international publications, and a member of the National Computer Security Association AntiVirus Developers Council (NCSA AVPD).

InterActive Agency, Inc.
www.iagency.com
2701 Ocean Park Boulevard, Suite 201
Santa Monica, CA 90405
310-664-6710; 310-664-6711 Fax

UNSUBSCRIBE INFORMATION

InterActive Agency continues to provide up-to-the-minute news on our cutting-edge clientele and projects. We always encourage you to send us feedback about this listserv, our clients, and our company. Correspondence should be sent to iaa@iagency.com.

To subscribe or unsubscribe, please send e-mail to awall@iagency.com. Include the words *subscribe* or *unsubscribe* without quotes in the subject or body of your e-mail. If you continue to receive announcements after unsubscribing, please call us at 310-664-6710.

For help, please reply to this e-mail and change your subject line to read *Help*.

MEASURING THE EFFECTIVENESS OF PUBLICITY EFFORTS

Most PR professionals sigh when their corporate managers ask them to justify and quantify the results of a public relations campaign. That's because there are very few tools available to measure campaign effectiveness. However, the online world has several tools and strategies that can be employed to measure the reach of the program.

The Web site can be used to track public relations activities that appear online or in other media by using these strategies:

Create Separate Sites with Unique URLS for Each Press Release and Communications Document

Benefit: Track the effectiveness of each message and medium.

Discussion: Each press release or communications document should refer to a unique Web site to contact for more information. For example, a press release sent to the trade press could ask readers to see www.mycompany.com/press1.html, while a press release sent to a consumer publication could carry the Web address www.mycompany.com/press2.html.

This information can be used to find out which publication venue or message is more effective at reaching your audience and prompting them to take action. The results can be shared with the advertising department at your company so they can target their ad dollars effectively.

Action: Create targeted Web sites with a message for each targeted audience. Add a counter to track the number of visits.

Create Infobots with Unique Addresses for Targeted Audiences and Reporters

Benefit: Same as above.

Discussion: Same as above, with the added benefit that some of your stakeholders who have e-mail accounts won't have access to the World Wide Web or your site. This strategy lets them get the information they request promptly.

Similarly, inquires could be sent to infobots with the following tags:

- infopack1@mycompany.com
- infopack2@mycompany.com

The infobots should contain information tailored to suit the prospect's interests. You will know that a certain writer is a dealer because he sent e-mail to an address that only a dealer would have access to. Therefore, you can send a response that answers his most frequently asked questions and uses keywords that appeal to dealers. Likewise, if a consumer from a woman's magazine responds, you can tailor the message appropriately.

Action: Create the infobots.

Create Specific Messages on Web Sites and Infobots for Each Audience You Target via the Previous Methods

Benefit: Your audiences will get information they need without having to wade through generic or irrelevant material.

Discussion: Let's say you issue a press release for a new product. The trade press wants to know feature and benefits; the business press wants to know how this announcement will affect the stock price; dealers want to know about their special pricing and advertising discounts. If you put all this information in one release, you might as well write a book! You would be sending lots of paper or bits to people who couldn't care less. However, if you create separate press releases and white papers for each audience and post them to unique Web sites or infobots, you will be able to deliver to each stakeholder the information he needs most. Thus you can incorporate one-to-one marketing programs much more effectively.

Action: Create the Web pages and infobots. Post the unique addresses on press releases, being careful to send the correct release to the correct audience.

NEW PUBLICITY OPPORTUNITIES ONLINE

The Internet and commercial online services are creating new media properties that corporate communicators can use as publicity outlets. Opportunities exist to place company representatives as guests on conferences sponsored by these publications as well as to place news and feature articles about companies and products.

Search for New Media Opportunities to Promote Your Product or Company

Benefit: Exposure to targeted audience.

Discussion: New publications are springing up every day on the Internet and commercial online services. They welcome informed guests who can provide information that benefits their audiences.

Action: Search for these new opportunities by checking newsgroups, search engines, and PR Newswire, Business Wire, and Canadian Corporate Newsnet. Study their formats to see what kind of information they want or what type of appearance (interview) would be appropriate. Pitch the topic. Prepare the host and spokesperson with sample questions. Promote the appearance both before and after the event.

Online Versions of Traditional Print Publications

More than 1,000 daily newspapers are now online, and thousands of trade publications and TV and radio stations are joining them as well.

These publications exist in the real world and post online editions. In some cases they print the same news as in the print edition; in others they add more stories and host archives of old editions. Several offer online discussions with experts or chats between online members.

- Computer press—Many top-tier publications are online. Most update their online publications at least once a day. *PC Week* is updated with new material twice a day!
- Business press—*BusinessWeek, Fortune, Forbes, Inc.,* and many others appear online.
- Daily newspapers—The *New York Times, Wall Street Journal, San Jose Mercury News,* and *San Francisco Chronicle* are online.
- Consumer publications—*Playboy, Car and Driver, Road and Track*—all online!

New Media Publications

These publications exist *only* online. They might have large or small readerships but should be courted as readers are devoted followers and passionate about the subject.

- One group of publications is called *e-'zines,* short for *electronic magazines.* One of the most prominent, *Slate,* published by Microsoft and edited by a noted journalist, joins hundreds of e-'zines dedicated to diverse interests and audiences. Be on the lookout for new publications. Before pitching them, read the e-'zine to see if the audience is appropriate. If it is, then determine which message the publication would most likely want to write about.
- Dozens of private newsletters exist on hundreds of topics. These are published by consultants. They could interview your experts or reprint information articles.
- Web sites produced by trade groups, associations, and the like could also be venues for articles and links.

Internet Radio Shows

Audio is becoming a more prevalent feature on the Internet. As a result, online radio stations are being created that offer shows on such diverse topics as current events, technology, music, business, personal finance, and sports.

- The Web Chat Broadcasting Network, www.wbs.net, offers a variety of live radio programs via the Internet on such topics as business, Internet marketing, current events, health, and relationships. These shows could be venues for your company executives. Shows have featured well-known individuals from the worlds of government, politics, arts, and media, including Senator Arlen Specter, National Public Radio commentator Susan Stamberg, and author Anne Lamott. Each guest is interviewed by a host who is an expert in the area. Questions from the audience are taken. A transcriber transcribes all questions and answers for the public to read as the comments are spoken. After the guest has departed, readers are invited to stay online and continue the discussion. The entire transcript is recorded and can be purchased.
- Off the Record, www.mediapool.com/offtherecord/, is an interview program featuring high-tech topics. The site features an audio version of the interview as well as a printed transcript, highlights, and links to related material.

Radio Stations

- Several dozen radio stations simultaneously broadcast their shows on the Internet via Audio Net, www.audionet.com. These shows include talk radio, sports, commentary, politics, food, and music. By pitching to these live shows you will be able to reach an audience on the Internet as well—especially if you promote the appearance.
- Hundreds of other radio stations have Web sites but they all seem to be advertisements and press kits for their on-air station. Look for these stations to begin broadcasting live on the Internet as technology improves.

TV Stations

- ESPN, CNN, NBC, and other broadcast outlets are online with print and/or audio editions. Look for more audio and video programming and original content online as technology improves.
- C|net is a hybrid in that the online service and TV show are developed simultaneously and intended to work off each other. The Web site, www.cnet.com, is one of the most innovative news sites on the Internet in terms of creating original content to meet the needs of its audience—those who are keenly interested in personal computing and enjoying the Internet.

Online Conferences

Forums on CompuServe, Prodigy, and America Online are always looking for experts to serve as guests on a wide variety of topics. These guests can be promoted for free on the service's "highlights" or "What's New" features. Really big guests can be promoted in *USA Today*'s cyberlistings, printed every day next to the TV schedule. Benefits include awareness from pre-event publicity, interacting with prospects at the event itself, and building relationships after the event with prospects who read the transcript of the event.

Conferences can be held in two venues:

1. People meet in a designated online area at an appointed time and interact by typing questions. A moderator fields questions and keeps order.
2. One expert is available for a set period of time, say a week, in a bulletin board area. He posts the beginning overview and questions for discussion. People answer those questions and add their own questions, thoughts, and observations. The guest can respond to messages as often as he likes, but at least once a day.

These conferences offer your company the opportunity to deliver its message, portray itself in a good light, and show its responsiveness to the community.

Best yet, whereas TV broadcasts messages to wide groups of people, online services can be used to broadcast and narrowcast messages. If your company appeals to a broad audience, like an entertainment organization, travel-related company, or the like, a conference can help. Small companies and consultants, speakers, and trainers can talk directly to highly targeted groups of prospects.

Online services love to feature big-name speakers and celebrities who attract large markets—and network charges. For example, Vice President Al Gore "spoke" on a moderated conference on CompuServe that drew 900 people. Jerry Seinfeld and Jay Leno participated in talks in Prodigy's entertainment area. Technology guru Esther Dyson participated in a conference on America Online. In an interesting use of integrated marketing, a Garth Brooks online conference, which drew 500 people to the NBC/McDonald's area on America Online, tied in with a McDonald's promotion to sell Brooks' CDs at their restaurants.

Be a Guest on a Conference

Benefit: Exposure to targeted audience.

Discussion: Forums on the commercial online services are always looking for interesting guests.

Action: Search for these new opportunities by checking newsgroups, search engines, and PR Newswire and Business Wire. Study their formats to see what kind of information they want or what type of appearance (interview) would be appropriate. Pitch the topic. Prepare the host and spokesperson with sample questions. Promote the appearance both before and after the event.

SUMMARY

Public relations strategies can be used online to build relationships with reporters, customers, and prospects. The Internet is changing the way reporters work and therefore PR people must change the way they work with reporters.

CHAPTER FIFTEEN

Writing and Distributing Interactive Publicity Materials Online

Now that you understand how online reporting operates, you are ready to begin writing online press materials and distributing them.

This chapter helps you build relationships with reporters by providing you with information on:

- how to write interactive press releases
- how to write effective e-mail pitch letters
- how to put an annual report online
- how to find reporters online
- how to distribute news materials online
- online video news releases
- how to stage a live events online

HOW TO WRITE INTERACTIVE PRESS RELEASES

Press releases in the real world are usually two pages long because reporters have requested that length. Writers can write a lot more than that, so a lot of good information never gets printed. However, in the online world, writers can create interactive press releases that contain links to information that wouldn't fit in a paper press release. If reporters are interested in the story, they will be interested in many of the links as well, as they crave information once they decide to write a story. Here are tips for writing an interactive press release:

Janal Communications
P.O Box 2108
Danville, CA 94526
510-648-1961

For immediate release

Contact

Daniel Janal
Janal Communications
510-648-1961
<u>dan@janal.com</u>

My Company Announces Record Profits

CITY—DATE—My Company today announced record profits on record sales. Sales jumped 30 percent and profit increased 50 percent.

"The increases are due to tremendous <u>cost cuttings</u> as well as anticipating the market demand for new products," said <u>Curtis Windmere</u>, president.

###

Figure 15–1. In this example, clicking on dan@janal.com would open an e-mail letter addressed to the author. "Cost cuttings" is a hyperlink that opens a press release explaining the cost cuttings. "Curtis Windmere" is a hyperlink that shows his biography and picture.

Turn the Press Release into an Interactive Press Release

Paper press releases contain only as much information as fits on the number of pages desired by the writer. Because many reporters demand that press releases be no longer than two pages, that has become the norm. But the restriction is based more on the mercurial demands of reporters than the public's right to be fully informed.

Interactive press releases can overcome the obstacles of the print media. This new breed of press release can offer more than the static press release because of hyperlinking. Here are several strategies to turn normal press releases into value-added press releases.

Add E-mail Addresses and Mailto Commands to Each Press Release for Each Contact Person

Benefit: Allows reporters to contact company representatives in a quick, efficient manner. The mailto command is an HTML command whereby the reader sends an e-mail to the person specified. For example, the HTML script:

Contact: <a href ="mailto:dan@janal.com">Dan Janal</a>, 510-648-1961

would appear on screen as:

Contact: <u>Dan Janal</u>, 510-648-1961

Action: Take all press materials and add the e-mail address and mailto commands.

Figure 15–2. Lexis-Nexis posts a menu of press releases on its Web site. Select a headline… (Copyright 1997, Lexis-Nexis, Inc.)

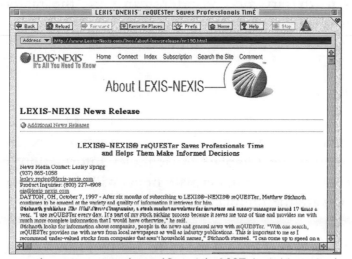

Figure 15–3. …to see the entire press release. (Copyright 1997, Lexis-Nexis, Inc.)

Print the Contact Information at the Top and Bottom of the Press Release

Benefit: Reduces the need to scroll.

Action: Type information into HTML and e-mail versions of press release.

Define Industry Terms with a Glossary

Benefit: Adds more information than could otherwise fit in a standard news release.

Action: Create the glossary and link keywords to it.

Link to Historical Articles and Related Issues on the Web Site

Benefit: Adds more information than could otherwise fit in a standard news release.

Action: Find and post the material. Create the links.

List and Link to Art, Graphics, Head Shots, Etc., that Illustrate Your Story

Benefit: A picture tells 1,000 stories. Putting the art on a press release page will slow down the time the article appears on the screen. By having links to the artwork, reporters can view the material they need when they need it.

Action: Upload files. Create links.

Create a Template for Press Releases

Benefit: Saves time. Whenever you need to write a new press release, simply open the template and type or copy your text from your word processor into the template. All contact information, copyright and license data, and other boilerplate items will be ready to use.

Action: Create the template.

Add a Password to Limit Access to Bona Fide Reporters

Benefit: Keeps unwanted people out of the media center.

Discussion: This is a delicate strategy. You might want to limit access to the press center only to reporters. Nike did this with its Olympic press site so reporters could find and retrieve digital pictures quickly and easily. If the entire world had access to these pictures, the competition to download the files would be huge and the wait time could affect reporters' deadlines. Oil companies do not permit the general public access to their press area for fear of environmental groups downloading pictures of company buildings, defacing them, and posting them online! If your press materials are not this widely demanded or sensitive, you probably would not want to add a password.

Action: Add a password screen. Contact key media people and give them passwords. Create a system to check credentials of new reporters who apply for a password. Consider creating mirror sites or adding additional computers to handle increased demands.

Formatting Do's and Don'ts

- Don't type in all uppercase. It looks like shouting and is hard to read.
- Use ### at the end of the release to indicate the end.
- Don't use -more- between screens to indicate a new page.
- Format the release as you would like to see it printed, because people will print it.

Convert Existing Press Releases to HTML Format

Discussion: In the old days of the Internet, formatting a press release for your Web site was an arduous task that required the help of the MIS department. With advances in software programs, every person who uses Microsoft Word can easily convert a press release into an interactive press release. Simply write your press release using Word 7.0 and save it as an HTML document. The command to do this is in the File, Save As menu. In seconds your work is saved in a format the Web can read and print. You don't have to understand HTML to perform this task. By doing this process, you will save time and money by reducing the number of people and operations to create the document.

Action: Convert all your press releases.

Add Contact Information on the Press Releases

Benefit: Reporters and key stakeholders can find contact personnel easily.

Discussion: Too many press releases on the Web don't have any contact information at all. Some PR people do this intentionally so they will not be flooded with inquires from the general public, who have access to this material. This tactic is a key mistake since reporters won't be able to find the information they need in a timely and easy manner. To correct this problem, use the approach of Bayou Steel Corp., which is represented by P.R. PR, a public relations agency in New Orleans: They list the e-mail addresses for the sales and marketing department, financial relations officers, administration, as well as media relations. (Figure 15–4.)

Action: Revise your press releases to include the appropriate contact information.

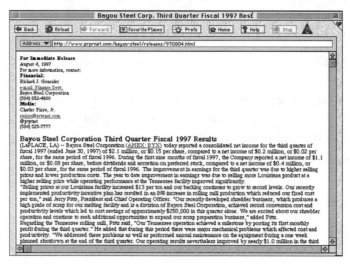

Figure 15–4. List contact number or e-mail addresses for all key departments on your press releases, as does Bayou Steel Corp. (Copyright 1997, P.R. PR, Inc., New Orleans.)

HOW TO WRITE EFFECTIVE E-MAIL PITCH LETTERS

A popular public relations strategy is to send reporters a pitch letter that describes what the news is and the action you would like them to take (write an article, interview the chairman, see a company representative at their offices, tour a new facility, etc.). This section describes how to write an e-mail pitch letter.

The Internet is primarily a text medium (although sound and pictures will become increasingly important). However, the standard rules of formal business writing do not apply! While good grammar and spelling will always be required, the tone of online writing is less formal and more conversational. Messages should be no longer than a screen unless something major is happening.

Case Study: Phase Two Public Relations

"Online communications gives you the ability to develop a close relationship and be more efficient. If I had to depend on a phone call, it would fall by the wayside by busy editors. A well-formulated e-mail gets a better response than a well-formulated voice mail. Giving good e-mail is essential. The more depth you give, the better response you will get," says Chris Boehlke, principal of Phase Two Public Relations in San Francisco. "It is so much more convenient for them to reply to us. It takes them a minute to say yes or no. With voice mail, the response is much lower. It is easier to click on 'reply.'"

Boehlke likes to limit pitch letters to three paragraphs maximum. "If they are interested, I'll come back with more detail. I equate it to training someone to talk on TV rather than in print. It is almost an alive medium," she says.

No one wants "It was great seeing you last week." They want "We'll be in town next week; let's get together." It has to be much more to the point.

Using e-mail, Boehlke is able to book 70 percent of her clients' media tours.

Tactic: Write Effective E-mail Pitch Letters to Reporters

Benefit: Gain favorable media attention and improve the chances of coverage.

Discussion: The worst way to approach reporters is the traditional method of sending voluminous press kits complete with backgrounders, white papers, and copies of previous press releases detailing the company's history. Instead, the proper approach is to send a short note explaining what is new and what you want the reporter to do. The entire note should be less than the depth of a computer screen (about 24 lines).

An effective e-mail pitch letter should go like this:

Optical Data Corporation is introducing two computer games that teach science, social studies, and math to children ages 3–8 next week at the Consumer Electronics Show. If you would like to schedule an appointment, review the games, or see the complete press kit online, please send an e-mail note to me or info@mycompany for an automatic response, call 555-1212, or visit our Web site, www.example.com.

This example gets to the heart of the matter (new product introduction) quickly, describes the benefits of the product and the target market, and then asks for action. Best yet, it accomplishes this task in fewer than 60 words! Reporters are intrigued by brevity. When they commit to writing a story, that's when they want tons of data. When the reporter responds, you can send the appropriate information.

If you are going to send information online, be sure to save the file as ASCII so that all reporters will be able to read the file into their word processor, whether it be a PC or a Macintosh. If you are going to send very long files, you can save time for yourself and the reporter by sending compressed files. A compressed file is one that has been truncated for transmission purposes with a program like PKZIP (for PCs), or Stuffit (for Macintosh). The recipient decompresses the files to see the original. Just be sure to ask reporters first if they can read those files and which computer system they use.

Dan,
Q: Which company lets you check your credit on the Web, enables you to shop for cars online (free), apply for financing in real time on the Internet, and has formed alliances with such industry powerhouses as Yahoo! and Netscape?

A: ADP, the $3.5-billion computing company, has leveraged its expertise in electronic commerce applications and created a comprehensive virtual automotive shopping mall with ADP AutoConnect, autoconnect.net. With more than 4,000 auto dealers online, and more than 800 links to auto manufacturers and other sites, ADP AutoConnect is the largest collection of automotive information on the Internet and great example of electronic commerce on the Web.

If you are interested in meeting the brains behind ADP AutoConnect, please give me a call at 312-240-2611 or e-mail rbenecke@edelman.com.

Following is more information about ADP AutoConnect: _____

With the growing number of consumers using computers and the Internet to research purchasing decisions, the hassle of car shopping has now been reduced to just a few keystrokes. And as a sure sign of the times, Internet powerhouses Yahoo! and Netscape have recently formed alliances with ADP AutoConnect to help Net users speed ahead on the information highway.

Tailor Your Message to Fit Individual Reporters' Needs

Benefit: Builds rapport with reporters; improves chances of gaining coverage.

Discussion: It is critical for you to realize that each reporter needs to develop her own story for her audience. One size story does not fit all reporters. Reporters can influence several audiences:

- the online community
- vertical markets
- general consumers
- rctailcrs and distributors

For example, the retail press looks for a story about how manufacturers offer incentives to retailers to sell their products; general consumer reporters are interested in new products that their readers will find interesting; the business reporter wants to know how the company's stock will be affected by the introduction of the new product. If you consider the reporter's target audience, you will be much more successful in dealing with reporters.

Action: Target the story.

Create a Compelling Subject Line

Benefit: Get attention.

Discussion: The subject line is the first piece of text displayed in a reporter's e-mail box. If you write an interesting subject line, reporters will read the message. If you don't, they will hit the delete key. A good subject line breathes life into the message. For example:

- Cybermedia CEO showing new Win 95 fix it program
- New Stormfront Bball game predicts Wall Series winners

"Idcntify what you bring to thc party," says Boehlke. "It is very much like TV or headline copy. Every word must be perfect. Messiness is not tolerated in e-mail."

Be careful not to be too cute or misleading. Nothing is worse than seeing a subject line that says "Sex" only to find a message that says

"Now that I've gotten your attention, let's talk about insurance," says Skye Ketonen, of the Niehaus Ryan Group.

Action: Write a great subject line.

Ask for Feedback

Benefit: Encourages dialog with reporters.

Action: At the end of the press release, ask reporters for comments. Include a mailto: form to ease the process.

HOW TO PUT YOUR ANNUAL REPORT ONLINE

Case Study: Annual Reports Online: Suncor Energy, Inc.

"The Internet is here to stay and lots of people are using it to get information, including financial information about companies. Brokers, analysts, fund managers and other investment professionals have been wired for years and they are increasingly using the World Wide Web to conduct research," says Ron Shewchuck, manager of external communications for Suncor, Inc., www.suncor.com, a major Canadian energy company based in Calgary. His company spent $250,000 to print an annual report but needed only $6,000–$8,000 to create an online annual report.

Each month, 300–400 people read the online annual report and 25–40 download the financial reports in Excel file formats. These numbers are large, considering the targeted nature of the audience and the material.

Here are Shewchuck's tips for success:

- Integrate the creation of your online annual report into your regular annual report production schedule and publish your online report on the same day as it is filed with securities commissions and mailed to shareholders.

- Publish the whole report, not pieces of it or a summary. Investors and potential investors want all the information they can get in a form that is easy to use. Organize the online report so it is Web friendly. That means structuring the information so users can get to the information they need, at the level of detail they need, in the shortest number of mouse clicks possible.

- Give users choices as to how they would like to view the material. Provide the report both as a downloadable Adobe Acrobat file and as a fully linked HTML document.

- Link, but don't over-link. Provide a minimum number of links in the overview material, like the chairman's message and operating highlights, because you don't want to distract people from your key messages. But make sure you link the notes to the financial statement to the appropriate parts of the statements themselves.

- Avoid bells and whistles, but provide cool ways to view your information. Make key charts and tables available as downloadable Microsoft Excel files so analysts can do what they want with your numbers. The key is to make it easy for them to know your company.

HOW TO FIND REPORTERS ONLINE

Now that you have written your press release and pitch letter, you need to send it to reporters. You can find out which reporters are online by several methods:

- Check the mastheads of magazines. More and more publications are listing their reporters' e-mail addresses in the print publications.
- Ask reporters for their e-mail addresses when you meet them at trade shows, conventions, and press conferences and when you speak to them on the phone.
- Look at their business cards or at the end of their articles.

Most reporters online are those from the technology press, with a smattering of technology reporters at daily newspapers. Consumer publication editors have not yet jumped online. However, this is changing almost daily. Many publications have realized they can make money by having an online presence. Once they launch the service, their reporters get online and can be contacted. America Online seems to be attracting a good number of consumer reporters.

Reporters welcome press releases and queries via e-mail because of these qualities:

- **Speediness:** They get the release faster than they would by mail.
- **Responsiveness:** Reporters can send questions by e-mail.
- **Editability:** The information can be imported into reporters' word processors where it can be edited, reformatted, or filed for later use.

Send Personal Pitch Letters to Multiple Recipients

Benefit: Reach many reporters quickly.

Discussion: Another advantage of e-mail is that you can send one pitch letter to hundreds of reporters in the time it takes to send one

note. First you target the reporters, find out their e-mail addresses, and follow your favorite online service's steps for sending a mailing list.
Action: Create list, write pitch letter, and send letter.
Warning: Make sure that the reporter sees only the copy addressed to him. The last thing you want is to let the reporter see he is part of a 100-person routing list. Depending on the service, he might see the names of each person on a separate line before he sees your message. That means the reporter sees the first 100 lines, the equivalent of two sheets of paper, or four computer screens. That is a sure turnoff.

HOW TO DISTRIBUTE NEWS MATERIALS ONLINE

Send the Press Release to a News Wire Service for Distribution

Benefit: Exposure
Discussion: BusinessWire, www.businesswire.com, PR Newswire, www.prnewswire.com, and Canadian Corporate Newsnet, www.cdn-news.net, distribute company press releases for a fee. These press releases are posted to several online services and the Internet, where reporters and the public can read them. Both U.S. services are so well established that the Securities and Exchange Commission considers transmission of business information on these services a primary requirement for complying with its rules to make information available to the public in a timely and equal manner. Both services send the press releases to more than 2,000 media outlets, the online services, and 85 electronic database services.

There are many advantages to using such a service. You reach reporters quickly and relatively inexpensively. Many reporters read these wires to get leads for writing news stories and features. You save a great deal of time, money, and labor by not having to print and mail press releases.

All press releases are carried by a number of online news services. Many online discussions in marketing forums center on which service is more effective, and the results are always split. So you can feel free to select either one and know that the service will be comparable. There is no need to put a release on both services as there is a great degree of duplication of media outlets.

Both services charge by the word. There is a minimum fee for the first 400 words and an additional fee for each additional 100 words. Different prices exist for selecting specialized news lists, such as those for sports, entertainment, automotive, health, legal markets, and for certain parts of the country. Because prices can change, please call the services for more information: Business Wire's number is 800-237-8212; PR Newswire's number is 800-832-5522.

To use either service, follow these basic steps:

1. Create an account with either service.
2. Write your press release.
3. Transmit the press release to the company via fax or modem.
4. Discuss with your account executive which lists of reporters should receive the press release and when.
5. Your account executive will call you after the release has been sent.
6. Check the online service to make sure the press release has indeed been distributed and there aren't any errors.

These two services target high-technology reporters:

- *Newstips,* www.newstips.com, a weekly tip sheet of hot news from the computer industry companies, is distributed to 2,000 reporters. For information, send e-mail to winston@newstips.com or call 216-338-8400.
- GINA, the Global Internet News Agency, www.gina.com, provides public relations professionals with requests from reporters who need sources for technology stories.

ONLINE VIDEO NEWS RELEASES

Video news releases (VNRs) perform a service to companies by creating videos of products and spokespeople and distributing the tapes to TV stations. This service is being morphed into an online version as well. Companies are creating graphic images—photos, graphics, audio, and full-motion video—for clients and pitching them to online news publications.

One of the leaders, DS Simon Productions, www.dssimon.com, 212-727-7770, says online publications want to use material from video news releases to highlight stories. This agency promotes its client's videos the old-fashioned way, with these steps:

1. blast fax and e-mail to editorial contacts
2. focus on 25 of the most appropriate reporters
3. pitch by phone
4. track usage

Case Study: Online VNRs—PR's Newest Tool

With the rapid rise and growing influence of the Internet, the placement opportunities for public relations people are enormous. Here's why: Due to the explosive growth of Web sites, the outlets for placing stories beyond the usual TV, radio, and print outlets has expanded exponentially, according to Gene R. Sower of DS Productions.

Aside from the many new Web sites filled with news and information, practically every conventional newspaper, TV, and radio station now has companion Web sites; the *New York Times* has CyberTimes, CNN has CNN Interactive, etc.

Any media site worth its bits and bytes now contains original stories, reporting, and content unique to that site, unavailable in the original, nondigital versions. With the multimedia capabilities of the World Wide Web, it's now common to find content spiced up with animations, video, and sound clips. Herein lies the opportunity to utilize online VNRs.

In order to attract and maintain visitors to their sites, Web publishers must maintain a steady stream of timely information, stories, pictures, and features. Having a media Web site with outdated content is like playing the same newscast day after day or publishing the same newspaper for a week.

PR professionals who can identify and service the needs of these new media outlets will reap the rewards for their clients. Of course, all the usual tenets of good PR still apply, if not more so: Know who you're pitching and the type of stories they write and report on. Be familiar with the content of the site. Don't offer cooking stories to a personal finance site. And most importantly, shape the story so that it has genuine news value. Pitching a story to a Web site must pass muster with the usual set of journalistic criteria, namely, why should my Web site audience care about your story? What's the news or other useful and relevant information?

Assuming your story is newsworthy and relevant, the opportunities for placement are also richer with possibilities than traditional media. Web sites, unlike their single-medium counterparts (radio–audio, newspaper–print, TV–video, etc.) can utilize multimedia elements. Web sites often combine text, graphics, photos, audio, and video. Those PR professionals who can not only walk the walk and talk the talk but who can navigate the pitching process and offer Web-ready multimedia elements will have the most success in bringing their client's message to an Internet audience. Here's one way to do exactly that:

The online VNR is a new public relations tool that offers Web-ready video, audio, stills, graphics, and text to Web sites, the most important component being a mechanism that includes Web-site notification and tracking of results.

One of the first companies to utilize the online VNR was computer software manufacturer Symantec. Symantec's online VNR, titled "Virus Protection for Windows 95," explained the company's new Norton Anti-Virus, Norton Utilities, and Norton Navigator products introduced for Windows 95. It featured video clip interviews of Symantec's president and CEO Gordon E. Eubanks, Jr., Benjamin Miller of *PC Computing,* and Sean Fulton of *HomePC,* derived from an earlier video news release/satellite media tour campaign.

In addition to the video clips (AVI and Quicktime for Windows and MAC) that were made available on the DS Simon Productions Web site, www.dssimon.com, the online VNR included an assortment of photo images (GIFS), detailed information about the products (HTML), a link to Symantec's Web site, and a consumer information 800 number.

Reporters can download the Web-ready video for preview or point their audience to the links for their own downloads. They can also get story ideas, identify local angles, and even print out scripts and press releases. They can grab accompanying Web-ready graphics and text to embellish their own stories or use the piece as is. Consumers can also view the product in use and then be instantly linked to Symantec's Web site for more information, ordering, etc.

"We found the online VNR to be an innovative way to reach media and consumers," says Michael Sweeny, director of public relations for Symantec. "It's a powerful tool for Internet exposure and we used it effectively to educate people about Norton Utilities for Windows 95."

One of the crucial elements of the online VNR is that it comes packaged with an extensive notification and monitoring effort. A combination of e-mail, phone calls, and faxes is directed to more than 300 relevant news-related Web sites, with a more targeted focus on 25 online publications of strategic importance. This is supplemented with more than 750 faxes to television reporters who are notified of the existence of the online VNR and its address on the Internet (URL). Relevant newsgroups, bulletin boards, and areas of America Online are then seeded with information that draws people to the online VNR site. By offering Web publishers Web-ready materials that are newsworthy, timely, and relevant to their audiences, PR professionals can extend their influence and deliver their clients' message on this rapidly growing worldwide communications medium.

HOW TO STAGE LIVE EVENTS ONLINE

The interactive nature of the Internet allows companies to present live events to their customers, investors, and employees. For many years companies held press conferences, meetings, and seminars by typing messages to one another. This was called chatting. The introduction of audio and Internet telephony now allows companies to hold these events with voice and audio.

Companies can broadcast their meetings using real voice. If their customers have multimedia computers, modems, and Internet connections, they can actually hear the meeting and ask questions just as if they were talking to the company by a telephone.

Case Study: Bell and Howell

Bell and Howell, www.bellandhowell.com, became the first company to host its annual meeting on the Internet in 1996. It went so well, they did it again in 1997. Here's the inside story on how they did it and how your company can go online successfully.

"Bell and Howell is a high-tech company. By putting our annual meeting online, we are able to act like a high-tech company," says Hank D'Ambrosio, vice president of administration for Bell and Howell Company.

"If you are interested in communicating with your shareholders on a global basis, broadcasting your annual meeting on the Internet may be an inexpensive way to communicate your corporate image," he says. "Corporate America's new attitude is to keep it brief, simple and keep costs low. Our approach was to limit presentations of year-end financials and spend more time communicating vision and company culture. We also wanted to leave plenty of time for questions and answers from our shareholders. The logical solution was to utilize the Internet. This forces you to keep the message short. It is cost effective. And you may reach investors around the globe."

"In 1997 there were 1,761 people who listened live to our annual meeting broadcast. In addition, 25 percent of our shares were voted online. In 1996, 230 people listened to the broadcast."

The broadcast is similar to a remote radio broadcast requiring phone connections, PCs for the Internet, and e-mail questions and a mixing board for the Web broadcast. The recipient needs a PC, a real audio player, which can be downloaded off the Web, and some form of Internet connectivity.

The live audience and the Internet audience were able to view a slide show while listening to the annual meeting broadcast. E-mail questions could be sent from two days before the meeting all the way through it. All questions were read in their entirety by the chairman and answered in the order they were received.

"While there is a considerable amount of planning involved, the event has gone very smoothly and has been very well received by shareholders, investors, and the media," D'Ambrosio says.

The key ingredients for success were to:

- Keep visual materials simple.

- Plan the presentation for people who have the least effective technology.

- Plan well in advance.

- Install ISDN lines, phone lines, and backups in case something goes wrong.

- Have a technical support team at the site.

- Rehearse.

D'Ambrosio credits the success of the program with having a reputable broadcast partner (Audio Net) and knowledgeable project management (The Reynolds Communications Group).

The event was promoted by a colorful invitation that stood out in the annual report, along with notices on the Web site and through traditional public relations.

"It is amazing the amount of publicity we got from this event," he said. The meeting archives are kept on the Web site for several months and are then removed.

SUMMARY

Writing online press material is challenging because it must be brief. Never has a communicator's skill for transmitting messages clearly and succinctly been so put to the test—the delete key is so close! Fortunately, the rules for writing for rapport with editors are manageable if you are willing to choose each word with care.

CHAPTER SIXTEEN

Building Relationships with Reporters

Despite the aggressive, wolf-pack image you might have of the media because of TV news crews and made-for-TV movies, it isn't difficult to build rapport with reporters.

This chapter will show you easy strategies for and case studies about doing just that.

RAPPORT BUILDING STRATEGIES

Don't Lie

Benefit: Builds credibility.
Discussion: Reporters will find out if you are lying. When they do, they won't ever speak to you again.
Action: Tell the truth.

Be a Reporter's Resource

Benefit: Build rapport, improve chances of gaining coverage.
Discussion: A great way to build rapport with reporters is to become their trusted resource. This means you:

- Return phone calls as soon as possible.
- Provide reporters with the information or products they need.
- Grant access to people at your company who have information.
- Know everything there is to know about your company and its products and, if you don't, get the answer by deadline.

- Know about competitors' products and talk knowledgeably about them.
- Know about the industry and provide gossip and tips.
- Admit when you do not know the answer and promise to find it.
- Never cover up.
- Always tell the truth!

Interview: Skye Ketonen, Niehaus Ryan Group

Skye Ketonen is one of the new breed of online public relations agents. The key to her success is her ability to create rapport with reporters. Her clients are regularly featured in top-tier publications like *BusinessWeek* because she has developed a personal relationship with reporters.

"I build relationships with reporters as people, not as editors," she says. "I become friends with reporters. We send e-mail about things that have nothing to do about this industry."

She also approaches the relationship as an equal, not as a PR leech. "We're both passionate about this industry," she says. "I am important to you. You are important to me. Let's be friends."

The results pay off handsomely. "They get to trust me, believe me, and trust me as a real person."

If you build rapport correctly, the payoff can be enormous.

Send Press Releases, Pitch Letters, and Notes via E-Mail Instead of Calling

Benefit: Build rapport with reporters.

Discussion: E-mail is a great way to build rapport with reporters. Here's why:

Reporters spend a good deal of time away from their desks covering stories, attending meetings, and—especially if they are in the trade press—at trade shows and conventions that may keep them away from the office for as long as a week.

This being so, you are more likely to speak to their voice mail than to them. When they return they are faced with dozens of messages. Naturally, reporters organize those notes into callbacks and discards. To jump ahead of the pack, you must use e-mail.

Many reporters check their e-mail several times a day, even when they are on the road. E-mail has a sense of urgency to it, so reporters read it first. Because e-mail can be answered quickly, reporters can cut through piles of it in a hurry.

Reporters who cover high tech welcome information via e-mail. As time goes on, reporters who cover other topics will be online as well. We are seeing a big leap in use by reporters whose publications are online, such as the *New York Times, U.S. News & World Report, Chicago Tribune, Car and Driver,* and others.

Reaching reporters via e-mail is efficient because you do not have to play phone tag. Time zones do not matter; people can read and respond to messages at their leisure. Answering e-mail is faster and less expensive than calling on the phone.

In fact, I have even conducted pitches for which all the communication took place online. I wrote a pitch letter on MCI Mail to Kerri Karvetski, who wrote for *Computer Retail Week*. She sent a positive response back via e-mail. I confirmed the time with her. She interviewed Bob Kersey, president of Optical Data Corporation, on the phone a few days later and told me when the article would appear. When the date passed and the article was not in that issue, I sent her e-mail asking her what was up (something I would be too shy to do on the phone). She wrote back that the issues for the next few weeks would be small but that the article would appear after that time. True to her word, the article did run. This shows that all the phases of product pitching and follow-up can take place online.

E-mail can be used to pitch products, set up appointments, follow on product reviews, answer questions, tell about seminars and dealer programs, and provide news, including earnings reports, high-level executive appointments, contracts signed, strategic partnerships, and the like.

Talk to Reporters via E-Mail

Benefit: Build rapport.

Discussion: You can create conversations with editors privately through their e-mail accounts. While it might not be appropriate to pitch stories, you can begin to develop rapport with reporters by showing them you read their articles, are familiar with their work, and are an expert in your field.

Action: To implement this strategy, create a list of the most important editors in your universe. Find out if they have e-mail accounts or if their publications have online forums. Send them notes to engage them in dialog. Examples include comments on recent articles and columns they have written and suggestions for stories about trends you see emerging. They will value this information as good for background or as a lead for a story idea. You don't have to plug your own company to build rapport!

Warning: Gratuitous, self-serving messages will not be appreciated. How do you know when you've crossed the line? Ask yourself: "If I were a reporter, would I value this letter, or would I toss it?" The answer is obvious. The second litmus test is the Oh,-what-the-heck test, as in "I don't know if he'll want to read this, but what the heck—it doesn't cost anything." Wrong. It can cost you your credibility, a commodity that cannot be recovered after it has been spent.

Find Out How Reporters Want to Receive Information

Benefit: Builds rapport.

Discussion: Few actions irritate reporters more than sending their press material in the wrong channel. Some reporters like to get e-mail while others prefer fax. Still others prefer a phone call. If you send e-mail to a reporter who wants a fax, you will upset him. It may sound picky to you and me, but that is a fact of life. You must learn to deal with it.

Media Map, a public relations resource for the high tech industry, surveyed reporters and found that 20 percent of technology reporters wanted information sent via e-mail (760 of 3,874). Media Map and PR Newswire created a distribution service that delivers your press release to reporters along their preferred routes.

Action: Find out how reporters want to be contacted. Ask them or use a reference source like Media Map if they cover technology.

Don't Abuse E-Mail

Benefit: Builds rapport.

Discussion: While e-mail is an easy medium to use, it is possible to make faux pas that will land you in a reporter's doghouse. Charles Pizzo, head of P.R. PR in New Orleans, warns:

- Do not send e-mail to dozens of reporters at the same time, as all the addresses will appear on the screen. This act tells each reporter that everyone else has the story and therefore he is not unique. Also, seeing dozens of names before the story slows down the time to actually read the story. This leaves a bad impression.
- Do not send e-mail to a periodical's reader feedback e-mail address. The message probably won't be delivered to the reporter.

If you participate in newsgroups or mailing lists, identify yourself as a company spokesperson; otherwise, reporters will think you are a consumer, which could cloud issues.

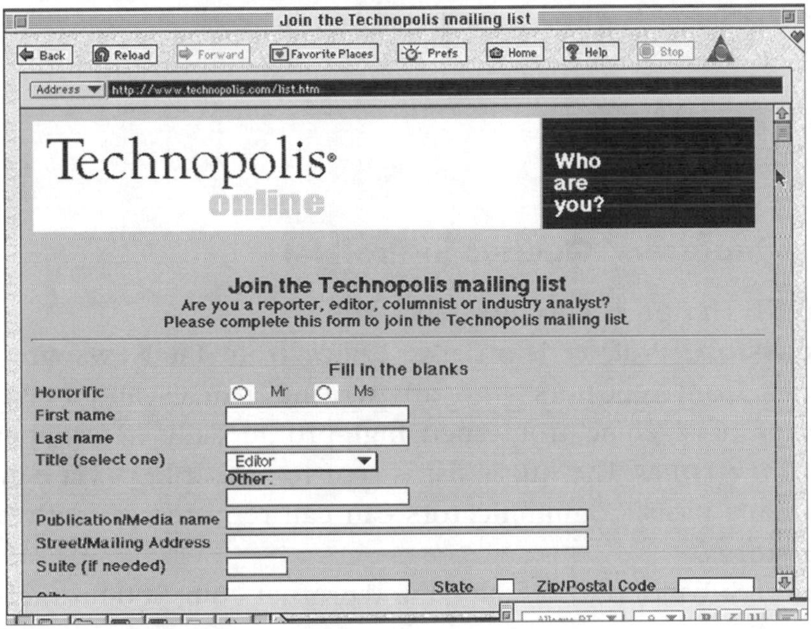

Figure 16–1. Technopolis Communications asks reporters how they want to be contacted and what kind of information they want to receive in a comprehensive registration form located on its Web site. (Copyright 1997, Technopolis Communications, Inc.)

Look for Reporters' Queries in Newsgroups and Mailing Lists

Benefit: Get press coverage.

Discussion: Savvy online reporters post query notices in forums to find subjects to interview for articles.

Action: Scan your favorite message areas and answer appropriate queries.

Example: Here's an actual post on a mailing list, reprinted with permission of Scott Hample:

Subject: Marketers marketing themselves
From: scott.hample@atlwin.com (Scott Hample)
To: Market-l@nervm.nerdc.ufl.edu (Multiple recipients of list Market-l)
Marketing Consultants: How do you market yourself or your company? Relationship marketing? Word of mouth? Direct mail? Database marketing? Ads in the trade journals and other business press? Does your organization practice TQM?

What are some of the typical methods you use to get your name known? There's gotta be something more than publishing articles and/or attending seminars!

Do you speak at seminars? Publish books and cassettes à la Nightingale Conant? What are some of the most unusual ways you market yourselves?

Please respond via e-mail at scott.hample@atlwin.com.
Thanks!
Scott
Whaley Research
404-814-3031

Look for Reporters' Queries in ProfNet

Benefit: Get press coverage.

Discussion: ProfNet is a daily service from PR Newswire that lists queries from reporters who are writing articles and need sources. Queries have come from such high-profile daily newspapers as the *New York Times.* The query list is sent to subscribers via e-mail or fax on a daily basis. Communicators can call reporters directly and pitch their stories.

Action: Subscribe to ProfNet, info@profnet.com, 800-Profnet.

Participate in Online Chats with Editors

Benefit: Build rapport.

Discussion: Many editors host online chats and conferences at their publication's site or as guests on other sites. By participating in these conferences, you might be able to build a relationship with an editor as you impress her with your knowledge of the industry by asking intelligent questions (not by promoting your product directly, unless asked).

Action: Look for notices of conferences, think of dynamite questions, and attend.

Example: Lawrence Custis

Teamwork consultant Lawrence Custis, custisen@teleport.com, used the Internet to market his services nationwide.

"The one feature of online services that has enhanced my efforts is live chat conferences. I've used this medium to meet magazine editors and staff and have become a conference giver myself," he says. "Since then I have received calls from firms in California and have been interviewed for articles in *Entrepreneur* magazine and *Home Office Computing* magazine. Also, I have received invaluable advice on using media releases and other marketing strategies, live, from Scott DeGarmo (editor/publisher, *Success* magazine), Jay Conrad Levinson (Guerrilla Marketing), Dennis Esko (editor-in-chief, *Home Office Computing* magazine), and many others."

SUMMARY

By being a resource instead of a pest, you can build credibility with reporters and maintain a relationship that can help your company achieve its marketing goals online.

CHAPTER SEVENTEEN

Interactive Public Relations Strategies for Your Communities

Public Relations will enter a Golden Age, thanks to the widespread use of the Internet and commercial online services. PR practitioners will not only be able to create strong relationships with reporters through the instant communication and information-on-demand capabilities of the online medium but will also be able to reach their communities directly— without the intervention of the editor and reporter who act as both gate- keeper and censor of information.

The Internet provides a communications tool for companies to talk directly to their communities. As communications professionals, we can only hope that reporters will print our press releases. But the truth is that but a small percentage of informative press releases is ever printed in newspapers or magazines.

This chapter helps you connect with your community (investors, dealers, distributors, consumers, employees, and other people in your target market) by providing strategies for building relationships, prospecting for new cus- tomers, building product and brand awareness, distributing product informa- tion, and building sales.

THE FAILING OF THE MASS MEDIA

When the media act as gatekeeper, they can do a disservice to the public. Let's look at what can happen when you send a press release to a reporter. He can:

- throw it out—which happens more times than PR pros care to admit
- print it in full—a dream that rarely occurs in real life
- print parts of it, without additional comments
- print parts of it, with comments by competitors who downplay your story
- print parts of it, with comments by analysts who change your perspective
- print parts of it in a roundup with competitors, thus diluting your message
- delete the key messages that support your main point
- introduce typos and errors

So there you have eight actions, seven of which are negative or potentially negative. That should be enough reasons for you to want to speak to directly to your audience. But if you are not convinced, let's look at a case study.

America Online (AOL) recently sent a press release over PR Newswire announcing its purchase of the Global Network Navigator from O'Reilly and Associates—a major story in the online community. The company-written press release ran approximately 1,300 words and included quotes from Steve Case, president of AOL, and Tim O'Reilly, president of O'Reilly and Associates.

Reuters felt this was a worthy story. They took the release, cut out the quotes, and printed a mere 410 words, less than one-third of the original story.

Did the reader get a fair assessment of the AOL story? Hardly. Does the investment community understand more or less because of the editing by the gatekeepers? Obviously less.

What's a PR practitioner to do?

Plenty.

Distribute Your Press Release on a Newswire

Benefit: Avoid the media; speak directly to your audience.

Discussion: Your audience can access all press releases sent over PR Newswire via the Internet and CompuServe by using simple searches on keywords. So make sure you send releases over PR Newswire. The cost is generally less than $500.

Example: Intellisystems

Intellisystems, a leading provider of expert-based help systems for high technology companies, issued a press release on PR Newswire. It was printed on PointCast, a news service that prints all press releases offered by PR Newswire.

Executives with buying authority at a major commercial online service read the press release on PointCast. They called the company and asked the president, Michael Beare, to fly to their offices for a meeting. Beare says he had been trying to get an appointment with that company for years but couldn't get in. Because of the newswire service, he got the appointment.

Post Press Releases on Your Web Site

Benefit: Your community can read the press release.

Discussion: Your readers can access press releases you post in your Web Site. Many, many, many high-tech companies do this today. If you aren't following this tactic, you are giving your competitors an advantage.

Post Press Releases on Forums that Cover Your Topic

Benefit: Your community can read the press release.

Discussion: To reach your customers directly, post the press release in message boards or USENET newsgroups and mailing lists that appeal to them. To do this you must first find message boards that attract your target audience and make sure the system operator (sysop) allows press releases. To gain permission, send a private note to the sysop.

Create a One-Way Mailing List of Your Community Members

Benefit: Maintain close relationships with customers, retailers, editors, and other VIPs by notifying them of news.

Discussion: A mailing list is an electronic tool that allows you to broadcast your press releases to customers' e-mailboxes. When you post a new press release or have interesting news, you can send a message to your list. The message can contain the entire content of the press release or instruct the recipients to visit a specific page of your Web site.

Because e-mail can be sent to any online system, you can converse with members on CompuServe, a local Internet service in Mexico City, or a dedicated Internet connection at your home office.

Companies must be committed to maintaining this dialog for the relationship-building process to work.

Warning: Make sure you get permission from each customer. Online consumers hate junk mail. Netiquette says that "Information that is UNsolicited in UNappreciated." Follow it as if your life depended on it, because if people get upset, they can and will tell 30,000 of their closest online friends with the click of a few keystrokes.

Create Information Files

Benefit: Increases exposure and credibility; possible source of leads.

Discussion: Good members of the online community give back to the community. Marketers can do well by doing good. Companies can create information-packed articles and reports that help consumers solve problems. These articles don't sell the company or product directly; instead, they sell the concept that empowers the company.

Action: Write a file that helps people solve a problem or provides them with useful, original information. These files can be stored.

Example: Let's say you are a tour guide who gives walking tours of San Francisco. You could write 500-word articles that describe sample tours with each stop explained. Another idea is to list areas to avoid because of crime, congestion, or image. As most forums are happy to accept relevant material, send a polite query letter stating your topic and asking if the forum wants to review it for the library. If yes, send it, along with a 50-word description of the article. Consultants should include their positioning statement as well. This descriptive information is posted to the library file so that readers can see a description of the material before deciding to read it. For example:

Jane Green conducts walking tours of San Francisco for her company, Green Ways, 800-555-1212.

Create a "Ten Commandments" Article for Libraries

Benefit: Prospecting. Increases exposure and positions you as an expert.

Discussion: This kind of article is a fact-based information piece that explains a topic of interest, such as "Ten Ways to Cut Your Taxes" for a tax accountant; "Ten Commandments for Reducing Stress" for a psychologist, masseuse, physical therapist, or sports trainer; or "Ten Keys to Financial Freedom" for a certified financial planner or investment adviser. People love these articles because they contain good information and are easy to read quickly. You'll love them, too, because they are easy to write. The format calls for you to write an opening paragraph that presents a problem. Next, write ten ways to solve the problem. Other good headline words are secrets, tips, hints, rules, and laws.

Action: Propose article; write the article, description, and keywords.

Example: Here is an example of a "Ten Commandments" article written by a stress management consultant for an audience of accountants and tax professionals:

As April 15 rolls around, accountants are under a great deal of stress. With the impending deadline of tax filing season, they work 20-hour days, seven days a week, and must deal with clients who are disorganized and frenzied. Tax accountants must cope with this tension. Here are ten ways to cut agita:

1. Exercise.
2. Eat healthy foods.
3. Avoid caffeine, sugar, and other stimulants and depressants.
4. Breath deeply.
5. Take short breaks.
6. Think pleasant thoughts.
7. Focus on how well you will feel on April 16.
8. Think of how you are helping people solve their problems.
9. Think of how you will enjoy the money you are earning.
10. Think of how you'll appreciate free time when you are done!

This article was written by John Peterson of Peterson and Associates, an accounting firm based in San Francisco.

Notice that the tips can be as short as one or two words. If you like, this information can be expanded to paragraphs containing several sentences. There is no negative effect in writing a longer article. However, a maximum of 250–500 words will ensure that your readers won't lose interest.

Here's a sample e-mail pitch letter for the sysop:

As April 15 rolls around, accountants will be under a great deal of stress. I can help your readers with a 250-word article called "The Ten Rules of Reducing Stress." Can I send a copy to you to post in the library? I am qualified to write this article because I have experience as (FILL IN).
Thanks.
Your Name
Signature file

Here's a sample description that would be attached to the file:

Are you stressed out as April 15 rolls around? This article will show you ten ways to cut stress. The article is written by John Peterson of Peterson and Associates, an accounting firm based in San Francisco.

Keywords are words that describe your article. Readers can search libraries by selecting keywords. If the system prompts you for keywords, select as search terms your name, the general field you are writing about, and who should read the article. For example:

Keywords: stress, accountants, tax preparers, exercise, bookkeepers, John Peterson.

Encourage Republication of Your Files

Benefit: Increases exposure and can be a source of leads.
Discussion: If one article in one library is good, then one article in many libraries must be better! Encourage readers to post your articles in other areas of interest, such as:

- mailing lists and newsgroups (If they post the article, then members will regard it as being noncommercial. If you post it, it might be viewed with suspicion.)
- local bulletin boards
- special-interest bulletin boards
- newsletters published by nonprofit groups, associations, and businesses
- relevant publications

You won't get paid for this editorial service, but you aren't in the business of making money from your writing. You are in business to sell your products or services. That's where the long-term benefit will come. To let people know they can reprint the work, include this line at the end of the article:

This article can be reprinted provided it is not edited in any manner and if proper credit is given. This includes listing my name as the author and my contact information.

If you like, you could instead ask people who want to reprint the article to call you and request permission individually. This way, you will know when and where the article will appear.

To protect your work, place a copyright notice at the beginning of the piece so that people can see it clearly and unmistakably. A sample copyright notice would look like this:

Copyright © 1997 Your Company
All rights reserved.
Published in the United States of America

Action: Encourage properly credited republication of your articles; attach the preceding copyright information paragraph to them.

Example: Warren Reid, Management Consultant

Warren Reid, Encino, California, a management consultant specializing in information technology, consult@primenet.com, spoke on the legal aspects of the year 2000 to a computer conference. His speech was so well received that he was asked to turn it into a 2000-word article that was published as the lead piece in the Year 2000 Web site, www.year2000.com. That article led to requests for reprint rights by KMPG/Canada, EDS, and Unisys, among others, who then printed it on their Web sites and in their internal newsletters on the Intranet.

Since that time, Reid has been catapulted to fame, interviewed by the *Wall Street Journal,* and asked to write a book and lead a series of seminars for companies and conferences.

"I've moved from being the keynoter on the second day to the keynoter, period. It was the Internet that did it," Reid says.

Write Articles for Online Magazines and Forums

Benefit: Increased exposure.
Discussion: Online publications welcome content that is objective and useful to their readers. By publishing articles in other venues, you can

increase your exposure to audiences of prospects and raise your credibility. For example, a financial planner could write an article about how to save money on taxes and submit the article to the Smart Business Center, www.smartbiz.com.

Action: Find appropriate publishing venues, select a topic, and query the editor. Based on your conversation with the editor, write the article.

ONLINE CONFERENCES

The Internet and commercial online services can hold conferences with their customers using a variety of tools. Companies that have their own forums can use those resources as well as the chat areas of the commercial online services. The Internet has Internet Relay Chat. One of the more interesting tools is WebChat, www.wbs.net, which enables conference participants to add pictures and sound to their text-based discussions. Using this tool, a company's support personnel could, for example, send FAQs that explain how to correct a problem and show a screen shot showing what the finished product would look like. Salespeople can conduct real-time chats with prospects by showing them pictures of products and sending audio clips of testimonials from consumers.

To hold a successful conference, companies should take a great deal of care to let consumers know what will be discussed, when the conference will take place, and how to use the tools. This information can be placed in a FAQ file that consumers can read at their convenience.

Hold Press Conferences and Annual Meetings Online

Benefit: Your community will hear the whole story.

Discussion: By holding a meeting online, your community will have access to every word and chart available to people in the audience. Most of this information would have been distilled by the media, so this is a terrific opportunity for your company to tell its story directly to the people who really care.

Example: Bell and Howell hosted the first online annual meeting. Shareholders listened to the meeting with free software offered by the company and e-mailed questions to board members stationed in Ann

Arbor, Michigan. "This is the way of the future," says William White, CEO of Bell and Howell. Many major newspapers reported that B&H hosted the online meeting, thus creating good exposure for the company.

Be a Guest at Online Conferences and Educational Seminars

Benefit: Prospects and increased exposure.

Discussion: Many forums hold online conferences to help members learn about topics of special interest. They have a lot of time and space to fill. If you submit an appropriate idea, you may be rewarded by getting increased exposure to your audience. Forum operators benefit as well because your session will generate traffic.

Action: Send a query note to the sysop with a conference topic, sample questions, and a list of what users will learn. Propose several dates.

Example: As companies lay off workers in today's difficult economy, those workers need to know how to get new jobs. My company helps people find new jobs by teaching them to write resumes that get responses. I would like to host an online conference for your members that will teach them what works and doesn't work in resumes, which buzzwords are old and tired and which ones are new and exciting, and how to stand out from the crowd. I've noticed you hold forums on Thursday evenings. Would October 18 or 25 work?

You will want to schedule the conference well enough in advance for the sysop to publicize the meeting to members. This could take about a month. To promote the conference, you might send a file to the library that describes your company and its services or provides tips on your area of expertise.

SUMMARY

While the press acts as a necessary filter to edit the news and provide objectivity, companies have a vested interest in telling the rest of the story. Online services provide a great many tools—e-mail, mailing lists, and chats—that allow their stories to be told—and found—by online communities.

All these steps allow you to create long, lasting relationships with your publics. They will come to rely on you as a source of information they can't get from the daily newspapers and trade publications. Further, you'll save money through these tools, compared to the expense of printing and mailing hundreds or thousands of press releases via snail mail.

There are many tools and strategies for dealing directly with your audience. The next two chapters offer additional strategies to be used by e-mail and with newsgroups, mailing lists, and forums.

CHAPTER EIGHTEEN

Building Relationships with E-mail and Private Mailing Lists

E-mail is the common denominator for reaching people in a cost-effective manner. After all, it is the one tool that everyone has and it's easy to use. There aren't any confusing commands to learn or navigation routes to be guided through. E-mail doesn't even care whether you use a PC or a Mac or UNIX computer system. E-mail, comprising of text, photos, and even audio messages, can be sent to people on different online systems. E-mail, therefore, is the way many companies communicate with consumers to create relationships.

E-mail helps companies by permitting the free flow of information without the barriers of time and space. People can send and receive e-mail at any time of the day or night. The recipients can answer at their leisure.

In this chapter, you will learn:

- what e-mail is
- benefits of using e-mail in the marketing mix
- how to create one-to-one relationships with prospects and customers
- strategies for integrated marketing
- strategies for creating effective messages
- e-mail netiquette for online marketers
- how to use private mailing lists to build relationships
- Congressional consideration of privacy laws

WHAT E-MAIL IS

E-mail is the most universal application on the Internet and commercial online systems. It is the first online tool people use and, for many, the only tool they will ever use. People are often introduced to e-mail through their companies, which may use it extensively. Reports show that about 80 million people use e-mail while only about 40 million people have access to the Web. If you direct people to your Web site, you might be missing a large segment of the market that doesn't have access to the World Wide Web.

How can people have e-mail but not have access to the Web? Here are several reasons:

- Their company has e-mail accounts for all employees, but doesn't want them surfing the Web.
- They use school computers that are limited to e-mail use.
- Free e-mail services, like Juno and Rocketmail, attract people to the world of online services but don't offer access to newsgroups or the World Wide Web.

Do not confuse e-mail with direct mail. The direct mail marketing techniques that work so well in the real world are the kiss of death on the Internet.

BENEFITS OF USING E-MAIL IN THE MARKETING MIX

Electronic messages are a terrific way for online marketers to interact with consumers. A variety of tools exist for marketers, including e-mail, forums, bulletin boards, newsgroups, and mailing lists. These can be used to dispense information about new products and services, company background, help files, and any other material you can create to foster a relationship.

The benefits of using e-mail to converse with consumers include:

- Prospecting for leads by introducing consumers to your product or service.
- Converting prospects to customers by providing them with requested information, such as company overviews, product backgrounders, press releases, reports, surveys, and media reviews.

- Building relationships and developing brand loyalty by informing consumers of new products or services, sales, discounts, seminars, events, and the like.
- Conducting market research by reading consumers' messages.
- Creating and maintaining one-to-one relationships with customers and prospects.

In an integrated marketing environment, e-mail can be used as a direct communications link with prospects. Let's look at the steps involved in an integrated marketing campaign.

HOW TO CREATE ONE-TO-ONE RELATIONSHIPS WITH PROSPECTS AND CUSTOMERS

1. E-mail is the beginning point in this building process. At its simplest, people who have questions about your product send you an e-mail. They might have seen the address on your letterhead, advertisement, product package, billboard, or business card, or your signature file attached to a message you posted on a discussion area.

   Responding to each message individually helps develop one-to-one relationships with consumers.

   After a while, you might notice that many people ask the same questions most of the time. Instead of writing an individual letter, you can access a library of texts written to account for most situations. As you receive a message about the product warranty, for example, you cut and paste the prepared answer that explains the warranty. What used to take you five minutes to write now takes you five seconds.

2. The next step up this ladder is automation of the process. You have a library of prepared answers to the most common questions. Customers can receive those answers when they send e-mail to a specific e-mailbox. For example, if they send a message to warranty@mycompany.com they will receive the answer in seconds. This is possible due to a software program called a mailbot or infobot. Your Internet Service Provider (ISP) can provide you with this service, as can many third-party companies that you can find through Yahoo! (search on "mailbot"). You might think of this service as an online cousin to the fax response systems in which you dial a company's

fax machine, type in your fax number, and the numerical code that requests a particular communication to be faxed back to you in seconds.

This process can save you time and money. If people read the response and still have questions, they can send a new request to a company representative who can personally answer the difficult questions. Thus your staff spends its time dealing with the more complex questions while the routine questions are handled by the infobot.

Any kind of file can be sent via e-mail, whether it be text, photo, or sound. E-mail can thus provide more information than a customer support representative talking on a telephone.

You can also provide answers to customers just at the moment they are most interested in developing a relationship with your company—even if that happens to be 2 A.M. on Sunday, when your customer support staff is at home and asleep.

3. All this time, your computer is recording the e-mail addresses of all persons who send a request. You are building a database of valuable information on where people can be contacted and what their key interests are. (You know this because they have sent e-mail to a specific e-mailbox. You therefore know that a certain person was interested in the seminars you offer, but not the books. Or they are interested in the seminar in Chicago, not the one in New York.)

The tactic of using a separate mailbox for information replies can also be used to track the number of responses from a particular source. For example, if you have two ads and list a different mailbox address in each ad, you'll be able to see which drew more responses. You can do this with articles, fliers, brochures, and any other marketing material.

4. As your database grows, you might want to establish closer lines of communication with individuals by contacting them directly via e-mail. You might send them coupons for your products that entice them to order directly from you, or lead them into one of your distributor's stores. You might build a relationship by sending a newsletter every month or quarter that gives them interesting new ways to use your products and services. You could even let them know that you've updated your Web site with information that will enhance their personal or professional lives. You could encourage them to participate in surveys so you can determine where the market is heading and what new features and benefits are sought.

You could also use this material to track who actually buys your products to see if a marketing effort is successful or if your pitches need to change.

Use these mailing list newsletters after the sale to reinforce the buying decision, educate the customer on additional features and uses of the product, and to sell additional products and upgrades.

Striking while the iron is hot is a key point in sales. The Internet and commercial online services have great tools to make this happen by giving people information when they need it.

STRATEGIES FOR INTEGRATED MARKETING: E-MAIL, INFOBOTS, PRIVATE MAILING LISTS

Here are strategies you can use to integrate e-mail in your marketing program.

Send E-mail to Yourself to See How It Looks

Benefit: Avoid embarrassment.

Discussion: Before you send e-mail to customers or reporters, send it to yourself to make sure the material is formatted properly and displays properly on the screen. It is all too easy to hit the wrong key on your word processor and send 500 lines of computer characters instead of a press release, or have your lines wrap badly or have paragraph markers disappear.

Make Each E-mail Look Individual

Benefit: Creates a feeling of intimacy.

Discussion: If you send e-mail to a list of 100 people, each person will see the name of every other person on the list and know this is not a personal correspondence, which lowers the intimacy factor. Also, they will see the names of the 100 people before they see your message, which means they will have to scroll past 100 lines before they can read your important message. This will increase the tick-off factor tremendously. Off-the-shelf e-mail programs don't do a very good job of explaining how to turn off the bcc (blind carbon copy) function, so test this activity thoroughly before sending messages.

Netmailer from Alpha Software, www.alphasoftware.com, merges database capabilities with personalized e-mail and might be the solution for mass mailings.

Action: Send your message to a list of dummy names at your company first to make sure the blind carbon copy has turned off the names of each other recipient.

Use ASCII Text for All Documents

Benefit: Ensure data is transmitted properly.

Discussion: With so many computer systems and word processors in the world, it is fairly easy to send a file that the recipient can't read. While some people love pages designed with high-end design programs, most people don't have the software to read it. Your best choice is to send everything in the lowest common denominator format, which is ASCII. Don't compress files with the ZIP format unless you are sure the recipient has the uncompress utility that makes the file readable. Also, don't send files as attachments; people don't like opening them for fear of contracting a virus. If they don't have a program that can read the file, it will look like garbage and your chance for making a good impression will be lost.

Action: Save all files to ASCII (or TXT) before sending.

Use HTML Formatted Files

Benefit: Messages look better and create a more positive impression than ASCII messages.

Discussion: E-mail messages can now look like Web pages, with different sized type, different colors, pictures and graphs, and links to Web sites and e-mail addresses. Use your HTML editor or Microsoft Word to create the files (use the "save as HTML command" to save your work) and send it to your lists. There is one problem with this format: Not everyone has an e-mail program that can read it. People who upgrade their browser software or e-mail software will be able to read the files easily. People who use early versions of programs will see the message as a series of cryptic commands. You might need to offer two versions of these files: one for users of old software who will need an ASCII version, and users of newer software, who will appreciate the HTML versions. Figures 18-1 is an example of an e-mail file sent as an HTML formatted document.

Action: Create and distribute the files with HTML formatting.

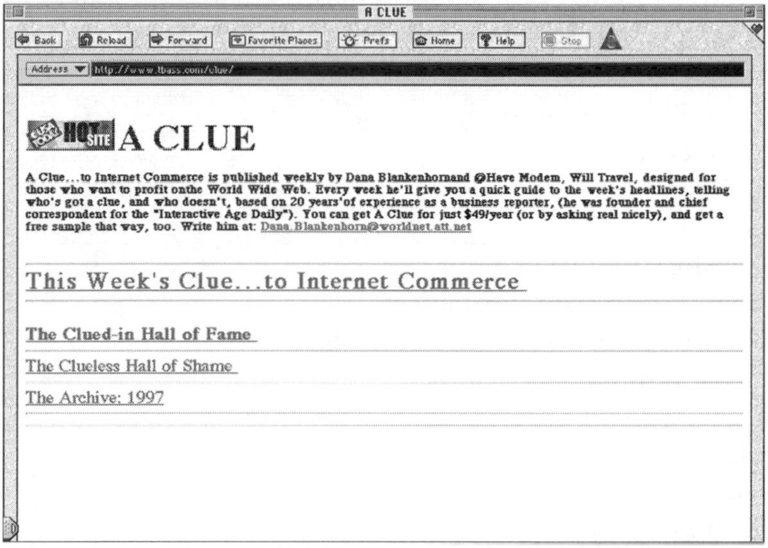

Figure 18–1. Dana Blankenhorn's "A Clue to Internet Commerce" is a weekly newsletter sent via e-mail that incorporates HTML formatting. Notice the large headlines, different fonts, and links to material on other Web sites (Copyright 1997, Dana Blankenhorn).

Create Information Packages Available via E-mail and Downloading

Benefit: Prospects get needed information when they want it without delay.

Discussion: The interactivity of consumer dialogs means that people will ask you for information about your company and its products or services. You can respond via regular mail or e-mail. Your company might already have a kit ready to be sent by mail or courier service to hot prospects but will also need one for the online consumer. You can let the customer access this information by creating files and storing them in forums or on your Web site. An alternative is to let customers send you e-mail with a note in the subject line saying "send info pack one." You can create an automatic response system in which your mailbot sends the appropriate file to the customer as soon as it receives the query. If you prefer to use a commercial online service, there isn't any automatic mail system. However, you can have an operator check messages and respond as soon as feasible. In either case, prospects will get the information they need in a timely manner—when they are hot to buy.

You must consider what kind of information should be included in this message. Each business will have a different set of considerations. Here are ideas:

- press releases
- data sheets
- sales sheets
- dealer sheets
- company financial information
- reviews from newspapers and magazines
- tables of contents (for books)
- catalogs
- brochures
- photos
- testimonial letters
- independent reports
- newsletters
- annual reports
- message from the president

The final consideration in this matter is: Should the material be rewritten for an online audience? Could the information be made interactive? Could you add multimedia, sound, or video to spice up the presentation? The answers, of course, are all *yes*.

Action: Create information packages that reinforce the integrated marketing message.

Create Signature Files to Add Positioning Statements to Your Messages

Benefit: A signature file tells people who you are and what you do.

Discussion: While every online system lets you put your name and e-mail address in the mail header, that information is next to useless to the reader. That's because there is no context for, say, joe@yourcompany

.com. Is he the chief cook or bottle washer? And just what does his company do, anyway?

Fortunately, netiquette does allow mail senders to include a signature, but don't confuse this with your John Hancock. An online signature or tagline is a four-line message printed at the bottom of your message area in which you can present information of any kind. It is commonly used by people in business to tell others who they are and what they do. A suitable use for online marketers is to print your positioning statement and contact information. The benefit of this signature is that you can subtly let people know who you are and what you do without being a pest. There are no downside risks since netiquette deems this an acceptable practice. Here is an example:

Daniel Janal *   Janal Communications   *   510-648-1961
Author, Speaker, Marketing Consultant Specializing on the Internet
Online Marketing Handbook
101 Successful Businesses You Can Start on the Internet
www.janal.com   dan@janal.com

Signature files can also be used at the end of each message you send to a mailing list or newsgroup.

Action: Create a signature file. Each software system allows for a different method. It would be impossible to list them all here. If you use Netscape Navigator or Microsoft Internet Explorer, create the sig file with your word processor. Save it as a text file, not as a Word file. Use the browser's e-mail preferences options to select that file as the sig file. It will be appended to all your messages. With Netscape Communicator, use the commands edit/preferences/identity. You'll see a fill-in box that asks you for the location and name of the signature file. With Microsoft Internet Explorer, go to mail, select "options," click on "signature" tab, select Text, then type your signature and press "ok."

Don't Buy Bulk E-mail Lists

Discussion: A number of direct mailers have compiled massive lists of e-mail addresses based on people who have posted messages in mailing lists and newsgroups. They sell these lists to advertisers, claiming these people are all interested in a given topic. This is a bad strategy for advertisers as most online citizens don't like their e-mailboxes filled with advertisements. Any advertiser who uses this tactic risks offending more people than they could ever actually sell to.

STRATEGIES FOR CREATING EFFECTIVE MESSAGES

There is plenty of ways to go with the flow of the online community and promote your business without violating netiquette. Here are strategies to increase the effectiveness of your one-on-one marketing:

Create a Compelling Subject Line

If people's mailboxes are overflowing with messages, they will weed out the unimportant or uninteresting ones. Use strong action words to convey your message. Avoid dull headers.

- Good Examples
    - My Company announces new product
    - My Company announces record profits
    - My Company holds semiannual sale
- Bad Examples
    - Get rich quick!
    - Important! Read this now!

Write Short Paragraphs

Short paragraphs are easy to read. The white space on the screen is a pleasant reading environment, as distinct from a solid block of text.

Keep the Message Short

People seem to dislike messages longer than one screen. As online writing tends to be informal, it is easy to truncate messages and avoid the paper-wasting headings, addresses, and salutations.

Ask for Action

Ask and ye shall receive. If you want to be successful with online marketing, you must ask or suggest that the prospect do something, like subscribe to a mailing list, visit your Web site, send e-mail for more information, order a product, or provide comments. If you do, you might convince the prospect to do something he might not have thought to do.

Ask Questions and Ask for Feedback

Discussion: When someone sends you a note, reply as soon as you can with the information and then ask a question to keep the conversation alive. Even a simple "What do you do?" or "What do you think?" will encourage the person to reply. If you don't ask these kinds of questions, the conversation will die. If you ask them, you will learn more about prospects so you can fill their needs.

Reply to Questions Quickly

Discussion: The online world expects and demands fast response to questions—about 24 hours seems to be the norm for new content in response to a personal question (as distinct from canned responses sent via an infobot). If you don't respond quickly, you could lose credibility and frustrate customers. A middle ground is to send a quick response via an infobot saying "We have received your message and will respond within 24 hours."

Action: Commit to answering messages quickly. Make this mandate known to all employees who deal with the public.

Track Responses with E-mail

Benefit: Accurate tracking of leads from various sources.

Discussion: The harshest criticism of public relations is that it is difficult to measure. You can begin to measure public relations by creating several e-mail accounts and using them in tandem with each message you use.

Example: Let's say you want to test the price of a product and place ads in printed publications or in legitimately posted messages on online systems. You have three ads; they are the same except for the three different prices and the three different e-mail addresses. People who are interested see only one ad and send an e-mail note to the corresponding account. By tallying the number of messages in each mailbox, you can determine which test price worked best. This method also works for testing leads or inquiries from articles published about your company or product, or articles you have written and placed in online libraries. You can also then track the respondent's actions after they receive your marketing materials to determine which source of leads works best.

Action: Contact your service provider to create additional accounts.

E-MAIL NETIQUETTE FOR ONLINE MARKETERS

Here are guidelines for writing and posting effective e-mail and messages in newsgroups and forums.

- **Be polite:** E-mail almost always sounds harsher than it's meant. Your comments can appear caustic and jokes might be read as criticism because the reader can't see your facial expressions or vocal intonations. Therefore, be exceedingly polite. Err on the side of good taste. Assume that anything that could be seen as negative will be taken as such.
- **Be brief:** Online communication tends to be short. Many formalities of letter writing are not used, such as headings, greetings, salutations, and closings. Short sentences, action verbs, and messages of one screen length are desirable.
- **Be grammatically accurate:** Nothing looks worse than a typo. Check your spelling and grammar.
- **Be case-sensitive:** DON'T TYPE IN UPPERCASE. It looks like you are shouting.
- **Be specific:** Headlines will attract readers to your message or drive them away. "Need Help with Creating Ads" is better than "Help Wanted."
- **Be yourself:** Use your real name, not a CB handle or nickname. People deserve to know who they are talking to. That means using your real name, business, and gender. It is difficult to conduct a serious conversation with someone named Hot Pants. A member of a commercial online service might call himself as John73141 so that people won't know who he is. If you want to be respected, use your real name.
- **Be informative:** People like to read information, not ads, online.

Put Emotion into Messages with Smileys

E-mail messages generally sound harsher than you intend because the medium does not project the voice inflections and body language that make spoken communication efficient. Online members have developed a special symbolic language that allows writers to show a kinder, gentler side. The language is called *emoticons*, short for *emotion* plus *icons* (called *smileys*). An emoticon is a combination of keyboard symbols that looks like a stick figure. When viewed by tilting your head sideways, these characters appear to be faces that smile, wink, or grimace. Emoticons are used by the sender to add an emotional tone that might otherwise be lost in the emotionless world of terse e-mail messages. Dozens of emoticons convey different subtle messages. Here are a few examples (tilt your head to the left for best results):

:-)	**smile**
;-)	**wink**
:- >	**very happy**
:- <	**disappointed**
:-D	**laughing**

One minor warning: Some people hate smileys because they are too cute.

E-mail Shorthand

A variation on emoticons involves using specialized constructions of letters to convey emotions. For example, a writer can avoid being misinterpreted as having written a sarcastic message by adding a grin, <g>, to indicate she is only kidding.

To write messages faster and avoid repetitions, an e-mail shorthand has developed that involves using abbreviations for often-used phrases. Here are several popular conventions and examples in average sentences:

- IMHO: in my humble opinion
  IMHO, the 49ers will win the Super Bowl.

- LOL: laughing out loud
  Did you see Seinfeld last night? I was LOL!

- ROFL: rolling on the floor laughing
  You think that was funny? How about Kramer and the cigar? I was ROFL!

- INAL: I'm not a lawyer (usually followed by legal advice)
  INAL but I think you should sue for back wages.

- TIA: thanks in advance
  TIA for your help in finding those files for me.

- BTW: by the way
  BTW, the price is $49.95, not $99.95

- PMFJI: pardon me for jumping in (when a new person enters a conversation)
  PMFJI, but I have experience in this area and thought you would like to know.

For example, a note might read:

> *BTW, I read in today's paper that the lawyers will use the insanity defense. INAL, but IMHO, this is ridiculous! I'm ROFL. What do you think? TIA.*

Using these e-mail expressions shows that you are a member of the community who understands its mores. Using symbolic language will help you get your messages across.

HOW TO EFFECTIVELY USE PRIVATE MAILING LISTS TO BUILD RELATIONSHIPS

Companies can create private mailing lists to keep in touch with their communities. Here are two strategies:

Create a One-Way Mailing List of Your Community Members

Benefit: Maintain close relationships with customers, retailers, editors, and other VIPs by engaging them in dialogs.

Discussion: A mailing list is an electronic tool that allows you to interact with your communities and lets each community member talk to the others. You can send press releases and product information, answer questions, let people know what's new on your Web site, and even let customers talk among themselves to help solve problems.

As a mailing list owner, you are a publisher who can freely distribute marketing materials without fear of reprisals or flames. After all, people want to be on your list because they want to receive information in the first place.

To create a mailing list, you must work with an Internet service provider who has the proper software to track subscriptions as well as manage the mailing functions. The three major programs are Listserv, Listproc, and Majordomo.

You will also need to create an information/welcoming message to new members. This message tells new and prospective subscribers what the list covers and who should join. This will help you and them make the best use of their time and resources so they don't join a list that doesn't meet their needs, or yours. The message also should contain information on how to unsubscribe and FAQs about the mailing list itself. This message should be set up as an information piece that is sent automatically to anyone who sends mail to information@mycompany.com.

The next step is to get members. You'll have to publicize the mailing list to attract subscribers. Consider these strategies:

- Posting notices in relevant newsgroups and mailing lists. Be sure to point out that this is a free service so you don't run afoul of netiquette.
- Including information in your signature file.
- Letting your customers know about the mailing list through press releases, letters, newsletters, ads, and other communications both on the Internet and in your printed materials.
- Posting information and sign-up forms on your Web site.

These strategies will help to create word of mouth, one of the best marketing methods, as satisfied subscribers will tell their colleagues about the service.

Be sure to include directions for subscribing and unsubscribing. For example:

To subscribe to CHAT LINES send e-mail to "lists@mycompany.com" with a blank subject line, and a message body of "subscribe chatlines." To unsubscribe, send e-mail to "lists@mycompany.com" with a blank subject line, and a message body of "unsubscribe chatlines."

Create a Two-Way Mailing List of Your Community Members

Discussion: The benefits and actions are the same as above. The added benefit of a two-way mailing list is that customers can talk to one another as well as with you. They can help solve each other's problems and discuss your company's strengths and weaknesses. It is a tool that can help you gauge customer interest and sentiment. You can also influence opinions by offering advice, news, and contacts with product managers or other company officials.

CONGRESSIONAL CONSIDERATION OF PRIVACY LAWS

Congress is considering a law that would enable consumers to prohibit online information being collected about them. Marketers would have to provide conspicuous notice that any data is intended for reuse or sale under the Privacy Bill of Rights for the Information Age, introduced by Representative Edward Markey (D-Massachusetts).

Companies that sell e-mail lists gathered from newsgroups and other sources are engaging in a battle with online services over the right to send bulk e-mail commercial messages. The commercial online services are opposed to mass advertising because their members don't want their e-mail boxes jammed with ads. Direct marketers contend they have the right to send e-mail to whomever they want. The issue will be resolved by the courts.

SUMMARY

E-mail is an effective means of creating relationships with people who seek out your company's product or service.

CHAPTER NINETEEN

Building Relationships with Newsgroups and Forums

Communities of like-minded people form on the Internet and the commercial online services just as naturally as cliques form in high school. In the online world, these people join discussion groups where they read and write messages to one another.

Marketers can use these areas to prospect for new customers, study market trends, and contribute information to the community. However, selling or conducting commerce is not allowed in most of these areas. Do not violate this cardinal rule of netiquette.

In this chapter, you will learn:

- what newsgroups, forums, SIGs, bulletin boards, and clubs are
- how to find target groups online
- benefits of using newsgroups in your marketing plan
- how to respond correctly to messages
- marketing strategies that conform to netiquette

WHAT NEWSGROUPS, FORUMS, SIGS, BULLETIN BOARDS, AND CLUBS ARE

Each commercial online service and the Internet have areas where people can post messages to one another and discuss topics of their mutual concern. There are more than 15,000 of these groups and their number grows daily. A microcommunity exists for virtually every hobby, political issue, lifestyle, race, and age that marketers would be interested in reaching.

Each system's services are remarkably similar in nature, although their structures and name conventions are not. In fact, based on the names, you wouldn't even guess that we were talking about the same areas. To help you get up to speed quickly, here is a table showing each service and the names given to each message area:

Service	Name	Messages
Internet	USENET Newsgroups (also called newsgroups), public mailing lists, and private mailing lists	Post articles
CompuServe	Forums or SIGs (special interest groups)	Message
America Online	Forums and Clubs	

For simplicity's sake, let's call them newsgroups except when we're pointing to specific matters concerning an individual area. Whatever the terminology, these are places where marketers can find potential prospects for their products.

Finding people online with special interests can be relatively easy to do, as they participate in forums catering to their needs. The online world is full of niches of people in different age groups, like senior citizens and high school students; jobs, like doctors and farmers; hobbyists, like mountain climbers and wine aficionados. People congregate into niche markets that online marketers can harvest if they follow the right steps.

HOW TO FIND TARGET GROUPS ONLINE

This table explains how to find niche markets congregated in forums:

Service	To find groups, type:
CompuServe	Go "directory" select menu option for either "search for list" by typing "topic" or "list all indexed topics" for a complete list.
America Online	Select "goto" from menu bar, select "directory of services," type "topic," press "enter" key.

Service	To find groups, type:
USENET Newsgroups	• A searchable collection of more than 54,000 mailing lists and newsgroups is located at the Liszt Web site, www.liszt.com.
	• You can also search Yahoo! for the topic. You might find newsgroups and mailing lists listed there. Or you could find Web sites devoted to that topic that have links to newsgroups and mailing lists.
	• The two leading browsers, Netscape Navigator and Microsoft Internet Explorer, both have newsgroup functions.
Internet Mailing Lists	• A list of mailing lists can be found www.neosoft.com /internet/paml.

BENEFITS OF USING NEWSGROUPS IN YOUR MARKETING PLAN

Online marketers consider newsgroups virtual gold mines on the digital frontier. They can benefit from reading messages in these highly focused forums in these ways:

- **Prospecting and retaining customers:** Marketers can reach hundreds and thousands of current and potential customers with one message.
- **Market research:** By reading messages you can find out what is hot, what people are talking about, and what their feelings are. While most messages are placed by members interested in finding answers to problems, you can also raise your own questions to find out what people are thinking about a topic of interest to you.
- **Crisis control and prevention:** By monitoring conversations you can find out what people are saying about your company and its products. If the word is bad, you can attempt to control the crisis by providing information and trying to solve the problem.
- **Building relationships:** By answering customers' questions you can help solve problems. By providing them with information you can enrich their experiences or empower them.

- **Publicity:** You can lead people to your related forum, Web site, or commercial site, provided that you do so in an informative, nonintrusive manner.
- **Becoming a recognized expert or leader in an industry:** This is a good strategy for consultants, as they can become known to hundreds or thousands of people, or to a select number of people in their specialized area of interest.

HOW TO RESPOND CORRECTLY TO MESSAGES

The arcane technology of posting messages can be confusing. Here are two tips for avoiding mistakes:

1. Some responses should go to the entire list; others should be sent to the poster's private e-mailbox. Be careful to do what you intend to do!

   Example: If the original post says "I've got this brilliant brochure I'd be happy to send to the people on this list. Send me e-mail if you'd like a copy," send your reply to the brilliant brochure maker, not the entire list!

2. When commenting on a post, quote only as much as absolutely necessary to make your points. Usually a line or two will do the trick.

   "When reading your reply, we all want to see your new contribution to the discussion, not the message we have already read," says Christina O'Connell, a marketing consultant. "Remember that many HTMARCOM [a mailing list devoted to High Tech Marketing Communications] members pay per message or per character for each and every post, so when you waste bandwidth by ignoring the above, you also cost members money. This is not the way to make a good impression on your professional colleagues on HTMARCOM."

Netiquette in a Nutshell

The golden rule of netiquette can be summed up in five words: Don't advertise in inappropriate areas. That seems pretty simple, but to drive the point home, here are a few definitions and examples of inappropriate advertising that should be avoided:

- blatant promotion of products

  Hi. I sell seashells by the seashore and online. Does anyone want to buy seashells? I can make you a good offer. Please send me e-mail and I'll respond quickly, or call 800-555-5555.

- blatant self-promotion of consultants

  Hi, I prepare taxes for small businesses. If you are a small business, I'll do your taxes.

- messages inappropriate to the group

  I know this group is for people who play bagpipes, but you must be concerned with health. I sell a power drink that increases stamina while you play bagpipes.

- get-rich-quick schemes

  You can make a fortune selling my product. Call me and I'll tell you how.

Those messages would probably be killed by the system administrators on the commercial networks before they reached the public, so if you tried to send them, you would be wasting your time. If you sent those messages to USENET newsgroups, they would be posted and read by people who have an inherent distaste for advertising. You probably would incur the wrath of hundreds of members, who would flame you with hate mail filled with profanity.

The effective online marketer respects the rules of the commercial online services and the netiquette of the Internet. Like karate masters, they learn to use the power of the force instead of fighting it. Three considerations should be added for online marketers: message length, appropriateness of topic, and spamming.

Message length: Because electronic mail is the main form of communication between parties on an online system, members get many pieces of mail each day. Message length becomes an issue. Messages should be short, not longer than 24 lines, which is about the size of a computer monitor. This works out to about 240 words, almost the same as a double-spaced sheet of regular typing paper. Messages should provide the gist of the material to be covered and ask readers if they want more information. Once permission is given, the follow-up message can be as long as needed to tell the story properly. If you follow this procedure, you will not be a victim of the kill file.

Appropriateness of topic: When you visit a discussion group, you will see a subject line indicating the topic at hand. It could be anything from "need advice" to "looking for a job" to "new and need help." What these messages have in common is that people are looking for answers to specific questions. It is considered rude to jump into a conversation with a topic that doesn't match the one in the subject line. If you want to discuss something, send a private note or start a new message with a new subject.

Spamming: Spamming is a technique of posting your messages to many discussion groups. You might think that multiple messages are a good way of blanketing your target audience. However, if you do this, you will incur wrath. People don't want to spend their time reading the same message over and over or to waste time and money killing duplicate messages. The rule is: Send your message once. If you forget this rule, some members will remind you—and not so nicely.

Here are rules to help you post well-mannered messages:

- **Be commercial in the right places:** Advertising is not allowed on most message boards. If you have a commercial announcement, place it only in message areas designed for that purpose, such as an Internet USENET newsgroup devoted to listing classified advertisements of computers for sale. It is possible to announce products or services in the few forums and newsgroups that specifically allow classified advertising. If in doubt, check first. Read the FAQs (frequently asked questions) and lurk (read messages) for a few days or weeks before posting an article.
- **Be focused:** Stay on the subject topic. If the topic is coffee, don't reply with a message about your favorite restaurant. Save that for a new topic.
- **Be redundant:** If you are responding to a message, summarize part of the message to which you are replying. Because people get so much mail, this will help remind the sender of the information and bring other people up to speed. However, don't include the entire

message, just a relevant excerpt or a paraphrase. Use arrows to indicate that this is text from an earlier message. For example:

>>On March 15, Dan Janal wrote:
>>Where's the best place to get a cappuccino in Danville?
The best place is Susan's Kitchen Cafe.

Many new versions of software automatically insert the previous message and arrows if you select the forward or reply options.

- **Be a giver:** Contribute to the community. Answer people's questions and calls for help. If you do, you will become a welcome member and build credibility in the group, which can help you promote your own business in a noninvasive manner.
- **Be singular:** Don't post the same message twice on the same forum. There are personal and technical reasons for this. People don't like wading through repetitive messages, especially when they are paying for each minute they are online or paying for each message received. The technical reason is that message boards have limited space. Once the queue is filled, older messages roll off the board and are replaced by new ones. If you waste space, you knock off messages that might actually help people.
- **Be quiet:** If you answer "Thanks" and "I agree" to every message, you will inadvertently force other people's responses off the board. When appropriate, send private mail, or use the term TIA for "Thanks in advance." The same is true for online conferences. Don't announce your comings and goings, and don't respond with "Hi" and "Bye." If there are a dozen people in the conference and all of them send greetings, the conversation grinds to a halt. Don't spam or send copies of letters to several forums or newsgroups. People get upset if they see the same note posted; additionally, the act of posting takes away from system resources and mailbox space that could be put to better use.
- **Be legal:** Obey the forum's rules on advertising, self-promotion, and etiquette. Scams, pyramid schemes, and stock fraud are as illegal online as they are in other media.
- **Be informed:** Read messages for a while to get a feel for the discussion before jumping in. Read help files or FAQs (Frequently

Asked Questions) to learn how the system operates and what is allowed.

Using proper netiquette shows that you are a member of the community who understands and respects its traditions.

MARKETING STRATEGIES THAT CONFORM TO NETIQUETTE

Lurk (Read Messages)

Benefit: Avoid being flamed.

Discussion: To make sure you don't violate netiquette, lurk (read) around the newsgroup for a few days to understand what the group discusses. You'll also avoid the faux pas of beginning a conversation about a topic that has been beaten to death.

Action: Go to your A-List of message boards; read messages, library files, FAQs, and other background files.

Answer Messages on Forums, Even If You Can't Promote Your Product

Benefit: Introduces you to the community as a model citizen. You raise your credibility when you answer questions that don't benefit you.

Discussion: Be a helpful neighbor. The best way to build credibility is to offer information. You might not actually be promoting your business or service, but you will be promoting yourself and building credibility. That will come in handy when people ask you what you do. They will be more apt to believe you because you are a member of the community.

Example:

I need to find a sales trainer who can teach my sales staff how to prospect without wasting time. Does anyone know someone who can do this?

You answer:

Gordy Allen of Leads Plus conducts great sales seminars and has written great workbooks for the sales staff and for the sales manager. You can reach him at 800-548-4571.

You also get exposure by displaying your signature file.

Action: Read newsgroups and answer questions that other members raise.

Answer Questions from Members that Lead Them to Your Product or Service

Benefit: Prospecting and increased exposure.

Action: Look for messages that you can answer with authority and that allow you to promote your product or service. When I mention this strategy at my seminars, someone always comes up to me afterwards and tells me how they used newsgroups to find information on buying tires, or planning trips to Europe, or the like. For example:

I have to write a business plan and I've never done one. Can someone suggest a software program that will do this?

Answer: Yes, try Biz Plan Builder from JIAN Software for Tools.

Answer: I write business plans for a living. My clients have included many start-ups and medium-sized companies. Please send a note if you would like more information.

Scan Message Areas for Mentions of Your Company

Benefit: Increased exposure.

Discussion: By looking for messages you can participate in and contribute to, you will help promote your company and product. It is not a violation of netiquette to join in a discussion about your own company or product.

Action: Check DejaNews daily to check messages that might affect your company. Create a list of forums on each commercial online service that reaches your audience. Assign the task of monitoring these areas to an employee trained to deal with sensitive issues and irate customers.

Create a Member Profile

Benefit: Prospecting. Inbound prospecting. People will get to know you better and faster.

Discussion: Most people online are merely names and numbers. They can be more than that. Forums allow you to create a member profile, which includes your interests, from professional to personal. Member profiles can be searched so people can find others who have similar interests. If you fill one out on yourself, other people can find you. The policy on this varies from forum to forum and system to system. Professional forums frequently allow you to post a description of yourself, which can include descriptions of your product or service. Check with the forums that feature topic headings like "Resumes," "Introductions," and "I'm new and here's what I do." If you use these options, you'll find prospects and they'll find you.

Action: Find forums that would attract your target audience. Follow the rules for creating a profile for yourself. Follow instructions for finding other members. Send them polite e-mail that strikes up a conversation. For example, let's say that you sell sailboats and supplies. You might send this message: "I see that you like to sail. I do too. I have a model x-200 and sail in San Francisco. Where do you sail?" If you get a response, you can begin to develop a relationship. As this relationship matures, you can then mention what you do and propose ways to help your new friend.

Ask for Additional Resources

Benefit: Prospecting.

Discussion: By posting questions that ask for additional sources on other forums, you might find more opportunities to interact with even more prospects. The answers might lead you to other areas on that system, to other online services, or to bulletin boards operated by enthusiasts or vendors.

Example: Let's say you sell mountain climbing equipment. You could search for sports, hiking, outdoors, exercise, vacations, and travel. Send a message:

Does anyone know of a local BBS or mailing list that covers mountain climbing?

Action: Post questions on those message boards asking if members know of other message boards for that audience.

Volunteer to Become a Sysop

Benefit: Increased exposure, credibility, and sales.

Discussion: You can increase your credibility and stature in your industry if you are part of the administration of the forum. This is a particularly good strategy for consultants, speakers, trainers, and other service providers. To become a sysop, first think of a topic that has long-lasting appeal on a message board that your prospects are likely to visit. This must be a topic that you are an expert on.

CASE STUDIES

Case Study: Bates Information Service

You can build rapport with people by answering questions people raise, just as Mary Ellen Bates of Bates Information Services did. She finds information for people who don't have the time or expertise to find the information themselves. She is an active member of several communities on the Internet and CompuServe.

"I participate when appropriate, usually giving recommendations of places to find information, names of trade associations and the like, and add that I'm an independent researcher who also does this for a living," says Bates. "There's plenty of value when I say, for example, in response to someone's query about finding market information on the XYZ industry, 'Here are several sources: the XYZ Trade Association, the XYZ Office at the Department of Commerce, and the BUSDB database on CompuServe. You might also want to contact an independent researcher to handle this research.' This establishes that I am enough of an expert that he can trust my advice and if he decides he doesn't want to do the work himself, he knows someone who can. I never post my phone number in these messages—just my name and company name. People e-mail me if they want more information."

Bates has landed clients on CompuServe and the Internet by using this approach. "There's a big difference between posting an ad, on the one hand, and posting an informative message with a mention at the end that this is what I do for a living. I've gotten some great clients this way and they're already convinced that I know what I'm doing because they've seen me in action," she says. "The bottom line is that people will listen to your messages and will think well of you if you add value to the discussion. There's no value added when someone posts an ad."

Case Study: Canyon InterWorks

Online marketers are master searchers. They search through forums that reach their target audiences, read messages to get a sense of the group, and wait for a relevant topic. They join the discussion with information about what they do. For instance, let's say your audience is small businesses and you see this note:

> Subj: business cards
> Date: 94-07-29
> From: Daniel241
> Gee, I wish I had a business card. Does anyone know where I can get them good but cheap?

You could respond as Chris Erichson did.

> Subj: daily Internet commerce
> Date: 94-07-30 20:35:30 EDT
> From: CANYONIWORKS@delphi.com
> To: Daniel241
>
> My company sells Internet Laser Cards—perforated cardstock sheets of 10 business cards—50 sheets per box. Each card displays a colorful "Internet Citizen" design—just feed the sheet through your laser or Inkjet printer, print your Internet address, name/company, telephone, etc. And pop them out. Crisp, clean edges, very professional and EXTREMELY useful.
>   If you want to get a better idea of what I am talking about, just leave mail, include your street address, and I will make sure we send you a sample.

"The key points are to answer their questions and help them," says Erichson, canyoniworks@delphi.com. "I offer my service/product in a way that relates to their needs. People pitch to me when I ask questions. I know they pitched me but they provided a highly probable solution to my problem in a helpful, nonaggressive way. It's all tact."

"I learned the golden rule: Net etiquette = Net success. Treat people with respect and read the FAQs," says Erichson, "I advertise on carefully researched USENETs and offer my product tactfully in related discussion threads. From this alone, I receive e-mail requests for info/samples with street addresses from around the world. I promptly mail them info and receive orders through the mail quickly and with a very high request-to-order ratio."

Case Study: Christina O'Connell

Newsgroups, forums, mailing lists, and the like can give PR pros considerable direct access to their customer base. "Bringing your message, in your own words, to these audiences can be extremely successful," says Christina O'Connell, an online public relations consultant. "*If* you know what you're doing! Hype, sales pitches, rehashes of stilted press releases don't cut it online, but ongoing availability to your customers, providing a genuine resource to appropriate audiences, etc., does.

"As Corporate Communications Manager for a computer hardware company, I initiated a broad online campaign that included daily monitoring of appropriate CompuServe forums, participation in discussions that involved our product line, e-mailed product information when requested, etc.

"One area where we were really successful was the promotion of new memory products. At the time, Apple was introducing several new PowerBooks, each with different memory configurations. Our company manufactured PowerBook memory boards. In a section of AOL that focused on PowerBook topics, I posted messages explaining the new configurations, giving advice on how to identify in-spec memory boards and what to do if you were sold out-of-spec boards. These messages were not pitches for our product but rather consumer-oriented posts on the lines of 'No matter who you buy memory from, here's what to ask when ordering.'

"The results included increased sales—folks trusted us because we knew what we were talking about and they knew where to find us; great corporate image boost as consumer-oriented and as engineering pros; a better-informed consumer base, which was valuable to us as quality manufacturers; and a nomination as 'Service Heroes' for being so helpful."

SUMMARY

To take advantage of the vast resource of targeted communities on newsgroups, forums, and the like, you must become a contributing member. If you provide people with answers to their questions, they will be quite receptive to learning more about your company and its services. If you provide information, not persuasion, you will be accepted.

CHAPTER TWENTY

Promoting Your Web Site

There are tens of thousands of Web sites on the Internet and they are all fighting for attention. Without a concerted marketing and promotion effort to promote it, your Web site could resemble a ghost town.

Fortunately, Web sites are relatively easy to promote. This chapter explains numerous strategies for getting attention. Even better, most of these methods are free, except for the employee time needed for execution.

HOW TO ATTRACT ATTENTION TO YOUR WEB SITE

When someone goes to a search engine and types "pasta" and finds 2,000 listings of companies selling pasta on the Internet, you'd like your site to be ranked first. Some search engines list all companies alphabetically, so you have no chance of being ranked first if your name is Ziti "R" Us. You'd have a much better shot if your company were called "Angel Hair Pasta, Inc." Because naming a company might be beyond the scope of activities you can perform, you need more ammunition. This chapter shows you ways to promote your site and have visitors return.

Here are 51 effective low-cost or no-cost strategies:

- Registration Tactics
  1. Register with search engines.
  2. Register under the appropriate category on Yahoo!
  3. List your Yahoo! Registration in two additional categories.
  4. Create compelling keywords.
  5. Add the META tag to your Web site.
  6. Create mission statements for proactive search engines.
  7. Create a title for each page.

8. Register with automated registration tools.
9. Register each product from your site.
10. Register with location-specific search engines.
11. Register with topic-specific search engines.
12. Check to see where your site is ranked.
13. Create a list of links.
14. Link to complementary sites.

- Publicity Strategies
  15. Notify the press about your new site.
  16. Notify the press about new content additions.
  17. Notify the press about new awards and distinctions.
  18. Encourage sites to reprint your information articles on their sites, or create links to your articles.
  19. Create a signature file.
  20. Post notices in newsgroups and mailing lists.
  21. Answer questions in newsgroups and lists.
  22. Win a "Cool Site of the Day" designation.

- Site Management Strategies
  23. Ask viewers to bookmark your site.
  24. Make your site the starting point for your customers.
  25. Create a personal mailing list and send updates to subscribers.
  26. Create a domain name that is easy to remember.
  27. Hire a professional firm to promote your site.

- Advertising Strategies
  28. Advertise the site on the Internet.
  29. Advertise the site in traditional media.
  30. Send direct-mail postcards to your customers or prospects.
  31. Create joint promotions with complementary sites.
  32. Pay commissions to other sites to refer people to your site.

- Promotion Strategies
  33. Print address on all marketing communications materials.
  34. Offer free products.
  35. Offer free information.
  36. Contribute funds to charity for each visit.
  37. Create your own awards.

38. Use novelties to keep your site address in front of people.
39. Add fun stuff.
40. Personalize the site.

- Strategies To Promote Return Visits
41. Create compelling content.
42. Create a "Cool Tip of the Day" page.
43. Update information on your page.
44. Notify people via e-mail when you update content.
45. Notify people via e-mail when you find information or offer new products they have requested.
46. Create an "insiders only" area that requires registration.
47. Operate surveys.
48. Conduct contests.
49. Require an offline activity to be performed before proceeding online.
50. Give coupons, discounts, and rebates.
51. Eliminate risks of buying.

REGISTRATION TACTICS

Register Your Web Site on the Search Engines

Purpose: Build traffic.

Discussion: Search engines are the *TV Guide*s of the Internet. They are vast databases of sites that can be searched by company name, industry, or keyword. Many people use search engines to begin their relationship-building experiences. By registering with search engines, people who didn't know you existed five minutes ago can visit your site. This service is free. The search engines generate revenue by selling advertisements. There are two kinds of search engines.

1. Passive search engines require you to register your site. Examples are:
   - Yahoo!, www.yahoo.com
   - Webcrawler, www.webcrawler.com
   - Lycos, www.lycos.com (When you register with Lycos, it will index each page on your site automatically.)

2. Proactive search engines explore the Web for new sites and list them automatically. You don't need to register your page at these sites because these engines add it automatically. In fact, you might want to search these engines now and see if your company is listed! Examples are:

- Alta Vista, www.altavista.digital.com
- Hotbot, www.hotbot.com
- InfoSeek, www.infoseek.com
- Excite, www.excite.com

There are several hundred search engines on the Internet. For a listing and descriptions, refer to the WebStep Top 100, www.mmgco.com /top100.html. However, the ones listed here get most of the traffic from consumers. There might be some search engines or directories that focus on your industry and you should make a special effort to find those and register your Web site with them. Search a major search engine with the words "directory" or "free links" to find additional promotional opportunities.

Search engines can be extremely effective tools to get people to learn about your company and go to your Web site. Lawyer Steven L. Kessler promoted his Web site on only one search engine, Yahoo!, and received more than 500 visits a month. Those visitors included several lawyers who wanted to network and a request from a trade magazine editor who asked him to write an article.

Trucost, a reseller of computer hardware and software, wanted to build business in a rollout process. It registered on Alta Vista and Yahoo! and received 150,000 visits the first month and 300,000 the second, which generated more business than it could handle.

Action: Registering your site is a simple process that involves a few easy steps. Here is the process for registering on Yahoo!:

- Write name of site, e.g., My Company.
- Write the address (URL, or Uniform Resource Locator), e.g., www.mycompany.com.
- Add keywords, which are comparable to index headings or topics. For example, a children's software company might use the keywords *software, children, learning,* and *math.* A financial investment service might use the keywords *money, investing, stocks,*

income, and *retirement.* Each search engine allows a different number of keywords. To be safe, create at least five.
• Add a two-sentence description of what your company does and what people will find at your site. For example, Joe's Travel Agency, specializing in vacations to Hawaii, offers readers a coloring book and ten tips on how to cut travel costs.
• For Yahoo!, select the category you want to be listed in, e.g., Business_and_Commerce:Public Relations Agencies.
• List your contact information (your name and e-mail address)
• Submit your form by clicking on the submit button.
• You will receive a confirmation note via e-mail.

Register Under the Appropriate Category on Yahoo!

Purpose: Prospects can find you easily.
Discussion: Yahoo! maintains a strict categorization of companies. This is good for marketers as all competitors are listed in the same area so customers can do comparison shopping.
Action: Go to Yahoo! and take these steps:

1. Find the category you want your site listed under. If you are not sure which category is appropriate, type the name of your closest competitor and see which category it is listed in. That might be the same category you should use.
2. Go to that category and make sure this is where you want your site located. Click on the "Add url" image and enter all the pertinent information.

List Your Yahoo! Registration in Two Additional Categories

Purpose: Increased exposure, more likely for prospects.
Discussion: Yahoo! lets you list your Web site in a total of three categories. This is beneficial for companies that sell multiple products. If you sell cookware, cookbooks, and cooking supplies, you can list your Web site in all three categories. It also helps companies that sell to multiple audiences. For example, a software company selling children's software could be listed under software, educational software, and games. You might find it useful to see which categories your competitors are listed in.

To do that, type in the name of your competitor. Yahoo! will display the categories.

Action: Go to Yahoo! and:

- Browse through Yahoo! to find the proper wording for each of the categories you want to be listed under.
- Write down the categories exactly as they appear. Register with Yahoo! There is a fill-in box on the registration form that asks for the titles of the categories to be listed. Write them in.

Create Compelling Keywords for Search Engines

Purpose: Your target audience can find your Web site more easily.

Discussion: When creating keywords, most business people think of nouns (e.g., travel, airplanes, cars, hotels). To go one step beyond your competitors, think like your customers and create keywords based on benefits. For example, a travel agency might use the keywords *travel, vacation, adventure, romance,* and *relaxation.*

Each search engine indexes on a different number of search terms, from five to about ten. Some Web masters decide to include every possible keyword on their site in the hope that search engines will expand their listings.

Use these keywords as well: your company name, each product name, names of competing products, names of competitors. That way, if a prospect types the name of a competing product or company she will see your company as well as the intended one. Many consumers, especially business-to-business consumers, will look at your site to see how it compares to the intended company. If you offer better quality or prices, you might get an order from a person who didn't even know you existed a few minutes ago! You can find the keywords your competitors use by going to their sites and using the browser's commands to view the document source.

Another strategy that worked at one time but is no longer effective is to list the top search terms several times. Search engines used to list the finds in order of how close a match there is. For example, a site that lists the keyword "publicity" five times will show up as a better match than a site that lists the same keyword only once. That no longer works because search engines decided to penalize this strategy, which is called "stuffing."

Action: Create the keywords, list them on your META Tags (described in the next section).

Add the META Tag to Your Web Site

Purpose: Aids search engines in identifying your keywords.

Discussion: META tags are HTML commands that contain your keywords and thus help search engines categorize your Web site so that prospects can find your pages. Most of the proactive search engines rely on the META tag to categorize your Web site. Customers don't see these commands; they are part of the HTML code, which is hidden from their view. The syntax is:

```
<META name="description" content="We specialize in grooming pink poodles.">

<META name="keywords" content="pet grooming, Palo Alto, dog">
```

The search engine will:

- index both fields as words, so a search on either poodles or dog will match.
- return the description with the URL. In other words, instead of showing the first couple of lines of the page, a match will look like the following:

Pink Poodles, Inc.

We specialize in grooming pink poodles.

www.pink.poodle.org/—size 3k—29 Feb 96

- index the description and keywords up to a limit of 1,024 characters.

Action: For a complete description of how to insert a META tag into your Web site, read instructions in the advanced section of Alta Vista, www.altavista.digital.com.

Create Mission Statement for Proactive Search Engines

Purpose: Helps your audience find you.

Discussion: These search engines take the first two or three lines from your site and list them on their directories as a short abstract. When people type your company name, they will see whatever your leading lines are. For example:

> My Company, the leading provider of travel services to Hawaii, offers Internet users a free listing of helicopter tours.

Place them at the top of the home page so the search engine will display them when people search for your site. If your first two lines read, "Welcome to our site. We are glad you came here," that is what readers will see as the result of a search on the search engine. However, if your first two lines read, "Our Company is the Internet's leading seller of cookware on the Internet. You'll find lots of bargains here," that's exactly what people will see when they search a search engine. Which would you rather they see?

Action: Create two sentences that will really grab your prospects.

Create a Title for Each Page

Discussion: Search engines read the HTML tag "title" and present that information on their searches. If your titles are descriptive, they can lure people to your site. Consider using your company name and brief description of what you do or a key benefit—for example, Widget Company, the leading manufacturer of widgets. If you have a lot of good information, consider using this format: YOUR COMPANY: How to save money on taxes.

The command looks like this:

```
<HTML>

<HEAD>

<TITLE>Widget Company: The leading manufacturer of widgets</TITLE>
```

If you do this, searchers will find out exactly what you do and will have a reason to go to your site. This tip might make the difference between someone visiting your site or visiting a competitor's site.

Action: Create title descriptions for each of your pages.

Register with Automated Registration Tools

Purpose: Saves time.

Discussion: Several software programs and services on the Internet automatically register your Web site with other search engines. The key benefit is that you can reduce the amount of time needed to register with dozens or hundreds of search engines. A possible disadvantage is that the page might not be registered accurately in these one-size-fits-all formats. For the maximum return on your time, register with the top eight services by hand and consider using a service to do the rest. Programs that perform this function include:

- Submit-it, www.submit-it.com
- Postmaster, www.netcreations.com/postmaster
- Site Promoter, www.sitepromoter.com

Action: Complete forms.

Register Each Product from Your Site

Purpose: Multiple exposures on search engines.

Discussion: Instead of merely registering your home page, register each product that has its own page on your Web site. This way, people can find out about more products more easily.

Action: Create a page for each product. Register each page using the tips from this section.

Register Your Web Site with Location-Specific Search Engines

Purpose: Increased exposure.

Discussion: If your Web site serves the residents or tourists in a specific geographic area, you should register your site with a search engine that meets the needs of that area. For example, businesses in Iowa can register with Iowa Online, www.iowa.net/links.submit. This strategy can bring new customers to your site who are planning to vacation in your area, start a new business, or are searching for specialty items from your neck of the woods.

Action: Use the major search engines to find these specific search engines. Register your site.

Register Your Web Site with Topic-Specific Search Engines

Purpose: Increased exposure.

Discussion: Many professions and industries have their own search engines, indexes, or list of links. By registering on these tools, prospects will find your business. An example of this is Find Links, www.find-links.com, which offers links to many different types of businesses and services.

Action: Use the major search engines to find these topic-specific sites.

Check To See Where Your Site Is Ranked.

Discussion: An online tool called Rank This, www.rankthis.com, shows you where your site is ranked on various search engines. That is, when people type "pasta" you'll find out exactly where you stand. If your ranking is low, people probably will not wade through hundreds of listings and learn about your site. If this is the case, you can use this information to your benefit by realizing that you need to take additional steps to improve the site's ranking, such as adding titles, keywords, mission statements, and other tactics described in this chapter.

Action: Go to the Rank This site and use the service. It is free.

Create a List of Links

Purpose: Increases attention and return visits.

Discussion: People love links. They love to follow links and find new things. Now you may be wondering why you should create links that allow people to leave your site after you've spent so much time, energy, and money to get them to your site in the first place. After all, Macy's doesn't have big signs in their shoe department pointing the way to the Kenneth Cole store in the mall. However, on the Web, you can be sure of one thing: people will leave your site. You can make that fact a pleasant experience by creating a list of invaluable resources for them to pursue. Obviously, you don't want to link to your competitors, but you can link to associations, news sources, and other related sites. By doing this, you are creating an invaluable resource for your readers, who will come back to check for updates. They also will tell their friends and colleagues about this resource.

Action: Create the list of links. Use a search engine to find relevant sources.

Link to Complementary Pages

Purpose: Increases exposure to prospects.

Discussion: If I sell Italian suits and you sell Italian shoes to the same audience, then we can complement each other by telling our customers about each others' services. We can each leverage off the investment the other has made in attracting and building an audience. Further, we don't risk losing these prospects to the complementary site because they are not competitors. (Don't link to another site selling suits, of course.) There is no charge for this service if you find friendly sites. The standard has been to give free links. However, as paid advertising becomes more prevalent on the Internet, some companies are charging for this service. You can see which sites have links to your Web site by typing in your company name or URL in any search engine. You'll find your own listings as well.

For example, CDnow is "the premier music seller featured on Yahoo!" Yahoo! will offer links to CDnow from music-related search pages and music category pages. CDnow will also prepare editorial material for inclusion in users' "My Yahoo!" pages, including lists of top-selling albums and other content elements.

Barnes & Noble and Lycos agreed to a three-year cross-promotional pact. Lycos will present users of its Internet search service with a list of books that match topics that users seek online.

Action: Find complementary pages by looking in the search engines. Send a short message to the Web master, the person who runs the Web site, asking if she would be interested in a reciprocal link. If she is, place a link from your site to hers.

PUBLICITY STRATEGIES

Notify the Press about Your New Site

Purpose: Phenomenal exposure to new audiences.

Discussion: This is one of the best methods to attract people to your site because the medium reaches so many people. If you send the press release to the media in your industry, you will reach a highly targeted audience as well. When McDonald's and Hyatt launched Web sites, *USA Today* wrote about them. When Pizza Hut announced you could order a pizza on the Internet, they received front-page publicity in nearly every top-tier newspaper and television station in the country—even though only one store in Santa Cruz, California, was participating in this offer! When *USA Today* wrote about the Miss America Web site to promote the annual pageant, the site received more visits than it had by any other marketing method, according to Nola Armijo of JONA Group, the public relations firm that got the placement.

Fortunately, for many industries and in many towns, opening a store on the Web is still news. This might change as more and more companies go online.

So take advantage of this opportunity while it still exists. *USA Today* and *Advertising Age* regularly print articles about new Web sites in industries large and small. *NetGuide* and *Internet World* also print reviews in their nationally distributed magazines.

Action: Write a press release. Find your target media by browsing publications or by using Bacon's Media Tracker (available in libraries by calling 800-621-0561). Send the release to them via e-mail or regular mail. PR Newswire can send a press release to the technology press via e-mail, fax, or regular mail, depending on the reporter's stated preference (800-832-5522).

Press Release Primer

- **Headline:** tells the gist of the story in five or six words, written in active style, centered in larger type than rest of press release.
- **Lead Paragraph:** tells the essence of what is new and answers the questions who, what, when, where, why, and how. It also points out the benefits of the site to the reader.

The rest of the press release gives more explanation and examples of what is contained at the site.

The last paragraph includes background information about the company, such as when it was founded, what it is known for, awards, and other memorable achievements.

Be sure to include the Internet address, or URL, in the first paragraph so reporters can find the site quickly.

Follow the style in this example by substituting your own information and you'll have the basics of a good press release.

Sample Press Release
For immediate release

Contact
Your name, phone number and e-mail address

My Company Creates Web Site on the Internet

YOUR CITY—TODAY'S DATE—Mycompany, short positioning statement, today opened a store on the Internet at www.mycompany.com. The site contains information about the company and buying products online, by telephone, or by visiting the company's real store at 123 Main Street.

Guests will be able to read the company's history, its annual report, and about its role in the community. They also will be able to find out the latest specials, prices, and discounts on products. Children will be able to retrieve free games, contests, and coloring books. Current customers will be able to find answers to common problems and get customer support online at any time of the day, seven days a week.

"We are providing our customers with more information and service that helps make their lives more productive, interesting, and fun," said Big Boss, president of Mycompany.

Company backgrounder.

###

Notify the Media about New Content

Purpose: Increased exposure.

Discussion: As news about new Web sites become old hat, the media will increasingly report on what is new on existing Web sites. If you have a new game, article, sample, or the like, you could get coverage. Neuberger and Berman Management, Inc., a no-load mutual fund firm, commissioned a survey that showed baby boomers were not saving enough money to send their kids to college. They issued a press release with this information in conjunction with the launch of their Web site, www.nbfunds.com, which features a worksheet for estimating the cost of a college education. The press release was printed in daily newspapers, including the *San Francisco Chronicle*.

Action: See steps in previous strategy.

Notify the Press about New Awards and Distinctions

Purpose: Increased exposure.

Discussion: The media could cover news of your new awards and distinctions, like being named one of the Cool Sites of the Day.

Action: See steps in previous two strategies.

Encourage Sites to Reprint Your Information Articles on Their Sites or Link to Them

Purpose: Draws people and increases word of mouth from satisfied browsers.

Discussion: The more people see your article, the more chances you have of gaining new clients and customers.

Some people have a hard time with this one. They are concerned about copyright and think that any time anyone uses their work, those people must pay. Let me say this: You cannot pay people enough to post your work on their site. They are giving you a third-party endorsement, much like newspapers and magazines. You can't pay for that kind of credibility.

Action: Write the article. At the top of each article you write, post the following message:

This article can be reprinted on your Web site or in your print publication provided you:

- print my name and contact information
- print the copyright notice
- print this message
- notify me of the publication date
- send me a copy of the printed article

You can send e-mail to complementary sites that would attract your target audience or wait for enterprising souls to find your articles.

Create a SIG, or Signature File

Purpose: Useful in creating an identity for your soft-sell image in newsgroups and mailing lists.

Discussion: Targeted newsgroups and mailing lists are composed of your potential audience members. You need to communicate with them, but netiquette forbids the posting of advertisements in these areas. The first step to using these areas effectively is to create a signature file, also called a sig file. This is a four- to six-line message that tells people who you are, where you work, what you (or the company) do, and how they can contact you.

Action: Create your signature.

Example:

>>>

Daniel Janal * Janal Communications * 510-648-1961

Author, Speaker, Marketing Consultant

Online Marketing Handbook * *101 Successful Businesses You Can Start on the Internet*

http:/www.janal.com/   dan@janal.com

>>>

Post Information Articles in Newsgroups and Mailing Lists

Purpose: Increases exposure to your target audience.

Discussion: This strategy can be dangerous if used incorrectly. Newsgroups and mailing lists do not want to be commercial areas and forbid notices of a commercial nature. If you send a commercial announcement, you will receive hundreds of flames or hate mail. People could boycott your site and encourage their friends to do the same. So don't do it!

However, you *can* post notices that you have just created a site that would appeal to them, or have information on that site that would enhance their professional or personal lives.

Here are examples:

- **Not acceptable:** The Fly Fishing Store has opened a site on the Web, at www.fishing.com. Come to our store and find the lowest prices on the Web!

- **Acceptable:** The Fly Fishing Store has opened a site on the Web at www.xyzfish.com. Come and read about the best places to fish in Montana.

>>>

John Smith * Fishing Store * 800-555-1212

Complete Supply of Everything for the Enthusiast

http:/www.xyzfish.com/   john@xyzfish.com

>>>

Action: Find appropriate groups. Write messages. Post along with signature file.

Answer Questions in Newsgroups and Mailing Lists

Purpose: Builds credibility and exposure.

Discussion: Many people post questions of a noncommercial nature in mailing lists and newsgroups, such as, "Where is the best place to go fishing in Montana?" You can build credibility and exposure by answering the question; even if the question doesn't benefit you directly, answering it will benefit you because thousands of people will see your name and company information in the signature file. This strategy complies with the Internet rule of being a good netizen by contributing to the community and offering something of value for free.

Action: Look for appropriate newsgroups and mailing lists. Search for questions you can answer. Answer them. Attach your signature file.

Example:

>Dan Janal writes:

>Where is the best place to go fishing in Montana?

Try the Old Man's Fishing Hole, 30 miles east of Bozeman.

Happy trails!

>>>

John Smith * Fishing Store * 800-555-1212

Complete Supply of Everything for the Enthusiast

http:/www.xyzfish.com/   john@xyzfish.com

>>>

Special note: *Don't subvert the system* by having a friend post a leading question like "Can you recommend a telephone answering machine?" if you sell that equipment. You could answer the question, but someone will find out that the question was a plant and will expose you. Even worse, you don't control the conversation, so unhappy customers could vent their frustrations, thus exposing your product to damage. People who use competing products could also tell how much they like other products, so you can't win in the end if you use this bad, inappropriate gimmick.

Win a "Cool Site of the Day" Designation

Purpose: Adds credibility to your site and increases traffic.

Discussion: With thousands of Web sites on the Internet, viewers look to authorities to point them to the more interesting sites. At first, several companies issued their top picks, which were called "Cool Site of the Day" or the like. Today, more than 1,000 companies or people issue their picks for cool Web pages and tell their audiences every day or week. Some are well known, like Point's Top 5 Percent of the Web. Others look only at vertical market areas, like health care or dogs. Still others are issued by everyday people as a service to their friends. The two major browsers from Netscape and Microsoft also promote sites their staff consider hot. You can find these sites on the main tool bar of each browser.

When people read about these cool sites they visit them. When the Ketchum Kitchen, www.recipe.com, was featured on Netscape's "What's New" section, it received 40,000 hits, compared to its normal rate of 4,000 hits a day.

These companies also issue a postage-stamp-sized graphic that can be displayed on your site. This award will build credibility for your site as well.

Action: Search Yahoo! for the latest sites. Read the rules for entering your site in competition. Fill out the form. Search Netscape and Microsoft Internet Explorer for their hot sites and read information about how to submit your site.

For "What's New" at NCSA, send e-mail to: whats-new@ncsa .uiuc.edu.

For "Cool Site of the Day," send e-mail to cool@infi.net and describe your site.

SITE MANAGEMENT STRATEGIES

Ask People to Bookmark Your Site

Purpose: Encourages repeat visits among prospects and customers.

Discussion: If people visit your site once, they might visit again if they see a reminder in their bookmark section. A bookmark is a software tool that automatically loads the page it refers to.

Action: Place a notice on your home page or subpages saying "Bookmark this page!"

Encourage People to Mark Your Page as Their Starting Page

Purpose: Builds repeat visits to your site; builds brand awareness.

Discussion: Netscape Navigator and Microsoft Internet Explorer default to their home page when viewers sign on each session. However, this default can be set to any page. If you encourage people to set the start-up to your page, they will see your news and updates every time they sign on.

Why would they want to do this? Perhaps you can offer a contest or coupons that make it worth their while to see what you are up to. Be creative! While this might be difficult to do if you are a business that people will use only once in their lifetime, organizations that have a need for regular communications with their customers, employees, or members will not find this task difficult. For example, a trade association of human relations professionals offered free software to their members and set the start page to be their Web site. Members found this useful as they needed to be kept up to date on their industry's affairs.

Action: Post a message on your home page asking people to change their starting page to yours. Offer them benefits. Explain how to perform this function.

Create a Personal Mailing List and Send Update Notices to Subscribers

Purpose: Encourages repeat visits among prospects and customers.

Discussion: People may visit your site once but never again because of the competition for attention. Even if people bookmark for your site, they might not necessarily visit it often.

If you ask people to join your mailing list, you can send them e-mail notifying them of new articles and offerings at your site. This strategy can build repeat traffic from people who have identified themselves as being interested in your company. Another strategy is to simply send the newsletter out to your subscribers, thus saving them the effort of going to your Web site. This tactic also reaches out effectively to people who only have e-mail systems but don't have access to the World Wide Web, which is a fairly common practice at many organizations.

Action: Add a form to your site that asks people to subscribe for free to your update service. Compile the list. Update the page. Send out the notices.

CASE STUDY: FLYING NOODLE PASTA

We are a gourmet pasta and pasta sauce retailer, have been online since December 1995, and our site generates 30 percent of our total sales. The remainder is from direct mail.

A commercial Web site should focus on many things; two of the most important are bringing new people to the site and giving all visitors a reason to return.

The main reason to update your site is to keep it interesting for repeat visitors. First-time visitors don't know how fresh your information is and, frankly, don't need to know.

Hence, there is no point in updating your site unless you have a way to tell previous visitors that you have added new information.

What we, and many other sites do, is offer a free e-mail newsletter to help drive people back to the site. Every two months we send out a newsletter with the following information:

1. prize winner name
2. article relevant to food/pasta
3. recommended food site
4. "Noodle News"
5. sale items
6. how to order
7. how to get off this list

The hook to get people to subscribe to our newsletter is the drawing from our sub-scriber list for a free month in our Pasta Club.

The article gives the publication credibility and gives the reader something useful. Recent articles have dealt with olive oils, balsamic vinegars, what makes one pasta bet-ter than another, how to jazz up boring supermarket sauces, etc.

The recommended food site is often a place that we have traded links with—generally commercial, always food-related. Often the other site will mention us in their newsletter.

Then we get to the good stuff. The Noodle News section deals with updates to our site, new products we are offering, recent publicity on our company, and any other news-worthy happenings.

The sales items are offered for a limited time to subscribers of the newsletter only and are different from the sales items on our Web site. We always refer people to the Web site sale items as well.

The other two items are self-explanatory.

When the newsletter goes out (we have around 2,000 subscribers) there is always a flurry of new sales and our visitor stats take a jump for a few days.

We find that sending the newsletter out every two months is often enough, without being intrusive, and isn't so often to be a logistical problem.

So, by all means update your site—just don't do it in a vacuum.

Raymond K. Lemire, The Big Parmesan, flying@ici.net, www.flyingnoodle.com, 1-800-566-0599

Create a Domain Name that Is Easy to Remember

Purpose: People will come to your site more easily if they remember its name.

Discussion: A domain name is the name by which the Internet user finds your site. An example is *http://www.janal.com*. "HTTP" stands for hypertext transfer protocol; it is assumed to precede Web addresses. "WWW" stands for World Wide Web. "Janal" is my company name. "Com" stands for commercial (or business). Your first choice should be to pick your company name to be your domain name and register it with InterNIC, the central registration agency of all domain names on the Internet. If that name is taken, you might be able to use a variation of the name. For example, if Janal were taken, I might have used Janal-Communications instead, or Janalcompany or Janalinc. If a product is more well known than your company, you might register that instead, such as "Tide" instead of "Proctor and Gamble." Some companies use their slogans, like Southwest Airlines, which uses www.iflyswa.com. This is worthwhile only if customers remember your slogan. You can also register your category, if people think of that first. For example, I helped Cambridge Publications, Inc., a company that writes documentation for computer software companies, register the domain www.documentation.com.

Action: Register your domain name or names by calling your ISP or InterNIC. Fees are $100 to register the name and $50 a year to maintain the name.

Hire a Professional Firm to Promote Your Page

Purpose: Saves you time.

Discussion: Most of the techniques described in this chapter are so simple that anyone can effectively promote his site. However, you might want to hire a professional company that specializes in this service to save time and leverage off their expertise. It might make sense to hire an expert so you can concentrate on running your business, selling products, or doing whatever it is that you do best. Also, if the task involves conducting a lot of online research, like reading newsgroups and mailing lists for opportunities to mention your product or contribute to the community, then a professional might be more economical.

Action: Hire a firm. Check Yahoo! for companies in this category; ask for references and check them out. Compare prices.

ADVERTISING STRATEGIES

Advertise the Site on the Net

Purpose: Ads expose your message to new audiences.

Discussion: Banner ads are becoming more evident on the Internet with each passing week. By placing ads on search engines and sites that attract your target audiences, you can convince them to visit your site as well.

Delta Point, www.deltapoint.com, bought a banner ad on Yahoo! to build awareness for its Web site authoring tool, Dynaweb. Within two weeks it had 20,000 free downloads of the demo version of their product. The ad "exceeded all expectations," said Eric Larsen, elarsen@ncom .com, a consultant to the company.

Action: Create the ad banner. Study the demographics of various sites to find the right fit. Negotiate the advertising rate. Study the number of hits you receive and whether or not they result in leads or sales. Read Chapter 12 for information on how to create great ads.

Advertise the Site in Traditional Media

Purpose: Increases exposure.

Discussion: More and more companies are displaying their Internet address in classified and display advertising sections of daily newspapers, business publications, and trade media. Advertisers range from small tax preparers to large car companies. Even TV ads are featuring Web addresses. Nearly every movie from Hollywood has a Web site filled with games and press materials. The studios run the typical ad for the movie but end it with the Web site address. Companies like MCI, Toyota, and IBM list their Web site address on their TV ads as well.

Action: Talk with your advertising department or agency about including the Web site address on all ads in all media. Buy advertising in a publication that reaches your audience.

Send Direct Mail Postcards via U.S. Mail to Your Customers or Prospects

Purpose: Increases attention.

Discussion: If you don't have the e-mail addresses of your target audience, you can send them postcards via the U.S. mail to let them know about the creation of your Web site and all the new features and free services. If they are not online, your wealth of offerings might convince them to get accounts!

The *Wall Street Journal* announced its interactive edition by sending a 5.5 x 8.5-inch postcard (presorted, first class rate) to subscribers of their noninteractive print edition. The postcard offered two months free if people signed up before a certain date. The teaser read, "After that, it'll pay for itself." Subscription prices followed, as well as a toll-free number for more information and how to access the Web.

You can send electronic postcards through e-mail as well. Go to a postcard site, like Greet Street, www.greetstreet.com, and send your advertising information in the postcard and include a picture. Suggest the recipient visit your site to get a free item or free information. This idea is still novel so you might gather a good many visits.

Action: Create the postcard and send it to your mailing list.

Create Joint Promotions with Complementary Sites

Purpose: Increases traffic to both sites.

Discussion: If I sell shoes and you sell hats, we can agree to post coupons of discounts that would lead people to each other's sites. This can be done in any number of ways: mention my site and get a discount; buy something at my site and get a discount at the other site.

Action: Find complementary sites. Offer a promotion. You are limited only by your imagination.

Pay Commissions to Other Sites to Refer People to Your Site

Purpose: Increases traffic.

Discussion: If a complementary site has done a good job in attracting qualified prospects, you might be able to lure them on to your site by paying to put a link or ad on the complementary site. Prices for this type of service are very elastic, so negotiate heavily.

Action: Find complementary sites. Send e-mail to Web master with proposal.

PROMOTION STRATEGIES

Print Web Site Address on All Marketing Communications Materials

Purpose: Exposure to people who use your products.

Discussion: Companies print their Web addresses on their marketing communications material and anything that doesn't move (and some things that do!). Print the address on your press releases, brochures, advertisements, letterheads, envelopes, and business cards. Molson prints its URL on a billboard leading from the Toronto airport to downtown. Joe Boxer weaves the URL into the waistband of its underwear and on roadside billboards (which yielded 15,000 e-mail requests in San

Francisco and Los Angeles). Other companies print the URL on trinkets like pens, mouse pads, and Frisbees. Distinct Corporation printed its address on coasters given to trade show attendees. Fernwood, an interactive soap opera on the Web, distributed its URL on bars of sample-size soap.

Action: Call your graphic artist and incorporate the address into appropriate materials. Be creative!

Offer Free Products

Purpose: Draws people and increases word of mouth from satisfied browsers.

Discussion: If location, location, location are the three magic words in real estate, then free, free, free are three magic words in online marketing. You can lure people to your site by offering them free samples or information.

The Seattle FilmWorks Company, www.sfw.com, lured people to its site by offering them two free rolls of film. Not only did this have the intended effect of drawing people to the site, it also meant that people had to divulge their names and addresses to receive the film! SFW went a few steps further to build customer support by offering a free screen saver that turned pictures into images that would appear on their computers. Everyone who uses the Internet has a computer and loves the idea of getting more software for it, especially if it is free. Software companies are changing the way their products are being distributed by offering software that runs for a short period of time via the Internet.

However, you don't have to be in the software industry to offer software. During the presidential primaries, Bob Dole offered his supporters free screen savers and wallpaper showing him standing outside the White House.

Most major record producers, like Warner Bros. and RCA, offer 30-second sound clips and personal messages from their top performers via the Web sites and forums on CompuServe. The files are available before the record is released so the online world feels like it is getting something special. The record company benefits as well, as top fans create word of mouth on the new song.

Small, independent musicians post free files of their songs so new audiences can hear a sneak preview. If they like the music clips, they can order the entire CD.

Software companies release demo versions of their software for free, hoping satisfied users will buy the full version of the product.

Action: Contract to create these files and post them on your site. Post notices of their availability in appropriate newsgroups, mailing lists, and forums.

Offer Free Information

Purpose: Draws people and increases word of mouth from satisfied browsers.

Discussion: Information-based companies, such as those that print reports, can post a press release announcing a major news item. Many research companies do this on the Internet, as they realize their audiences will be attracted to the headline but need deeper levels of statistics and explanation than are included in the press release.

Companies not in the information industries can also post files that help enhance the lives of their customers and prospects. If you sell gas grills, list dozens of barbecue recipes. The Windmere Real Estate Company, www.windmere.com, posts files on how to improve a house's curb appeal. The idea is that the information attracts prospects; the noncommercial nature of the article builds trust and credibility that turns them into clients.

Consultants and speakers also post information articles. My site, www.janal.com, features my latest thinking on online marketing topics. Prospects and clients can read the articles for free. If they know that the site will be updated regularly, they come back periodically and tell their associates.

Action: Write articles and post them on your Web site.

Contribute Funds to Charity for Each Visit

Purpose: Publicity.

Discussion: Media Synergy, www.mediasyn.com, a Toronto-based software company specializing in graphic tools for the PC, contributes ten cents to the Hunger Project for each person who visits their Web site and fills out a form. The form asks people for suggestions on how they might use the company's product, which allows people to send multimedia messages over the Internet. The best suggestions are published. This helps the company gather research information and customer input.

This is an example of a strategy that can get publicity in traditional media as well as create a positive word-of-mouth campaign on the Internet. It also proves the adage about doing well by doing good.

Action: Find a worthy cause. Issue a press release to media that cover your industry, the charity's target group, and other relevant audiences.

Create Your Own Awards and Issue Them to Cool Sites

Purpose: Creates exposure on complementary site; positions your company as an authority.

Discussion: As long as everyone and her brother are creating awards, why not create one yourself and notify the happy winners? You will be seen as an authority and will build traffic to your site from people who are looking to find previous winners.

Action: Search for the sites using Yahoo! or another search engine. Read and rate the sites. Create a clever logo. Notify winner. Create an index of all top winners so people can link to them as well.

Case Study: Dog-e-zine

Creating legitimate awards can take a fair amount of time, as a researcher must find, read, and rate sites. However, the results can be worth it. Wildwood Interactive created the Dog-e-zine, www.dog-e-zine.com, to promote sales of its CD-ROM, The Wizard of Dogs.

By creating the rating system, Wildwood built an editorial database that gives the site validity as a place to visit. Instead of giving stars as signs of the merit of the award, they give bones. Four bones is a great site.

A logo was designed for the awards and sent to the winners.

Winners were so pleased with the accolades that they posted the logo on their page. The logo included a link back to the Dog-e-zine. In this manner, the audience of the four-bone winners became readers of the Dog-e-zine. The number of visits grew exponentially with a new award given each week.

Use Novelties to Keep Your Web Site Address in Front of People

Purpose: Increases impressions of your company while providing a useful device for consumers.

Discussion: Putting your Web site address on something that will be seen often is a great benefit. While the easy options are mouse pads and coffee cups, other companies are getting very creative without spending a fortune. Smartbiz, www.smartbiz.com, a site that offers thousands of free documents for marketers, keeps its name on desks by offering a free tent card with space for people to write their user ID and passwords for a dozen sites that require this information. At the top of the list is Smartbiz. When I first received the card, I thought it was a dumb gimmick—until I couldn't remember my codes! Then it became invaluable and earned a spot on my desk.

Action: Brainstorm! Or talk to your novelty sales person for ideas.

Add Fun Stuff

Purpose: Create word of mouth.

Discussion: In addition to information, Pacific Bell Voice Mail offers fun stuff at their site, www.pbvoice-mail.com/fun. You can type in your phone number and receive a printout of what the number spells (each number being related to a set of three letters on the telephone keypad).

Action: Brainstorm for an idea that is fun and relates to your product or service.

Personalize the Site

Purpose: Builds relationships.

Discussion: Lafeber Corp., www.lafeber.com, an upscale bird food manufacturer, personalizes a cartoon with the person's name after a visitor signs the guest register. Visitors can then order T-shirts with their personal cartoon.

Action: Brainstorm!

STRATEGIES TO PROMOTE RETURN VISITS

Create Compelling Content

Purpose: Encourages repeat visits.

Discussion: If the purpose of your site is to create brand awareness or if people usually buy your products only after numerous impressions, it is essential that you convince prospects to return. If you give people great content or clear benefits for visiting your site, they will return. Great content could be interesting and useful articles, like L'Oreal, www.loreal.com, offering hints on makeup and skin tones. UPS, www.ups.com, allows you to check the status of a package. Wells Fargo Bank, www.wellsfargo.com, permits you to find the balance on your checking account. Many sites offer free stock quotes and news, like Scudder, www.scudder.com. Several companies have adopted a soap opera story that hooks readers into coming back day after day, like "As the Lasagna Bakes" at Ragu, www.eat.com. The History Channel, www.historychannel.com/today, shows what happened on this day in history. Century 21 Real Estate Corp. provides information on demographics, schools, and financing for 112 communities across the United States and Canada on its site on America Online (keyword: real estate). The San Jose Municipal Employees Credit Union, www.mecusj.org/javacalc.htm, lets people find out the cost of a loan by typing numbers into a calculator on their site (Figure 20–1).

Action: Brainstorm to think of the kind of content you can create for your site.

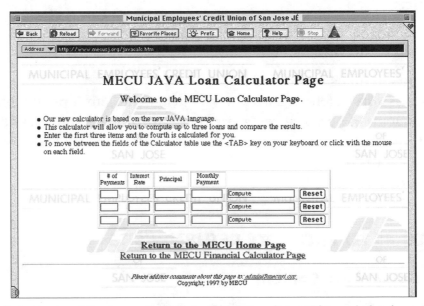

Figure 20–1. Municipal Employees Credit Union of San Jose lets members calculate loans. (Courtesy of MECUJC.)

Tell Jokes

Purpose: Generates repeat visits.

Discussion: People like to be entertained, no matter what industry they are in—even the dry realm of economics, which has jokes at www.etla.fi.pkm/joke.html. Rodney Dangerfield has a list of jokes at www.rodney.com/rodney/index.htm. People tell their friends about the joke sites and visit repeatedly.

Action: Develop the jokes. Add a new one each day.

Create a "Cool Tip of the Day" Page

Purpose: Encourages repeat visits.

Discussion: A "Cool Tip of the Day" page includes a neat new tip that enhances the reader's personal or professional life. It might be a sentence or a paragraph long. It could be information like how to be a better gardener or how to repair something around your home or how to market something on the Internet. If readers know the site is updated every day, they will come back for more information every day.

Examples:

- "Cool Marketing Tip of the Day" Page, www.wgi.com, lists excerpts from various Internet marketing books (including this one). Authors are happy because they get exposure to new markets. The Webster Group, which publishes the site, gets traffic to promote its marketing services. Everyone wins.

- Each week Merriam-Webster editors post a new Word of the Week, www.patmeier.com/wow/wodwelcm.htm. Editors provide the part of speech and a basic definition as well as a sentence using it in context and a "Did you know?" section offering a bit of interesting word lore. Previously posted words are kept in an archive so you can check the words for days when you didn't have a chance to get online.

Action: Create content. Then you will need to either manually update the tip each day or create or license software to do this for you automatically. Search the "tip of the day" sites (search Yahoo! or Alta Vista) to see if you can license the code from an existing site.

Update Information on Your Web Site

Purpose: Generates repeat visits.

Discussion: Adding new articles, games, and other content will increase the number of visits by prospects. No one knows how often a site should be updated. A good rule of thumb is once a month or once a week, if you adopt a magazine approach. If you offer time-sensitive information, like stock or mutual fund quotes, you need to update the page every few minutes. If you operate a business-to-business site that offers a solitary line of products and don't want to devote a lot of time to it, then you might update it only when new pricing, products, or specifications are announced.

Action: Update as often as necessary.

Notify People via E-Mail When You Update Your Web Site

Purpose: Generates repeat visits.

Discussion: People won't know that your site has been updated unless they take an active step and visit (which could be frustrating to them if you don't update the site as often as they check it). To encourage repeat visits, send out notification by e-mail whenever you post new information. You can gather e-mail addresses by asking visitors to register. HotWired, the electronic version of *Wired* magazine, sends out HotFlash, a weekly newsletter of events and information. You can join my free mailing list to read about updates to this book by sending e-mail to dan@janal.com.

Action: Create forms to gather e-mail addresses, store names, and send out information.

Notify People via E-Mail When You Find Information or Offer New Products They Have Requested

Purpose: Builds sales.

Discussion: For companies that sell products, consider asking customers to let you know what products they are interested in, should those products be out of stock or not yet created. You notify them when those products appear. Using this tactic will also let you build a database of customers' needs and desires.

Example: Amazon Books, www.amazon.com, asks readers to fill out a simple form about their interests or tastes so that the company can notify them when books from a particular author, genre, or topic are published. (Companies that sell videos, music, magazines, and the like can also use this strategy.) When it finds a book that matches your criteria, Amazon sends the following note:

Hi. Per your request, we at Amazon.com Books are notifying you of new books matching the following criteria:
Internet Marketing
Online Marketing Handbook

Action: Build the form.

Create an "Insiders Only" Area That Requires Registration

Purpose: Helps create a sense of exclusivity.

Discussion: By creating a password-protected area on your Web site, you give people the feeling of belonging to a special community. You can also gather demographic information from the members. Industry.Net offers a great deal of information to all visitors but requires them to register in order to download highly valued industry-specific software programs.

Action: Decide what content should be cordoned off. Talk to your Web site designer to implement the password system. Talk to your marketing staff to determine what demographic material is needed. As people don't necessarily like to fill out this information, create a priority of needs so that you get the information that is most important.

Operate Surveys

Purpose: Encourages repeat visits.

Discussion: People like to see what other people are thinking. That's why presidential polls are so popular. Web sites can survey their readers on issues of the day or topics in their industry. Surveys serve the additional purpose of gathering useful statistics from your target audience to use in marketing research. If the information is newsworthy, you can issue a press release announcing the findings.

Prodigy used this strategy effectively in a number of forums to find out people's thoughts of the day. Respondents had the option of identifying themselves by age, race, sex, and region of the country. The results could be searched on those categories as well to provide viewers with interesting insights. By tabulating results instantly, people had instant gratification.

The granddaddy of all polling firms, Gallup, maintains a polling site on the Internet, www.gallup.com, that lets people enter their opinions and read the results of famous surveys.

Action: Create a survey that ties into your integrated message or reinforces your company mission.

Conduct Contests

Purpose: Creates widespread attention and repeat visits.

Discussion: At any given time there are more than 1,000 companies offering contests to draw people to their sites. Prizes can range from $1 million in CompuServe's Hunt to two free tickets to a minor league baseball game sponsored by Commonwealth Bank in Virginia. Sunny Delight offers college-bound students an Internet scavenger hunt and a chance to win a $10,000 scholarship. This ploy received nationwide attention in *USA Today*.

Accutrade, www.accutrade.com, an online discount stockbroker, created a stock market trading game. Every participant was credited with $100,000 in play money. The person with the most valuable portfolio at the end of the game wins a free trade every day for life.

Microsoft created a contest for people who used their Front Page program to create home pages. This is a great idea because it caused people to buy the program and use it in order to have a chance at winning.

Contests are best when they reinforce the sponsoring company's mission or core values. For example, Amazon.com, the online bookstore mentioned earlier, conducted a contest in which customers wrote a segment to a short story begun by literary icon John Updike. The company awarded $1,000 to each winner, and entered all winners in a $100,000 lottery. More than 280,000 entries were received, which averages out to nearly 9,000 entries per day!

Crayola conducted a contest for adults to draw artwork with their crayons. The contest was judged by children. The company regularly conducts contest for children to create greeting cards—for example, for

Mother's Day. This type of contest helps encourage the use of the company's products, a very smart marketing move.

Contests can be conducted as simply as asking people to identify themselves; by filling in a form stating name, address, phone, and e-mail address so they can win in a random drawing; or as involved as a challenge or test of skills, as in the Crayola crayon coloring contests, trivia contests, and essay and photo contests.

One clever strategy could be to create a contest that asks people to tell why they desperately need a new copy of whatever you are selling. Give away a certain amount as prizes. The rest of the entrants become leads for your sales staff—equipped with the prime buying motive as stated by the prospects themselves!

Another benefit of all this contest activity is that winners can be promoted on local newspapers and television. In the case of Amazon, which has daily winners, there are numerous opportunities for publicity in many local markets.

Action: Create a useful contest. The more the contest relates to the company's products and mission, the more effective the overall result will be in reinforcing the marketing mission. For example, the Crayola coloring contests requires the use of crayons. This act reinforces sales and use of the company's products. A contest involving children in writing an essay about the use of crayons in folk art would not be as effective.

Case Study: Hotel Discounts

Hotel Discounts, www.hoteldiscounts.com, sells hotel rooms via the Internet. To stimulate traffic to their site, it created a contest in which business travelers were asked to write about their "Trip from Hell." The prize was a weekend vacation in Boca Raton, Florida.

More than 13,000 people either entered the contest or read the entries. All entries were posted online. The site was so popular that 50 people a day still visit the site even though the contest ended months ago.

The contest helped the company create a brand name and increased traffic, which resulted in sales.

"It was so successful, we will do it again!" said Larry Chase, president of Chase Online Marketing Strategies, larry@chaseonline.com, chaseonline.com.

They intend to run banner ads on the search engines with the headline: "Just when you thought it was safe: Trip from Hell 2."

Case Study: Readers' Digest

When I created a contest for the Readers' Digest Association to promote the new Complete Do-It-Yourself Manual on CD-ROM, I discovered a number of factors that must be considered before committing a company to a specific type of contest.

At first we thought it would be a good idea to have people submit something to win the grand prize, like write a short letter about the funniest thing that ever happened to them doing a home repair. We nixed the idea when we thought people wouldn't have the time to write or might not be comfortable with their writing skills.

Then we thought about having them submit before and after pictures of their home repair. That idea didn't pan out when we thought that people might not have taken pictures of their work.

We then realized that any kind of contest that required a submission would also require judging. That meant we had to line up a panel of judges, a manpower burden.

Even worse, we thought of the tremendous manpower that would be needed to open envelopes of submissions, take out the material, and sort it—let alone read the material to pick a winner!

We then decided that the easiest tactic would be to ask people to fill out an entry form online. They didn't have to submit anything but their name, e-mail address, and street address—after all, how could we send them the prizes if we didn't know where they lived?

The next step was to create a site to showcase the product and allow for order taking. To lead people to the site, we created a "Cool D-I-Y (Do-It-Yourself) Tip of the Day" page with 60 tips for the two-month run of the contest. Press releases, reviewer's quotes, and product information added heft to the site and credibility for the CD-ROM. We also added a quiz about home repair that showed off the content of the product. However, we didn't require anyone to fill out the quiz to enter the contest. It was just a fun thing to do. The quiz changed every week.

The contest met the company's goals of introducing the product to the online world and generating sales in the 1–2 percent range.

Require an Offline Activity to Be Performed Before Proceeding Online

Purpose: Assures repetition of the brand name.

Discussion: The Web site for the movie *Jumanji* hosted a multipart game, www.spe.sony.com/Pictures/SonyMovies/Jumanji/main.html. Users could download a part and play it offline. When they solved the part, they received a password. They could then go back online to get the next segment of the game by entering the password. This activity ensured that children visited the site over and over.

Action: Create a game, quiz, or test that encourages this type of repeat visit.

Give Coupons, Discounts, and Rebates

Purpose: Encourages repeat visits.

Discussion: People will come back to your site when they know you offer coupons, discounts, rebates, or other money-saving incentives. Casual Male, a retailer of clothing for big and tall men, stated that 23 percent of the 30,000 visitors to its Web site, www.thinkbig.com, downloaded coupons worth 25 percent off apparel. The Hyde Park, Massachusetts–based firm uses the site to lead buyers to the chain's 400 retail stores. L'eggs, the leading hosiery manufacturer for women, offers a 50-percent discount on its products to people via online ordering. Rail Europe, www.raileurope.com, offers special prices for online consumers.

Action: Create the incentive and promote it on the Internet and other media.

Eliminate Risk of Buying

Purpose: Generate repeat visits.

Discussion: If you eliminate the risk of buying when people visit your site, then they will come back for more. You can do this by guaranteeing the products and offering a no-questions-asked policy on returns, as all the large department stores and mail order companies do.

Action: Post notices on your site.

SUMMARY

There are many ways to publicize your site and draw people to it. Most strategies are free, except for your time and energy.

If you have ideas for promoting a Web site, please send me the strategy, action steps, and results. I'll be happy to include the strategy on my site and put a free link to yours! Readers can find updates to this chapter by going to this address: www.janal.com/articles.html.

CHAPTER TWENTY-ONE

Crisis Communications

Crisis.

Even the sound of the word strikes fear into the hearts of corporate communications managers.

While these managers have traditionally used the media of print, television, and radio and the tools of press releases, press conferences, and good old-fashioned phone calls to handle catastrophes and calamities, even the best crisis communications program can be improved by using Internet tools. When integrated with traditional crisis communications procedures, the Internet-savvy company has a much greater variety of choices and strategies to combat their crises.

This chapter describes how to use the Internet to handle a crisis. We'll explore tools and strategies to:

- prepare for crisis
- find the crisis
- respond to the crisis
- evaluate the response
- averting online crises

PHASE 1: PREPARE FOR CRISIS

When I teach my PR class at Berkeley, I always ask my students when the best time is to deal with a crisis. Even neophyte classes responded, "before the crisis happens." The Internet can help you deal with crises in a timely manner—before they happen.

According to the Institute for Crisis Management, the majority of business crises are not accidental or sudden; they develop well before they thrust an organization onto the evening news.

A number of crisis can be anticipated, such as dismal earnings reports, accidents and deaths, shareholder suits, and strikes. During the planning phase, the Internet can help you with:

- strategies for creating policies and messages
- strategies for training personnel
- strategies for media relations

Let's look at these areas.

Strategies for Creating Policies and Messages

Use E-mail and Word Processors to Plan and Write Messages

We've all wasted so much time on voice mail that many of us have been looking for an alternative. That alternative is e-mail. By sending electronic messages about how to deal with potential crises to coworkers, we can transmit our thoughts to one or many with the press of a button. Our coworkers can read the messages when they are ready and respond with considered thoughts instead of shooting from the hip. If many people are involved in the process, a paper trail can show each person's thoughts and logic at various stages of the process.

To document the process, consider using a word processor instead of a standard e-mail program. Most word processors have a revision function that shows the changes each person makes to the document. Each person's changes are displayed in a different color, so you'll know if the comment came from the chairperson or anyone else. When changes are approved, you can easily accept them and discard the rejects. Standard e-mail packages don't have this function.

Conduct Strategy Meetings with Electronic or Video Conference

Imagine e-mail on steroids. You now have an electronic conference where participants can type messages in real time. Positions can be stated, debated, and rated. When you are done, you'll have a transcript of the event. This strategy can be extremely useful for companies with participants in several offices.

Why would you want to do an online conference instead of a conference call? You could do either, really, with great benefit. A possible advantage of the online conference is that all people can participate, including the shy ones or the ones who can't get a word in edgewise over more vocal people. Plus you get a transcript.

One disadvantage is that online communications can't transmit the passion in a person's voice. The subtlety of a comment might be lost online. A joke might be taken as an insult. Be careful.

In the not-too-distant future, you might consider using Internet phone services to conduct long-distance meetings in real time. Right now, the sound quality is a bit weak. The advantage over regular phone service will be a much lower expense rate.

Place Materials Online For Access by Media

Create material to distribute to the press online—press releases, backgrounders, slides, and sound clips. These materials can be prepared in advance for planned crises such as layoffs and earnings reports. The documents can be disseminated to the media and other audiences (like employees, analysts, and the community, if that is appropriate) when the timing is appropriate.

Decide If the Media Need Passwords to Access Materials

While full access is generally a good rule of thumb to follow in responding to crises, in some situations you might want only a limited group to read certain files. For example, you might want to limit access by the general public so that the access time to read information and download large picture or video files is not hindered. If this is the case, then use a password system that enables reporters to enjoy full access to the material only after you have made it generally available to them. You will need to create a password system with your information technology department or Internet service provider and issue passwords to beat reporters who would need to access the information when a crisis develops. The area should be kept empty until the appropriate personnel declare that crisis materials can be viewed by reporters.

If you create a media distribution list in advance, you can e-mail the password to reporters. They can all have the same password to ease the registration and confirmation process.

You can also set up passwords for selected key groups such as investors, dealers, and employees. The material stored in each directory can be molded to meet their needs. By doing this you fulfill your obligation to provide timely information to your key audiences without slowing access by the media.

Strategies for Training Personnel

Every person at your company should know how to respond to the media and the public when a catastrophe occurs. That's because when a crisis first breaks, the security guard or janitor could be interviewed by reporters. Even if you don't want the nonprofessional staff to talk to the media, they need to be trained to refer questions to the proper authorities. The first person a reporter sees at an accident site might very well be a security guard at the main gate. That person needs to know what to say, even if it is "No comment" or the name and phone number of the public affairs person in charge of media relations.

The Internet can help you train your spokespeople to deal with crisis situations. If all your material is available to all possible speakers on the Internet, then everyone can read from the same playbook and tell the same story.

Use the Internet To House Crisis Communications Documents

You can use the Internet to store training files like the text of sample interviews, question-and-answer sheets, company backgrounders, and so on. Today you can post these files as text, audio, or even video. Material can be presented as interactive training sessions to be studied individually or as a group in a conference setting.

This procedure can help you save money by delivering training materials to employees in remote locations. You don't have to fly them in to your main office or send a trainer on the road to visit a dozen locations.

Use the Internet To Train Employees

Through a computer-based training program you can teach employees how to respond in times of crisis. Course material can be stored online. Employees can take the training and answer test questions to show they understand the materials. By using audio and video, they can see and hear how to act and respond during a crisis.

Strategies for Media Relations

Build Relationships with Reporters Before the Crisis

The best time to build relationships with reporters is before the crisis develops. As reporters have limited time to do their jobs, many rely on e-mail correspondence to find information and further their relationships. As an online professional, you must find out which reporters cover your company and industry and build relationships with them. If they have e-mail addresses, you can curry favor with them by providing useful information and insight into industry trends. When a crisis develops and the reporters turn to you as a source, you will have established a degree of credibility and rapport.

Find Reporters' E-mail Addresses

To find reporters' e-mail addresses, ask them, or look at their signed columns, publication mastheads, and business cards. Keep addresses stored in an e-mail folder so you can contact reporters quickly.

Find Out How Reporters Want To Be Contacted

Ask which method of correspondence they prefer. Some reporters have distinct preferences for e-mail, fax, phone, or mail for general correspondence and a different set of priorities for crisis calls. Find out the favored method and add to your credibility.

Assign Passwords (If Applicable)

At the very least, even the most hard-bitten reporters want to know who to contact during a crisis. You can provide them with your regular contact information as well as tell them about your online command center that will be stocked with vital information that they can access as needed. If you will require them to use a password, this would be a good time to tell them their code. All codes should be easy to remember, such as the reporter's name or the words *crisis* or *media*.

PHASE 2: FIND THE CRISIS

A communications professional's worst nightmare is to learn about a crisis by picking up a phone and hearing the bad news directly from a reporter. The Internet provides professionals with many sources to find crises:

- online newspapers and archives
- Web sites operated by competitors and associations
- newsgroups and forums

Online Newspapers and Archives

The Internet is one of the largest news sources available to any public relations professional. More than 1,000 daily newspapers and thousands of trade publications have online editions that are updated daily or even hourly. This vast resource library helps you find potential crises at your company and in your industry much faster than waiting for the morning paper.

By contracting with any number of news services online, you can get updates on news stories affecting your company virtually every minute of the day. If you do this, you won't be surprised by reporters who find out about crisis before you do.

Web Sites Operated by Competitors and Associations

Web sites of competitors or special interest groups can also contain misinformation about your company or its products. Use the downloading software programs to monitor those sites and ensure that the truth is being told. Be sure to check product comparison sheets, which can hold many errors.

Web sites run by your competitors could contain inaccurate information about your company or products. Check the product feature lists to ensure that they don't claim their product is the only one to provide a benefit or was the first to do so (provided your company can back up its own claim).

Reporters and the public can read this information and regard it as fact. Comparison charts also should be checked for accuracy. When I handled the PR for a computer company, a competitor printed a comparison chart in an advertisement that said its computer could display 64 colors. Under the box for my client's features, the ad merely said *yes*. However, that computer could display *millions* of colors. This simple act made the competitor's computer look more powerful when in fact it was inferior!

If competitors or special interest groups issue press releases over PR Newswire or Business Wire, you will be able to catch them by using a news filter.

Web sites operated by industry associations and trade groups can print breaking news and contain invaluable information about industry statistics and resources.

If you check your competitors' sites, you won't be blindsided.

Newsgroups and Forums

Controversies can also be found in the tens of thousands of newsgroups, mailing lists, and forums, which are online bulletin boards for people interested in specific topics such as computers, fly fishing, or raising kids. People post messages stating opinions or asking questions. Their comrades respond in writing. The world can see the printed transcript of the dialog and add their own comments.

While these dialogs are a wonderful exercise in free speech and the sharing of information, they can also become breeding grounds of controversy for companies. For example, if a dissatisfied customer posts a message saying he is not happy with your product, the whole world can see it.

A surprisingly large number of people use newsgroups to find information and opinions about products they intend to buy—from automobile tires to classical music selections to stereo equipment. Not surprisingly, a lot of inaccurate information is sent unintentionally, as are personal likes and dislikes about products. One recent search found people debating the merits of Diet Snapple. Current events also are discussed in newsgroups as people give their opinions on news stories they read about in newspapers and see on television. For example, the sex discrimination suit at Mitsubishi was discussed in newsgroups that discuss women's issues.

It is vitally important for companies to monitor these newsgroups for libelous or inaccurate material because unchallenged statements will be quoted and regarded as truth. Consumers who read those postings could be negatively influenced about your company or product. Companies can also be the targets of special interest groups that hold opposing points of view on certain issues, such as tobacco, the environment, home schooling, abortion, and the like.

Even worse than simply affecting the millions of newsgroup subscribers, reporters from daily newspapers and trade publications frequently read newsgroup postings to find out what customers are saying about products. If they read many negative messages about your company or product, the good reporters will call you for a comment. The sloppy reporters will print the flames without calling you to set the record straight.

Companies need to respond and set the record straight because these messages can be seen by hundreds of thousands of people today and in the future; messages can be retrieved forever by using special tools and services such as DejaNews, a database of all messages posted to newsgroups.

When you enter a query, DejaNews responds with the e-mail address of the person who wrote the article, the newsgroup in which it appeared, and the title of the article. Both the e-mail address and the headline are linked to additional information. By clicking on the headline, you will be able to read the entire text of the article. You can then find additional articles that commented on this one so you can see how people reacted to the posting. Did they agree, or disagree, or did the subject die? You can also find every article the writer ever posted to any newsgroup by clicking on his e-mail address. This might be useful in developing a profile of the writer. You might discover that the writer works for a competitor! You might be able to ascertain whether the writer is a crank or a credible person with a legitimate complaint.

While there is a strong bias against advertising and commerce in newsgroups, no one objects to the right of companies to defend their good name or set the record straight. Care should be taken in selecting the appropriate rank of the responder.

- If the problem involves inaccurate information, a product manager or public relations person can correct the price of a product or talk about its features.
- If the situation involves a more serious matter, such as company policy, the president, chairman, or division vice president should respond.
- In only the rarest of matters should an attorney respond because the title *attorney* sends a message that could be misinterpreted as a threat.

Not only is it important for the appropriate person to respond, but that person must have her own e-mail account. Nothing looks cheesier than to have a message signed by the president of the company, but have the header read "Joe Doe, Public Relations." Readers will think Joe wrote it and tried to pass it off as coming from the executive office. If the president of the company doesn't have an e-mail account, he won't have any credibility with his message posted on another person's account.

There is no similar service for mailing lists or forums on the commercial online services.

Another type of online crisis that communications managers must deal with on the Internet comes from the new breed of net celebrities whose sizable audiences rely on their opinion. If these opinion leaders blast your product or company, you will want to contact them to set the record straight and minimize damage.

Investor relations managers also need to monitor the Internet and commercial online services, which are breeding a new crop of investment analysts who promote stocks. Their recommendations can lead to a surprising surge in trading volume.

The Motley Fool area on America Online is one of the most heavily trafficked sites. Columnists there suggest stock selections. In one case, "MF Boring" recommended a stock called Zytec (NASDAQ: ZTEC), a manufacturer of electronic power supplies for electronic industries—and it rose from $27 to $46 1/2 in less than two weeks. When Boring announced he would sell it, his fans dumped the stock and it plunged 9 11/16 in one day! It should be noted that Boring does not try to manipulate the stock; he announces his buys and sells the night before he places orders so his fans can buy at the same time (or even before, depending on the time zones in worldwide markets). As Zytec is a thinly traded stock, the effect of hundreds of online investors can be hard felt. Investor relations managers will want to monitor the Motley Fool and other opinion leaders to see if their stock is selected—and subject to wild swings, which would invite the scrutiny of a business reporter.

While the Internet, commercial online services, and newsgroups can be breeding grounds of rumors and inaccurate statements that could lead to controversies and crises, smart public relations professionals will use the Internet to quell rumors, set the record straight, and build positive relationships.

PHASE 3: RESPOND TO THE CRISIS

Crisis communications managers will want to respond to crises using traditional media and public relations tactics as well as online tools, and respond to the media by disseminating information online. Here are the online tools and how they can augment a traditional crisis communications plan:

- e-mail and mailing lists
- news wires
- Web sites
- conferences
- newsgroups

Let's look at these tools and strategies that can be developed.

E-mail and Mailing Lists

E-mail can be an effective tool to send reporters press releases, back-grounders, alerts, and contact information because information can be sent and received in a matter of seconds. Notes can be prepared in advance and sent to reporters on a moment's notice.

To save time, you could create a mailing list or a distribution list of key reporters. Write one message and broadcast it to reporters on the list.

By using e-mail, you can contact 5 or 500 reporters at the same time so that no one can complain that they weren't notified before another reporter. If you do this, be sure to remove the cc: or carbon copy that tells the reporter they are one of 500 reporters to get the release. Nothing makes a reporter feel more insignificant than being on a list like this.

You can also create mailing lists of key audiences such as employees, stockholders, vendors, and VIPs to keep them informed of the latest events.

News Wires

All press releases should be transmitted to PR Newswire or Business Wire because they distribute these materials on the Internet. The media and key audiences can find the releases via a keyword search or by checking their individual news papers.

Web Sites as Crisis Communication Hotlines

The Internet allows you to turn your Web site into a 24-hour crisis communications online hotline. This area can contain all your printed materials as well as updates. It can also contain picture, audio, and video files that reporters can download and either print or put on the air in a timely fashion.

In addition to helping out in crisis mode, the Web site can be a resource to reporters and key audiences if it contains such information as company news, press releases, annual reports, financial statements, product information, quotes from customers and analysts, reprints of reviews, and other tools of public relations and marketing. By making this material available and updating it appropriately, your key publics and the media will learn to go to your site first when disaster strikes.

Online Press Conferences

Online press conferences give reporters the opportunity to ask questions of company officials. While phone and in-person press conferences can also be used to field questions, online press conferences offer several advantages, although most companies probably wouldn't use this as their first or only tactic in disseminating information during a crisis. Online press conferences allow an unlimited number of attendees to attend at their own expense (a local phone call) and save a printed transcript of all comments. While the press may not attend these online conferences, they still might have value for your various publics, like employees, stockholders, and distributors.

A chat session is an online dialog conducted by invited participants who converse by typing messages. Chat sessions can be used by a company to present its views in a dialog with the press and consumers. Internet Relay Chat is one such system, although primitive. A better choice would be Web Chat from Web Chat Broadcasting Network, which has been used by at least one Fortune 500 company to broadcast its annual meeting via the Internet.

Phone services via the Internet are increasing in popularity. Several companies offer patrons the opportunity to talk over the Internet by placing a local phone call to their Internet service provider. Please note that both parties must use the same product and schedule the call in advance, as they will have to meet at a designated online location. As you can imagine, this system has the potential to help disseminate news and build relationships via the Internet, but the technology is still hard to use and the quality marginal.

These two strategies are presented as possibilities that no doubt will become more effective as technology improves.

Newsgroups

Newsgroups should be included in your plan to distribute information if your audience is likely to read one in particular. For example, your customers probably want to hear the news of your product recall directly from your company instead of from the daily newspaper, which might print a shortened version of your announcement.

Monitor Newsgroups

Communications professionals should monitor newsgroups for offending or misleading comments posted by outside observers. Check these areas several times a day, as people post messages frequently. Also, people from different time zones could sign on after your normal business hours and post questions. The sooner their questions are answered, the better.

Paying attention to the tone of the message is vitally important. Because emotion doesn't come through in online communications, messages can seem direct and harsh. Messages can seem friendlier if you use an informal tone and avoid business or legal jargon.

Rally Your Troops

Another useful strategy is to rally your troops of loyal customers. Identify your evangelists in advance. When crisis strikes, ask them to respond to other people's complaints about the products with their own testimonials. They will be seen as impartial observers, whereas your employees might be seen as biased.

You might give these evangelists a special commendation or prize for helping out. However, chances are that your loyal customers will want to respond without hesitation as they want to show they made the correct choice in buying your product.

Don't Hide Identities

If your employees answer questions, they must identify themselves as employees. They should not pretend to be customers. As we have seen with DejaNews, every message can be traced and there are some newsgroup denizens whose only purpose in life is to find examples of shady corporate manipulation. If employees pose as customers, they will be found out!

PHASE 4: EVALUATE THE RESPONSE

After the crisis has passed, or when it is showing signs of abatement, you can monitor the situation by using the Internet as well as traditional sources. Check newsgroups for the quality and quantity of communication. Is the tone friendly or hostile? Have messages decreased in number, or are there still many postings?

If your company is public, you can check the stock market news services for trading volume and price direction. However, be aware that most stock services offer quotes on a 20-minute delay.

Case Studies

While most crisis communications professionals will be able to use the Internet to aid them in the fight against real-world crises, it should be noted with extreme diligence that the Internet itself can be a breeding ground of controversy that winds up on the front pages of daily newspapers and nightly news reports. Intel and Quicken, two leading companies in the computer hardware and software arenas, found their names on the front pages of hundreds of daily newspapers because of controversies that began with online postings in newsgroups. In both cases, customers complained that the products didn't work properly. Intel chose to ignore the problem and it festered, causing the company much embarrassment and a momentary decline in the price of their stock. Quicken chose a different approach, which calmed the storm quickly—so well that few people remember the problem at all, while Intel continues to fight flames from outraged consumers. Let's look at each crisis, the steps the companies chose to use to fight the problems, and how the Internet played a part in the crises.

Case Study: Intel Pentium Chip Flaw

Problem: A university professor claimed to have found a bug in Intel's Pentium chip. He said the mathematical functions for a complex formula were not accurate on a consistent basis. The company denied there was a problem. The professor posted a notice on a newsgroup asking others if they could duplicate the problem. They could. Word spread to the university community and then to the trade press and general press.

Steps taken: Intel denied there was a major problem and said that the situation would affect only a few people. They refused to take responsibility or replace the affected chips.

Because Intel had spent hundreds of millions of dollars on a consumer advertising campaign promoting "Intel Inside" as a standard by which to judge computers, and because they are the leading computer chip vendor, the mainstream media picked up the story and placed it prominently. The *New York Times, Wall Street Journal,* and *USA Today* all gave the story front-page coverage. These stories stoked fires on other newsgroups as well as around office water coolers as people wondered if their computers were tainted.

The story refused to go away. Intel refused to replace the chips, saying it would cost a fortune (never mind the lost value of their advertising campaign or the amount of bad publicity they were receiving). The company stock dropped nearly 20 points in a few weeks. Intel, however, stuck to its story that the problem affected only a few people. The company also said that every chip had bugs and the Pentium was no different. Meanwhile, jokes mocking Intel appeared in newsgroups. No one was buying Intel's story.

Just as it appeared that the story was dying, IBM announced it would not use Intel chips in its computer. The article appeared on the front page of the *New York Times.* Within a matter of days, Intel reversed its position and agreed to replace chips at no cost to consumers. In a few weeks, Intel's stock price returned to its pre-crisis level and then went higher.

Analysis: Intel mishandled the entire affair from the very beginning. First it denied the problem, then admitted there was a problem, but a minor one. It refused to accept responsibility, saying it would be expensive to replace the chip, but suffered untold costs in terms of lost credibility and the sudden worthlessness of their multimillion-dollar advertising campaign. These are classic missteps in handling a crisis.

In terms of the ramifications for online relations, this affair shows that consumers will talk among themselves online, even if the company doesn't want to hear the story. Also, reporters will find out about the controversy and find sources willing to talk on the record about their problems. Because of the chatter in newsgroups, the story refused to die. Also, because all newsgroup messages are saved and are searchable, people can read thousands of messages about the controversy and might decided that the existence of the bug is a reason to buy a competitor's product—or boycott the company because of its malignant attitude.

Case Study: Quicken

Problem: A bug in Quicken's tax preparation software was discovered and publicized in forums by users who asked if other people had the same problem. Reporters saw the messages. Business sections featured the story on lead pages.

Steps taken: Quicken took fast action to admit the problem, fixed it, sent free copies of the updated program to users, and offered to pay any penalties or interest incurred by taxpayers whose returns were affected. They issued press releases.

Outcome: The story died in a few days.

Analysis: Quicken showed what happens when you take responsibility for your actions: the public forgives you. By accepting all financial blame they stemmed any negative criticism and received accolades instead. Few people remember this incident. Many people remember the Intel fiasco.

AVERTING ONLINE CRISES

While the bulk of this chapter is devoted to using online services as a tool in your overall crisis communications plan, this section discusses potential crises that might develop as a *result* of your company being online. We'll look at:

- spoofing
- spamming
- boycotts
- domain name stealing
- competitive snooping

Spoofing

Spoofing is what happens when someone posts a Web site that looks and feels like your Web site. For example, Bob Dole had a site for his election efforts. An unknown party posted a site lampooning Dole. The site looked like it could have been for Bob Dole until you read the text and found out that Dole was the "ripe man for the job" and that links to "family values" took you to the Marilyn Monroe Home Page! U.S. West faced a similar problem when a disgruntled customer posted the "U.S. Worst" home page.

Due to freedom of speech laws in the United States, there is little you can do to stop these actions unless the pages are libelous or steal your artwork, which would violate copyright laws. However, you can protect your company by registering domain names that could be used by spoofers. For example, the stretch from U.S. West to U.S. Worst is something that any high school sophomore could have thought of. But if you own the domain www.usworst.com, then the sophomore can't use it. Register every conceivable name that would spoof your company.

Spamming

Spamming is the act of sending out mountains of unsolicited junk mail to people's e-mail boxes. This is a violation of netiquette and has been discussed at length throughout this book. If your company participates in this activity, angry recipients might very well tell their friends on newsgroups and give you a black eye. Fortunately, this action doesn't have to occur. Just don't spam.

Boycotts

If you don't heed the previous warning about not spamming, your company could be the victim of a boycott via the net. Companies that spam are listed on a boycott page. Your company can avoid this disaster simply by practicing good netiquette.

Domain Name Stealing

On the Internet, people send e-mail to my domain name, dan@janal.com, or find my Web site by typing www.janal.com. If you are smart and fast, you can easily register your domain name with InterNIC, the official organization that assigns all domain names. Someone could register your company name as its domain name if they are there first. Regulations prevent a registered trademark from being used as a domain name by any party other than the official holder, but if a company that has a similar name has registered it before you, then you are out of luck. For example, if Bob Avis wants to register avis.com he can, provided the rental car company hasn't registered it already. If Bob has registered it, then the other Avis will continue to be in second place and won't get the registration no matter how hard it tries. However, if Bob Avis tried to register hertz.com, InterNIC would not give him the name.

Companies might steal your name without even realizing it—or it can be a deliberate act. To protect yourself, register your company name as the domain name as soon as you can. Don't forget to register your association's letters (i.e., American Association of Associated Associations would be aaaa.com) too.

Competitive Snooping

When you create a Web site, the entire world can see what you have written—including your competitors. There are two steps to take to minimize snooping:

1. Limit the amount of information to that which you wouldn't mind revealing to a stranger at a trade show booth. You have to figure your competitors are getting all your public information anyway. Just decide what the general public needs to know and don't print anything else.
2. Limit access to your site to people who register and tell you who they are and where they work. You can decide whether or not you want them to visit your site. This is not unlike a realtor who shows multimillion-dollar houses by appointment only. She wants to make sure buyers are qualified before investing her time and effort. This is a good strategy for a business-to-business company because you want to identify and qualify each visitor. It is a bad strategy for a general consumer site that wants to sell products and services, as you might scare off potential customers.

Online Sources of Crisis Communications Material

- Data Bank, www.scils.rutgers.edu/de/databank/cristop.html, contains information and links.
- PRSIG, CompuServe: go prsig, contains library files on how to deal with crises.

SUMMARY

Crises can start online or offline and brew online. Companies should take great care in monitoring relevant discussion areas to deal with negative comments because bad news travels fast—even faster online. In a short time, these errors look like facts because the information—or misinformation—is repeated. Companies that don't respond quickly can face serious risks. Fortunately, a great many tools and strategies can be used to combat crises.

PART 5

Online Selling

CHAPTER TWENTY-TWO

Designing Your Web Site To Increase Sales

Good design is essential for presenting sales information in a comfortable, convenient manner on the Internet. Because the online services are consumer-driven media, it is essential that information be used as the main persuasion and education tool and presented in a manner that is easy to find and absorb. The Internet offers a variety of tools to make finding and using information fast and efficient for consumers.

In this chapter, you will learn:

- how to create a Web site or hire a designer
- what information marketers need to put on a Web site
- tips for designing Web sites
- the latest research on guidelines for effective Web sites
- You will also tour successful marketing sites.

HOW TO CREATE A WEB SITE

Creating a Web site is a relatively straightforward process. Here are the steps:

1. Determine the goal of the site. Will it be used to sell products, create an image, or as a library for company information?
2. Create content that supports these goals.
3. Convert the files into an HTML (hypertext markup language) program. Learning to write this code is beyond the scope of this book. For good references and tutorials, read any book written by Laura LeMay.
4. Load the site onto a computer server that is connected to the Internet. Your Internet Service Provider (ISP) can do this for you.

In a very short while, you might not have to deal with any coding for HTML. That's because software programs are being developed that create programs without the user having to know any codes. The programs prompt the user for information such as the name of the company, background, and mission statement. Programs in this category include Microsoft Front Page, Netscape Navigator Gold, InContext Spider, and Delta Point Quick Site.

If you are not comfortable with the technical and artistic aspects of creating a Web site, don't worry. Outside companies can handle all these details.

A cottage industry for creating sites is springing up. These companies offer complete site creation and supporting materials. They go by several names, such as Internet presence providers, database marketers, and malls. Advertising agencies offer Web creation and management services.

The advantages of hiring consultants to create these materials are plentiful. As they already know how to use the software, they save you the time, expense, and hassle of learning it. Their familiarity enables them to use the software to its fullest potential so that your products are displayed in the most advantageous manner available. For the same reason, consultants are able to create and complete the project for you quickly. Because they have designed projects for other companies, they will be able to draw on that experience to create a better presentation for you. Finally, because their business depends on their being well informed, consultants know about the latest technological improvements and how these can help you.

Select a site design consultant as you would choose any consultant: Ask for referrals from your colleagues, ask the consultants for references, look at their previous work, determine your level of rapport, and ask for the price structure. After you've selected the top two or three consultants you feel can do the job, begin negotiating their fees. Bear in mind that you don't want to cut the price so low that they will not want to work with you or will have to cut corners to complete the task.

Budget Considerations

Budgeting for the creation of the Web site must include line items for creating content, converting it to HTML format, and connecting it to the computer server. Here are important factors to consider.

- **Creating content**. Creating content can be done in-house with the marketing team determining which products and messages to feature. In-house artists and graphic designers can create the visual elements. Companies that don't have artists can hire consultants.

- **Creative and technical consulting**. Consultants can help companies create Web sites from start to finish or just complete parts of the puzzle. For example, large companies with in-house advertising departments may be adept at creating text and graphics files but may lack the expertise to convert files to HTML format or to place the files onto a computer server and connect it to the Internet. That might be the time to call in a consultant.

    For smaller companies, farming out the entire process can be a boon as the company can focus on what it does best and the consulting team can do what it does best.

    The cost of hiring a consultant varies greatly depending on the amount of material you need to create and the negotiating ability of the consulting firm. If you have a simple site with few items and links, the consultant might be able to complete the job in a few hours. A more intricate job could take days or weeks. As with any immature industry, prices have yet to become standardized. Consultants can and will charge whatever they think the market will bear. Prices vary across the country and range from $50 to $125 an hour plus expenses. The time to create a Web site for a small or home-based business could range from 6 to 100 hours depending on the complexity of the project.

- **Updates**. A key benefit of electronic information is that it can be changed easily whenever you want. However, each time you change information, you have to pay for the artist's time. Most companies have dynamic information; it changes with each modification in the product line, price, or availability. Your budget should account for the technician's time to update material. If you decide to undertake this task in-house, you have to account for training and actual time spent on this function.

INFORMATION MARKETERS NEED TO PUT ON A WEB SITE

Behind all the cool graphics and clever writing of a Web site lies a basic business strategy designed to sell. Good sites have a mission to provide information in an entertaining and interactive manner that helps to not only make a sale but create a customer for life.

The term *site* is misleading. A home page is really a table of contents or directory to your store. This opening page is actually longer than a computer screen and can be quite long. The advantage is that you can display a great deal of information in a precise location. It is important for you to think in screenfuls of content so navigation is easy for consumers. Small companies with one product have only one long page. Companies with more content can use additional pages—called *subpages* or *Web pages*. The home page and subpages together form the Web site.

The Web site should contain the following information displayed as headlines or buttons and linked to subpages with more detailed information:

- Name of company.
- Logo.
- Mission statement—explains what your business does and the market it serves. The statement should be printed in full on the home page.
- Headlines of the information and products on your site. These headlines link to descriptions and pictures of products.
- Notice of special events—entice people to visit your store and explore its contents.
- Sales—tells people at a glance what the hot buys are this week. This information should be printed on the home page.
- "What's new"—tells viewers what information has been added or changed. This information should be printed on the home page as headlines and linked to related pages.
- Message from the president—can show the true character and nature of the company, giving it a personal, as opposed to impersonal, feel. This line links to the actual message.
- Press releases—give people a depth of understanding of the products and the company that might not be contained in sales materials. This line links to the press releases section.
- Sales materials—give broad and deep information about the products or services. This line links to the sales materials section.
- Catalogs—show the full range of products in your store, with descriptions, prices, and ordering information as well as transaction capabilities. This line links to the catalog section.
- Registration form—asks people to identify themselves so you can build a relationship with them. Forms should ask only a few questions, such as name, address, e-mail address, and the scantiest of

demographic material; the more questions you ask, the fewer answers you will get. Remember that people value their privacy and might not want to reveal their identities. If you require that people identify themselves before you allow them into your store, they might walk on by. This line links to the registration form.

- Testimonials—to your products and services by satisfied customers can help convince prospects to invest in your company. This line links to the testimonials section.
- Employment notices—show descriptions of jobs that are available at your company. This line links to the employment section.
- E-mail response form—so people can contact you directly and create a one-to-one relationship that can last for life.
- Links to other sites—listings of information sources on the Internet your readers will find interesting. These links tie into other Web sites.
- Coupons, discounts, and sales items.
- Fun stuff—a well-rounded site includes diversions like contests, trivia, cartoons, and jokes to entertain customers.
- Contact information—your company's physical address, telephone, and fax numbers. This information should be included on all pages because people print out individual pages, not the entire site. If they include your product spec sheet in their report, it is handy to have the contact data readily available so they can call to place the order.
- Map—showing your company's location on a street map, along with directions.
- Date of last update—so people will know if anything has changed since their last visit.
- Copyright notice—protects your work.

TIPS FOR DESIGNING WEB SITES

A well-designed Web site is essential to attracting customers and guiding them to intelligent buying decisions. Designing sites is partly subjective and partly formula. Let's look at two key areas:

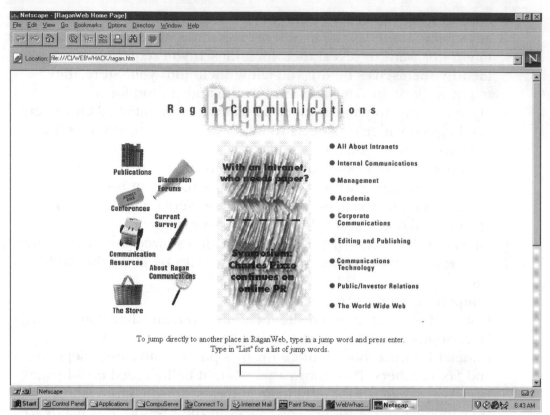

Figure 22–1. Ragan Communications, www.ragan.com, is an example of the latest design styles, which include a search engine on the site so readers can find information quickly. This large site contains information for corporate communicators. (Copyright 1997, Lawrence Ragan Communications)

1. **Content:** What you want to say and strategies for getting people to return.
2. **Interface:** How you present the information visually and how the user interacts with it. This is the organization, menu, and icons.

Content

Time and space are two critical concerns for marketers—usually. When they buy advertising time on a TV show, it is very expensive. When they plan to print a brochure, space is expensive. When they plan a newspaper ad, every word and picture is at a premium. These elements don't matter on the Web because space is unlimited.

Therefore, when creating the content for a Web site, you (the marketer) must ask different questions:

- What material will you place online? Do you place your entire catalog or just the highlights? If your Internet service provider charges
  the going rate—which is inexpensive and getting more competitive
  all the time—you can afford to place every nut and screw in your
  inventory online. This is a boon to companies with large invento-
  ries, such as bookstores, music stores, and technical component suppliers. However, the more products you offer, the harder it can be to
  find specific products. You can avoid this dilemma by using menus
  that allow consumers to find what they are looking for. For example, a music lover could drill down through menus labeled Records,
  Classical, Symphonies, Beethoven and then hear the opening strains
  of the Fifth Symphony. This can also be accomplished by providing
  search capabilities.

- How much information will you use to describe the material—a single line, a paragraph, or a full page? Again, with unlimited space you
  can provide customers with the answers to every question they
  could think of. You can use short descriptions written for consumers and pages of technical specifications and schematic drawings for engineers. For example, a stereo speaker could be described
  with an appeal to emotion, as in, "Impress your friends with the best
  sound available." It can also be sold to the audiophile who demands
  to know the technical specifications of each component.

- Pictures present a professional image and add to the wow factor.
  However, they should be small pictures, as large ones take too long
  to appear on the screen—a turn-off. If you use pictures, create large
  and small versions of the same pictures and display only the small
  picture. Let the reader know he can see the larger picture if he
  wants to by clicking on the small one. Pictures saved in gif89a and
  .jpg file formats load faster than those in other formats. People
  become frustrated if your site sends a large file because it is slow to
  appear on the screen. Part of this reaction can be circumvented if
  you let people know how large the file is and how long it will take
  to transmit. That way they can decide to retrieve it and wait more
  patiently for it to appear.

- Will sound or video enhance the shopping experience? For an
  entertainment company or a training company, a video might do a
  better job of selling than any brochure could because the customer
  can see a clip from a movie or a training session in action.

Interface

An interface is the visual display of digital information. It is the way marketers communicate with consumers through the computer. If the interface is fun, exciting, and pretty, and if it leads the consumer to a highly interactive experience, the interface is a success. If consumers are confused, the interface is a failure.

A good user interface is critical to the success of a Web site, as it is to all forms of sales communications on all the commercial online systems.

Bad interfaces, like bad clothes that stand out and hide the person, detract from the message. Good interfaces, like good clothes that don't intrude and don't take attention away from the person, don't distract the reader from the message. A badly designed interface reminds people that they are dealing with a machine. A well-designed interface is so unobtrusive that people can concentrate on the information instead of the computer.

Fortunately, there are keys to good interface design. The best way to understand good design is to browse through Web sites and play with them. Make notes on what you like and what you don't.

The first generation of Web sites used text only with a gray background. The next generation added cartoon-like images or photos. Recently designers have begun using white or colored backgrounds to avoid the ugly gray ones. They are also designing pages like magazine pages to include white space near the borders of the screen like a printed page. Another nice look is the addition of text wrapped around art. Look at the *New York Times* site, www.nytimes.com, for ideas for creating attractive pages.

An area of concern is the use of colors and backgrounds. A great many Web sites sport unattractive black backgrounds with hideous colored fonts (like purple or brown). Not only are these sites ugly, they are nearly impossible to read. This is a case of people who don't know how to market taking control of the site. Another faux pas is the use of busy backgrounders or watermarks. These devices make pages hard to read. This is an example of people using tools just because they are available, even though the effect is counterproductive. Just think—if backgrounds and dense watermarks were effective presentation tools, don't you think the print world would have adopted them? There is a reason you don't see these devices in magazines and newspapers: they don't work!

Frames are used to display information in three windows on a screen. Although the layouts can vary, the top frame is usually horizontal and the bottom two frames are adjoining squares. The top frame is used for the corporate logo while the left frame includes a table of contents or directory and the right frame holds the data. Some designers feel this is an efficient way to display data while keeping the company logo fresh in people's faces; others feel that the frames take up too much space on the screen and don't allow for enough data to be seen at any one time. The frames also take a long time to load and therefore should be avoided if your audience has slow modems or bad phone service.

An alternative to frames are tables, which present information in two- or three-column formats. Tables are faster to load than frames and can actually display more information because they don't require the borders used by frames. Given the choice, I'd choose tables every time.

Other considerations:

- **Awards**. If your site wins an award from a recognizable service like "Cool Site of the Day," you might want to display the award icon on your page. However, be aware that this picture will add to time loading your page displays. I've seen some pages that have so many awards that load time seems interminable.
- **Icons for other companies**. Some sites add icons from companies like Netscape, Microsoft, InfoSeek, and Yahoo! so that people who visit can then visit their sites! Ask yourself if these icons help you more than they help the other company (these are unpaid advertisements!). However, if you want your viewer to go to another page to download an application, like Real Audio conferencing software, then these icons and links serve a vital marketing function and should be used.

Icons

Because there are no instruction manuals on how to use each Web site, icons should be used to help readers find information quickly.

"People recognize symbols rather than text," says Bill Linder of Columbus PBX, a one-stop information resource center that creates Web sites in Columbus, Indiana. "Imagine seeing a road sign from 100 feet away. You notice its size, shape, and color. Is it a stop sign or perhaps a yield sign? You begin to act on that information. As you get closer to the sign, you see the word *stop* but you've already begun to apply the brakes. "To complete the analogy, think of the international symbol set. Even without a word, you know that a picture icon means, for example, skiing or no parking. The same is true with icons on the Web. Customers understand their meanings faster and make decisions faster with pictures."

You don't have to design a page from scratch. Numerous icons, buttons, and backgrounds are available as shareware, which means you can test-drive the material and pay for it if you decide to continue using it.

Menus, Site Maps, and Search Engines

Menus are an easy way for customers to find information. Successful strategies include creating an overall menu that leads customers to deeper levels of information. Each menu also should have information on ordering so that once the customer is convinced she should buy the product, she can do so without having to wade through additional materials.

Two Web sites do a particularly wonderful job of presenting menus so you can find your way around the site easily: the *Wall Street Journal,* www.wsj.com, and Cnet, www.cnet.com.

When you design product menus, put your best products at the beginning or the consumer might never see them. Remember that a page can be longer than a screen and that anything below the bottom of the screen will not be seen unless the reader scrolls to it or hits a hotlink.

The best way to do this is to create a menu that has a short description of each major product area. For example, an appliance store could have menu listings for irons, toasters, blenders, coffee makers, and can openers. Each item could lead to another menu that lists the brand names of each of five models. If the customer selected blenders, he would see listings for five different models, complete with pictures of the units and a two-line description that included the price. If he wanted more information, another menu could reveal such information as operating instructions, recipes, and comparisons to other models.

Each menu should have information on how to purchase the item. This can be done as an online ordering form that can be completed and returned to the store via e-mail, fax, or snail mail (e.g., "To order, call 1-800-555-1212 or e-mail to orderform@estore.com."). Menus should also give users a link to return to the top of the page.

As Web sites get bigger and contain more information about more products and services, it is important to create navigation tools to make finding data fast. You can use a site map, which looks like the tree structure used in outlining. Another way to find information on really large sites is to use a search engine. Users type the term they want to find and the search tool finds all references on the site.

Personality

Marketers add personality to their Web sites to give products and service a bit of pizzazz. Perhaps the best example is Ragu, www.eat.com, which has created an Italian theme embodied in a fictional character named Momma. Visitors enter her kitchen and see text (or hear it with Real Audio) and learn about Italian history, art, architecture, movies, language, and menus. A number of companies selling beer have adopted pub atmospheres and graphics—see Molson, www.molson.com. Direct mail copywriter Ivan Levison uses graphics that look like coupons on his site, along with a strong writing style that gives you a sense of him as a person and a feel for what he can do.

Figure 22–2. Ivan Levison's home page displays a feel for his personality. (Copyright 1997, Ivan Levison and Associates)

Test Drive/Usability

To ensure usability, the Web site should be tested before it goes online. A test-drive will show whether the typical user understands the icons and can follow the scheme of things. For the best results, let a nontechnical person try to use the system. Be sure to test the site with different browsers to ensure its proper display; each browser displays text, color, and spacing slightly differently. You must test your site against the leading programs to ensure that the browser doesn't frustrate your artist's scheme by pushing text off the screen, bumping pieces of artwork into one another, or causing other unforeseen problems. As different browsers print text in different colors, be sure not to confuse your readers by saying, "If you click on the green text, you'll see the related information." The text might actually appear in red on some browsers. Instead, say, "If you click on the highlighted text"—italicized text.

LATEST RESEARCH: GUIDELINES FOR EFFECTIVE SITES

Systems Research Corp., www.Webanalytics.com, 201-909-3755, conducts focus groups for companies that want to test their Web sites with target audiences. Here are the findings of Daniel Sklaire, the company's president, dans@systemsresearch.com:

1. Make the corporate identity clear on the home page or first screen. *There should be no mystery about who's sponsoring the page.* However, it should not be larger than four square inches; logos this size, which are typically graphics based, will take up too much download time. Excessive download time will cause viewers to hit the stop button and skip to another site. [Editor's note: Some sites feature their advertisers' banners more prominently than their own logo! This is a big mistake.]
2. Make all Web designers test Web pages with a 14.4K modem. If they get impatient with a slow download, their graphics are too large and cumbersome.
3. One of the goals of a Web site should be to impart positive recognition, image enhancement, and increased awareness for the sponsor. There are several strategies to accomplish this. One key strategy is to generate return visits to a Web site, which, if accomplished, would be evidence of high effectiveness and interest. Sites that are

returned to generally get more word of mouth, one of the most powerful (but undirectable) methods of publicity.

4. Contentwise, Web sites should be viewed as final destinations for information, not interim places. If, for example, your company is 3M and places an ad with a URL for windows security film, don't lead the viewer to an 800 info number—give them an info sheet or downloadable ad instead!

5. Realize that the Web is direct marketing. It is an immediate response vehicle where viewers get addresses and take action. When writing and designing Web pages, make them every bit as actionable as a direct mailer that would be sent via the U.S. Postal Service.

6. Design using progressive rendering. This means that nongraphics text appears immediately when the page is accessed, allowing the viewer to begin reading immediately and before graphics are displayed. The graphics will catch up—but after you have the viewer already engaged. As on newspaper front pages, get your best shot or story up top.

7. The use of long pages should be encouraged, with button links that lead the viewer down further on the page, and less to subsequent pages. This provides for faster access to information than loading new pages.

8. Always use buttons to identify items that link to major underlying pages in the site. Without identifying buttons, viewers do not necessarily know to click on a topic. Highlighted words alone are not enough. Keep graphics for buttons at a minimum to reduce download times.

9. Don't be afraid to use the words "Click Here" to ask for action. There is many an icon on a Web site that viewers have no idea is hot unless they feel it. Don't make the reader work at using your site.

10. Iconize the most important subjects on the page, thereby prioritizing them for the reader. The largest icon should bring the viewer to the content that the sponsor feels is most important. Keep icons simple and not too large, again reducing download time.

11. The use of large and small graphics is interesting to viewers. Use one or two major graphics at most, followed by a series of smaller graphics or icons that lead to subsequent content. Again, keep graphics on a diet, not more than 6K per image.

12. Provide compelling text at the top of the page, so that the viewer sees this first when the graphics are being downloaded. The download time should be viewed much the same as a 30-second commercial on TV: You have a limited attention span, so make the most of it while they are waiting for your graphics! Give them something to read!

13. If your site is large (many underlying pages), always provide a site map showing linked pages and the content that lies therein. This is an easy way to have viewers find what they need quickly. Sites that cause frustration due to long search times will undoubtedly be avoided on successive surf runs. Use the term *site guide* or *site map* to clearly identify it.

14. Content on a site must be compelling. If you have no really interesting content to offer, provide some sizzle features such as multimedia or cool graphics. For example, the use of audio or motion on graphics will get positive reviews. Netscape allows for downloadable audio clips or multimedia.

15. The provision of links to other sites is a good idea, but remember that you are taking the viewer away from your site. Place linkages to other sites further into your own site so that the viewer has to see at least a few screens of your own content first.

16. Make use of the long page format. Web pages can be a full 8 x 14 or longer but very few sites take advantage of this. With the longer format you have the opportunity to get more content to the viewer in a single download and a greater chance of exposing them to your messages. Put the most important information and selection buttons on top.

17. Provide for a response vehicle on all pages in the form of either a linked e-mail icon or response form. Allow for a memo spot for open-ended text. Also allow for e-mail for comments to your Web master, who can forward info to appropriate parties in your company if sent. Web masters must be responsive and forward any messages the day received to appropriate parties.

18. Offer downloadable documents, giving the viewer a souvenir to take away with pertinent information about your company, products, or services. If your company is in technical markets, this might be a white paper.

Ten Ways to Increase Sales on Your Web Site

1. **Who are you?** You'd be surprised how many Web sites don't list the name of the company, what it does, and how it is unique. Most list this information somewhere on the Web site, but not on the front page. Why force people to find out who you are?

2. **What's in it for them?** Similarly, these sites for sore eyes don't tell viewers how they will benefit from visiting the site. Here's a hint: People will stay because you save them time, save them money, inform them, or entertain them.

3. **Is the art appropriate?** Everyone knows not to put large graphics on the site, because it takes tooooooo long to display. However, many sites have art for art's sake, even though it has nothing to do with what the company does. I'm not talking about cute buttons and navigation bars, but 3 x 5 pictures of people sitting behind computers. You can have a funky-looking site by offering a colored background, which takes absolutely no time to load.

4. **Grammar.** Typos can make your page look amateurish, yet many pages have grammatical errors and bad punctuation and capitalization. Check and double check. This is a very common problem, even with sites that are magnificent marketing tools.

5. **Links.** Do your links work? Surprisingly, internal links might not work because of sloppy coding. Test and test again. Check external links as well; sites can go out of business or change their URL.

6. **Interactivity.** Is your site interactive or is it merely a brochure? Unlike other marketing gurus, I don't mind an online brochure. I feel that if the customer wants to be educated, then text is the most interactive medium available. However, a site can be much more to a prospect if you add a calculator, quiz, fun facts, screen saver, wallpaper, or information article.

7. **Too much searching.** One particularly bad site forced users to go from a press release to the site instead of back to the press release menu. Give users the option of where to go. Put a full slate of navigation buttons at the bottom of the page.

8. **Who you gonna call?** Put contact information at the bottom of each page. You never know which page people will print. When they need to contact you, they'll have the information at their fingertips, not at the end of an Internet connection.

9. **Who specifically are you gonna call?** The prospect picks up the phone—and winds up in voice mail jail. Tell them who they should ask for. It could be Jane Smith, director of sales, or Operator 115.

10. **Ask for the order.** Sure, the Internet works because it is a soft sell, not a hard sell. But if you don't ask for the order by offering incentives, freebies, discounts, coupons, consulting, or the like, you decrease your chances for success. If you don't ask for the order—and offer incentives—you won't get the order.

GUIDED TOURS OF WEB SITES

The best way to understand the World Wide Web and its implications for shopping and to begin thinking about organizing your Web site is to visit several existing sites. This section takes you on a guided tour of several Web sites that clearly illustrate how to make shopping interesting, fun, and interactive. The examples come from a variety of categories that show that the Web can be home to many different products, from mass market items, like film and hot sauce to business market products, such as real estate, software, and consulting.

Seattle FilmWorks

To get a good understanding of a Web site, take a tour of one that does it right. Let's look at Seattle FilmWorks, www.filmworks.com/. This site was selected because it has the following important elements:

- It entices viewers with a visually stunning interface—in this case, photographs.
- It promotes interactivity by sponsoring contests and free offers. By offering two free rolls of film, the company received hundreds of orders from as far away as Czechoslovakia and Switzerland. The contest changes every month, so new people can enter and win prizes.
- The company gathers the names and addresses of its readers through interactive features.
- It encourages repeat visits by containing a library of information on photography. This is a natural, as everyone who visits this site is interested in taking better pictures.

If your Web site is designed correctly, your customers will be able to see an attractive and inviting catalog of the products and services that you offer. Let's look at various elements.

Each site can be compared to the table of contents of a well-designed magazine or brochure. There are no set rules or formats for designing a site. You have complete artistic control over the design, look, and feel of the page.

Figure 22–3. Beautiful graphics invite readers to see Seattle FilmWorks.

In this example you see the Seattle FilmWorks logo at the top of the screen. This logo is carried through on each page to present a unified look to the entire presentation. The colors are bold and the typeface easy to read.

Many sites have the following elements: a company logo at the top of the screen, titles that explain what information can be found, and pictures that show various products. The page is about the size of a computer screen. The full range of colors is available as well as an unlimited amount of space to print text. Let's look at the opening graphic. Notice how it contains buttons for Gallery, Picture, Contest, Special, and Table of Contents. A consumer who clicks on a button will be whisked to the corresponding page.

For now, let's stay on this page, because there is more here than meets the eye.

One interesting design consideration is that the page can extend longer than the screen, though not wider. This means that you actually have a great deal of room to work with beyond the depth of the user's screen. You must make a decision about what the user first sees on the screen and what she can see when she scrolls down the page—if you want her to scroll down the page.

In this example, the site does indeed contain more information than can fit onto a screen. You'll notice that the top of the film graphic appears near the bottom of the screen. The elevator bars at the far right show computer-literate readers that they can navigate downward to see more of the page. Less computer-literate readers will see that there is more art and realize that they can see this material by scrolling. Unfortunately, there are no computer manuals on a site. Readers must be given explicit instructions if you want them to interact with your site. As the reader scrolls further down the page, he reads about the highlights of the site.

Do you want to continue to view Photoworks with graphics or <u>without?</u>

PhotoWorks Gallery

PhotoWorks reveals three never-before-published photos of Marilyn Monroe.

Pictures On Disk

Seattle FilmWorks introduces an easy, low-cost way to get your own photos on a floppy disk.

Internet Photo Contest

See previous winners. Your photo could soon win you $250.

Seattle FilmWorks Photographer's Special

Get up to 24 of your images digitized free with your first film developing order.

Figure 22–4. To save time, give readers the choice of seeing a text-only site.

The site asks readers if they prefer to have the page delivered without pictures (Figure 22–5). It also provides a table of contents for the rest of the information at this site. Even though this site relies heavily on photos to make its impression—after all, people who come to this site are interested in taking pictures—it is important for every site to offer this feature.

Because pictures can take a long time to display, readers might not want to kill an hour waiting for them. Remember that people have short attention spans—even shorter when they are paying online and telephone charges! In the case of this site, the opening page took nearly ten minutes to transfer on a 14.4-kilobaud modem in the middle of the day. Other pictures and graphics took equally long periods of time. When you design your pages, you must consider whether or not people are willing to trade time for value. In this case, many people are interested in seeing good photographs and will probably wait for them to transmit. Will they do so at *your* home page? Are the pictures valuable additions to your information-gathering and distribution processes? Do they enhance the interactive experience? Or are they cute, visually interesting place-holders that don't really add a whole lot? You need to decide (or test the page with others and act on the results). In fact, Seattle FilmWorks later revised its pages, tossing out the fancy photographs and replacing them with faster-loading color images.

One work-around solution to the problem of large art files and slow transmission is to use small, thumbnail-sized art and give the reader the opportunity to click on it to see a full-screen version.

Figure 22–5. Offering free samples is a great way to attract people.

The special offer (Figure 22–6) is located on a page offering two free rolls of film. Notice how the company banner ties the subpage to the home page and enforces the uniform look. It also helps to build logo and brand identity.

The order form is sweet and simple. Anyone can understand it. There is no legal gobbledygook. If you want the film, you fill out the coupon. The form asks for the reader's name, postal address, and e-mail address.

The designers realized that people will fill out a simple form but might hesitate if it takes too long or asks a lot of questions. Two buttons at the bottom of the screen allow the user to send the request or stop the process. In either case, consumers are sent back to the site, where they can make more choices. This screen fulfills one of the most important functions in marketing: It captures the reader's name and contact information. The Web has no provision for identifying readers. If you want to know who has visited your site, you must ask them.

"What's really important is capturing information from people who visit the site," says Dan Fine of Fine Communications in Seattle, the database marketer who created the FilmWorks site.

Free PhotoWorks Software

Photography enters the digital age. When you develop your film at Seattle FilmWorks, you can also order up to 24 digitized images for just $3.95. Try this service today and your first disk is absolutely free.

PhotoWorks software lets you display digitized images, use them as screen-savers or send them out over the Internet. To receive your own complimentary copy of the PhotoWorks software, simply click here to download the PKZIPped program onto your computer.

Figure 22–6. Free software is sure to draw people to your Web site.

The site offered readers free software (Figure 22-6) to turn their photos into screen savers—a naturally great idea for this audience (offer might not be valid when you read this book). To receive the software, readers were told to "click here" after reading a description of the program. Behind the scenes, the computer did the rest. Downloading the software was easy.

Tell viewers the size of the file and include a general estimate on how long it will take to download so they can plan their time accordingly. People won't get upset over a long transmission if they can budget their time in advance.

One of the key points in designing a Web site is to add value to the reader's experience. The free offer accomplishes this task in several ways. It offers:

- **A free, useful product.** Most people who visit this site will want the film because they shoot pictures. This is a great lure.

- **Interactivity.** Readers get the chance to participate in a contest where they can submit their photos—or see winners. To make the contest current, prizes are given each month. This ensures that people will have something new to look at and have another chance to enter.
- **Free information.** Distributing free information is a cherished tradition on the Internet, so this tactic works well by dispensing information that has obvious value. In this case, the information answers questions about photography.
- **Free software.** If people like free information, they love free software. This tactic not only draws people to the site, it ties in with its general theme. The software is truly useful and reinforces the marketing message of letting this company develop your film so that you can use the images on your computer.

Hot! Hot! Hot!

Lobo Enterprises operates a World Wide Web site that offers hot sauces for sale at www.hothothot.com/hot/. It is an excellent example of a catalog that features easy access to its contents through a menu, clear instructions, and imaginative and fun artwork. The site hits you right between the eyes with vibrant artwork in hot colors (Figure 22-7). The introduction tells you about the hot sauces available, like Bat's Brew, Nuclear Hell, and Ring of Fire.

The catalog's opening screen (Figure 22-8) grabs attention immediately with its vibrant colors. Rather than use a simple table of contents like a printed catalog, the graphic is linked to each succeeding page so that users can select hot sauces by heat level, origin, ingredients, or name, with appropriate graphics to illustrate the themes. The product description (Figure 22-9) provides short overviews, with three icons that help readers see at a glance the various ratings for heat and other factors, a text description of the ingredients, and the best cooking use for the product. Size and price are displayed so that readers can see them easily. Notice the order button on the page. This page is not cluttered and gives readers the information they need quickly.

Welcome to Hot Hot Hot, the Net's coolest hot sauce shop!

(brought to you by <u>Presence</u>)

We want to welcome you to the Internet's first "Culinary Headshop!" Here you'll find fiery foodstuffs you never thought existed. Please come in and browse!

We have over 100 products of fire and the list is always growing. With names like Bats Brew, Nuclear Hell, and Ring of Fire, we're sure you'll find something you like.

Figure 22–7. Main menu for Hot! Hot! Hot! Catalog.

The Net's Coolest Hot Shop

We have one of the largest collections of international hot sauces for you to discover; best of all it's here, online and always available.

Hot Hot Hot Holiday Specials!

Figure 22–8. Main menu for the catalog. (Courtesy of Presence)

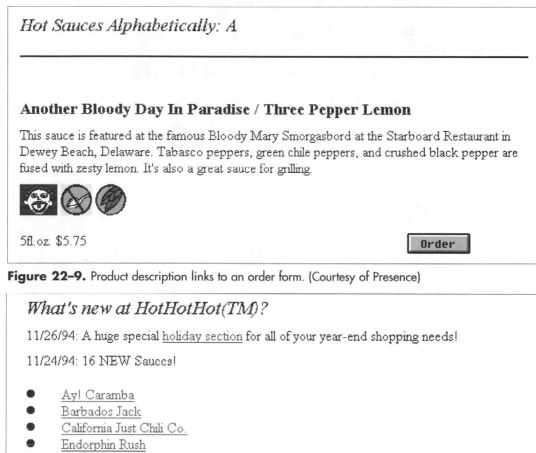

Figure 22–9. Product description links to an order form. (Courtesy of Presence)

What's new at HotHotHot(TM)?

11/26/94: A huge special holiday section for all of your year-end shopping needs!

11/24/94: 16 NEW Sauces!

- Ay! Caramba
- Barbados Jack
- California Just Chili Co.
- Endorphin Rush
- Flavors of the Rainforest Papaya
- Gib's Bottled Hell
- Gib's Nuclear Hell
- Island Soy Sauce
- Melinda's Amarillo Hot Sauce
- Mongo Hot Sauce
- Montezuma Habanero Chipotle
- Oso Hot Sauce
- Papaya Curry

Figure 22–10. "What's New" tells people about offerings. (Courtesy of Presence)

The "What's New" page (Figure 22-10) is dated so that people can see if the listings have changed since their last browse. Products are listed with text only, so the page displays quickly. Each title is a hotlink that, when clicked, leads the consumer to a description of the hot sauce. Traditional marketing shows its hand here with clever titles. Who can resist a hot sauce named "Endorphin Rush"?

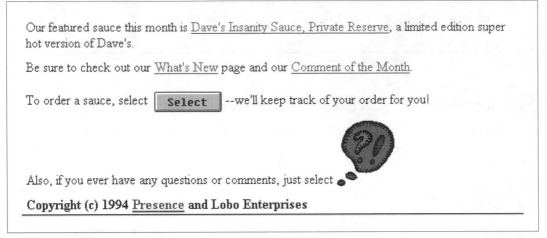

Our featured sauce this month is <u>Dave's Insanity Sauce, Private Reserve</u>, a limited edition super hot version of Dave's.

Be sure to check out our <u>What's New</u> page and our <u>Comment of the Month</u>.

To order a sauce, select [Select] --we'll keep track of your order for you!

Also, if you ever have any questions or comments, just select

Copyright (c) 1994 <u>Presence</u> **and Lobo Enterprises**

Figure 22–11. Merchants feature sale items, just as in a store. (Courtesy of Presence)

The online version of an end-cap display in a retail store is seen in the featured product area (Figure 22–11) that highlights an item the merchant wants to showcase. Consider doing this to your selected products.

SUMMARY

To make the sale, build credibility, or ensure a successful transaction, good design and content are essential ingredients of any Web site. This chapter showed the basic ingredients needed to create a site for marketing purposes. The next three chapters show how companies selling consumer products, services, and business-to-business are using the Internet with great success.

CHAPTER TWENTY-THREE

Strategic and Operational Issues for Online Selling

Merchants have a ground-floor opportunity to build brand identity and sales to an online audience that is wealthy, growing, and eager to buy products online.

In this chapter, we will explore:

- the World Wide Web: interactive selling at its best
- the benefits of online shopping
- sales figures and projections
- companies on the Web
- security and transaction issues
- online malls
- simulating the sales process online: organizing strategies

THE WORLD WIDE WEB: INTERACTIVE SELLING AT ITS BEST

Clearly, the most exciting interactive sales and marketing tool to date is the Internet's World Wide Web. The Web lets you create a virtual shopping experience through a combination of text, pictures, and sound that consumers can access to learn more about your company and its products and to place an order. A Web site can be compared to a catalog or to a store because customers can read about products, see them in action, and place an order. A site usually includes an overview of the company as well as point-and-click access to product or service information, online catalogs, product order forms, and other literature.

The Web can help you create an interactive sales presentation for a prospect because he selects the information he is interested in. The customer can pick and choose the product he wants to see, read as much information as he wants, and ask questions (and find answers) at any time of the day or night—and place an order from anywhere in the world. He can do this by pointing and clicking on designated words and graphics in a document located on a computer miles, or countries, away. He can place the order on the spot or can go to discussion groups and ask others about their experiences and recommendations.

Because of the high degree of interactivity, companies have the luxury of creating sales presentations tailored to each customer's individual needs. Also, marketers can create multiple selling propositions—a different reason to buy for each customer. In this manner, everyone who visits the Web can get personal treatment.

At its best, the Web creates a personal selling experience. Customers can see a demonstration of the product in full color. They can hear a step-by-step explanation of how to use the products to cook a better meal, listen to the eggs cracking, and watch a happy family eating the food.

Best yet, creating a Web site doesn't cost an arm and a leg. With the right tools and training, anyone can design a site and have it loaded onto a computer server for the whole world (literally) to see. The Web is truly every person's printing press.

THE BENEFITS OF ONLINE SHOPPING

The exciting promise of online marketing is the ability to make the sale. The Internet and commercial online services can deliver this today! Whether it be a trip to the virtual mall or a browse through an online catalog, marketers can use online services to make money.

"You are never going to get more attention from any customer than when they are online. Both their hands are on the keyboard and both their eyes are on the monitor," says Carol Wallace, program manager of communications for Prodigy. "You are interacting with them. They have preselected you. They want to see you. This is a very intimate selling situation."

Eastern Mortgage Securities, www.eastmorg.com, received 50–100 home equity loan applications a week only five months after it started up. It received 11,000 applications in the first quarter of 1996; 75 percent were approved in 24 hours. The site reads like a direct marketing letter, offering a free offer (24-hour approval) and a strong call to action with an online application. The cost of attracting prospects online is much lower than through traditional approaches. A completed loan application by mail costs $150 but only $10 on the Internet.

That sure is a big change from 1984, when online shopping first began and customers were suspicious. They didn't like the idea of not being able to see and touch products. They weren't sure about sending their credit card information over the computer line. While they might have appreciated the time they saved on shopping, there wasn't a large supply of products to select from.

All that has changed. Hundreds of merchants offer products online—from clothing to books to vacations. Big names like B. Dalton, Lands' End, and J.C. Penney offer online shopping. Small companies selling T-shirts, self-published mystery novels, and computer software also offer their wares online. Technology is improving to the point where people can see pictures of products and read or hear descriptions. Data encryption is developing to the point where it can reliably protect sensitive information such as customer credit card information.

Online shopping offers several advantages over shopping in person:

- Comparison shopping is quick and easy.
- Consumers can order directly from the comfort of their home or office, 24 hours a day, from anywhere in the world.
- The store never closes.
- There are no traffic jams, no parking places to fight over, and no waste of time.

Shopping has never been easier for consumers. They can order products directly from the merchant using a computer and a modem. They can browse at their own pace and can't be hassled by pushy salespeople. Orders are paid for by credit card, which merchants can verify before processing the order. Many companies offer toll-free telephone order services for customers who prefer them. Delivery varies by merchant but is usually made by a recognized carrier such as Federal Express or UPS so that companies can track receipts. Consumers usually get their products within 72 hours.

Online information can be delivered immediately to consumers via e-mail; they don't have to wait three weeks for a catalog to reach them by mail. They can view the information and make a buying decision immediately. In this way, online services help fulfill demand.

Merchants benefit as well.

- Merchants gain an additional distribution channel for their products.
- Online shoppers tend to have more disposable income than the average consumer.
- Online marketers can keep track of their best customers and alert them to sales and special promotions.
- Vendors can build relationships with customers through online sales, support, and service.
- The flexible publishing platforms of the Internet and commercial online services offer the marketer the chance to build relationships by publishing unlimited amounts of information for consumers to devour at their own pace.

The Internet and online commercial services offer different concepts in selling. They range from a totally interactive medium on the Internet's World Wide Web, complete with multimedia presentations, to graphics and colorful drawings on Prodigy, America Online, and CompuServe. The ability to sell with the tools of sound and motion picture presentations is in the works on all the commercial online services. Someday the computer will achieve television's ability to deliver commercials complete with sound and synchronized pictures. The commercial online services also are exploring sales opportunities involving CD-ROM. These storage devices contain audio and video files that would otherwise take too long to transmit over the phone lines.

One key to the success of an online store is interactivity. "Online marketers need to make their information informative, engaging, and nonintrusive. Because the services, products, etc., are interactive, shoppers must want to surf these areas. If the information does not engage them, they won't scan the area. it's as simple as that," an America Online company spokesman says.

SALES FIGURES AND PROJECTIONS

Transactions on the Web are expected to exceed $46 billion in sales by the year 2000, according to Montgomery Securities. Ad-supported sites will approach $5 billion. Fee-based sites and premium or subscription services will grow to $214 million by 1997 and nearly $1 billion by 2000.

Women shoppers will spend $368 million online in 1996, according to "Women Online: Developing Content for an Emerging Market," a report by Jupiter Communications. By 2000, Jupiter forecasts that this figure will grow to nearly $3.5 billion, based on the ever-increasing numbers of women going online. In 1996 women accounted for an estimated 37 percent of users of online services, including both commercial online services and the World Wide Web. This translates into 13.8 million women online. By 2000 women will represent nearly 47 percent of total online services users, or 43.3 million.

Forrester Research predicts that by 1999, 50 percent of all software will be delivered online. Microsoft figures the value of software distributed electronically could reach $5 billion. Software publishers Sierra On-line and Electronic Arts say that in the next three to five years they expect 30–50 percent of revenues will come from online.

COMPANIES ON THE WEB

More than 75 percent of Fortune 1000 companies expect to process online transactions by 1997, according to Forrester Research. More than 20,000 businesses have Web sites—including 30 percent of the Fortune 500. They range from large companies, like General Motors, Intel, and Proctor & Gamble, to small businesses like mine. People are even putting their resumes online to find jobs in the high-tech industries. How's that for advertising?

Many industries, including travel, entertainment, auto, financial investment services, professional sports, books, and software, are adopting the Internet in a big way with integrated advertising, marketing, and customer support and retention programs.

Faceless Transactions: Benefit or Hindrance?

The computer offers the opportunity for sales to be conducted completely without a human operator at the sales center. This is great for companies that want to cut personnel costs. Also, some customers simply don't like aggressive salespeople and prefer ordering online.

However, faceless and voiceless transactions might cost some companies more in the long run. "Vendors don't want faceless transactions. Customer service operators build customer rapport, add-on sales, and sell service," says Marc Fleischmann, president of Internet Distribution Services, Inc., of Palo Alto, California, a marketing design technology company that helps companies market their services on the Internet. Some groups of consumers actually do want to talk to a person, even if it is over the phone, so they can have pertinent questions answered.

These reasons reinforce the belief that online marketing is but one part of the marketing mix and another channel of distribution—not the only one.

SECURITY FOR ONLINE ORDERING

More than 75 percent of people surveyed by Dataquest say they would not buy anything on the Internet by sending the credit card information over the computer lines for fear of the information being stolen. Although there has not been a single reported case of a consumer having a credit card stolen over the Internet, the fear persists.

Despite this study, a number of merchants report healthy sales via the Internet. Internet Shopping Network's founder Bill Robinson says more than 100,000 consumers have given credit card information over the Internet.

Merchants should make it easy for customers to buy products in the manner they prefer: calling an order center via a toll-free number, sending an e-mail note, completing an online order form, or printing out an order form and sending it in via fax or phone, putting it in the mail, or using COD.

The specter of fraud exists for the merchant as well. She might receive calls from thieves who are placing orders with stolen credit cards. Good business practice calls for merchants to call the credit card authorization center to make sure the card is valid. However, fast thieves can place many orders online before the card's original owner realizes the card is missing and calls in to report the disappearance. By that time, many merchants could be liable for a lot of money.

Just as in any credit card transaction, there are certain risks. Proponents of online shopping say the security of credit card numbers is just as reliable—or unreliable—as traditional transactions. After all, thieves can steal credit card numbers from carbons tossed into the garbage in a restaurant or store. Unscrupulous employees can steal credit card numbers given to them over the phone or sent in via mail order. All businesses have risks.

The commercial online services assert that they have secure systems that cannot be violated by hackers trying to steal credit card information. The Internet does not make such claims.

Because of potential risks, banks also are wary about online transactions and have established stiffer-than-usual requirements for new merchants who sell products online. They are taking a hard-nosed approach to granting credit card processing terminals to companies that do business on online services.

Merchants can protect themselves from fraud by following these steps:

1. Send the product by a carrier that gets a signed record of delivery. Customers can't claim they never received the product. If they honestly didn't receive the product, the shipper's records can be traced.
2. Call the credit card authorization center to verify the credit card number before shipping the product.
3. Ship the product quickly. People change their minds and then claim they never ordered the product.
4. Ask for the customer's address for verification purposes. This is especially important for online orders of information products or other products that are transmitted to the customer over the online system, like newsletters, software, and research and consulting services. In those cases, the merchant or consultant probably wouldn't have thought to make a record of the address because he isn't mailing or shipping anything over a normal shipping route to the customer.
5. Ship the package COD (cash on delivery).
6. Request payment in advance.

Online marketers can employ other strategies to fight fraud. One method that seems to work is the membership program. Using this approach, you permit access to the shopping ordering area to members only. To become a member, the customer has to submit her address and credit card information in advance to the merchant, who ascertains the validity of the information. The new member receives a membership number and password that she must use to place an order. As it is unlikely that the wrong person could get both password and number, the system is safe.

Third-party companies also are brokering this service so that consumers don't have to register with each merchant individually.

TRANSACTION ISSUES

Secure transactions are available on the Internet by a variety of methods. Netscape offers secure servers; software companies have technologies for encrypting data sent over the phone lines. More companies are offering solutions every day. It is beyond the scope of this book to discuss in detail all the issues related to digital money. There are books that cover this topic and the entire field of electronic data interchange (EDI). For the latest information, check the home pages for these companies:

- First Virtual Internet Payment System, www.fv.com
- Digicash, www.digicash.com
- Ecash, www.digicash.com/ecash/ecash-home.html
- Cybercash, www.cybercash.com

Merchants are creating relationships with companies like these that accept money from consumers and put the dollars into an account that the consumers can draw on when they visit sites that accept this financial transaction. Security is built into the system to prevent unauthorized usage. Mastercard, VISA, and American Express also are working on secure payment programs.

ONLINE MALLS

Virtual malls on the Internet are gaining in popularity and scope. Many companies are creating their own electronic realty offices and opening malls. These malls are collections of businesses accessed by the consumer through a common address. According to Forrester Research, there are 601 malls, with an average of 18 stores per mall, representing 7500 merchants. Mall owners take 5–15 percent commission.

Malls can be based on a number of similar elements:

- *products,* such as Hearthnet, www.hearth.com/
- *industries,* such as Industry.net, www.industry.net
- *geographic regions,* such as Eureka Springs, Arkansas, www.DiscoverEureka.com
- *products and geography,* such as Interart, www.interart.com, which features Sante Fe food and art
- *dissimilar products,* which should be avoided because they might not be able to attract the people who are interested in your products or services.

IBM, Time-Warner, and AT&T are all reportedly building malls.

Pros and Cons of Joining a Mall

There are many reasons for merchants to want to be in a mall.

- A large amount of traffic comes to a mall site because people know they will find common types of products.
- Merchants can take advantage of a business structure that handles technology as well as accepting and verifying orders. Malls should have designers available for hire who can create and update merchant sites.
- As mall operators upgrade equipment, merchants benefit as the costs are spread out among many players.

On the down side, if mall operators don't promote the site or are bad landlords, your store will suffer. "There's nothing a mall could do that an individual store owner couldn't do on his own," says Emily Green, Forrester analyst.

How to Select a Mall

A good mall provides management, marketing, and security for its merchants. If you decide to select a mall, make sure it offers these features:

- Affordable, high-quality connectivity through T1 lines—and lots of them, if the mall has many merchants. As more merchants sign on and more consumers join, the transmission times slow considerably.

If the mall doesn't offer fast access, your consumers could get turned off by long transmission delays.

- Attractive and easy user interface.
- Software tools for providers that make it easy to put up and maintain the site, or access to technicians who will update the site for you at a reasonable cost.
- Security mechanisms, including authentication and encryption.
- Experience in the business. Many start-up companies bill themselves as malls but don't have the depth of knowledge, expertise, or hardware needed to help a merchant.
- Experience in publicizing and promoting the site.
- Reliability of hardware systems and the ability to fix hardware problems quickly. If the site is down, no one can buy from you.
- An easy-to-type address. For example, an easy address is www.mycompany.com. A difficult address is: www.somemall.com/level2/eastwing/mycompany.

Compare mall operators on the basis of how much commission they take, transaction charges, download or access charges, and payment schedules.

SIMULATING THE SALES PROCESS ONLINE: ORGANIZING STRATEGIES

The Web site can be an instrumental tool in building sales, according to Kristin Zhivago, editor of *Marketing Technology* in Menlo Park, California, kristin@zhivago.com, 415-328-6000. Here are her views on how online activities affect marketing and how to coordinate online presences to build sales:

"Online marketing is not just going to fit into the marketing mix. It is going to drive the marketing effort. If you think of the selling process from the customer's viewpoint, it is a buying process. Online marketing has the potential to remove the barriers a customer normally encounters while trying to buy something.

"The customer sees the buying process in three distinct phases: recognizing a need, searching for the solution, and making a purchase. Using traditional buying methods, the search for the solution can be time-consuming and frustrating. There is a lot of back-and-forth with vendors.

"Throughout the buying process, the customer is seeking answers to specific questions in a particular order. The vendors provide their answers through salespeople, tech support, literature, videos, demos, and other promotional pieces. Once the questions are answered satisfactorily, the customer will make a buying decision.

"If your Web site is well-designed, customers can quickly get answers to their questions. While the need is still fresh in their minds, they will be transformed from people with a problem to people who have identified, and want to purchase, a particular solution. This compresses the buying cycle and will have a profound effect on marketing practices.

"Your Web site will be a successful marketing tool only if you organize it to conveniently answer all of the customer's questions. That may seem obvious, but considering how poorly standard marketing materials have provided answers in the past, we are not expecting Web sites to be any better. Organizing the presentation of the information so that it matches the customer's question sequence is particularly important with online marketing because it is an interactive medium. It puts the customer in the driver's seat. The last thing you want to do is make your customer drive all over cyberspace waiting for downloads, and getting lost, locked out, and ticked off.

"As you start to organize your Web site, don't assume that you already know how your customers ask questions or that your salespeople will be able to tell you. Salespeople usually talk to customers who are already partway through their buying process. Your site needs to start at the beginning of the process and progress unobtrusively as your customers work their way toward a purchase.

"Call customers and ask them about their buying process. Tell them you are designing your Web site and you want it to make sense to them. Listen carefully.

"By the tenth phone call, the proper structure should be obvious. There will be clear, identifiable patterns. Use this information to design your Web site, and you will be rewarded with sales from grateful customers. You will have removed the frustration and confusion from their buying process.

"Talking to customers will also make you confident that you are doing the right thing. I guarantee that the customer's view of the buying process is different from your company's view of the selling process. You will have to fight for the customer's interests in internal meetings.

"If you do not know your customers well, you will not be able to make the logical, fact-based arguments needed to win. The company-centric view will prevail and customers will be frustrated when they visit your site. If you have spoken with customers you will not only know what to do but you will be able to use real-world examples when the arguments start. Anecdotes have an incredibly powerful effect on coworkers, many of whom are holding tightly to cherished but incorrect ideas about who the customers are and how the customers buy.

"Online marketing has the potential to become your most profitable marketing vehicle because it shortens the buying cycle and can provide detailed sales tracking data (which has been lacking with other marketing vehicles). But it also requires a substantial investment. Because it is interactive and online, customers expect it to be kept up to date and refreshed substantially every few weeks. You will need a Web master to do that.

"You will also need a Netmonitor to constantly watch the various bulletin boards, sites, and discussion lists for questions on your types of products. When appropriate, your Netmonitor should be able to jump in and answer those questions, using preapproved copy and/or ideas.

"So, you will need at least two more people in your marketing department devoted exclusively to your online marketing efforts. And you can't afford to stop using your standard broadcasting vehicles, which will bring customers to your Web site. Because all of your traditional marketing communications work will need to continue, your total marketing budget will have to be increased.

"However, online marketing will decrease the amount of time the salespeople and technical people spend answering questions. This should reduce the total amount of money and resources your company devotes to making the sale."

SUMMARY

Increasing numbers of people want to shop online, and increasing numbers of merchants are setting up shop to accommodate them. This chapter reviewed the basic concerns and issues for online merchants. The next chapter offers more case studies and examples.

CHAPTER TWENTY-FOUR

Selling Consumer Products and Services Online

Companies in many industries are selling products and services to a willing online audience. This chapter continues our examination of examples and strategies.

In this chapter we will explore:

- the online catalog
- case studies

THE ONLINE CATALOG

Online data can be seen as an electronic version of the company catalog—complete with pictures that entice the eye, words that inspire the imagination, and prices that don't make consumers think twice. Electronic information is less expensive to deliver than catalogs: there aren't any printing or postage costs. Online marketers with wry senses of humor are fond of saying they don't like to spend money mailing dead trees to customers.

The lowered cost of doing business online means that some merchants can enjoy a larger profit margin while others pass the savings along to consumers in the form of lower prices. Still others view the online systems as another distribution channel that features the same pricing structure as catalogs or direct mail.

Merchants can change information, product lineups, and pricing immediately to take advantage of market trends, price tests, and the like. Some companies, of course, would like to move quickly but can't because of internal operations, though at least the promise is available.

Print isn't outdated yet. Hard-copy catalogs can display color more attractively than computers. Print catalogs can be read on the bus or in the bathroom. Also, consumers can flip through pages more easily and see several pieces of information at once. This is handy when, say, they are looking at the order form and then need to flip back to page 20 to find the product number for the kite they want to buy. Yet online consumers can find information quickly by linking from one page to the next and can order directly from each page.

Regardless, the elements of proper advertising must be present for online marketing to work effectively.

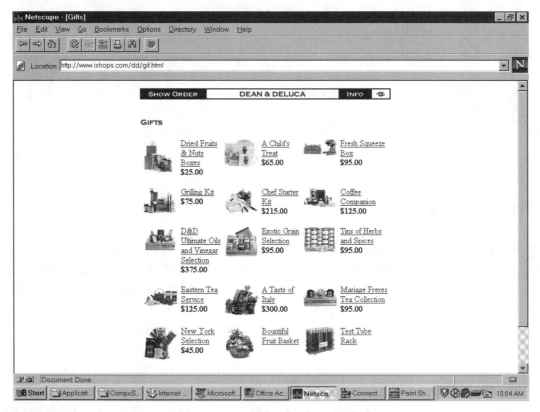

Figure 24–1. Consumers can order a variety of fine foods and gifts from Dean & DeLuca, www.ishops.com/dd. (Courtesy of Dean & DeLuca.)

Case Study: Dean & DeLuca Fine Foods

Dean & DeLuca, of New York's SoHo district, offers roughly 600 fine food products and specialty kitchen tools through local markets across the country as well as through a catalog printed several times a year.

Dean & DeLuca decided to present its inventory online, hoping to tap the electronic market of gourmet cooks. "We liked the idea of having the world's finest food emporium available at all times to anyone interested in cooking," notes Pat Roney, president and CEO. "And when we learned that we could be up and running with our entire product line within a month, we jumped at the chance."

Dean & DeLuca chose to build its online presence using the iCat Commerce Suite, a software package of Web publishing and delivery tools. The company contracted with iCat Corporation's Technical Services Group (TSG), www.icat.com, in Seattle to handle production, on a very tight deadline.

The company wanted the premium image of their print catalog reflected in the online version, so they had their own designers supply TSG with the appropriate graphics and the art department directed the production work. TSG extracted product names, descriptions, prices, and other text elements from the QuarkXpress files of the print catalog and transferred the information into a database in iCat Commerce Publisher. Transferring the product text into the database involved a tagged import process using text-only or ASCII files.

To add product images to the site, TSG batch-converted .pict files provided by Dean & DeLuca to the Web-friendly .gif format. The conversion process took roughly half a day. From there, TSG linked the graphics to the database through an automated import process and added ordering templates to the layout for secure online transactions.

Dean & DeLuca's full electronic catalog was created in roughly 2 1/2 weeks by one member of TSG with just five HTML templates. Three templates incorporate the iCat Command language and serve to produce all of the product pages for the entire 600-product catalog; one additional HTML template acts as the home page and the other provides company information.

The founders of Dean & DeLuca hope that cooks who have never heard of the company will discover it through their Web site. They are also expecting to introduce home cooks to new tools and ingredients, encouraging them to experiment more in their cooking. And, of course, they're planning to see orders from the Web site.

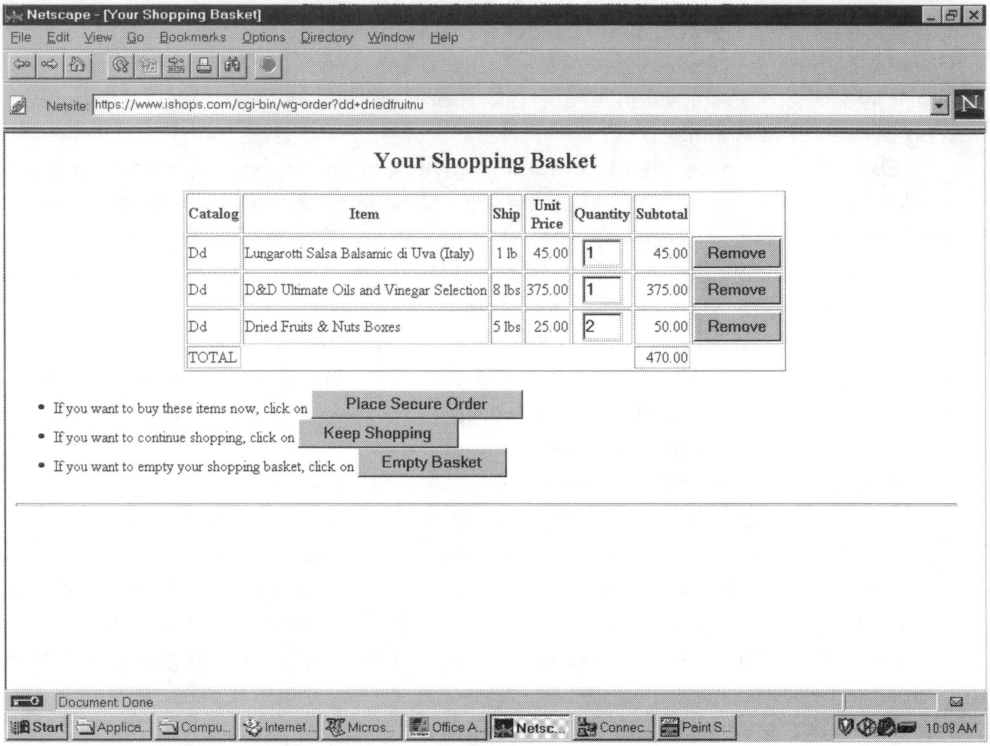

Figure 24–2. As consumers browse through the Dean & DeLuca catalog, they can see their accumulated order, complete with totals for the sale. (Courtesy of Dean & DeLuca.)

Case Study: Quote.Com

Quote.Com, Inc., is a provider of financial information that helps investors on the Internet. It is an example of a company that charges for access to its service on the World Wide Web. Most Web sites offer free information in hopes of making money from advertisers who want to reach their readers, or by offering information that will build a relationship in which the reader becomes a customer. As business models take shape on the Internet, Quote.Com, www.quote.com, is one to study.

"One of the reasons I started Quote.Com was because I noticed that investors were becoming more actively involved in their investment decisions," says Chris Cooper, president. "I've tried to create a place on the Internet where investors can find all of the tools they need to be as informed as a broker on Wall Street. The Basic Plus service, at $33.95 per month, bundles professional tools at a price an individual investor can afford." Members pay a fee and are given a password that allows them to use the services in Quote.Com.

Cooper studied the market and found that more people than ever before are investing their money in the stock market. "Returns on more traditional means of investing are simply not enough to keep up with inflation. Factor in large commissions from full-service brokers and there is not much money left. As a result, many people have taken control of their finances by using discount brokerage houses. To succeed in this scenario investors have to take an active role in their portfolios, including research, analysis, and awareness of breaking news," he says.

In response to these needs Quote.Com created several levels of service, called packages, which include news services, Business Wire and PR Newswire, quotes, portfolio tracking, research tools, one-year price histories for stocks, commodities, and mutual funds, Hoover's Company Profiles, and Standard & Poor's Marketscope. Packages can also include e-mail notification of news from portfolio items, price limits, and end-of-the-day pricing. This is an excellent example of using technology to add value. Prices range from $9.95 to $39.95 per month.

Like most successful sites, Quote.Com offers a free service to turn prospects into customers—a complimentary membership in the Quote.Com financial market data service. When users register, they can retrieve five quotes a day from any of the U.S. exchanges, symbol searches, and limited balance sheet data. In addition to the Basic Service subscription, users can choose from an à la carte menu of optional services and pay an additional fee by the month or by the individual one-time usage. By following this strategy, the company neared the breakeven point after four months of operation.

Case Study: GolfWeb

GolfWeb has been in operation since the beginning of 1995 and originated as a site devoted to addressing the interests of golfers. The site has grown consistently each month and has more than 25,000 pages of information content. The revenue model is based on advertising sales and retail operations.

Visitors come to GolfWeb to review tournament results, access historical data, read editorials on the golf world, and use its international database of golf course information to plan vacations. The company believes that its content draws readers and drives sales. Retailers are setting up shop on the Web in record numbers, but GolfWeb's success is based on drawing readership to the site rather than drawing shoppers. The entire GolfWeb site can be accessed without charge and there are no membership fees or individual charges of any sort unless a customer wishes to make a retail purchase, a spokesman said.

GolfWeb has leveraged its readership by providing links into the Pro Shop from other sections of the site, as appropriate. A typical example is when an editorial column refers to a product that is for sale in the Pro Shop, a direct link to the Pro Shop is supplied so the reader can learn more about the product and make a purchase on the spot, if he wishes.

GolfWeb's Pro Shop area was developed in-house with the needs of golfers in mind. Despite the many variables involved in categorizing golf clubs, a menu-drive system was designed that allows golfers to choose clubs in the same manner as any simpler product, such as books, shirts, and gifts. Customers designate items they wish to purchase by placing them in a metaphoric shopping cart.

GolfWeb claims to have competitive advantages by offering automated shopping over the Internet, along with the ability to transmit a completed order with credit card payment information directly to its offices. GolfWeb offers 250 distinct products with over 800 varieties and styles. It accepts orders 24 hours a day by telephone and over the Internet, and e-mail queries are reviewed seven days a week to respond to customer inquiries and to send quotations.

The site is secure, using Netscape's Secure Commerce server and Cybercash; this encryption system alleviates customer concerns about Internet security. Customers are also offered alternate options for ordering, including a mechanism that allows them to print out a shopping list, fill in a credit card authorization area, and fax the order to GolfWeb. Another option allows the customer to e-mail a competed shopping list to their own address to retrieve and review at a later date.

GolfWeb successfully anticipated a large international demand for name-brand golfing equipment and has been accepting and shipping international orders since the store opened. Orders have been filled for destinations throughout Europe and Asia, Russia, South Africa, Guatemala, and Australia. GolfWeb has been successful in negotiating favorable worldwide shipping rates and is distinct among competitors in its ability to provide high-quality products and services at excellent prices.

Case Study: 1-800-FLOWERS

1-800-FLOWERS is one of the most successful direct sales businesses on the Internet. The site also supports the company's integrated marketing program. Donna Iucolano, the manager for interactive services and supervisor of a staff of 12, answered our questions. The Web site URL is www.1800flowers.com.

Consumers are greeted at the site by a cheery message—"Welcome to our world"—and an equally cheery image of the entrance to a nursery. They then select Shop Our Store. In that section they can choose from four main categories:

1.   Seasons' Best, an assortment of bouquets with enticing names like "Fields of Europe," "Fresh Noble Fir Wreath," and "Dried Floral Winter Centerpiece."

2.   Shop by Occasion, including birthday, anniversary, congratulations, best wishes, thank you, new baby, get well, and sympathy.

3.   Shop by Product Category, such as flowers, roses, plants, gift baskets, gourmet items, balloons, and decorative keepsakes.

4.   Shop by Price Range, from under $25 to $65 and over.

Each product is accompanied by a photo and enticing descriptive catalog copy. Each arrangement can be ordered in small, medium, and large sizes. Prices and shipping charges are clearly visible.

To purchase, consumers select the product and quantity. They then click the Add button. After each selection, an invoice pops up showing the products ordered, total price, and service charge. When they've finished selecting, consumers click the Go to the

Checkout Lane button to pay for their purchases by filling in their name, address, phone number, and credit card information. If they make mistakes, they can reset the form to empty their shopping basket.

The company allows purchases through Netcape's Commerce Server and a standard transfer protocol for people who don't use Netscape. It has a joint marketing arrangement with United Airlines, so members can get 300 miles for purchases over $29.95.

Q: What was 1-800-FLOWERS' mission in going online?

A: The original reason for going online was to pursue new media and showcase our products online using interactive media. Our first interactive project was in 1992 with CompuServe. Since that time we've made substantial investments in the interactive services division.

Q: Has it met its goal?

A: We are at $25 million as a division. I think we are doing all right. That figure represents 10 percent of company sales. We are on 16 electronic ventures, all major commercial online services, interactive TV trials, multimedia kiosks, PDAs, wireless, and cellular.

Q: How did the idea get started?

A: As a company we are pretty innovative and big technology users. We saw this as a new and innovative thing. We run a very state-of-the-art facility on the telecom side. We embrace technology.

Q: How has the cost of technology affected your product costs and consumer prices?

A: We realized that technology reduces the costs of service and we pass along the savings to customers. It is less expensive to order online than over the phone. We made a decision very early on that savings would be passed along to customers.

Q: Was it difficult to get approval from corporate to go onto the Web?

A: Not really. We came to the Internet in April after spending 3 1/2 years online. It wasn't our first venture online. A lot of companies are having trouble selling it [a Web site] internally because they don't have any experience online.

Q: Which department has responsibility for maintaining the site?

A: Interactive marketing, which is a hybrid of marketing and has a staff of 12 with a wide variety of skill sets.

Q: Was the site created internally or was an outside contractor hired?

A: It was created with an Internet development company, Fry Multimedia, for the back end and Erin Edward for the creative.

Q: What criteria do you look for in a vendor?

A: We certainly want them to have experience with the Internet, multimedia art and design, and transactional applications. They should be able to support our marketing efforts and work with our larger ad agency of record. We look at their work for other clients and check referrals. We also ask for recommendations.

Q: What would you do differently?

A: We are constantly rebuilding the page. That is very important because a month or two in this environment is a long time. New developments happen all the time. We make changes daily. As new technologies are available, we are comfortable making enhancements and changes.

Q: What improvements or features will you add in the near future?

A: Better searching capabilities. We're looking at intelligent agents. We want to cut the time customers spend online. I think it will be good when we have better compression technology to make art and images smaller and more performance oriented. We'll implement alternative payment methods and digital cash. When things like that are here, shopping online will be better.

Q: What role does the site play in the integrated marketing program for 1-800-FLOWERS?

A: It has a big role. It is more than just a shopping application. We have a lot of floral info online. We promote our retail stores and post help wanted information. It is a comprehensive application. It talks about the company as a whole and allows us to publish information about the industry, flower giving, and gifts.

SUMMARY

Anyone who doubts that companies are receiving money on the Internet doesn't have to look far for examples that can inspire others to similar successes. The next chapter examines business-to-business selling on the Internet.

CHAPTER TWENTY-FIVE

Business-to-Business Selling Online

This chapter rounds out the advice given throughout the book on how to use the Internet to build relationships and sell products. Because every business claims to have its own unique obstacles, no one chapter could possibly be all things to all people. Therefore, this chapter presents highlights of business-to-business selling through statistics and case studies. We trust you will be able to glean a few tidbits from other industries to help make you a success.

In this chapter, you will see.

- business-to-business selling opportunities online
- who's doing business online
- case studies
- additional marketing strategies

BUSINESS-TO-BUSINESS OPPORTUNITIES SELLING ONLINE

"The new business customer—the knowledge worker with access to computers and the Internet—is ready to spend billions on online services," says Chris Elwell, publisher of SIMBA Information, Inc. "Consumer online sales totaled $1.2 billion. Business online revenues already exceed $14.5 billion and companies are building the infrastructure to support widespread use of computer-based services. Once this network is in place—and SIMBA projects over 20 million business people will have access to online and Internet services by 2000—the opportunity to sell information and transactional services to this market will explode."

WHO'S SELLING BUSINESS-TO-BUSINESS

Companies in virtually every industry are using the Internet to create relationships with prospects and customers and to sell products. Searching through Yahoo! on your industry will yield invaluable links to other companies whose strategies you can explore on your own. Here are examples of how companies are using the Internet to sell products to businesses:

- *Wilkins Outdoor Advertising,* www.outdoor-ad.com, advises companies on how to buy billboard ads on the highway, not on the Internet, but uses the World Wide Web to showcase its expertise.
- *Newsweek* sought out media buyers at magazines by hosting a Web site called Mediaspot, www.mediaspot.com. The site prints information about restaurants and night life in cities where *Newsweek* has offices, as well as bios of editorial and sales staffers. The Web site also ties in with an integrated advertising program including print ads, postcards, and promotional contests.
- *Career Mosaic,* www.careermosaic.com, a job listing service, charges companies between $40 and $150 to list job openings. The site receives seven million visitors a month.
- *AMP,* www.amp.com, features 64,000 computer and stereo parts. It attracts 200 new customers a day and repeat customers are growing by 15–20 percent each month. The company is one of the more sophisticated sites on the Internet; it offers such options as asking a customer to type in his language, country, and company to produce an interface that will, for example, account for the person's language, local shipping costs, and preferred pricing lists.
- *Softbank,* operator of the Comdex computer trade show, allows businesspeople to register via the Internet, thus saving the company the costs of postage and labor to type information.

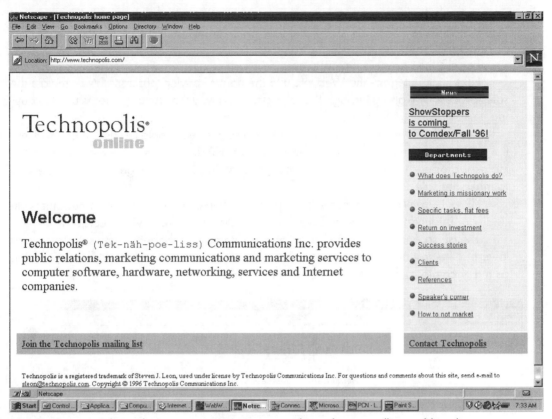

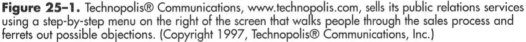

Figure 25–1. Technopolis® Communications, www.technopolis.com, sells its public relations services using a step-by-step menu on the right of the screen that walks people through the sales process and ferrets out possible objections. (Copyright 1997, Technopolis® Communications, Inc.)

Case Study: Hewlett-Packard

Hewlett-Packard (HP) is a worldwide leader in computer manufacturing. Its Web site draws 35,000–40,000 people a day and transmits 16 billion bits of information in the form of product information, schedules, photos, catalogs, and software updates.

The site has 10,000 pages and adds 10 percent more each month. Thirty percent of visitors are outside the United States. Between 40 and 60 people at HP are involved in the marketing and commerce of the Web site.

"We've made a significant investment and have made a significant payback," a company spokesman said. "We are looking at this as a business-to-business medium." That includes every business from small office/home office to data centers.

The spokesman dispels the thoughts of having a cool site, opting for one with a corporate look and feel. Ironically, he says a colleague at another company with a cool site was under pressure to turn it into one that looked more like HP's!

Instead of opting for cool, HP looks to metrics. "You should focus on what you want to accomplish. Cool is not a basic objective," he says. "Who is setting the goals? Technologists, artists, marketers, or customers?"

For HP, the answer is the customers.

HP tries to integrate the Web site into the normal buying process. "We simulate the sales process by walking through the sales steps in a way that the customer is used to buying."

Research showed that in order to make the sale, three people needed to be involved: the engineer, the manager, and a finance person. HP decided to created pages that met the needs for each participant in the sales process. This helped HP get the buy-in needed to make the sale.

HP put up technical documents to provide after-sales support for its customers. In addition, it found that prospects used the information to make buying decisions!

The HP spokesman sees the benefit to his customers as shortening the sales cycle and lowering the cost of doing business. HP saves "tens of millions of dollars" by not printing as many catalogs, thanks to Web browsing.

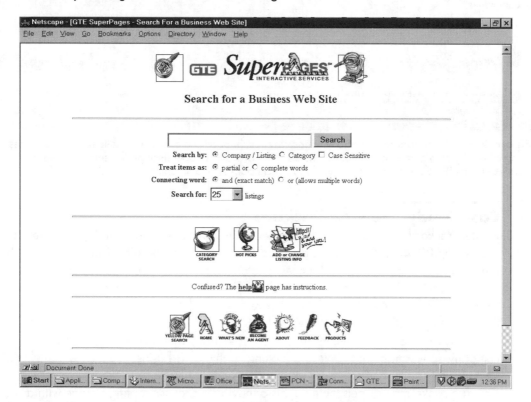

Figure 25-2. GTE SuperPages, www.superpages.gte.net, lets businesses find other businesses anywhere in America. (Copyright 1997, GTE Directories Corp.)

Case Study: GTE Superpages

Feature-rich, interactive business services that are now accessible on the Internet's World Wide Web provide a powerful new tool for both consumers and businesses.

Patrick Marshall, GTE Directories vice president for new media services, says GTE's SuperPages interactive business directory, www.superpages.gte.net, and its competitors have created a new marketing vehicle with enormous potential for exploiting the reach, cost-effectiveness, and interactive capabilities of the Internet and the World Wide Web.

"SuperPages' interactive directory enables businesses to reach more consumers and markets than they ever thought possible," Marshall said. "With SuperPages, a local or regional company can become a national and even international company almost overnight."

SuperPages' interactive directory works much like an electronic Yellow Pages, but with many more capabilities. For one, the SuperPages directory includes listings by category for most U.S. businesses—about ten million listings. Users can search for a company in numerous ways: by category, name, phone number, city, state, even zip code. The SuperPages directory also features a fast search tool to browse the Internet's World Wide Web.

Soon after the test version went online, Marshall said, it developed its first user success story. An American expatriate living and working in Indonesia told GTE via e-mail that for some time he had been trying to locate a particular manufacturer of socks. Clothing stores had advised him that the company was no longer in business.

When the SuperPages interactive business directory came online, the man in Indonesia searched electronically for the socks company and found it was still going strong in New York. Twelve pairs of the company's socks were soon on their way to Indonesia.

"The SuperPages interactive directory is a major innovation in online directories. Like radio or television when they first appeared on the scene, nobody can predict the Internet's full potential or impact on our daily lives," Marshall said. "Already we can see that SuperPages can give consumers, including business-to-business consumers, more choices and options than they ever had."

In addition to the search function, the SuperPages directory includes a host of other services and features that offer essentially one-stop shopping for consumers and for small- and midsized businesses that want to have a presence on the Internet.

SuperPages offers extended listings of up to five lines of information, simple ads, links to Web sites, keyword searches, and even faster searches. In addition, advertisers can obtain help with Web site development and hosting, domain registration, Internet access, chat, and e-mail.

GTE has adopted an aggressive pricing strategy designed to attract small- and mid-sized businesses. For example, an advertiser can get an interactive listing with five lines of copy free for six months and only $25 per month thereafter. A display ad costs as little as $35 per month plus set-up charges; a site of up to three screens costs as little as $45 per month plus set-up charges.

Numerous other SuperPages interactive directory options and add-on features fully exploit the visual and interactive capabilities of the Internet and World Wide Web.

"Consumers will warm up quickly to SuperPages directory because it is fast, comprehensive, and easy to use," Marshall said. "Advertisers will like SuperPages interactive directory because it adds a whole new dimension to their marketing mix at a very reasonable cost."

ADDITIONAL MARKETING STRATEGIES FOR BUSINESS-TO-BUSINESS

It is vitally important for businesses to qualify the people who come to their site so salespeople can follow up, as no one will ever buy a piece of capital equipment solely over the Internet. Companies must require the prospects to identify themselves by title, purchasing power and authority, and other factors relevant to their industry.

Here are two strategies to add to others found throughout the book:

1. Require registration for access to the site's meatier subjects.
2. Offer a form for a free evaluation. The evaluation is really a sales call with information provided by the user and helps the company to qualify the user.

Case Study: Easy Analytic Software, Inc.

Easy Analytic Software, Inc. sells demographic reports to marketers via the Internet. The Internet is the only marketing source for this new company, which also combines public relations as a way to get people to the site (www.easidemographics.com).

"The *San Francisco Chronicle* ran an article about us and we got 60 leads in three days," says sales director Greg Gergen. "I've been in sales most of my career and I've never had it so easy."

Visitors to the site must fill out a registration form that includes specific questions that help salespeople qualify the leads. Upon filling out the form, users can see a demographic report of their choice. The next day, they receive an e-mail from the company which reminds the prospect about the company and reinforces the company's image. On the third day, the prospects get a phone call from Gergen. This is an excellent example of an integrated sales and marketing program.

SUMMARY

The Internet is a viable source of commerce for companies in the business-to-business area. Not only are companies doing a landmark business today in terms of sales and sourcing but also projections call for this trend to continue as more companies and prospects go online.

CHAPTER TWENTY-SIX

International Marketing Online

People from around the world can access information about your company and its products as the Internet turns commerce into a global village.

In this chapter you will learn:

- the opportunities for worldwide sales
- Internet hosts per country
- 15 steps to increase marketing efficiencies internationally

THE OPPORTUNITIES FOR WORLDWIDE SALES

We all know the World Wide Web, but how many of us underscore the *world* and appreciate the Internet as a medium that reaches surfers in Australia as well as in Hawaii?

The truth is that a goodly number of leading-edge consumers and companies log on to the Internet in countries around the world. The marketer who doesn't appreciate this fact is one who is losing out on opportunities.

Software publishers realized long ago that overseas sales can account for 50 percent of revenue and a large percentage of the growth of their product line. The same can be true for producers of other products as well.

International consumers generate 30 percent of gross sales for Cbooks, www.cbooks.com/home.html, because books are cheaper to buy in the United States than in their own countries, even with shipping costs.

AMP catalog added Japanese, Mandarin Chinese, and Korean to its list of English, French, Spanish, German, and Italian versions. The result: The percentage of visits in these languages went from 0 to 2 percent of the total number of visits in just one month.

The Milne Jewelry Company of Utah found a ready audience for its products in Japan and Germany, where customers place larger orders than U.S. residents do. It offers its pages in several languages.

"The emerging international online business is on the brink of mirroring the explosive growth seen in the North American market over the next five years," says SIMBA in its report "Online Services International Markets 1996." International home-based users of the Internet and online services will reach 20.8 million by 2000, a 400 percent increase from year-end 1995.

"Expanding into these new markets, however, does pose new obstacles," the research firm states. "Challenges for online services will extend far beyond language and cultural differences. Extremely high telecommunications costs, low PC/modem penetration, and phone bills that are delivered just once every three months are among the difficulties that face online companies as they attempt to capitalize on this growth opportunity."

INTERNET HOSTS PER COUNTRY

Ranking	Country	Hosts
1	United States	6,053,402
2	Germany	452,997
3	United Kingdom	451,750
4	Canada	372,891
5	Australia	309,562
6	Japan	269,327
7	Finland	208,502
8	Netherlands	174,888
9	Sweden	148,877
10	France	137,217

Source: CyberAtlas, www.cyberatlas.com/geographics.html

15 STEPS TO INCREASE MARKETING EFFICIENCIES INTERNATIONALLY

What can you do to increase sales internationally? Here are 15 tips:

1. Make your site available in several languages. On the site, add buttons that allow customers to select the language of their choice. To be culturally sensitive, don't label the button *German* but rather *Deutsch*. Have the page written or edited by a native speaker who will catch errors in usage, connotation, and denotation.

2. Be considerate of cultural differences. What you take for granted might be offensive to people in other countries. For example, a woman's bare leg or arm could be seen as pornography in Muslim countries. A U.S. businessperson was tossed in jail in one such country for showing tapes of the *Love Boat* TV show, which featured women in bikinis walking in the background of sets.

3. Be conscious of word choice and idioms. We've all heard the anecdote of the Chevy Nova not selling in Mexico because *no va* means *doesn't go*. I've also heard half a dozen versions of the negative connotations the red and white Coca-Cola logo has in China.

4. Be aware of colors. Certain colors and combinations that are effective in the United States don't mean the same things or stir up the same feelings in other countries. Red, white, and blue mean patriotism here but don't say anything in Brazil, whose national colors are green and yellow.

5. Be aware of international laws. In Spain you can't use the country's flag in ads. In Germany it is against the law to compare your product to a competitor's product.

6. Make it easy to take money. Put your prices in local currency. Be sure you account for the change in exchange rates; update these figures regularly.

7. Make it easy to accept money. While Canadian companies often have bank accounts that draw on U.S. dollars, many other prospective buyers don't have such ready access. Make it easy to make a transaction by accepting credit cards, which are payable in U.S. dollars at the current exchange rate. You might not need to be as concerned with international buyers' reluctance to share credit card information over the Internet as with U.S. customers'. I've received credit card orders for my books from people in Germany, Australia,

and Israel. I can't recall a single order from the United States that included a credit card. Still, offer your phone or fax numbers as ways to accept orders.

8. Make sure you can do business in other countries. Do you need a license? Can you sell your products internationally without violating U.S. law?

9. Refer business to local operatives. It might be easier to send international business to your local distributor or office. Be sure to list the local addresses and phone numbers. Be sure to remove toll-free numbers that work only in the United States.

10. Create the right product mix for an international audience. If your U.S. catalog lists bikinis, sweaters, and ski parkas in equal ratio, you might want to reconsider the offerings for a page viewed in Norway or Ecuador. Hard-to-find items seem to sell well on the Internet, so a New England syrup that is a slow seller in the United States might find a ready audience in a country that doesn't have maple trees.

11. Be attentive to sounds. The beeps in Lotus 1-2-3 were considered offensive in Japan. Lotus had to change the sounds to sell software in that country.

12. Test the page with native speakers. They understand the language far better than a staffer in the United States who studied the language in high school.

13. Test the page with a browser that displays the appropriate alphabet set to ensure that the text is readable. One good program is Internet with an Accent by Accent Software.

14. Don't use a lot of images. People in most countries on the globe have spotty, expensive phone service with noisy lines. Tell your story with text; you'll have a better chance of getting your message across without encountering a disconnect.

15. Create forms for addresses that use the appropriate headings. For example, Canada doesn't have states; it has provinces.

SUMMARY

Marketers can generate additional sales by selling to the worldwide online community. However, they must be prepared to conduct business internationally and to be mindful of the differences in culture and customs across borders.

CHAPTER TWENTY-SEVEN

Building Brand Online

In this chapter you will see how to:

- build brand on the Internet for your existing product
- build a new brand online

BUILDING BRAND ON THE INTERNET FOR YOUR EXISTING PRODUCT

Brand is the value of a company or product above and beyond the worth of its physical assets, according to JBW Communications. Having a positive brand image can translate into a higher stock valuation. Even children recognize brands. Test show that two-year-olds can recognize brands such as Mickey Mouse and Disneyland, among others. Adults are affected by brands as well. Every time a consumer has to make a choice between several products, the one with the stronger brand image will win. Think back to a time when you needed to buy film for a must-have event. Did you buy a trusted name brand like Kodak or Fuji, or did you buy the generic brand? When you are in a foreign country, do you drink the water or order a Pepsi or a Coca-Cola? That's the value of a good brand image.

A brand's total equity can have a direct influence on a parent, company selling price, revenue, profit potential, retail price, and even corporate debt rating, according to Lynn Upshaw in the book *Building Brand Identity*.

Building brand is critically important for these reasons. The Internet can be used to help build brands to existing audiences by reinforcing consistent messages and themes in banner ads and on Web sites. Companies can also use the Internet to reach new audiences.

Companies that create Web sites should be sure to take advantage of their brand. Copy your logo, colors, typeface, slogans, and characters to your Web site, which should have the same look and feel as your other marketing materials. Customers expect to see the familiar look they have grown used to in the real world when they visit the company's Web site. When they see different images, they might wonder if they have visited the wrong spot by mistake.

One of the best examples of extending the value of the brand on the Internet comes from Southwest Airlines, www.lflyswa.com. Its Web site uses the same typeface and colors as its entire marketing program. Even its Web site address is the same as their slogan: www.lflyswa.com. While it is doubtful that anyone would have thought to type that slogan to get to their Web site instead of southwestairlines.com or a similar address, there is no doubt that once their loyal customers realize that the address is the same as the slogan, they will remember it forever. Southwest's core values are that it is a friendly airline and it is affordable. Southwest is known for being an airline with a personality, and the Web site shows that as well. The site features a personal message from the company chairman, Herb Kelleher.

Many Fortune 500 companies understand the value of creating a consistent image across all media, including the Internet and their Web sites. IBM, Microsoft, 3M, and many others print their logos and typefaces in the same typeface, color, and size on their Web sites as they do in their other marketing programs. These three companies have another trait in common—they print their logo or company name on the top of *each* page on the Web site. Not only does this help readers navigate the site more easily but also they get numerous impressions of the company. Another unintended benefit of printing the logo on each page is that it reminds readers that they are still at the company site. This sounds a bit odd until you realize that many pages have links that take readers to other companies' Web sites. For example, a company might link to a news article that appears on a magazine's site. In this still-new era of the Internet, many people still don't realize they have left the corporate site and are now at a different company's site! When logos are placed at the top of each page, readers will know where they are at all times.

An example of a company that doesn't quite get branding right on the Internet is Ragu. While they do print their distinctive red and yellow logo on its front page, the logo does not appear on other pages. Even worse, they have created a character called Momma, who is a congenial, witty, sharp-tongued persona. She presides over "Momma's Cucina." *Momma* is repeated on each page, but not *Ragu*. One final note on this matter is that Momma exists only on the Internet. If you go to the supermarket, you will see neither

Momma nor the Cucina. Ragu is creating a brand that exists only on the Internet instead of either using the Momma character in the integrated marketing program or integrating existing materials into the Web site.

Consistency is an important factor in creating brand. Only in extreme cases or very good reasons should brand be violated. I came across one good example when I conducted a seminar for America Express. The people there told me that for their campaign to reach college students, they created a site that had funkier graphics, bolder graphics, and a cooler writing style than used in their regular Web site. But what really makes this interesting is the fact they put sunglasses on their famous logo, Mercury. However, the art department or marketing department couldn't make this change by themselves. They needed the permission of the chairman of the board of American Express before they could change their famous logo. Companies should be very careful when making changes of this magnitude because trademarks and copyrights could be affected by improper use of this type of intellectual property.

The Internet offers new opportunities for companies to create brands. One new facet is the idea of building communities online. This topic is covered in detail in chapter 13. In a nutshell, a company must determine its core values and what its core customers really want from the company and its products, not what the company thinks it produces. In other words, Reebok decided its customers would not visit its site to read about sneakers. Instead, it realized that its customers were concerned with sports fitness, so it created numerous features that enhanced customers' abilities to be more physically fit. Sample ideas included a personalized fitness schedule based on activities the person likes to perform.

Pzifer, www.allergy-info.com, wanted to create a brand identity for its customers who are allergy sufferers. It created an Allergy Information Center site that includes value-added information showing the pollen count in various cities.

Rotorooter, www.rotorooter.com, offers plumbing and maintenance tips as well as a plumbing game called Pipe Dreams.

Betty Crocker, www.bettycrocker.com, is the ultimate homemaker, so it makes sense to build a site that contains hundreds of recipes, a menu planner, and a tool that creates a shopping list from chosen recipes.

Clinique, the number-two vendor of women's cosmetics in department stores, uses the Internet to build brand image and fill a void in its marketing campaign. Its site at www.clinique.com appeals to consumers aged 16–25 who do not go to department stores as often as the company's main consumers. The site offers personalized product consultations. The Web site is a bargain compared to print and broadcast budgets, which cost $15 million. The site budget is reported to have cost $250,000 to build and to cost another $150,000 to $200,000 per year to maintain. The site looks similar to the company's packaging and advertisements, using the same pale green color. By hosting a site Clinique can extend its brand image, appeal to a new customer base, and develop relationships with them.

American Express, www.americanexpress.com, builds brand identity with its travel-related services. Its site lists the benefits and services of card ownership but creates a real sense of identity by offering a variety of travel services such as special events, travel and events, shopping services, tips on traveling, lists of articles, and message boards where visitors can share tips with other travelers. The site makes good use of the Internet by allowing travelers to search for hotels in London and to read reviews in major tour-guide books like Fromer and Fodor. The site is updated once a week as articles are added to the 10,000-article database. Although the main purpose of the site was to build the brand of American Express as the leader in travel services, the company also received applications for 15,000 new cards in less than a year!

BUILDING A NEW BRAND ONLINE

Branding will become increasingly important in cyberspace, where many companies are new and have no identity. Right now people are willing to experiment with these new companies. It has been said that small companies can compete effectively with large companies on the Internet because people only know them by the quality of their marketing materials. A new company can look credible in cyberspace without having a storefront if it has great-looking information online.

Many new companies have opened storefronts on the World Wide Web and have captured market share and significant sales. Success stories have been printed in many magazines about companies like Virtual Vineyards, Hotel Discounts, Travelocity, Auto-by-Tel, and Software.net. These companies certainly deserve their good fortune.

But as more people go online, will they buy from a company they've never heard of, or will they gravitate toward companies they know and trust? Would you buy from a new online auction house on the Internet or from Christie's? Would you buy travel services from a Web site that is new to you, or would you go to the Hilton site and make reservations directly?

Would you be willing to risk your hard-earned money at a cyberstore in another country that has no guarantees for returns, or would you choose a product from L.L. Bean's catalog?

If you are creating a new business on the Internet, it is vitally important to create your brand image early in the game, before your real-world competitors jump onto the Internet bandwagon and steal your customers because they have a better-known name.

Several companies have done a marvelous job of creating brand identity on the Internet: Amazon.com, (www.amazon.com), CDnow, (www.cdnow.com), and OnSale, (www.onsale.com), have emerged as leaders in selling books, audio CDs, and auctions, respectively.

Case Study: Amazon Books

Amazon.com sells books on the Internet and *only* on the Internet. It bills itself as the "World's Largest Bookstore" with more than 2.5 million books. It realized its members' core values included a love of books and created a community by offering chats with authors and a writing contest to finish a book started by John Updike. Thousands of people entered the contest.

Amazon built relationships with its customers by creating its "Eyes" program, which notifies them via e-mail of books they might be interested in. The company also created a referral marketing program in which readers can earn commissions from Amazon if they review books on their own Web sites and the readers ordered the books from Amazon (Amazon sends the HTML code to make this a very easy process).

The company met with success in many areas: incredible customer loyalty, more than 10,000 book review associates, and publicity in virtually every publication imaginable. That success translated into a very successful stock offering in which the stock price went from 18 to 29.5 in the first day. Amazon founder Jeff Bezos was worth $324 million on that day.

However, there is more to this success story. On the day Amazon went public, competitor Barnes and Noble announced that its Web site would offer chats with authors and also sued Amazon, claiming Amazon infringed on its slogan. Barnes and Noble later dropped the suit.

The problem with being creative in creating brand is that once you have shown your cards, the competition can copy the tactic as well.

SUMMARY

The Internet can be used to build brand in the real world. Web sites should leverage on the brand's core assets and even its look and feel.

PART 6

The Future

CHAPTER TWENTY-EIGHT

The Future of Online Marketing

One of the best parts about writing a chapter on the future is that it can also serve as the first chapter in the next edition of this book! This chapter explores the future of marketing online as new technologies and strategies develop. For free updates, see my home page, www.janal.com.

INTEGRATING MEDIA AND TECHNOLOGY INTO THE SALES CYCLE AND CUSTOMER SUPPORT

E-mail will get more robust. You will soon be able to control the fonts and colors in e-mail messages. That will mean you will be able to control the look and feel and design of sales messages. Your e-mail can look more like a direct-mail piece or a full-page print advertisement. Maybe a hybrid format will develop that will take the medium of direct mail to the next level.

You'll also be able to send voice, picture, and video with e-mail files so your ad can offer the vocal inflections needed to convey tone and image to a prospect. These tools will remove the monotone feel of printed e-mail.

Now imagine the integration of telephone technology via the Internet. With the free distribution of Internet telephone products from Netscape and Microsoft, the two largest distributors of browsers, people will be able to send and receive telephone messages via the Internet (at the cost of the call to their local Internet Service Provider, not the long-distance call normally associated with this activity on a telephone). Imagine using the inexpensive calling features of Internet telephony to return customer support calls for a fraction of the price demanded by long-distance telephone carriers! You'll also be able to broadcast messages to customers (helpful in announcing sales, updates or recalls). Naturally, you'll be able to leave voice messages in a person's message center as well, so if he isn't in when you call, he can hear your message at his convenience.

Now let's put them all together. You place an ad in a magazine for a trip to Hawaii. A prospect reads the ad and sends e-mail to your mailbot (automated e-mail responder). She reads the response message and sees attached pictures of the hotel. She wants more information that isn't in the e-mail package so she presses a hyperlink that calls your customer service representative and they chat in real time over the Internet phone.

The customer service rep sends audio files of Hawaiian music to play over the prospect's computer system speakers to put her in the mood. While answering questions orally, the rep also sends pictures and videos to the prospect so she can see the view from the room, read the menu in the gourmet restaurant, and look at a live picture of the day care facilities.

Convinced she will have a relaxing vacation, the prospect gives her credit card number to the rep, who closes the deal.

This scenario is not farfetched. The technology exists to make it happen today. The only thing missing is an innovative company that is willing to integrate these tools from various media to make a bold marketing statement.

GREATER USE OF SOUND IN ADVERTISING AND CUSTOMER SUPPORT

With so many computers being sold as multimedia systems with high-speed modems and stereo sound speakers, the market is ripe for advertisers to put audio on their Web pages (see Score, www.ccnet.coom/~score). Audio can be used in the sales cycle to create a mood so that when a person enters the drag racing page, he hears the sound of engines revving, thus putting him in the right frame of mind for presentation. Imagine hearing jazz music upon entering the New Orleans visitors' site and you get the idea how this technique can be used for any company.

Moving past the subtle background music, let's use audio the way radio does. Put up a 30-second commercial that people hear when they visit your site. Time will tell what kinds of persuasion techniques (humor, information, fear, benefit) will work best. Add pictures (stills or video) and text or text links, and you have a powerful information/sales tool.

As video gets better (faster delivery and better-quality images), you'll have the makings of an infomercial via the Internet—which people will have requested.

Audio technology will help customer support operations as people will be able to hear responses to their questions, record them, and play them back when needed. Expect a tight integration of text-linked menu options to lead to audio instructions for solving the problem. For example, "If you need help with returning an item by Federal Express, press 1; by UPS, press 2; by Airborne, press 3."

BETTER DEMOGRAPHIC STATISTICS

Each survey of Internet users conflicts with every other survey—usually by wide margins, as some surveys say there are 30 million people on the Internet while others say there are only 10 million. These surveys will get better because marketers will pay for good data to help them accurately plan online marketing campaigns.

A NEW WAVE OF MEASUREMENT TECHNIQUES AND STANDARDS

Publishing sites must offer verifiable demographics of their viewers for marketers to become truly comfortable spending large dollars on the Web. Because publishers want to make that day come sooner than later, they will be creating measurement tools and devising ways of identifying consumers and their demographics. Many companies are scurrying for position as they try to create these products. For lists of new companies and products in this area, search Yahoo! on a regular basis.

TIGHT INTEGRATION OF PERSONAL NOTIFICATION SERVICES VIA E-MAIL, PAGERS, AND FAX

E-mail, pagers, telephone, and fax will be tightly integrated so that personal notification services (like news, stock quotes, and requested advertising information) can be sent immediately to the customer via his preferred method. To help pay for this service, information providers might offer advertisements to be placed somewhere in the message. For example, "This free stock alert is being set to you courtesy of XYZ Company, the leading provider of mutual funds."

COOP DOLLARS FLOW TO WEB ADS

Manufacturers will begin to see the value in advertising on the Internet and will open cooperative advertising programs to include funding of Web sites, banner ads advertising links back to the manufacturers' home page, and new techniques that will evolve.

CABLE MODEMS

Cable modems offer the promise of faster transmission times that will convert the World Wide Wait into a medium that rivals television in terms of access time and picture quality. Every expert disagrees on the timing of this development—anywhere from yesterday to 1999.

CUSTOMIZED WEB SITES

Creating individual Web sites on the fly for customers based on their registration numbers will become increasingly important for companies and even expected by consumers. This tactic will go well beyond today's limited techniques of saying "Hi, Dan. You are calling from CCNet." Instead, the computer will remember what products I am interested in and tell me what is new.

GREATER USE OF ALLIANCES

As larger companies take a stronger position on the Internet, smaller companies will need to form alliances to match the marketing muscle of the big guns. Expect links to and from smaller companies who can leverage off each other's audiences. This is much like the link to the complementary sites strategy explained earlier in this book. The difference is that cooperation today is a nice thing to do; in the future it will be a requirement.

INTEGRATION OF INTERNET AND PAY-PER-VIEW CD-ROMS

Information providers (Internetese for publishers of news, information, or entertainment) will send CD-ROMs to their customers. These disks will contain software, music, research reports, and movies that are too cumbersome to download off the Internet. Companies will install a payment system so that customers can find the promotional material online and proceed to the CD that contains the actual file. They will install payment systems and unlocking codes to track payments and guard against piracy of intellectual property. This technique could be useful for companies that have a wide variety of entertainment products. If the customer orders one title, he can also receive the CD-ROM that contains many more. If he likes the first, he is likely to buy the additional titles—especially if he can get instant gratification by having access to the material.

LOCAL MEDIA OUTLETS BECOME NATIONAL OUTLETS

As radio stations go online via Real Audio and Audio Net, people across the country (and the world) can hear broadcasts from distant places. A consumer in San Francisco can listen to WOR-AM in New York City and hear the Dolans' financial program. A sports maven in New England can hear the Jimmy Johnson show from Miami. Local and regional newspapers will also attract a national audience, especially those that cover large niche markets, such as the *San Jose Mercury News,* which covers high technology; the *Detroit Free Press,* which covers the automobile industry; and *Florida Today,* which covers the space industry. These media can sell advertisements on a national basis. Local merchants should also consider the reach of these local properties as well for additional sales opportunities.

REPORTERS WILL BECOME MORE DEPENDENT ON ONLINE RESOURCES

Reporters in various industries are becoming more comfortable with online tools like e-mail and Web surfing. They will expect to find press releases and pictures online that they can copy and edit into their articles. As more publications go online, reporters will have an insatiable need to fill an unlimited amount of space and keep up with competitors who also have 24-hour news services.

HELP DESKS AND INFORMATION CENTERS WILL BE INTEGRATED WITH THE INTERNET

Companies that use software to distribute their products or services (like stock brokerage companies that update prices and charts and software companies that sell consumer and business-to-business software applications) will tie the consumer's computer into an online service for support services, such as help systems, program updates, and announcements. This process will help cut the delivery costs of new products and information and give consumers access to the latest help files available. This application would work well for any company that publishes information that quickly goes out of date.

SUMMARY

The field of online marketing is new and constantly changing. As new tools develop and evolve, so will the strategies marketers use to win new customers and to build long-lasting relationships with existing consumers. Check my home page for free updates and strategies and to subscribe to my free newsletter, Dan Janal's Online Marketing Newsletter! The address is: www.janal.com.

Happy marketing.

Glossary

Baud: The speed at which modems transfer data. The speed is listed in BPS or bits per second.

Browser: The software program that allows users to read pages on the World Wide Web.

Download: Retrieve files from a computer.

FAQ (Frequently Asked Questions): A file that contains questions and answers about specific topics.

Flame: Abusive hate mail.

FTP: File Transfer Protocol: send and retrieve files from the Internet

HTML: Hypertext Mark-up Language: The standard format for documents on the World Wide Web.

Hypertext: A system where documents scattered across many sites are directly linked.

Hypermedia: A system where documents, pictures, sound, movie and animation files scattered across many sites are directly linked.

ISDN (Integrated Services Digital Network): Technology that makes it possible to move multiple digital signals through a single, conventional phone wire.

Leased line: A permanently installed telephone line connecting a LAN to an Internet Service Provider.

Lurking: Reading messages in a forum or newgroups without adding comments.

Modem: A device that connects a computer to a phone line and enables users to transmit data between computers.

Mosaic: A software program that allows users to browse the World Wide Web.

Netiquette: The etiquette of Internet.

Newbies: Newcomers to the Internet.

Service Provider: A company that provides connections to the Internet.

Signature or **.sig:** A personalized address at the bottom of a message often containing contact information and a short commercial description.

SLIP and **PPP (Serial Line Internet Protocol and Point-to-Point Protocol):** Two common types of connections that allow your computer to communicate with the Internet.

Smileys and **emoticons:** Typographical versions of faces that display emotions in text messages.

Spam: Posting or mailing unwanted material to many recipients. A flagrant violation of Netiquette.

TCP/IP (Transmission Control Protocol/Internet Protocol): The standardized sets of computer guidelines that allow different machines to talk to each other on the Internet.

Sysop (SYStem Operator): The person who administers a forum. Same as Webmaster.

Upload: Send a file from your computer to another.

URL (Uniform Resource Locator): A type of address that points to a specific document or site on the World Wide Web.

Usenet: A collection of discussion areas (bulletin boards) known as newsgroups on the Internet.

WAIS (Wide Area Information System): A system that allows users to search by keyword through the full text contained on many databases.

World Wide Web (WWW or **W3** or **The Web):** A hypertext and hypermedia system that enables users to find information about companies.

Biography

Daniel Janal is a speaker, author and marketing consultant specializing in Internet Marketing.

He is the author of two best-selling Internet marketing books: *Online Marketing Handbook* and *101 Businesses You Can Start on the Internet*. He is writing a book on crisis communications called *Risky Business: How Companies Can Protect Themselves from Fraud and Attacks on the Internet*. It will be published in March by John Wiley and Sons.

He has provided online marketing consulting services for the *Reader's Digest*, Panasonic, and Biltmore Estates. He was on the publicity team that launched America Online.

He has delivered online marketing training seminars to the publicity staffs of American Express/IDS, U.S. Postal Service, and IBM. His public seminar clients include AT&T, Pacific Bell, DCI Expos, and Ragan Communications. He has addressed trade groups and associations including Public Relations Society of America, Credit Union Executives Society, and National Ski Areas Association. He lectures at the University of California at Berkeley. He has addressed audiences in Mexico, Canada, and Brazil.

Mr. Janal has provided public relations consulting services for more than 100 software publishers, hardware manufacturers and publishing companies over the past 13 years, including launching Grolier's Multimedia Encyclopedia, the first piece of consumer software available on CD-ROM. Other clients include AT&T Multimedia Software Solutions, Bell Atlantic Creative Services, Prentice-Hall Home Software, and The Learning Company.

He also has written *How to Publicize High Tech Products and Services* (10K Press/Janal Communications, 1991), considered the definitive training manual for public relations novices. He is the codeveloper of *Publicity Builder* software (JIAN, 1993).

He has contributed articles to trade magazines, including *PC Laptop Computing, InfoWorld, Accounting Technology, PR Tactics, Ski Area Management,* and *Credit Union Executives Society*.

He has been profiled in many periodicals, including the *New York Times, USA Today,* and *Success* magazine. He has been quoted in numerous publications including the *Los Angeles Times, Investor's Business Daily* and *Cyber-Times,* published by the *New York Times*.

He has been featured on dozens of television and radio talk shows, including CNBC's *Money Club* and *Today's Business.*

Before starting a career in public relations and marketing, Mr. Janal was an award-winning newspaper reporter for the *Today* newspaper in Cocoa, Florida, news editor of the Port Chester (New York) *Daily Item* and business news editor for the Rockland County (New York) *Journal-News.* He has won writing awards from the National Education Association and the Hearst Foundation. He holds bachelor's and master's degrees in journalism from Northwestern University's famed Medill School of Journalism.

Janal Communications Seminars, Consulting

Daniel Janal, author of Online Marketing Handbook, *is one of the most sought-after speakers on the Internet training and consulting circuit. He has presented lively, interactive workshops for American Express, IBM, the U.S. Postal Service, and Pacific Bell Network Integration. He also lectures at the University of California at Berkeley and the University of California at Santa Cruz.*

Call Daniel Janal today to find out how he can train your staff or help your company present public seminars. Send e-mail to: dan@janal.com or call 510-648-1961 during normal business hours in California.

Index